D0781931

INTRODUCTION TO DIGITAL FILTERS

WITH AUDIO APPLICATIONS

JULIUS O. SMITH III

Center for Computer Research in Music and Acoustics (CCRMA)
Department of Music, Stanford University, Stanford, California 94305 USA

INTRODUCTION TO DIGITAL FILTERS

WITH AUDIO APPLICATIONS

JULIUS O. SMITH III

Copyright © by Julius O. Smith III, 2007

Third printing, January 2012
W3K Publishing (`http://books.w3k.org`)

ISBN 978-0-9745607-1-7

Printed in the United States of America by
BookSurge Publishing (`http://www.booksurge.com`).

Printed from PostScript™ files generated by LaTeX 2_ε and dvips using standard
10-point book format, and the packages vmargin, fancyheadings, graphicx,
subfigure, makeidx, latexsym, html, multicol, and boxedminipage.

Contents Overview

Preface	xv
1 The Simplest Lowpass Filter	1
2 Matlab Filter Analysis	25
3 Analysis of a Digital Comb Filter	47
4 Linear Time-Invariant Filters	83
5 Time Domain Representations	97
6 Transfer Function Analysis	121
7 Frequency Response Analysis	149
8 Pole-Zero Analysis	175
9 Implementation Structures	199
10 Filters Preserving Phase	219
11 Minimum-Phase Filters	231
Appendices	243
Bibliography	443
Index	451

Appendices

A Background Fundamentals   243

B Elementary Audio Digital Filters   253

C Allpass Filters   299

D Laplace Transform Analysis   309

E Analog Filters   319

F Matrix Filter Representations   335

G State Space Filters   347

H Linear Time-Varying Filters   377

I Recursive Digital Filter Design   383

J Matlab Utilities   397

K Digital Filtering in Faust and PD   417

L Links to Online Resources   441

Contents

Preface   xv

1   The Simplest Lowpass Filter   1
   1.1   Introduction 1
   1.2   The Simplest Lowpass Filter 3
   1.3   Finding the Frequency Response 5
      1.3.1   Sine-Wave Analysis 7
      1.3.2   Mathematical Sine-Wave Analysis 8
      1.3.3   Amplitude Response 12
      1.3.4   Phase Response 13
   1.4   An Easier Way 14
      1.4.1   Complex Sinusoids 14
      1.4.2   Complex Amplitude 15
      1.4.3   Phasor Notation 16
      1.4.4   Complex Sinusoids as Circular Motion 16
      1.4.5   Rederiving the Frequency Response 18
   1.5   Summary 21
   1.6   Exercises 22

2   Matlab Filter Analysis   25
   2.1   Matlab Filter Implementation 26
   2.2   Matlab Sine-Wave Analysis 30
   2.3   Complex Sine-Wave Analysis 39
   2.4   Practical Frequency-Response Analysis 42
   2.5   Exercises 45

3   Analysis of a Digital Comb Filter   47
   3.1   Difference Equation 48
   3.2   Signal Flow Graph 48
   3.3   Software Implementation in Matlab 49
   3.4   Software Implementation in C++ 50

3.5	Software Implementation in Faust	53
3.6	Impulse Response	56
3.7	Transfer Function	58
3.8	Frequency Response	59
3.9	Amplitude Response	60
3.10	Phase Response	61
3.11	Pole-Zero Analysis	63
3.12	Alternative Realizations	65
	3.12.1 First-Order Parallel Sections	66
	3.12.2 Parallel, Real, Second-Order Sections	74
	3.12.3 Parallel Second-Order Signal Flow Graph	78
	3.12.4 Series, Real, Second-Order Sections	81
3.13	Summary	81
4	**Linear Time-Invariant Filters**	**83**
4.1	Definition of a Signal	84
4.2	Definition of a Filter	85
4.3	Examples of Digital Filters	86
4.4	Linear Filters	88
4.5	Time-Invariant Filters	90
4.6	Showing Linearity and Time Invariance	90
4.7	Dynamic Range Compression	92
4.8	A Musical Time-Varying Filter Example	94
4.9	Analysis of Nonlinear Filters	94
4.10	Conclusions	95
4.11	Exercises	95
5	**Time Domain Representations**	**97**
5.1	Difference Equation	97
5.2	Signal Flow Graph	99
5.3	Causal Recursive Filters	100
5.4	Filter Order	100
5.5	Direct-Form-I Implementation	100
5.6	Impulse-Response Representation	100
5.7	Filter Stability	101
5.8	Impulse Response Example	102
5.9	Implications of Linear-Time-Invariance	102
5.10	Convolution Representation	106
5.11	FIR Digital Filters	109
	5.11.1 FIR impulse response	111
	5.11.2 Convolution Representation of FIR Filters	111
	5.11.3 FIR Transfer Function	112
	5.11.4 FIR Software Implementations	113

5.12 Transient and Steady State Response 114
    5.12.1 FIR Example 115
    5.12.2 IIR Example 116
    5.12.3 Transient and Steady-State Signals 116
    5.12.4 Decay Response, Initial Conditions Response 118
    5.12.5 Complete Response 118
5.13 Summary and Conclusions 119
5.14 Exercises 120

6 Transfer Function Analysis   **121**
6.1 The Z Transform 122
6.2 Existence of the Z Transform 123
6.3 Shift and Convolution Theorems 124
6.4 Z Transform of Convolution 125
6.5 Z Transform of Difference Equations 126
6.6 Factored Form 127
6.7 Series and Parallel Transfer Functions 127
6.8 Partial Fraction Expansion 129
    6.8.1 PFE to Real, Second-Order Sections 131
    6.8.2 Inverting the Z Transform 132
    6.8.3 FIR Part of a PFE 133
    6.8.4 Alternate PFE Methods 136
    6.8.5 Repeated Poles 136
    6.8.6 Alternate Stability Criterion 140
    6.8.7 Summary of the Partial Fraction Expansion 141
    6.8.8 Software for Partial Fraction Expansion 142
6.9 Exercises 146

7 Frequency Response Analysis   **149**
7.1 Frequency Response 149
7.2 Amplitude Response 151
7.3 Phase Response 152
7.4 Polar Form of the Frequency Response 152
7.5 Frequency Response as a Ratio of DTFTs 153
    7.5.1 Frequency Response in Matlab 154
    7.5.2 Example LPF Frequency Response Using `freqz` . . 157
7.6 Phase and Group Delay 160
    7.6.1 Phase Delay 160
    7.6.2 Phase Unwrapping 161
    7.6.3 Group Delay 163
    7.6.4 Group Delay Examples in Matlab 165
    7.6.5 Vocoder Analysis 168
    7.6.6 Numerical Computation of Group Delay 169

7.7	Exercises	171

8 Pole-Zero Analysis — **175**
8.1	Filter Order = Transfer Function Order	176
8.2	Graphical Amplitude Response	177
8.3	Graphical Phase Response	181
8.4	Stability Revisited	184
	8.4.1 Computing Reflection Coefficients	185
	8.4.2 Step-Down Procedure	186
	8.4.3 Testing Filter Stability in Matlab	187
8.5	Bandwidth of One Pole	189
8.6	Time Constant of One Pole	189
8.7	Unstable Poles—Unit Circle Viewpoint	190
	8.7.1 Geometric Series	190
	8.7.2 One-Pole Transfer Functions	191
8.8	Poles and Zeros of the Cepstrum	193
8.9	Conversion to Minimum Phase	195
8.10	Hilbert Transform Relations	195
8.11	Exercises	196

9 Implementation Structures — **199**
9.1	The Four Direct Forms	200
	9.1.1 Direct-Form I	200
	9.1.2 Direct Form II	202
	9.1.3 Transposed Direct-Forms	204
	9.1.4 Numerical Robustness of TDF-II	206
9.2	Series and Parallel Filter Sections	207
	9.2.1 Series Second-Order Sections	207
	9.2.2 Parallel First and/or Second-Order Sections	209
	9.2.3 Formant Filtering Example	210
	9.2.4 Butterworth Lowpass Filter Example	215
	9.2.5 Summary of Series/Parallel Filter Sections	216
9.3	Exercises	217

10 Filters Preserving Phase — **219**
10.1	Linear-Phase Filters	219
10.2	Zero-Phase Filters	220
	10.2.1 Example Zero-Phase Filter Design	222
	10.2.2 Elementary Zero-Phase Filter Examples	224
10.3	Odd Impulse Reponses	225
10.4	Symmetric Linear-Phase Filters	225
	10.4.1 Simple Linear-Phase Filter Examples	226
	10.4.2 Software for Linear-Phase Filter Design	227

10.5 Antisymmetric Linear-Phase Filters 227
10.6 Forward-Backward Filtering 228
10.7 Phase Distortion at Passband Edges 229

11 Minimum-Phase Filters   **231**
  11.1 Definition of Minimum Phase Filters 231
  11.2 Minimum-Phase Polynomials 232
  11.3 Maximum Phase Filters 233
  11.4 Minimum Phase Means Fastest Decay 234
  11.5 Minimum-Phase/Allpass Decomposition 234
  11.6 Linear Phase Audio Filters 235
  11.7 Creating Minimum Phase 240

A Background Fundamentals   **243**
  A.1 Signal Representation and Notation 243
    A.1.1 Units 243
    A.1.2 Sinusoids 244
    A.1.3 Spectrum 244
  A.2 Complex and Trigonometric Identities 246
    A.2.1 Complex Numbers 246
    A.2.2 The Exponential Function 247
    A.2.3 Trigonometric Identities 248
    A.2.4 Half-Angle Tangent Identities 249
  A.3 Sinusoids as Eigenfunctions of LTI Systems 250
    A.3.1 Proof Using Trigonometry 250
    A.3.2 Proof Using Complex Variables 251
    A.3.3 Phasor Analysis 252

B Elementary Audio Digital Filters   **253**
  B.1 Elementary Filter Sections 253
    B.1.1 One-Zero 254
    B.1.2 One-Pole 256
    B.1.3 Two-Pole 258
    B.1.4 Two-Zero 263
    B.1.5 Complex Resonator 264
    B.1.6 The BiQuad Section 269
    B.1.7 Biquad Software Implementations 270
  B.2 Allpass Filter Sections 272
    B.2.1 The Biquad Allpass Section 272
    B.2.2 Allpass Filter Design 273
  B.3 DC Blocker 273
    B.3.1 DC Blocker Frequency Response 274
    B.3.2 DC Blocker Software Implementations 274

B.4   Low and High Shelf Filters 279
B.5   Peaking Equalizers 280
B.6   Time-Varying Two-Pole Filters 283
      B.6.1   Normalizing Two-Pole Filter Gain at Resonance . . 285
      B.6.2   Constant Resonance Gain 286
      B.6.3   Peak Gain Versus Resonance Gain 287
      B.6.4   Constant Peak-Gain Resonator 290
      B.6.5   Four-Pole Tunable Lowpass/Bandpass Filters 295
B.7   Exercises 295

C Allpass Filters   299
C.1   Allpass Examples 300
C.2   Paraunitary Filters 302
C.3   MIMO Allpass Filters 303
      C.3.1   Paraunitary MIMO Filters 304
      C.3.2   Paraunitary Filter Examples 306
C.4   Allpass Problems 307

D Laplace Transform Analysis   309
D.1   Existence of the Laplace Transform 310
D.2   Analytic Continuation 311
D.3   Relation to the z Transform 313
D.4   Laplace Transform Theorems 314
      D.4.1   Linearity 314
      D.4.2   Differentiation 314
D.5   Laplace Analysis of Linear Systems 315
      D.5.1   Moving Mass 315
      D.5.2   Mass-Spring Oscillator Analysis 317

E Analog Filters   319
E.1   Example Analog Filter 319
E.2   Capacitors 320
E.3   Inductors 321
E.4   RC Filter Analysis 322
      E.4.1   Driving Point Impedance 322
      E.4.2   Transfer Function 323
      E.4.3   Impulse Response 323
      E.4.4   The Continuous-Time Impulse 324
      E.4.5   Poles and Zeros 324
E.5   RLC Filter Analysis 325
      E.5.1   Driving Point Impedance 325
      E.5.2   Transfer Function 325
      E.5.3   Poles and Zeros 325

	E.5.4	Impulse Response	326
E.6	Relating Pole Radius to Bandwidth		326
E.7	Quality Factor (Q)		328
	E.7.1	Decay Time is Q Periods	329
	E.7.2	Q as Energy Stored over Energy Dissipated	330
E.8	Analog Allpass Filters		331

F Matrix Filter Representations   **335**
F.1	Introduction		335
F.2	General Causal Linear Filter Matrix		336
F.3	General LTI Filter Matrix		336
F.4	Cyclic Convolution Matrix		338
F.5	Inverse Filters		339
F.6	State Space Realization		340
F.7	Time Domain Filter Estimation		342
	F.7.1	Effect of Measurement Noise	343
	F.7.2	Matlab System Identification Example	345

G State Space Filters   **347**
G.1	Markov Parameters		348
G.2	Response from Initial Conditions		349
G.3	Complete Response		349
G.4	Transfer Function of a State Space Filter		349
G.5	Transposition of a State Space Filter		351
G.6	Poles of a State Space Filter		351
G.7	Difference Equations to State Space		352
	G.7.1	Converting to State-Space Form by Hand	353
	G.7.2	Signal Flow Graph to State Space Filter	355
	G.7.3	Controllability and Observability	356
	G.7.4	A Short-Cut to Controller Canonical Form	358
	G.7.5	Matlab Direct-Form to State-Space Conversion	358
	G.7.6	State Space Simulation in Matlab	359
	G.7.7	Other Relevant Matlab Functions	361
	G.7.8	Matlab State-Space Filter Conversion Example	362
G.8	Similarity Transformations		362
G.9	Modal Representation		364
	G.9.1	Diagonalizing a State-Space Model	365
	G.9.2	Finding the Eigenvalues of A in Practice	366
	G.9.3	Example of State-Space Diagonalization	366
	G.9.4	Properties of the Modal Representation	369
G.10	Repeated Poles		370
	G.10.1	Jordan Canonical Form	371
G.11	Digital Waveguide Oscillator Example		372

G.11.1 Finding the Eigenstructure of A 374
G.11.2 Choice of Output Signal and Initial Conditions . . . 375
G.12 Exercises 376

H Linear Time-Varying Filters   377
H.1 Introduction 377
H.2 Derivation 379
H.3 Summary 381

I Recursive Digital Filter Design   383
I.1 Lowpass Filter Design 383
I.2 Butterworth Lowpass Design 384
I.3 Bilinear A/D Transformation 388
    I.3.1 Bilinear Transformation 388
    I.3.2 Frequency Warping 388
    I.3.3 Analog Prototype Filter 389
I.4 Equation-Error Filter Design 390
    I.4.1 Equation Error Formulation 391
    I.4.2 Error Weighting and Frequency Warping 392
    I.4.3 Stability of Equation Error Designs 392
    I.4.4 An FFT-Based Equation-Error Method 393
    I.4.5 Prony's Method 395
    I.4.6 The Padé-Prony Method 396

J Matlab Utilities   397
J.1 Time Plots: `myplot.m` 398
J.2 Frequency Plots: `freqplot.m` 399
J.3 Saving Plots to Disk: `saveplot.m` 400
J.4 Frequency Response Plots: `plotfr.m` 401
J.5 Partial Fraction Expansion: `residuez.m` 403
    J.5.1 Method 403
    J.5.2 Example with Repeated Poles 405
J.6 Partial Fraction Expansion: `residued.m` 406
J.7 Parallel SOS to Transfer Function: `psos2tf` 407
J.8 Group Delay Computation: `grpdelay.m` 408
J.9 Matlab listing: `fold.m` 410
J.10 Matlab listing: `clipdb.m` 411
J.11 Matlab listing: `mps.m` and test program 412
J.12 Signal Plots: `swanalplot.m` 415
J.13 Frequency Response Plot: `swanalmainplot` 416

K Digital Filtering in Faust and PD   417
K.1 A Simple Faust Program 417

K.2 Generating Faust Block Diagrams 419
K.3 Testing a Faust Filter Section 422
K.4 A Look at the Generated C++ code 423
K.5 Generating a Pure Data (PD) Plugin 424
     K.5.1 Generating the PD Plugin 424
     K.5.2 Generating a PD Plugin-Wrapper Abstraction . . . 429
     K.5.3 A PD Test Patch for the Plugin Wrapper 429
K.6 Generating a LADSPA Plugin via Faust 432
K.7 Generating a VST Plugin via Faust 434
     K.7.1 Bypassing Windows 436
K.8 Generating a MIDI Synthesizer for PD 437
K.9 MIDI Synthesizer Test Patch 439

L Links to Online Resources   441

Bibliography   443

Index   451

Preface

This book was written for my introductory course[1] in digital audio signal processing, which I have given at the Center for Computer Research in Music and Acoustics (CCRMA) since 1984. The course was created primarily as a first course in digital signal processing for entering Music Ph.D. students in the Computer Based Music Theory and Acoustics program. Due to the nature of CCRMA research, this book will emphasize audio and music applications, although the material on the subject of digital filters itself is not specific to audio or music. A recommended co-requisite is [84], which contains a more detailed development of the mathematics of signals and spectra in the discrete-time case. A shorter precursor to this book was published in [79].

Outline

Below is an overview of the chapters.

1. **The Simplest Lowpass Filter** — a thorough analysis of an extremely simple digital filter using high-school level math (trigonometry) followed by a simpler but more advanced approach using complex variables. Important later topics are introduced in a simple setting.

2. **Matlab Filter Analysis** — a thorough analysis of the same simple digital filter analyzed in Chapter 1, but now using the matlab programming language. Important computational tools are introduced while the study of filter theory is hopefully being motivated.

3. **Analysis of Digital Comb Filter** — a thorough analysis and display of an example digital comb filter of practical complexity using more advanced methods, both mathematically and in software. The intent is to illustrate the mechanics of practical digital filter analysis and to motivate mastery of the theory presented in later chapters.

---

[1]http://ccrma.stanford.edu/CCRMA/Courses/320/

4. **Linearity and Time-Invariance** — mathematical foundations of digital filter analysis, implications of linearity and time invariance, and various technical terms relating to digital filters.

5. **Time Domain Filter Representations** — difference equation, signal flow graphs, direct-form I, direct-form II, impulse response, the convolution representation, and FIR filters.

6. **Transfer Function Analysis** — the transfer function is a frequency-domain representation of a digital filter obtained by taking the z transform of the difference equation.

7. **Frequency Response Analysis** — the frequency response is a frequency-domain representation of a digital filter obtained by evaluating the transfer function on the unit circle in the z plane. The magnitude and phase of the frequency response give the amplitude response and phase response, respectively. These functions give the gain and delay of the filter at each frequency. The phase response can be converted to the more intuitive phase delay and group delay.

8. **Pole-Zero Analysis** — poles and zeros provide another frequency-domain representation obtained by factoring the transfer function into first-order terms. The amplitude response and phase response can be quickly estimated by hand (or mentally) using a graphical construction based on the poles and zeros. A digital filter is stable if and only if its poles lie inside the unit circle in the z plane.

9. **Implementation Structures** — four direct-form implementations for digital filters, and series/parallel decompositions.

10. **Filters Preserving Phase** — zero-phase and linear-phase digital filters. Such filters largely preserve the shape of a signal in the time domain by delaying all frequency components equally.

11. **Minimum-Phase Filters** — minimum-phase digital filters, desired phase for audio filters, and creating minimum phase from spectral magnitude. Minimum phase gives "minimum delay" for a useful class of filters.

12. **Appendices** — elementary discussion of signal representation, complex and trig identities, closure of sinusoids under addition, elementary digital filters, equalizers, time-varying resonators, the dc blocker, allpass filters, introduction to Laplace transform analysis, analog filters, state-space models, elementary filter *design*, links to on-line resources, and software examples in the matlab, C++, and Faust programming languages (including automatic plugin generation).

Book Series Overview

This book is the second in my music signal processing series,[2] after [84]. The books can be loosely summarized by the following "design goals":

1. **Mathematics of the Discrete Fourier Transform**
   All about the DFT formula and its constituents, with frequent references to audio applications.

2. **Introduction to Digital Filters**
   A gentle introduction to the analysis and implementation of digital filters, with particular emphasis on audio applications.

3. **Physical Audio Signal Processing**
   Efficient computational physical models for delay effects and virtual acoustic musical instruments.

4. **Spectral Audio Signal Processing**
   Analysis, processing, and synthesis of audio signals in terms of spectral representations computed using a Fast Fourier Transform (FFT).

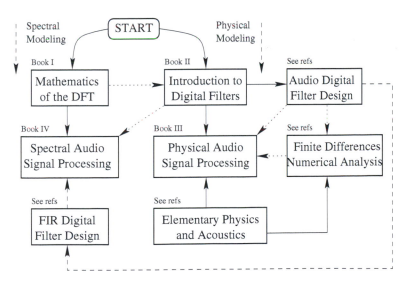

Figure 1: Schematic of interdependencies in the music signal processing book series, along with some closely related topics.

Figure 1 illustrates the dependencies. A solid line indicates a strong dependence, while a dotted line indicates a weaker (optional) dependence.

---

[2]http://ccrma.stanford.edu/~jos/pubs.html

The student is expected to pick up elementary physics [33] and programming skills [82, 15] elsewhere. In all books, the main chapters contain approximately what is covered in class, while the appendices provide both elementary background material and additional advanced topics.

Acknowledgments

With respect to the previously published precursor of this book [79], I would like to again express appreciation to John Strawn for his thorough editing assistance, and to Andy Schloss, David Jaffe, Andy Moorer, Janet Coursey, and Ken Shoemake for their helpful proofreading and suggestions. More recently, thanks to Vivian Woo and Matt Wright for especially helpful reviewing assistance, and to Mark Cartwright, Ryan Cassidy, Humane Chan, Nick Dargahi, David Gelbart, Peter Howard, Thomas Icking, Tim Janik, Christian Keil, Moonseok Kim, Arvindh Krishnaswamy, Andrew Leary, Dong In Lee, Poliang Lin, Gautham Mysore, Jim Murphy, Juhan Nam, John Nolting, Carlos Pita, Mathew Romaine, Volker Schatz, Andrew Simper, Lee Soulsby, Sook Young Won, and Larry Wu, for reporting errata they encountered in the earlier draft versions of this book.

The support of the Fannie and John Hertz Foundation during my graduate student years—when [79] was written—is gratefully acknowledged. Finally, the present version would not exist at all without the support of my wife Carol and son Harrison (who made sure I took plenty of breaks along the way ($\smile$)).

Julius Smith
September, 2007

Errata

Despite best efforts, errata will be almost surely be discovered over time. See http://books.w3k.org/filters1p3/ for known errata, clarifications, and other information pertaining to this book.

The author and publisher make no warranties, express or implied, regarding the contents of this book.

Chapter 1

The Simplest Lowpass Filter

This chapter introduces analysis of digital filters applied to a very simple example filter. The initial treatment uses only high-school level math (trigonometry), followed by an easier but more advanced approach using complex variables. Several important topics in digital signal processing are introduced in an extremely simple setting, and motivation is given for the study of further topics such as complex variables and Fourier analysis [84].

1.1 Introduction

Musicians have been using filters for thousands of years to shape the sounds of their art in various ways. For example, the evolution of the physical dimensions of the violin constitutes an evolution in filter design. The choice of wood, the shape of the cutouts, the geometry of the bridge, and everything that affects resonance all have a bearing on how the violin body filters the signal induced at the bridge by the vibrating strings. Once a sound is airborne there is yet more filtering performed by the listening environment, by the pinnae of the ear, and by idiosyncrasies of the hearing process.

What is a Filter?

Any medium through which the music signal passes, whatever its form, can be regarded as a filter. However, we do not usually think of something as a filter unless it can modify the sound in some way. For example, speaker wire is not considered a filter, but the speaker is (unfortunately). The different vowel sounds in speech are produced primarily by changing the shape of the mouth cavity, which changes the resonances and hence the filtering characteristics of the vocal tract. The tone control circuit in an ordinary car radio is a filter, as are the bass, midrange, and treble boosts in a stereo preamplifier. Graphic equalizers, reverberators, echo devices, phase shifters, and speaker crossover networks are further examples of useful filters in audio. There are also examples of undesirable filtering, such as the uneven reinforcement of certain frequencies in a room with "bad acoustics." A well-known signal processing wizard is said to have remarked, "When you think about it, everything is a filter."

A *digital* filter is just a filter that operates on digital signals, such as sound represented inside a computer. It is a *computation* which takes one sequence of numbers (the input signal) and produces a new sequence of numbers (the filtered output signal). The filters mentioned in the previous paragraph are not digital only because they operate on signals that are not digital. It is important to realize that a digital filter can do anything that a real-world filter can do. That is, all the filters alluded to above can be simulated to an arbitrary degree of precision digitally. Thus, a digital filter is only a formula for going from one digital signal to another. It may exist as an equation on paper, as a small loop in a computer subroutine, or as a handful of integrated circuit chips properly interconnected.

Why learn about filters?

Computer musicians nearly always use digital filters in every piece of music they create. Without digital reverberation, for example, it is difficult to get rich, full-bodied sound from the computer. However, reverberation is only a surface scratch on the capabilities of digital filters. A digital filter can arbitrarily shape the spectrum of a sound. Yet very few musicians are prepared to design the filter they need, even when they know exactly what they want in the way of a spectral modification. A goal of this book is to assist sound designers by listing the concepts and tools necessary for doing custom filter designs.

There is plenty of software available for designing digital filters [10, 8, 22]. In light of this available code, it is plausible to imagine that only basic programming skills are required to use digital filters. This is perhaps true for simple applications, but knowledge of how digital filters work will help at every phase of using such software.

Also, you must understand a program before you can modify it or extract pieces of it. Even in standard applications, effective use of a filter design program requires an understanding of the design parameters, which in turn requires some understanding of filter theory. Perhaps most important for composers who design their own sounds, a vast range of imaginative filtering possibilities is available to those who understand how filters affect sounds. In my practical experience, intimate knowledge of filter theory has proved to be a very valuable tool in the design of musical instruments. Typically, a simple yet unusual filter is needed rather than one of the classical designs obtainable using published software.

1.2   The Simplest Lowpass Filter

Let's start with a very basic example of the generic problem at hand: understanding the effect of a digital filter on the spectrum of a digital signal. The purpose of this example is to provide motivation for the general theory discussed in later chapters.

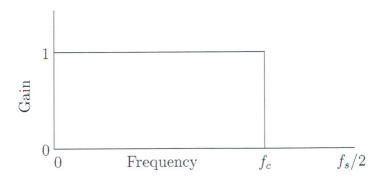

Figure 1.1: Amplitude response (gain versus frequency) specification for the ideal low-pass filter.

Our example is the simplest possible low-pass filter. A low-pass filter is one which does not affect low frequencies and rejects high frequencies. The function giving the *gain* of a filter at every *frequency* is called the *amplitude response* (or *magnitude frequency response*). The amplitude response of the ideal lowpass filter is shown in Fig. 1.1. Its gain is 1 in the *passband*, which spans frequencies from 0 Hz to the *cut-off frequency* f_c Hz, and its gain is 0 in the *stopband* (all frequencies above f_c). The output spectrum is obtained by multiplying the input spectrum by the amplitude response of the filter. In this way, signal components are eliminated ("stopped") at all frequencies above the cut-off frequency, while lower-frequency components are "passed" unchanged to the output.

Definition of the Simplest Low-Pass

The simplest (and by no means ideal) low-pass filter is given by the following *difference equation*:

$$y(n) = x(n) + x(n-1) \qquad (1.1)$$

where $x(n)$ is the filter input amplitude at time (or sample) n, and $y(n)$ is the output amplitude at time n. The *signal flow graph* (or *simulation diagram*) for this little filter is given in Fig. 1.2. The symbol "z^{-1}" means a delay of one sample, *i.e.*, $z^{-1}x(n) = x(n-1)$.

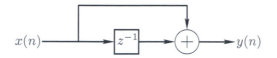

Figure 1.2: System diagram for the filter $y(n) = x(n) + x(n-1)$.

It is important when working with spectra to be able to convert time from sample-numbers, as in Eq. (1.1) above, to seconds. A more "physical" way of writing the filter equation is

$$y(nT) = x(nT) + x[(n-1)T] \qquad n = 0, 1, 2, \dots ,$$

where T is the sampling interval in seconds. It is customary in digital signal processing to omit T (set it to 1), but anytime you see an n you can translate to *seconds* by thinking nT. Be careful with integer expressions, however, such as $(n-k)$, which would be $(n-k)T$ seconds, not $(nT-k)$. Further discussion of signal representation and notation appears in §A.1.

To further our appreciation of this example, let's write a computer subroutine to implement Eq. (1.1). In the computer, $x(n)$ and $y(n)$ are data arrays and n is an array index. Since sound files may be larger than what the computer can hold in memory all at once, we typically process the data in blocks of some reasonable size. Therefore, the complete filtering operation consists of two loops, one within the other. The outer loop fills the input array x and empties the output array y, while the inner loop does the actual filtering of the x array to produce y. Let M denote the block size (*i.e.*, the number of samples to be processed on each iteration of the outer loop). In the C programming language, the inner loop of the subroutine might appear as shown in Fig. 1.3. The outer loop might read something like "fill x from the input file," "call `simplp`," and "write out y."

In this implementation, the first instance of $x(n-1)$ is provided as the procedure argument `xm1`. That way, both x and y can have the same array bounds $(0, \dots, M-1)$. For convenience, the value of `xm1` appropriate for the *next* call to `simplp` is returned as the procedure's value.

```
/* C function implementing the simplest lowpass:
 *
 *        y(n) = x(n) + x(n-1)
 *
 */
double simplp (double *x, double *y,
                int M, double xm1)
{
    int n;
    y[0] = x[0] + xm1;
    for (n=1; n < M ; n++) {
      y[n] =  x[n]  + x[n-1];
    }
    return x[M-1];
}
```

Figure 1.3: Implementation of the simple low-pass filter of Eq. (1.1) in the C programming language.

We may call xm1 the filter's *state*. It is the current "memory" of the filter upon calling simplp. Since this filter has only one sample of state, it is a *first order* filter. When a filter is applied to successive blocks of a signal, it is necessary to save the filter state after processing each block. The filter state after processing block m is then the starting state for block $m + 1$.

Figure 1.4 illustrates a simple main program which calls simplp. The length 10 input signal x is processed in two blocks of length 5.

You might suspect that since Eq. (1.1) is the simplest possible low-pass filter, it is also somehow the worst possible low-pass filter. How bad is it? In what sense is it bad? How do we even know it is a low-pass at all? The answers to these and related questions will become apparent when we find the *frequency response* of this filter.

1.3   Finding the Frequency Response

Think of the filter expressed by Eq. (1.1) as a "black box" as depicted in Fig. 1.5. We want to know the effect of this black box on the spectrum of $x(\cdot)$, where $x(\cdot)$ represents the entire input signal (see §A.1).

```
/* C main program for testing simplp */
main() {
  double x[10] = {1,2,3,4,5,6,7,8,9,10};
  double y[10];

  int i;
  int N=10;
  int M=N/2; /* block size */
  double xm1 = 0;

  xm1 = simplp(x, y, M, xm1);
  xm1 = simplp(&x[M], &y[M], M, xm1);

  for (i=0;i<N;i++) {
    printf("x[%d]=%f\ty[%d]=%f\n",i,x[i],i,y[i]);
    }
  exit(0);
}
/* Output:
 *      x[0]=1.000000        y[0]=1.000000
 *      x[1]=2.000000        y[1]=3.000000
 *      x[2]=3.000000        y[2]=5.000000
 *      x[3]=4.000000        y[3]=7.000000
 *      x[4]=5.000000        y[4]=9.000000
 *      x[5]=6.000000        y[5]=11.000000
 *      x[6]=7.000000        y[6]=13.000000
 *      x[7]=8.000000        y[7]=15.000000
 *      x[8]=9.000000        y[8]=17.000000
 *      x[9]=10.000000       y[9]=19.000000
 */
```

Figure 1.4: C main program for calling the simple low-pass filter `simplp`

$x(n) \longrightarrow$??? $\longrightarrow y(n)$

Figure 1.5: "Black box" representation of an arbitrary filter

1.3.1 Sine-Wave Analysis

Suppose we test the filter at each frequency separately. This is called *sine-wave analysis*.[1] Fig. 1.6 shows an example of an input-output pair, for the filter of Eq. (1.1), at the frequency $f = f_s/4$ Hz, where f_s denotes the sampling rate. (The continuous-time waveform has been drawn through the samples for clarity.) Figure 1.6a shows the input signal, and Fig. 1.6b shows the output signal.

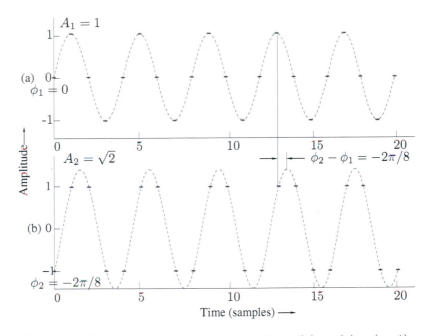

Figure 1.6: Input and output signals for the filter $y(n) = x(n) + x(n-1)$. (a) Input sinusoid $x(n) = A_1 \sin(2\pi f nT + \phi_1)$ at amplitude $A_1 = 1$, frequency $f = f_s/4$, and phase $\phi_1 = 0$. (b) Output sinusoid $y(n) = A_2 \sin(2\pi f nT + \phi_2)$ at amplitude $A_2 = 1.414$, frequency $f = f_s/4$, and phase $\phi_2 = -\pi/4$.

The ratio of the peak output amplitude to the peak input amplitude is the filter *gain* at this frequency. From Fig. 1.6 we find that the gain is

---

[1]Testing a filter by sweeping an input sinusoid through a range of frequencies is often used in practice, especially when there might be some distortion that also needs to be measured. There are particular advantages to using *exponentially swept sine-wave analysis* [24], in which the sinusoidal frequency increases exponentially with respect to time. (The technique is sometimes also referred to as *log-swept sine-wave analysis*.) Swept-sine analysis can be viewed as a descendant of *time-delay spectrometry*.

about 1.414 at the frequency $f_s/4$. We may also say the *amplitude response* is 1.414 at $f_s/4$.

The phase of the output signal minus the phase of the input signal is the *phase response* of the filter at this frequency. Figure 1.6 shows that the filter of Eq. (1.1) has a phase response equal to $-2\pi/8$ (minus one-eighth of a cycle) at the frequency $f = f_s/4$.

Continuing in this way, we can input a sinusoid at each frequency (from 0 to $f_s/2$ Hz), examine the input and output waveforms as in Fig. 1.6, and record on a graph the peak-amplitude ratio (gain) and phase shift for each frequency. The resultant pair of plots, shown in Fig. 1.7, is called the *frequency response*. Note that Fig. 1.6 specifies the middle point of each graph in Fig. 1.7.

Not every black box *has* a frequency response, however. What good is a pair of graphs such as shown in Fig. 1.7 if, for all input sinusoids, the output is 60 Hz hum? What if the output is not even a sinusoid? We will learn in Chapter 4 that the sine-wave analysis procedure for measuring frequency response is meaningful only if the filter is *linear* and *time-invariant* (LTI). Linearity means that the output due to a sum of input signals equals the sum of outputs due to each signal alone. Time-invariance means that the filter does not change over time. We will elaborate on these technical terms and their implications later. For now, just remember that LTI filters are guaranteed to produce a sinusoid in response to a sinusoid—and at the same frequency.

1.3.2   Mathematical Sine-Wave Analysis

The above method of finding the frequency response involves physically measuring the amplitude and phase response for input sinusoids of every frequency. While this basic idea may be practical for a real black box at a selected set of frequencies, it is hardly useful for filter design. Ideally, we wish to arrive at a *mathematical formula* for the frequency response of the filter given by Eq. (1.1). There are several ways of doing this. The first we consider is exactly analogous to the sine-wave analysis procedure given above.

Assuming Eq. (1.1) to be a linear time-invariant filter specification (which it is), let's take a few points in the frequency response by analytically "plugging in" sinusoids at a few different frequencies. Two graphs are required to fully represent the frequency response: the amplitude response (gain versus frequency) and phase response (phase shift versus frequency).

The frequency 0 Hz (often called *dc*, for *direct current*) is always comparatively easy to handle when we analyze a filter. Since plugging in a sinusoid means setting $x(n) = A\cos(2\pi f n T + \phi)$, by setting $f = 0$, we

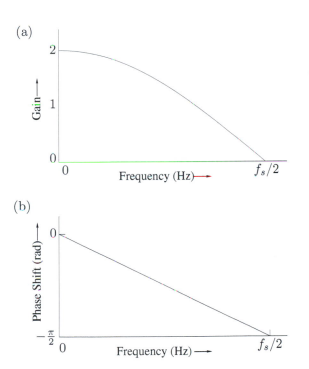

Figure 1.7: Frequency response for the filter $y(n) = x(n) + x(n-1)$. (a) Amplitude response. (b) Phase response.

obtain $x(n) = A \cos[2\pi(0)T + \phi] = A \cos(\phi)$ for all n. The input signal, then, is the same number $(A \cos(\phi))$ over and over again for each sample. It should be clear that the filter output will be $y(n) = x(n) + x(n-1) = A \cos(\phi) + A \cos(\phi) = 2A \cos(\phi)$ for all n. Thus, the gain at frequency $f = 0$ is 2, which we get by dividing $2A$, the output amplitude, by A, the input amplitude.

Phase has no effect at $f = 0$ Hz because it merely shifts a constant function to the left or right. In cases such as this, where the phase response may be arbitrarily defined, we choose a value which preserves *continuity*. This means we must analyze at frequencies in a neighborhood of the arbitrary point and take a limit. We will compute the phase response at dc later, using different techniques. It is worth noting, however, that at 0 Hz, the phase of every *real*[2] linear time-invariant system is either 0 or π, with the phase π corresponding to a sign change. The phase of a *complex filter* at dc may of course take on any value in $[-\pi, \pi)$.

The next easiest frequency to look at is half the sampling rate, $f = f_s/2 = 1/(2T)$. In this case, using basic trigonometry (see §A.2), we can simplify the input x as follows:

$$
\begin{aligned}
x(n) &= A \cos\left(2\pi \frac{f_s}{2} nT + \phi\right), \qquad n = 0, 1, 2, \ldots \\
&= A \cos\left(2\pi \frac{1}{2T} nT + \phi\right) \\
&= A \cos(\pi n + \phi) \\
&= A \cos(\pi n) \cos(\phi) - A \sin(\pi n) \sin(\phi) \\
&= A \cos(\pi n) \cos(\phi) \\
&= A(-1)^n \cos(\phi), \qquad n = 0, 1, 2, \ldots \\
&= [A \cos(\phi), -A \cos(\phi), A \cos(\phi), -A \cos(\phi), \ldots], \qquad (1.2)
\end{aligned}
$$

where the beginning of time was arbitrarily set at $n = 0$. Now with this input, the *output* of Eq. (1.1) is

$$
\begin{aligned}
y(n) &= x(n) + x(n-1) \\
&= (-1)^n A \cos(\phi) + (-1)^{n-1} A \cos(\phi) \\
&= (-1)^n A \cos(\phi) - (-1)^n A \cos(\phi) \\
&= 0. \qquad\qquad\qquad\qquad\qquad\qquad\qquad (1.3)
\end{aligned}
$$

The filter of Eq. (1.1) thus has a gain of 0 at $f = f_s/2$. Again the phase is not measurable, since the output signal is identically zero. We will again

---

[2] We may define a *real filter* as one whose output signal is real whenever its input signal is real.

need to extrapolate the phase response from surrounding frequencies (which will be done in §7.6.1).

If we back off a bit, the above results for the amplitude response are obvious without any calculations. The filter $y(n) = x(n) + x(n-1)$ is equivalent (except for a factor of 2) to a simple two-point average, $y(n) = [x(n) + x(n-1)]/2$. Averaging adjacent samples in a signal is intuitively a low-pass filter because at low frequencies the sample amplitudes change slowly, so that the average of two neighboring samples is very close to either sample, while at high frequencies the adjacent samples tend to have opposite sign and to cancel out when added. The two extremes are frequency 0 Hz, at which the averaging has no effect, and half the sampling rate $f_s/2$ where the samples alternate in sign and exactly add to 0.

We are beginning to see that Eq. (1.1) may be a low-pass filter after all, since we found a boost of about 6 dB at the lowest frequency and a null at the highest frequency. (A gain of 2 may be expressed in decibels as $20 \log_{10}(2) \approx 6.02$ dB, and a *null* or *notch* is another term for a gain of 0 at a single frequency.) Of course, we tried only two out of an infinite number of possible frequencies.

Let's go for broke and plug the general sinusoid into Eq. (1.1), confident that a table of trigonometry identities will see us through (after all, this is the simplest filter there is, right?). To set the input signal to a completely arbitrary sinusoid at amplitude A, phase ϕ, and frequency f Hz, we let $x(n) = A\cos(2\pi f nT + \phi)$. The output is then given by

$$y(n) = A\cos(2\pi f nT + \phi) + A\cos[2\pi f(n-1)T + \phi].$$

This input can be simplified as follows: Recall from the discussion surrounding Fig. 1.6 that only the peak-amplitude *ratio* and the phase *difference* between input and output sinusoids are needed to measure the frequency response. The filter phase response does not depend on ϕ above (due to time-invariance), and so we can set ϕ to 0. Also, the filter amplitude response does not depend on A (due to linearity), so we let $A = 1$. With these simplifications of $x(n)$, the gain and phase response of the filter will appear directly as the amplitude and phase of the output $y(n)$. Thus, we input the signal

$$x(n) = \cos(2\pi f nT) = \cos(\omega nT),$$

where $\omega \stackrel{\Delta}{=} 2\pi f$, as discussed in §A.1. (The symbol $\stackrel{\Delta}{=}$ means "is defined as".) With this input, the output of the simple low-pass filter is given by

$$y(n) = \cos(\omega nT) + \cos[\omega(n-1)T].$$

All that remains is to reduce the above expression to a single sinusoid with some frequency-dependent amplitude and phase. We do this first by using standard trigonometric identities [2] in order to avoid introducing complex numbers. Next, a much "easier" derivation using complex numbers will be given.

Note that a sum of sinusoids at the same frequency, but possibly different phase and amplitude, can always be expressed as a *single* sinusoid at that frequency with some resultant phase and amplitude. While we find this result by direct derivation in working out our simple example, the general case is derived in §A.3 on page 250 for completeness.

We have

$$
\begin{aligned}
y(n) &= \cos(\omega nT) + \cos[\omega(n-1)T] \\
&= \cos(\omega nT) + \cos(\omega nT)\cos(-\omega T) - \sin(\omega nT)\sin(-\omega T) \\
&= \cos(\omega nT) + \cos(\omega nT)\cos(\omega T) + \sin(\omega nT)\sin(\omega T) \\
&= [1 + \cos(\omega T)]\cos(\omega nT) + \sin(\omega T)\sin(\omega nT) \\
&= a(\omega)\cos(\omega nT) + b(\omega)\sin(\omega nT) \tag{1.4}
\end{aligned}
$$

where $a(\omega) \triangleq [1 + \cos(\omega T)]$ and $b(\omega) \triangleq \sin(\omega T)$. We are looking for an answer of the form

$$
y(n) = G(\omega)\cos[\omega nT + \Theta(\omega)],
$$

where $G(\omega)$ is the filter amplitude response and $\Theta(\omega)$ is the phase response. This may be expanded as

$$
y(n) = G(\omega)\cos[\Theta(\omega)]\cos(\omega nT) - G(\omega)\sin[\Theta(\omega)]\sin(\omega nT).
$$

Therefore,

$$
\begin{aligned}
a(\omega) &= G(\omega)\cos[\Theta(\omega)] \\
b(\omega) &= -G(\omega)\sin[\Theta(\omega)]. \tag{1.5}
\end{aligned}
$$

1.3.3   Amplitude Response

We can isolate the filter amplitude response $G(\omega)$ by squaring and adding the above two equations:

$$
\begin{aligned}
a^2(\omega) + b^2(\omega) &= G^2(\omega)\cos^2[\Theta(\omega)] + G^2(\omega)\sin^2[\Theta(\omega)] \\
&= G^2(\omega)\left\{\cos^2[\Theta(\omega)] + \sin^2[\Theta(\omega)]\right\} \\
&= G^2(\omega).
\end{aligned}
$$

This can then be simplified as follows:

$$
\begin{aligned}
G^2(\omega) &= a^2(\omega) + b^2(\omega) \\
&= [1 + \cos(\omega T)]^2 + \sin^2(\omega T) \\
&= 1 + 2\cos(\omega T) + \cos^2(\omega T) + \sin^2(\omega T) \\
&= 2 + 2\cos(\omega T) \\
&= 4\cos^2\left(\frac{\omega T}{2}\right).
\end{aligned}
$$

So we have made it to the *amplitude response* of the simple lowpass filter $y(n) = x(n) + x(n-1)$:

$$
G(\omega) = 2\left|\cos\left(\frac{\omega T}{2}\right)\right|
$$

Since $\cos(\pi f T)$ is nonnegative for $-f_s/2 \le f \le f_s/2$, it is unnecessary to take the absolute value as long as f is understood to lie in this range:

$$
\boxed{G(\omega) = 2\cos(\pi f T)} \qquad |f| \le \frac{f_s}{2} \tag{1.6}
$$

1.3.4 Phase Response

Now we may isolate the filter phase response $\Theta(\omega)$ by taking a ratio of the $a(\omega)$ and $b(\omega)$ in Eq. (1.5):

$$
\begin{aligned}
\frac{b(\omega)}{a(\omega)} &= -\frac{G(\omega)\sin[\Theta(\omega)]}{G(\omega)\cos[\Theta(\omega)]} \\
&= -\frac{\sin[\Theta(\omega)]}{\cos[\Theta(\omega)]} \\
&\triangleq -\tan[\Theta(\omega)]
\end{aligned}
$$

Substituting the expansions of $a(\omega)$ and $b(\omega)$ yields

$$
\begin{aligned}
\tan[\Theta(\omega)] &= -\frac{b(\omega)}{a(\omega)} \\
&= -\frac{\sin(\omega T)}{1 + \cos(\omega T)} \\
&= -\frac{2\sin(\omega T/2)\cos(\omega T/2)}{1 + [\cos^2(\omega T/2) - \sin^2(\omega T/2)]} \\
&= -\frac{2\sin(\omega T/2)\cos(\omega T/2)}{2\cos^2(\omega T/2)} = -\frac{\sin(\omega T/2)}{\cos(\omega T/2)} = \tan(-\omega T/2).
\end{aligned}
$$

Thus, the phase response of the simple lowpass filter $y(n) = x(n) + x(n-1)$ is

$$\boxed{\Theta(\omega) = -\omega T/2.} \tag{1.7}$$

We have completely solved for the frequency response of the simplest lowpass filter given in Eq. (1.1) using only trigonometric identities. We found that an input sinusoid of the form

$$x(n) = A\cos(2\pi f nT + \phi)$$

produces the output

$$y(n) = 2A\cos(\pi fT)\cos(2\pi f nT + \phi - \pi fT).$$

Thus, the gain versus frequency is $2\cos(\pi fT)$ and the change in phase at each frequency is given by $-\pi fT$ radians. These functions are shown in Fig. 1.7 on page 9. With these functions at our disposal, we can predict the filter output for any sinusoidal input. Since, by Fourier theory [84], every signal can be represented as a sum of sinusoids, we've also solved the more general problem of predicting the output given *any* input signal.

1.4   An Easier Way

We derived the frequency response above using trig identities in order to minimize the mathematical level involved. However, it turns out it is actually easier, though more advanced, to use *complex numbers* for this purpose. To do this, we need *Euler's identity*:

$$\boxed{e^{j\theta} = \cos(\theta) + j\sin(\theta)} \qquad \text{(Euler's Identity)} \tag{1.8}$$

where $j \triangleq \sqrt{-1}$ is the imaginary unit for complex numbers, and e is a transcendental constant approximately equal to $2.718\ldots$. Euler's identity is fully derived in [84]; here we will simply use it "on faith." It can be proved by computing the Taylor series expansion of each side of Eq. (1.8) and showing equality term by term [84, 14].

1.4.1   Complex Sinusoids

Using Euler's identity to represent sinusoids, we have

$$Ae^{j(\omega t + \phi)} = A\cos(\omega t + \phi) + jA\sin(\omega t + \phi) \tag{1.9}$$

when time t is continuous (see §A.1 for a list of notational conventions), and when time is discrete,

$$Ae^{j(\omega nT + \phi)} = A\cos(\omega nT + \phi) + jA\sin(\omega nT + \phi). \tag{1.10}$$

Any function of the form $Ae^{j(\omega t+\phi)}$ or $Ae^{j(\omega nT+\phi)}$ will henceforth be called a *complex sinusoid*.[3] We will see that it is easier to manipulate both *sine* and *cosine* simultaneously in this form than it is to deal with either *sine* or *cosine* separately. One may even take the point of view that $e^{j\theta}$ is *simpler* and *more fundamental* than $\sin(\theta)$ or $\cos(\theta)$, as evidenced by the following identities (which are immediate consequences of Euler's identity, Eq. (1.8)):

$$\cos(\theta) \quad = \quad \frac{e^{j\theta} + e^{-j\theta}}{2} \qquad\qquad (1.11)$$

$$\sin(\theta) \quad = \quad \frac{e^{j\theta} - e^{-j\theta}}{2j} \qquad\qquad (1.12)$$

Thus, *sine* and *cosine* may each be regarded as a combination of two complex sinusoids. Another reason for the success of the complex sinusoid is that we will be concerned only with real *linear* operations on signals. This means that j in Eq. (1.8) will never be multiplied by j or raised to a power by a linear filter with real coefficients. Therefore, the real and imaginary parts of that equation are actually treated *independently*. Thus, we can feed a complex sinusoid into a filter, and the real part of the output will be the *cosine* response and the imaginary part of the output will be the *sine* response. For the student new to analysis using complex variables, natural questions at this point include "Why e?, Where did the imaginary exponent come from? Are imaginary exponents legal?" and so on. These questions are fully answered in [84] and elsewhere [53, 14]. Here, we will look only at some intuitive connections between complex sinusoids and the more familiar real sinusoids.

1.4.2　Complex Amplitude

Note that the amplitude A and phase ϕ can be viewed as the magnitude and angle of a single complex number

$$\mathcal{A} \triangleq Ae^{j\phi}$$

which is naturally thought of as the *complex amplitude* of the complex sinusoid defined by the left-hand side of either Eq. (1.9) or Eq. (1.10). The complex amplitude is the same whether we are talking about the continuous-time sinusoid $Ae^{j(\omega t+\phi)}$ or the discrete-time sinusoid $Ae^{j(\omega nT+\phi)}$.

---

[3] Some authors refer to $e^{j\omega nT}$ as a *complex exponential,* but it is useful to reserve that term for signals of the form $Ar^{n}e^{j\omega nT}$, where $r > 0$. That is, complex exponentials are more generally allowed to have a non-constant *exponential amplitude envelope*. Note that all complex exponentials can be generated from two complex numbers, $\mathcal{A} = Ae^{j\phi}$ and $z = re^{j\omega T}$, viz., $\mathcal{A}z^{n}$. This topic is explored further in [84].

1.4.3   Phasor Notation

The complex amplitude $\mathcal{A} \triangleq Ae^{j\phi}$ is also defined as the *phasor* associated with any sinusoid having amplitude A and phase ϕ. The term "phasor" is more general than "complex amplitude", however, because it also applies to the corresponding *real* sinusoid given by the real part of Equations (1.9–1.10). In other words, the real sinusoids $A\cos(\omega t + \phi)$ and $A\cos(\omega nT + \phi)$ may be expressed as

$$A\cos(\omega t + \phi) \quad \triangleq \quad \mathrm{re}\left\{Ae^{j(\omega t + \phi)}\right\} = \mathrm{re}\left\{\mathcal{A}e^{j\omega t}\right\}$$

$$A\cos(\omega nT + \phi) \quad \triangleq \quad \mathrm{re}\left\{Ae^{j(\omega nT + \phi)}\right\} = \mathrm{re}\left\{\mathcal{A}e^{j\omega nT}\right\}$$

and $\mathcal{A}$ is the associated phasor in each case. Thus, we say that the *phasor representation* of $A\cos(\omega t + \phi)$ is $\mathcal{A} \triangleq Ae^{j\phi}$. Phasor analysis is often used to analyze linear time-invariant systems such as analog electrical circuits.

1.4.4   Plotting Complex Sinusoids as Circular Motion

Figure 1.8 shows Euler's relation graphically as it applies to sinusoids. A point traveling with uniform velocity around a circle with radius 1 may be represented by $e^{j\omega t} = e^{j2\pi ft}$ in the complex plane, where t is time and f is the number of revolutions per second. The projection of this motion onto the horizontal (real) axis is $\cos(\omega t)$, and the projection onto the vertical (imaginary) axis is $\sin(\omega t)$. For *discrete-time* circular motion, replace t by nT to get $e^{j\omega nT} = e^{j2\pi(f/f_s)n}$ which may be interpreted as a point which jumps an arc length $2\pi f/f_s$ radians along the circle each sampling instant.

> *Euler's identity says that a complex sinusoid corresponds to circular motion in the complex plane, and is the vector sum of two sinusoidal motions.*

For circular motion to ensue, the sinusoidal motions must be at the same frequency, one-quarter cycle out of phase, and perpendicular (orthogonal) to each other. (With phase differences other than one-quarter cycle, the motion is generally elliptical.)

The converse of this is also illuminating. Take the usual circular motion $e^{j\omega t}$ which spins counterclockwise along the unit circle as t increases, and add to it a similar but clockwise circular motion $e^{-j\omega t}$. This is shown in Fig. 1.9. Next apply Euler's identity to get

$$
\begin{aligned}
e^{j\omega t} + e^{-j\omega t} &= [\cos(\omega t) + j\sin(\omega t)] + [\cos(-\omega t) + j\sin(-\omega t)] \\
&= \cos(\omega t) + j\sin(\omega t) + \cos(\omega t) - j\sin(\omega t) \\
&= 2\cos(\omega t)
\end{aligned}
$$

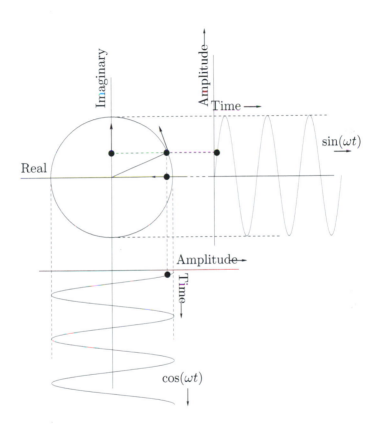

Figure 1.8: Relation of uniform circular motion to sinusoidal motion via Euler's identity $\exp(j\omega t) = \cos(\omega t) + j\sin(\omega t)$ (Eq. (1.8)). The projection of $\exp(j\omega t)$ onto the real axis is $\cos(\omega t)$, and its projection onto the imaginary axis is $\sin(\omega t)$.

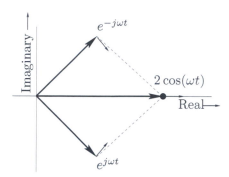

Figure 1.9: Opposite circular motions add to give real sinusoidal motion, $e^{j\omega t} + e^{-j\omega t} = 2\cos(\omega t)$.

Thus,

> Cosine *motion is the vector sum of two circular motions with the same angular speed but opposite direction.*

This statement is a graphical or geometric interpretation of Eq. (1.11). A similar derivation (subtracting instead of adding) gives the *sine* identity Eq. (1.12).

We call $e^{j\omega t}$ a *positive-frequency sinusoidal component* when $\omega > 0$, and $e^{-j\omega t}$ is the corresponding *negative-frequency component*. Note that both *sine* and *cosine* signals have equal-amplitude positive- and negative-frequency components (see also [84, 53]). This happens to be true of every *real* signal (*i.e.*, non-complex). To see this, recall that every signal can be represented as a sum of complex sinusoids at various frequencies (its *Fourier expansion*). For the signal to be real, every positive-frequency complex sinusoid must be summed with a negative-frequency sinusoid of equal amplitude. In other words, any counterclockwise circular motion must be matched by an equal and opposite clockwise circular motion in order that the imaginary parts always cancel to yield a real signal (see Fig. 1.9). Thus, a real signal always has a magnitude spectrum which is symmetric about 0 Hz. Fourier symmetries such as this are developed more completely in [84].

1.4.5   Rederiving the Frequency Response

Let's repeat the mathematical sine-wave analysis of the simplest low-pass filter, but this time using a complex sinusoid instead of a real one. Thus, we will test the filter's response at frequency f by setting its input to

$$x(n) = Ae^{j(2\pi f nT + \phi)} = A\cos(2\pi f nT + \phi) + jA\sin(2\pi f nT + \phi).$$

Again, because of time-invariance, the frequency response will not depend on ϕ, so let $\phi = 0$. Similarly, owing to linearity, we may normalize A to 1. By virtue of Euler's relation Eq. (1.8) and the linearity of the filter, setting the input to $x(n) = e^{j\omega nT}$ is physically equivalent to putting $\cos(\omega nT)$ into one copy of the filter and $\sin(\omega nT)$ into a separate copy of the same filter. The signal path where the *cosine* goes in is the *real* part of the signal, and the other signal path is simply called the *imaginary* part. Thus, a complex signal in real life is implemented as two real signals processed in parallel; in particular, a complex sinusoid is implemented as two real sinusoids, side by side, one-quarter cycle out of phase. When the filter itself is real, two copies of it suffice to process a complex signal. If the filter is complex, we must implement complex multiplies between the complex signal samples and filter coefficients.

Using the normal rules for manipulating exponents, we find that the output of the simple low-pass filter in response to the complex sinusoid at frequency $\omega/2\pi$ Hz is given by

$$
\begin{aligned}
y(n) &= x(n) + x(n-1) \\
&= e^{j\omega nT} + e^{j\omega(n-1)T} \\
&= e^{j\omega nT} + e^{j\omega nT}e^{-j\omega T} \\
&= (1 + e^{-j\omega T})e^{j\omega nT} \\
&= (1 + e^{-j\omega T})x(n) \\
&\triangleq H(e^{j\omega T})x(n),
\end{aligned}
$$

where we have defined $H(e^{j\omega T}) \triangleq (1 + e^{-j\omega T})$, which we will show is in fact the *frequency response* of this filter at frequency ω. This derivation is clearly easier than the trigonometry approach. What may be puzzling at first, however, is that the filter is expressed as a *frequency-dependent complex multiply* (when the input signal is a complex sinusoid). What does this mean? Well, the theory we are blindly trusting at this point says it must somehow mean a gain scaling and a phase shift. This is true and easy to see once the complex filter gain is expressed in *polar form*,

$$H(e^{j\omega T}) = G(\omega)e^{j\Theta(\omega)},$$

where the gain versus frequency is given by $G(\omega) \triangleq |H(e^{j\omega T})|$ (the absolute value, or modulus of H), and the phase shift in radians versus frequency is given by the phase angle (or argument) $\Theta(\omega) \triangleq \angle H(e^{j\omega T})$. In other words, we must find

$$G(\omega) \triangleq \left| H(e^{j\omega T}) \right|$$

which is the amplitude response, and

$$\Theta(\omega) \triangleq \angle H(e^{j\omega T})$$

which is the phase response. There is a trick we can call "balancing the exponents," which will work nicely for the simple low-pass of Eq. (1.1).

$$
\begin{aligned}
H(e^{j\omega T}) &= (1 + e^{-j\omega T}) \\
&= (e^{j\omega T/2} + e^{-j\omega T/2})e^{-j\omega T/2} \\
&= 2\cos(\omega T/2)e^{-j\omega T/2}
\end{aligned}
$$

It is now easy to see that

$$
\begin{aligned}
G(\omega) &= \left| 2\cos(\omega T/2)e^{-j\omega T/2} \right| \\
&= 2\left| \cos(\omega T/2) \right| \\
&= 2\cos(\omega T/2) = 2\cos(\pi fT), \qquad |f| \le f_s/2.
\end{aligned}
$$

and

$$\Theta(\omega) = -\frac{\omega T}{2} = -\pi fT = -\pi \frac{f}{f_s}, \qquad |f| \le f_s/2.$$

We have derived again the graph of Fig. 1.7 on page 9, which shows the complete frequency response of Eq. (1.1). The gain of the simplest low-pass filter varies, as *cosine* varies, from 2 to 0 as the frequency of an input sinusoid goes from 0 to half the sampling rate. In other words, the amplitude response of Eq. (1.1) goes sinusoidally from 2 to 0 as ωT goes from 0 to π. It does seem somewhat reasonable to consider it a low-pass, and it is a poor one in the sense that it is hard to see which frequency should be called the cut-off frequency. We see that the spectral "roll-off" is very slow, as low-pass filters go, and this is what we pay for the extreme simplicity of Eq. (1.1). The phase response $\Theta(\omega) = -\omega T/2$ is linear in frequency, which gives rise to a constant time delay irrespective of the signal frequency (see Problem 3 on page 22).

It deserves to be emphasized that all a linear time-invariant filter can do to a sinusoid is *scale its amplitude* and *change its phase*. Since a sinusoid is completely determined by its amplitude A, frequency f, and phase ϕ, the constraint on the filter is that the output must also be a sinusoid, and furthermore it must be at the same frequency as the input sinusoid. More explicitly:

> If a sinusoid, $A_1 \cos(\omega nT + \phi_1)$, is input to a linear time-invariant filter, then the output signal (after start-up transients have died away) will be a sinusoid at the same frequency, $A_2 \cos(\omega nT + \phi_2)$. The only possible differences between the input and output are in their relative amplitude and relative phase. Any linear time-invariant filter may thus be completely characterized by its gain A_2/A_1, and phase $\phi_2 - \phi_1$, at each frequency.

Mathematically, a sinusoid has no beginning and no end, so there really are no start-up transients in the theoretical setting. However, in practice, we must approximate eternal sinusoids with finite-time sinusoids whose starting time was so long ago that the filter output is essentially the same as if the input had been applied forever.

Tying it all together, the general output of a linear time-invariant filter with a complex sinusoidal input may be expressed as

$$
\begin{aligned}
y(n) \;&=\; (\textit{Complex Filter Gain}) \; \textit{times} \; (\textit{Input Circular Motion} \\
&\qquad \textit{with Radius A, Phase } \phi) \\
&=\; \left[G(\omega)e^{j\Theta(\omega)} \right] \left[A e^{j(\omega nT + \phi)} \right] \\
&=\; [G(\omega)A]\, e^{j[\omega nT + \phi + \Theta(\omega)]} \\
&=\; \textit{Circular Motion with Radius } [G(\omega)A] \textit{ and Phase } [\phi + \Theta(\omega)].
\end{aligned}
$$

1.5 Summary

This chapter has introduced many of the concepts associated with digital filters, such as signal representations, filter representations, difference equations, signal flow graphs, software implementations, sine-wave analysis (real and complex), frequency response, amplitude response, phase response, and other related topics. We used a simple filter example to motivate the need for more advanced methods to analyze digital filters of arbitrary complexity. We found even in the simple example of Eq. (1.1) that complex variables are much more compact and convenient for representing signals and analyzing filters than are trigonometric techniques. We employ a complex sinusoid $Ae^{j(\omega nT + \phi)}$ having three parameters: amplitude, phase, and frequency, and when we put a complex sinusoid into any linear time-invariant digital filter, the filter behaves as a simple complex gain $H(e^{j\omega T}) = G(\omega)e^{j\Theta(\omega)}$, where the magnitude $G(\omega)$ and phase $\Theta(\omega)$ are the amplitude response and phase response, respectively, of the filter.

1.6   Elementary Filter Theory Problems

1. *General Amplitude and Phase in Deriving Frequency Response:*
   Repeat the derivation of Eq. (1.13) without the simplifications $A = 1$, $\phi = 0$. That is, let

   $$x(n) = Ae^{j(\omega nT + \phi)}$$

   and find $y(n)$ from Eq. (1.1). Verify that the frequency response is the same.

2. *A Modification of the Simplest Low-Pass Filter:*
   Consider the filter

   $$v(n) = x(n) - x(n-1)$$

   which is identical to Eq. (1.1) except that adjacent input samples are sub- tracted rather than added. Derive the amplitude response and the phase response. How has the response changed? Would you call this a low-pass filter, a high-pass filter, or something else?

3. *Linear Phase Means Simple Waveform Delay:*
   Show that the phase response $\Theta(\omega) = -\omega T/2$ obtained for Eq. (1.1) corresponds to a waveform delay of one-half sample ($T/2$ sec) at all frequencies.

4. *Complex Numbers and Trigonometry:*
   Show how easy it is to derive the identities

$$\cos(a + b) \;=\; \cos(a)\cos(b) - \sin(a)\sin(b)$$
$$\sin(a + b) \;=\; \sin(a)\cos(b) + \cos(a)\sin(b)$$

   by using Euler's identity and the formula

$$e^{j(a+b)} = e^{ja}e^{jb}$$

   How would you derive the $\cos(a+b)$ identity, say, if you did not know the answer and did not use complex numbers?

5. *Filters with Coefficients:*
   The analysis for Eq. (1.1) will work for a larger class of filters. Try to get the frequency response for the filter

$$y(n) = ax(n) - ax(n - 2)$$

   where a is a constant but arbitrary gain. Plot the amplitude response $G(\omega)$. Would you call this a low-pass filter, a high-pass filter, or something else entirely? What is the effect on $G(\omega)$ when a is changed? How does the phase response $\Theta(\omega)$ depend on a?

Chapter 2

Matlab Analysis of the Simplest Lowpass Filter

The example filter implementation listed in Fig. 1.3 on page 5 was written in the C programming language so that all computational details would be fully specified. However, C is a relatively low-level language for signal-processing software. Higher level languages such as *matlab* make it possible to write powerful programs much faster and more reliably. Even in embedded applications, for which assembly language is typically required, it is usually best to develop and debug the system in matlab beforehand.

The Matlab (R) product by The Mathworks, Inc.,[1] is far and away the richest implementation of the matlab language. However, it is very expensive for non-students, so you may at some point want to consider the free, open-source alternative called Octave.[2] All examples in this chapter will work in either Matlab or Octave,[3] except that some plot-related commands may need to be modified. The term *matlab* (not capitalized) will refer henceforth to either Matlab or Octave, or any other compatible implementation of the matlab language.[4]

---

[1] http://www.mathworks.com

[2] http://www.octave.org

[3] Users of Matlab will also need the Signal Processing Toolbox, which is available for an additional charge. Users of Octave will also need the free "Octave Forge" collection, which contains functions corresponding to the Signal Processing Toolbox.

[4] In an effort to improve the matlab language, Octave does not maintain 100% compatibility with Matlab. See http://octave.sf.net/compatibility.html for details.

This chapter provides four matlab programming examples to complement the mathematical analysis of §1.3:

2.1: Filter *implementation*

2.2: Simulated *sine-wave analysis*

2.3: Simulated *complex* sine-wave analysis

2.4: Practical *frequency-response* analysis

In all four examples, the simplest lowpass filter, $y(n) = x(n) + x(n-1)$, is used as the specific filter for implementation or analysis, and the results obtained by simulations are compared to those obtained from theory in §1.3.

Note: The reader is expected to know (at least some) matlab before proceeding. See, for example, the Matlab Getting Started[5] documentation, or just forge ahead and use the examples below to start learning matlab. (It is very readable, as computer languages go.) To skip over the matlab examples for now, proceed to Chapter 3 starting on page 47.

2.1   Matlab Filter Implementation

In this section, we will implement (in matlab) the simplest lowpass filter

$$y(n) = x(n) + x(n-1), \ n = 1, 2, \ldots, N$$

(from Eq. (1.1)).   For the simplest lowpass filter, we had two program listings:

- Fig. 1.3 on page 5 listed `simplp` for filtering one block of data, and

- Fig. 1.4 on page 6 listed a main program for testing `simplp`.

In matlab, there is a built-in function called `filter`[6] which will implement `simplp` as a special case. The syntax is

```
y = filter (B, A, x)
```

where

x is the input signal (a vector of any length),

y is the output signal (returned equal in length to x),

---

[5]http://www.mathworks.com/access/helpdesk/help/techdoc/
[6]Say `help filter` in Matlab or Octave to view the documentation. In Matlab, you can also say `doc filter` to view more detailed documentation in a Web browser.

A is a vector of filter *feedback coefficients*, and

B is a vector of filter *feedforward coefficients*.

The `filter` function performs the following iteration over the elements of
x to implement any causal, finite-order, linear, time-invariant digital filter:[7]

$$
\begin{aligned}
\texttt{y}(n) \;=\; & \sum_{k=0}^{M_n} \texttt{B}(k+1)\texttt{x}(n-k) \\
& -\; \sum_{k=1}^{N_n} \texttt{A}(k+1)\texttt{y}(n-k), \quad n=1,2,\ldots,N_x \qquad (2.1)
\end{aligned}
$$

where $N_x \overset{\Delta}{=} \texttt{length(x)}$, $N_n \overset{\Delta}{=} \min\{N, n-1\}$, $M_n \overset{\Delta}{=} \min\{M, n-1\}$, $M+1$
is the length of B, $N+1$ is the length of A, and $\texttt{A}(1)$ is assumed to be 1.
(Otherwise, B and A are divided through by $\texttt{A}(1)$. Note that $\texttt{A}(1)$ is not
used in Eq. (2.1).) The relatively awkward indexing in Eq. (2.1) is due to
the fact that, in matlab, all array indices start at 1, not 0 as in most C
programs.

Note that Eq. (2.1) could be written directly in matlab using two `for`
loops (as shown in Fig. 3.2 on page 51). However, this would execute *much*
slower because the matlab language is *interpreted*, while built-in functions
such as `filter` are pre-compiled C modules. As a general rule, matlab
programs should avoid iterating over individual samples whenever possible. Instead, whole signal vectors should be processed using expressions
involving vectors and matrices. In other words, algorithms should be "vectorized" as much as possible. Accordingly, to get the most out of matlab,
it is necessary to know some linear algebra [58].

The simplest lowpass filter of Eq. (1.1) is *nonrecursive* (no feedback),
so the feedback coefficient vector A is set to 1.[8] Recursive filters will be
introduced later in §5.1. The minus sign in Eq. (2.1) will make sense after
we study *filter transfer functions* in Chapter 6.

The feedforward coefficients needed for the simplest lowpass filter are

$$
\texttt{B} = [1, 1].
$$

With these settings, the `filter` function implements

$$
\begin{aligned}
\texttt{y}(1) \;&=\; \texttt{B}(1) \cdot \texttt{x}(1) \\
\texttt{y}(n) \;&=\; \texttt{B}(1) \cdot \texttt{x}(n) + \texttt{B}(2) \cdot \texttt{x}(n-1) \\
&=\; \texttt{x}(n) + \texttt{x}(n-1), \quad n = 2,3,\ldots,\texttt{length(x)}.
\end{aligned}
$$

---

[7]These adjectives will be defined precisely in Chapters 4 and 5.

[8] As we will learn in §5.1, `A(1)` is the coefficient of the *current output sample*, which
is always normalized to 1. The actual feedback coefficients are `-A(2),-A(3),`....

```
% simplpm1.m - matlab main program implementing
%               the simplest lowpass filter:
%
%                     y(n) = x(n)+x(n-1)}

N=10;         % length of test input signal
x = 1:N;      % test input signal (integer ramp)
B = [1,1];    % transfer function numerator
A = 1;        % transfer function denominator

y = filter(B,A,x);

for i=1:N
  disp(sprintf('x(%d)=%f\ty(%d)=%f',i,x(i),i,y(i)));
end

% Output:
%    octave:1> simplpm1
%    x(1)=1.000000        y(1)=1.000000
%    x(2)=2.000000        y(2)=3.000000
%    x(3)=3.000000        y(3)=5.000000
%    x(4)=4.000000        y(4)=7.000000
%    x(5)=5.000000        y(5)=9.000000
%    x(6)=6.000000        y(6)=11.000000
%    x(7)=7.000000        y(7)=13.000000
%    x(8)=8.000000        y(8)=15.000000
%    x(9)=9.000000        y(9)=17.000000
%    x(10)=10.000000      y(10)=19.000000
```

Figure 2.1: Main matlab program for implementing the simplest low-pass filter $y(n) = x(n) + x(n-1)$.

A main test program analogous to Fig. 1.4 is shown in Fig. 2.1. Note that the input signal is processed in one big block, rather than being broken up into two blocks as in Fig. 1.4. If we want to process a large sound file block by block, we need some way to initialize the state of the filter for each block using the final state of the filter from the preceding block. The `filter` function accommodates this usage with an additional optional input and output argument:

```
[y, Sf] = filter (B, A, x, Si)
```

`Si` denotes the filter *initial* state, and `Sf` denotes its *final* state. A main program illustrating block-oriented processing is given in Fig. 2.2.

```
% simplpm2.m - block-oriented version of simplpm1.m

N=10;        % length of test input signal
NB=N/2;      % block length
x = 1:N;     % test input signal
B = [1,1];   % feedforward coefficients
A = 1;       % feedback coefficients (no-feedback case)

[y1, Sf] = filter(B,A,x(1:NB));       % process block 1
      y2 = filter(B,A,x(NB+1:N),Sf); % process block 2

for i=1:NB   % print input and output for block 1
  disp(sprintf('x(%d)=%f\ty(%d)=%f',i,x(i),i,y1(i)));
end

for i=NB+1:N % print input and output for block 2
  disp(sprintf('x(%d)=%f\ty(%d)=%f',i,x(i),i,y2(i-NB)));
end
```

Figure 2.2: Block-oriented version of the matlab program in Fig. 2.1.

2.2 Simulated Sine-Wave Analysis in Matlab

In this section, we will find the frequency response of the simplest lowpass filter

$$y(n) = x(n) + x(n-1), \quad n = 1, 2, \ldots, N.$$

using *simulated sine-wave analysis* carried out by a matlab program. This numerical approach complements the analytical approach followed in §1.3. Figure 2.3 gives a listing of the main script which invokes the sine-wave analysis function `swanal` listed in Fig. 2.4. The plotting/printing utilities `swanalmainplot` and `swanalplot` are listed in Appendix J starting at §J.13 on page 416.

```
% swanalmain.m - matlab program for simulated sine-wave
%                analysis on the simplest lowpass filter:
%
%                      y(n) = x(n)+x(n-1)}

B = [1,1]; % filter feedforward coefficients
A = 1;     % filter feedback coefficients (none)

N=10;               % number of sinusoidal test frequencies
fs = 1;             % sampling rate in Hz (arbitrary)

fmax = fs/2;     % highest frequency to look at
df = fmax/(N-1);% spacing between frequencies
f = 0:df:fmax;   % sampled frequency axis
dt = 1/fs;       % sampling interval in seconds
tmax = 10;       % number of seconds to run each sine test
t = 0:dt:tmax;   % sampled time axis
ampin = 1;       % test input signal amplitude
phasein = 0;     % test input signal phase

[gains,phases] = swanal(t,f/fs,B,A); % sine-wave analysis

swanalmainplot;    % final plots and comparison to theory
```

Figure 2.3: Main matlab program for computing the *frequency response* of the simplest low-pass filter $y(n) = x(n) + x(n-1)$ by means of *simulated sine-wave analysis*.

```
function [gains,phases] = swanal(t,f,B,A)
% SWANAL - Perform sine-wave analysis on filter B(z)/A(z)

ampin = 1;        % input signal amplitude
phasein = 0;      % input signal phase

N = length(f);          % number of test frequencies
gains = zeros(1,N);   % pre-allocate amp-response array
phases = zeros(1,N); % pre-allocate phase-response array
if length(A)==1
  ntransient=length(B)-1; % no. samples to steady state
else
  error('Need to set transient response duration here');
end

for k=1:length(f)      % loop over analysis frequencies
  s = ampin*cos(2*pi*f(k)*t+phasein); % test sinusoid
  y = filter(B,A,s); % run it through the filter
  yss = y(ntransient+1:length(y)); % chop off transient
  % measure output amplitude as max (SHOULD INTERPOLATE):
  [ampout,peakloc] = max(abs(yss)); % ampl. peak & index
  gains(k) = ampout/ampin;  % amplitude response
  if ampout < eps  % eps returns "machine epsilon"
    phaseout=0;        % phase is arbitrary at zero gain
  else
    sphase = 2*pi*f(k)*(peakloc+ntransient-1);
    % compute phase by inverting sinusoid (BAD METHOD):
    phaseout = acos(yss(peakloc)/ampout) - sphase;
    phaseout = mod2pi(phaseout); % reduce to [-pi,pi]
  end
  phases(k) = phaseout-phasein;
  swanalplot; % signal plotting script
end
```

Figure 2.4: Matlab function for performing *simulated sine-wave analysis*.

In the `swanal` function (Fig. 2.4), test sinusoids are generated by the line

```
s = ampin * cos(2*pi*f(k)*t + phasein);
```

where amplitude, frequency (Hz), and phase (radians) of the sinusoid are given be `ampin`, `f(k)`, and `phasein`, respectively. As discussed in §1.3, assuming linearity and time-invariance (LTI) allows us to set

```
ampin = 1;        % input signal amplitude
phasein = 0;      % input signal phase
```

without loss of generality. (Note that we must also assume the filter is LTI for sine-wave analysis to be a general method for characterizing the filter's response.) The test sinusoid is passed through the digital filter by the line

```
y = filter(B,A,s); % run s through the filter
```

producing the output signal in vector y. For this example (the simplest lowpass filter), the filter coefficients are simply

```
B = [1,1]; % filter feedforward coefficients
A = 1;     % filter feedback coefficients (none)
```

The coefficient `A(1)` is technically a coefficient on the output signal itself, and it should always be normalized to 1. (B and A can be multiplied by the same nonzero constant to carry out this normalization when necessary.)

Figure 2.5 shows one of the intermediate plots produced by the sine-wave analysis routine in Fig. 2.4. This figure corresponds to Fig. 1.6 in §1.3 (see page 7). In Fig. 2.5a, we see samples of the input test sinusoid overlaid with the continuous sinusoid represented by those samples. Figure 2.5b shows only the samples of the filter output signal: While we know the output signal becomes a sampled sinusoid after the one-sample transient response, we do not know its amplitude or phase until we measure it; the underlying continuous signal represented by the samples is therefore not plotted. (If we really wanted to see this, we could use software for *band-limited interpolation* [91], such as Matlab's `interp` function.) A plot such as Fig. 2.5 is produced for each test frequency, and the relative amplitude and phase are measured between the input and output to form one sample of the measured frequency response, as discussed in §1.3.

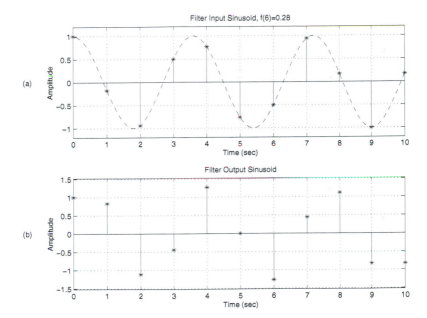

Figure 2.5: Input and output signals for the sixth test frequency $f(k) = f_s/4$ in the simulated sine-wave analysis of the simplest lowpass filter.

Next, the one-sample start-up transient is removed from the filter output signal y to form the "cropped" signal yss ("y steady state"). The final task is to measure the amplitude and phase of the yss. Output amplitude estimation is done in swanal by the line

```
[ampout,peakloc] = max(abs(yss));
```

Note that the peak amplitude found in this way is *approximate*, since the true peak of the output sinusoid generally occurs *between* samples. We will find the output amplitude much more accurately in the next two sections. We store the index of the amplitude peak in peakloc so it can be used to estimate phase in the next step. Given the output amplitude ampout, the *amplitude response* of the filter at frequency f(k) is given by

```
gains(k) = ampout/ampin;
```

The last step of swanal in Fig. 2.4 is to estimate the phase of the cropped filter output signal yss. Since we will have better ways to accomplish this later, we use a simplistic method here based on inverting the sinusoid analytically:

```
phaseout = acos(yss(peakloc)/ampout) ...
         - 2*pi*f(k)*(peakloc+ntransient-1);
phaseout = mod2pi(phaseout); % reduce to [-pi,pi)
```

Again, this is only an approximation since peakloc is only accurate to the nearest sample. The mod2pi utility reduces its scalar argument to the range $[-\pi, \pi)$,[9] and is listed in Fig. 2.6.

```
function [y] = mod2pi(x)
% MOD2PI - Reduce x to the range [-pi,pi)
  y=x;
  twopi = 2*pi;
  while y >= pi, y = y - twopi; end
  while y < -pi, y = y + twopi; end
```

Figure 2.6: Utility (matlab) for reducing a radian phase angle to $[-\pi, \pi)$.

In summary, the sine-wave analysis measures experimentally the gain and phase-shift of the digital filter at selected frequencies, thus measuring the frequency response of the filter at those frequencies. It is interesting to

---

[9]The notation $[a, b)$ denotes the *half-open interval*—the set of all real numbers between a and b, including a but not b.

compare these experimental results with the closed-form expressions for the
frequency response derived in §1.3.2. From Equations (1.6–1.7) we have

$$G(f) = 2\cos(\pi f/f_s)$$
$$\Theta(f) = -\pi f/f_s$$

where $G(f)$ denotes the *amplitude response* (filter gain versus frequency),
$\Theta(f)$ denotes the *phase response* (filter phase-shift versus frequency), f
is frequency in Hz, and $f_s = 1/T$ denotes the sampling rate. Both the
amplitude response and phase response are *real-valued* functions of (real)
frequency, while the *frequency response* is the *complex* function of frequency
given by $H(f) = G(f)e^{j\Theta(f)}$.

Figure 2.7 shows overlays of the measured and theoretical results.
While there is good general agreement, there are noticeable errors in the
measured amplitude and phase-response curves. Also, the phase-response
error tends to be large when there is an amplitude response error, since the
phase calculation used depends on knowledge of the amplitude response.

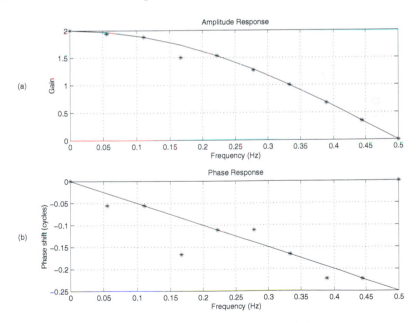

Figure 2.7: Overlay of measured and theoretical frequency response
when $f_{\text{max}} = f_s/2$.

It is important to understand the source(s) of deviation between the measured and theoretical values. Our simulated sine-wave analysis deviates from an ideal sine-wave analysis in the following ways (listed in ascending order of importance):

1. **The test sinusoids are *sampled* instead of being continuous in time:** It turns out this is a problem only for frequencies at half the sampling rate and above. Below half the sampling rate, sampled sinusoids contain exactly the same information as continuous sinusoids, and there is no penalty whatsoever associated with discrete-time sampling itself.

2. **The test sinusoid samples are *rounded* to a *finite precision:*** Digitally sampled sinusoids do suffer from a certain amount of round-off error, but Matlab and Octave use double-precision floating-point numbers by default (64 bits). As a result, our samples are far more precise than could be measured acoustically in the physical world. This is not a visible source of error in Fig. 2.7.

3. **Our test sinusoids are *finite duration*, while the ideal sinusoid is infinitely long:** This can be a real practical limitation. However, we worked around it completely by removing the start-up transient. For the simplest lowpass filter, the start-up transient is only one sample long. More generally, for digital filters expressible as a weighted sum of M successive samples (any *nonrecursive* LTI digital filter), the start-up transient is $M - 1$ samples long. When we consider *recursive* digital filters, which employ output feedback, we will no longer be able to remove the start-up transient exactly, because it generally decays *exponentially* instead of being finite in length. However, even in that case, as long as the recursive filter is stable, we can define the start-up transient as some number of time-constants of exponential decay, thereby making the approximation error as small as we wish, such as less than the round-off error.

4. **We measured the output amplitude and phase at a signal peak measured only to the nearest sample:** *This* is the major source of error in our simulation. The program of Fig. 2.3 measures the filter output amplitude very crudely as the maximum magnitude. In general, even for this simple filter, the maximum output signal amplitude occurs *between* samples. To measure this, we would need to use what is called *bandlimited interpolation* [91]. It is possible and practical to make the error arbitrarily small by increasing the sampling rate by some factor and finishing with quadratic interpolation

of the three samples about the peak magnitude.   Similar remarks apply to the measured output phase.

The need for interpolation is lessened greatly if the sampling rate is chosen to be unrelated to the test frequencies (ideally so that the number of samples in each sinusoidal period is an irrational number). Figure 2.8 shows the measured and theoretical results obtained by changing the highest test frequency `fmax` from $f_s/2$ to $f_s/2.34567$, and the number of samples in each test sinusoid `tmax` from 10 to 100. For these parameters, at least one sample falls very close to a true peak of the output sinusoid at each test frequency.

It should also be pointed out that one *never* estimates signal *phase* in practice by inverting the closed-form functional form assumed for the signal. Instead, we should *estimate the delay* of each output sinusoid relative to the corresponding input sinusoid. This leads to the general topic of *time delay estimation* [12]. Under the assumption that the round-off error can be modeled as "white noise" (typically this is an accurate assumption), the optimal time-delay estimator is obtained by finding the (interpolated) peak of the *cross-correlation* between the input and output signals. For further details on cross-correlation, a topic in *statistical* signal processing, see, *e.g.*, [77, 87].

Using the theory presented in later chapters, we will be able to compute very precisely the frequency response of any LTI digital filter without having to resort to bandlimited interpolation (for measuring amplitude response) or time-delay estimation (for measuring phase).

a)

b)

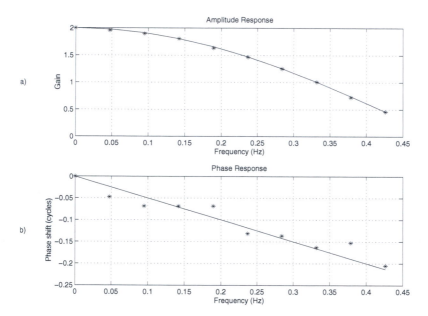

Figure 2.8: Overlay of measured and theoretical frequency response when $f_{max} = f_s/2.34567$.

2.3 Complex Sine-Wave Analysis

To illustrate the use of complex numbers in matlab, we repeat the previous sine-wave analysis of the simplest lowpass filter using complex sinusoids instead of real sinusoids.

Only the sine-wave analysis function needs to be rewritten, and it appears in Fig. 2.10. The initial change is to replace the line

```
s = ampin * cos(2*pi*f(k)*t + phasein); % real sinusoid
```

with the line

```
s = ampin * e .^ (j*2*pi*f(k)*t + phasein); % complex
```

Another change in Fig. 2.10 is that the plotsignals option is omitted, since a complex signal plot requires two real plots. This option is straightforward to restore if desired.

In the complex-sinusoid case, we find that measuring the amplitude and phase of the output signal is greatly facilitated. While we could use the previous method on either the real part or imaginary part of the complex output sinusoid, it is much better to measure its *instananeous amplitude* and *instananeous phase* by means of the formulas

$$A = |Ae^{j\theta}|$$
$$\theta = \angle Ae^{j\theta}.$$

Furthermore, since we should obtain the same answer for each sample, we can *average* the results to minimize noise due to round-off error:

```
ampout = mean(abs(yss)); % avg instantaneous amplitude
gains(k) = ampout/ampin; % amplitude response sample
sss = s(ntransient+1:length(y)); % chop input like output
phases(k) = mean(mod2pi(angle(yss.*conj(sss))));
```

The expression angle(yss.*conj(sss)) in the last line above produces a vector of estimated filter phases which are the same for each sample (to within accumulated round-off errors), because the term $e^{j2\pi f(k)nT+\phi}$ in yss is canceled by the conjugate of that term in conj(sss). We must be certain that the filter phase-shift is well within the interval $[-\pi, \pi)$; otherwise a call to mod2pi would be necessary for each element of angle(yss.*conj(sss)).

The final measured frequency response is plotted in Fig. 2.9. The test conditions were as in Fig. 2.7, *i.e.*, the highest test frequency was fmax = $f_s/2$, and the number of samples in each test sinusoid was tmax = 10. Unlike the real sine-wave analysis results in Fig. 2.7, there is no visible error associated with complex sine-wave analysis. Because instantaneous amplitude and phase are available from every sample of a complex sinusoid, there is no need for signal interpolation of any kind. The only source of error is now round-off error, and even that can be "averaged out" to any desired degree by enlarging the number of samples in the complex sinusoids used to probe the system.

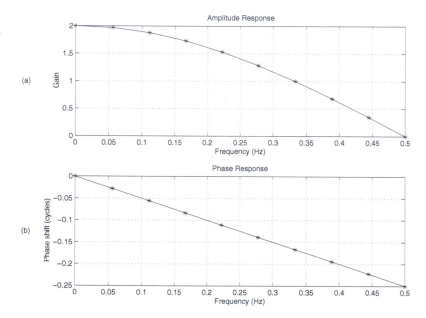

Figure 2.9: Overlay of measured and theoretical frequency responses of the simplest lowpass filter, obtained using *complex* sine-wave analysis.

This example illustrates some of the advantages of complex sinusoids over real sinusoids. Note also the ease with which complex vector quantities are manipulated in the matlab language.

```
function [gains,phases] = swanalc(t,f,B,A)
% SWANALC - Perform COMPLEX sine-wave analysis on the
%           digital filter having transfer function
%           H(z) = B(z)/A(z)

ampin = 1;      % input signal amplitude
phasein = 0;    % input signal phase

N = length(f);         % number of test frequencies
gains = zeros(1,N);    % pre-allocate amp-response array
phases = zeros(1,N);   % pre-allocate phase-response array

if length(A)==1, ntransient=length(B)-1, else
  error('Need to set transient response duration here');
end

for k=1:length(f)     % loop over analysis frequencies
  s = ampin*e.^(j*2*pi*f(k)*t+phasein); % test sinusoid
  y = filter(B,A,s); % run it through the filter
  yss = y(ntransient+1:length(y)); % chop off transient
  ampout = mean(abs(yss)); % avg instantaneous amplitude
  gains(k) = ampout/ampin; % amplitude response sample
  sss = s(ntransient+1:length(y)); % align with yss
  phases(k) = mean(mod2pi(angle(yss.*conj(sss))));
end
```

Figure 2.10: Matlab function for performing *complex* sine-wave analysis.

2.4   Practical Frequency-Response Analysis

The preceding examples were constructed to be tutorial on the level of this (introductory) part of this book, specifically to complement the previous chapter with matlab implementations of the concepts discussed. A more *typical* frequency response analysis, as used in practice, is shown in Fig. 2.11.

A comparison of computed and theoretical frequency response curves is shown in Fig. 2.12. There is no visible difference, and the only source of error is computational round-off error. Not only is this method as accurate as any other, it is by far the *fastest*, because it uses the Fast Fourier Transform (FFT).[10]

This FFT method for computing the frequency response is based on the fact that *the frequency response equals the filter transfer function $H(z) = B(z)/A(z)$ evaluated on the unit circle $z = e^{j\omega T}$ in the complex z plane.* We will get to these concepts later. For now, just note the ease with which we can compute the frequency response numerically in matlab. In fact, the length N frequency response of the simplest lowpass filter $y(n) = x(n) + x(n-1)$ can be computed using a single line of matlab code:

```
H = fft([1,1],N);
```

When N is a power of 2, the radix-2 FFT algorithm can be used for high-speed execution.[11] When $N > 2$, the FFT input is automatically "zero padded" in the time domain, resulting in *interpolation* of the frequency response [84].[12] In other words, the above line of code is equivalent to

```
H = fft([1,1,zeros(1,N-2)]);
```

when $N \geq 2$. The code in Fig. 2.11 carries out explicit zero-padding for clarity.

In both Matlab and Octave, there is a built-in function **freqz** which uses this FFT method for calculating the frequency response for almost any digital filter $B(z)/A(z)$ (any causal, finite-order, linear, and time-invariant digital filter, as explicated later in this book).

---

[10]http://en.wikipedia.org/wiki/Fast_Fourier_transform

[11]As a fine point, the fastest known FFT for power-of-2 lengths is the *split-radix FFT*— a hybrid of the radix-2 and radix-4 cases. See http://cnx.org/content/m12031/latest/ for more details.

[12]http://ccrma.stanford.edu/~jos/mdft/

```
% simplpnfa.m - matlab program for frequency analysis
%              of the simplest lowpass filter:
%
%                      y(n) = x(n)+x(n-1)}
%
%                  the way people do it in practice.

B = [1,1]; % filter feedforward coefficients
A = 1;     % filter feedback coefficients

N=128;     % FFT size = number of COMPLEX sinusoids
fs = 1;    % sampling rate in Hz (arbitrary)

Bzp = [B, zeros(1,N-length(B))]; % zero-pad for the FFT

H = fft(Bzp);   % length(Bzp) should be a power of 2

if length(A)>1 % we're not using this here
  Azp = [A,zeros(1,N-length(A))]; % but show it anyway.
  % [Should guard against fft(Azp)==0 for some index]
  H = H ./ fft(A,N); % denominator from feedback coeffs
end

% Discard the frequency-response samples at
% negative frequencies, but keep the samples at
% dc and fs/2:

nnfi = (1:N/2+1);      % nonnegative-frequency indices
Hnnf = H(nnfi);        % lose negative-frequency samples
nnfb = nnfi-1;         % corresponding bin numbers
f = nnfb*fs/N;         % frequency axis in Hz
gains = abs(Hnnf);     % amplitude response
phases = angle(Hnnf);  % phase response

plotfile = '../eps/simplpnfa.eps';
swanalmainplot;     % final plots and comparison to theory
```

Figure 2.11: Main program in matlab for finding the frequency response of the simplest low-pass filter $y(n) = x(n) + x(n-1)$ using the FFT. See §J.13 on page 416 for the final plotting utility.

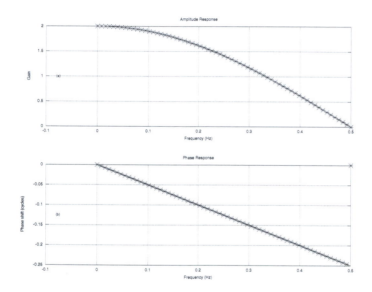

Figure 2.12: Overlay of theoretical and numerically determined frequency response using the FFT method.

2.5   Elementary Matlab Problems

1. Using the complex "test sinusoid"

$$x(n) = Ae^{j(\omega nT + \phi)},$$

   find the signal
   $$y(n) = x(n) - x(n-1) \tag{2.2}$$
   in polar form.

   (a) Regarding (2.2) as the definition of a digital filter, find its frequency response.

   (b) Find and plot (in Matlab or Octave) the amplitude response.

   (c) Find and plot the phase response.

   (d) What kind of filter is this? [Hint: It's not a lowpass filter.]

2. Translate the phase response obtained in the previous problem to *time delay* in seconds (as a function of frequency).

3. Consider now the digital filter

   $$y(n) = 3x(n) + 2x(n-2). \tag{2.3}$$

   (a) Find and plot (in Matlab or Octave) the amplitude response.

   (b) Find and plot the phase response.

4. Consider the arctangent function

   $$\theta = \tan^{-1}\left(\frac{y}{x}\right)$$

   where x and y can be any real number.

   (a) What is the range of θ?

   (b) What is the name of the matlab arctangent function whose output range is $-\pi$ to π?

5. Write a matlab script that generates a sinusoidal wave:

   (a) Set the sampling rate to 44100 samples per second.

   (b) Set the sinusoid length to 5 seconds.

   (c) Set the amplitude level to -6 dB (relative to maximum).

   (d) Set the frequency to 440 Hz.

   (e) Save the wave as a sound file named `mysound.wav`.

6. *Additive synthesis*
   A sum of cosine waves can be given by

$$x(t) = \sum_{k=1}^{N} A_k \cos(2\pi f_k t + \phi_k)$$

where A_k, f_k, and ϕ_k mean the peak amplitude, frequency, and initial phase of k_{th} sinusoidal component.
Write a Matlab function that implements this synthesis method and saves the result as an audio file. The syntax of your function should be:

```
function y = additive(f, A, fs, dur, name)
% f: vector of frequencies in Hz
% A: vector of complex amplitudes A*e^(j*phase)
% fs: sampling rate in Hz
% dur: total duration of the signal in seconds
% name: name of the output audio file
% f and Z must be of the same length:
% Z(1) corresponds to f(1) and so on.
```

Chapter 3

Analysis of a Digital Comb Filter

In Chapter 1, we extensively analyzed the simplest lowpass filter, $y(n) = x(n) + x(n-1)$ from a variety of points of view. This served to introduce many important concepts necessary for understanding digital filters. In Chapter 2, we analyzed the same filter using the matlab programming language. This chapter takes the next step by analyzing a more practical example, the *digital comb filter*, from start to finish using the analytical tools developed in later chapters. Consider this a "practical motivation" chapter—*i.e.*, its purpose is to introduce and illustrate the practical utility of tools for filter analysis before diving into a systematic development of those tools.

Suppose you look up the documentation for a "comb filter" in a software package you are using, and you find it described as follows:

```
out(n) = input(n) + feedforwardgain * input(n-delay1)
                  - feedbackgain * out(n-delay2)
```

Does this tell you everything you need to know? Well, it does tell you exactly what is implemented, but to fully understand it, you must be able to predict its *audible effects* on sounds passing through it. One helpful tool for this purpose is a plot of the *frequency response* of the filter. Moreover, if `delay1` or `delay2` correspond to more than a a few milliseconds of time delay, you probably want to see its *impulse response* as well. In some situations, a *pole-zero diagram* can give valuable insights.

As a preview of things to come, we will analyze and evaluate the above example comb filter rather thoroughly. Don't worry about understanding the details at this point—just follow how the analysis goes and try to intuit

the results. It will also be good to revisit this chapter later, after studying
subsequent chapters, as it provides a concise review of the main topics
covered. If you already fully understand the analyses illustrated in this
chapter, you might consider skipping ahead to the discussion of specific
audio filters in Appendix B, §B.4.

3.1   Difference Equation

We first write the comb filter specification in a more "mathematical" form
as a digital filter *difference equation*:

$$y(n) = x(n) + g_1\, x(n - M_1) - g_2\, y(n - M_2), \tag{3.1}$$

where $x(n)$ denotes the nth sample of the input signal, $y(n)$ is the output
at time n, and g_1 and g_2 denote the feedforward and feedback coefficients,
respectively. The signal flow graph is shown in Fig. 3.1.

3.2   Signal Flow Graph

Figure 3.1 shows the *signal flow graph* (or *system diagram*) for the class of
digital filters we are considering (digital comb filters). The symbol "z^{-M}"
means a *delay* of M samples (always an integer here). This notation for a
pure delay will make more sense after we derive the filter *transfer function*
in §3.7.

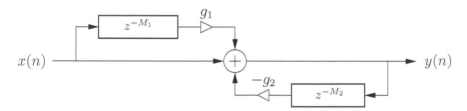

Figure 3.1: signal flow graph for digital filters having difference equations
of the form $y(n) = x(n) + g_1\, x(n - M_1) - g_2\, y(n - M_2)$ (digital comb filters).

3.3   Software Implementation in Matlab

In Matlab[1] or Octave,[2] this type of filter can be implemented using the `filter` function. For example, the following matlab[3] code computes the output signal y given the input signal x for a specific example comb filter:

```
g1 = (0.5)^3;              % Some specific coefficients
g2 = (0.9)^5;
B = [1 0 0 g1];            % Feedforward coefficients, M1=3
A = [1 0 0 0 0 g2];        % Feedback coefficients, M2=5
N = 1000;                  % Number of signal samples
x = rand(N,1);             % Random test input signal
y = filter(B,A,x);         % Matlab and Octave compatible
```

The example coefficients, $g1 = 0.5^3 = 0.125$ and $g2 = 0.9^5 = 0.59049$, are chosen to place all filter zeros at radius 0.5 and all filter poles at radius 0.9 in the complex z plane (as we shall see below).

The matlab `filter` function carries out the following computation for each element of the y array:

$$y(n) \;\; = \;\; \sum_{k=0}^{NB-1} B(k{+}1) \, * \, x(n{-}k) \qquad (3.2)$$

$$- \;\; \sum_{k=1}^{NA-1} A(k{+}1) \, * \, y(n{-}k) \qquad (3.3)$$

for $n = 1, 2, \ldots, N$, where `NA = length(A)` and `NB = length(B)`. Note that the indices of x and y can go negative in this expression. By default, such terms are replaced by zero. However, the `filter` function has an optional fourth argument for specifying the *initial state* of the filter, which includes past input and past output samples seen by the filter. This argument is used to forward the filter's state across successive blocks of data:

```
[y1,state] = filter(B,A,x1);        % filter 1st block x1
[y2,state] = filter(B,A,x2,state);  % filter 2nd block x2
...
```

---

[1] http://www.mathworks.com/access/helpdesk/help/techdoc/
[2] http://www.octave.org
[3] The term "matlab" (uncapitalized) will refer here to *either* Matlab or Octave [82]. Code described as "matlab" should run in either environment without modification.

Sample-Level Implementation in Matlab

For completeness, a direct matlab implementation of the built-in `filter` function (Eq. (3.3)) is given in Fig. 3.2. While this code is useful for study, it is far slower than the built-in `filter` function. As a specific example, filtering 10,000 samples of data using an order 100 filter on a 900MHz Athlon PC required 0.01 seconds for `filter` and 10.4 seconds for `filterslow`. Thus, `filter` was over a thousand times faster than `filterslow` in this case. The complete test is given in the following matlab listing:

```
x = rand(10000,1); % random input signal
B = rand(101,1);   % random coefficients
A = [1;0.001*rand(100,1)]; % random but probably stable
tic; yf=filter(B,A,x); ft=toc
tic; yfs=filterslow(B,A,x); fst=toc
```

The execution times differ greatly for two reasons:

1. recursive feedback cannot be "vectorized" in general, and

2. built-in functions such as `filter` are written in C, precompiled, and linked with the main program.

3.4   Software Implementation in C++

Figure 3.3 on page 52 gives a C++ program for implementing the same filter using the Synthesis Tool Kit (STK[4]). The example writes a sound file containing white-noise followed by filtered-noise from the example filter. Assuming the STK is installed in the usual place (as by Planet CCRMA), the following `Makefile` will compile and link it on a typical Linux system:

```
STK_LIB = -lstk
INCLUDE = -I/usr/include/stk

filterNoise: filterNoise.cpp
g++ $(INCLUDE) filterNoise.cpp -o filterNoise $(STK_LIB)
```

---

[4]http://ccrma.stanford.edu/CCRMA/Software/STK/

```
function [y] = filterslow(B,A,x)
% FILTERSLOW: Filter x to produce y = (B/A) x .
%        Equivalent to 'y = filter(B,A,x)' using
%        a slow (but tutorial) method.

NB = length(B);
NA = length(A);
Nx = length(x);

xv = x(:); % ensure column vector

% do the FIR part using vector processing:
v = B(1)*xv;
if NB>1
  for i=2:min(NB,Nx)
    xdelayed = [zeros(i-1,1); xv(1:Nx-i+1)];
    v = v + B(i)*xdelayed;
  end;
end; % fir part done, sitting in v

% The feedback part is intrinsically scalar,
% so this loop is where we spend a lot of time.
y = zeros(length(x),1); % pre-allocate y
ac = - A(2:NA);
for i=1:Nx, % loop over input samples
  t=v(i);    % initialize accumulator
  if NA>1,
    for j=1:NA-1
      if i>j,
        t=t+ac(j)*y(i-j);
        %else y(i-j) = 0
      end;
    end;
  end;
  y(i)=t;
end;

y = reshape(y,size(x)); % in case x was a row vector
```

Figure 3.2: Matlab function for implementing a digital filter directly.
Do not use this in practice because it is much slower than the built-in `filter` routine.

```cpp
// filterNoise.cpp - filtered white noise example
// Tested with STK 4.4.2

#include "Noise.h"  // Synthesis Tool Kit (STK) class
#include "Iir.h"     // STK class
#include "FileWvOut.h"  // STK class
#include <cmath>   // for pow()
#include <vector>

using namespace stk;

int main()
{
  Noise *theNoise = new Noise(); // Noise source

  /* Set up the filter */
  StkFloat bCoefficients[5] = {1,0,0,pow(0.5,3)};
  std::vector<StkFloat> b(bCoefficients, bCoefficients+5);
  StkFloat aCoefficients[7] = {1,0,0,0,0,pow(0.9,5)};
  std::vector<StkFloat> a(aCoefficients, aCoefficients+7);
  Iir *filter = new Iir;
  filter->setNumerator(b);
  filter->setDenominator(a);

  FileWvOut output("main");   /* write to main.wav */

  /* Generate one second of white noise */
  StkFloat amp = 0.1; // noise amplitude
  for (long i=0;i<SRATE;i++)   {
    output.tick(amp*theNoise->tick());
  }

  /* Generate filtered noise for comparison */
  for (long i=0;i<SRATE;i++)   {
    output.tick(filter->tick(amp*theNoise->tick()));
  }
}
```

Figure 3.3: C++ main program for computing filtered noise using the example digital filter. The Synthesis Tool Kit (STK), version 4.2, supplies the Noise and Filter classes used.

3.5   Software Implementation in Faust

The Faust language for signal processing is introduced in Appendix K. Figure 3.4 shows a Faust program for implementing our example comb filter. As illustrated in Appendix K, such programs can be compiled to produce LADSPA or VST audio plugins, or a Pure Data (PD) plugin, among others.

```
/* GUI Controls */
g1  = hslider("feedforward gain", 0.125, 0, 1, 0.01);
g2  = hslider("feedback gain", 0.59049, 0, 1, 0.01);

/* Signal Processing */
process = firpart : + ~ feedback
with {
  firpart(x) = x + g1 * x''';
  feedback(v) = 0 - g2 * v'''';
};
```

Figure 3.4: Faust main program implementing the example digital filter. (Tested in Faust version 0.9.9.2a2.)

As discussed in Appendix K, a prime (') denotes delaying a signal by one sample, and a tilde (~) denotes feedback. A colon (:) simply indicates a connection in series. The feedback signal v is delayed only four samples instead of five because there is a free "pipeline delay" associated with the feedback loop itself.

Faust's -svg option causes a block-diagram to be written to disk for each Faust expression (as further discussed in Appendix K). The block diagram for our example comb filter is shown in Fig. 3.5.

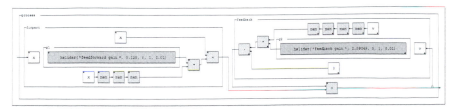

Figure 3.5: Block diagram generated by the Faust -svg option.

Compiling the Faust code in Fig. 3.4 for LADSPA plugin format produces a plugin that can be loaded into "JACK Rack" as depicted in Fig. 3.6.

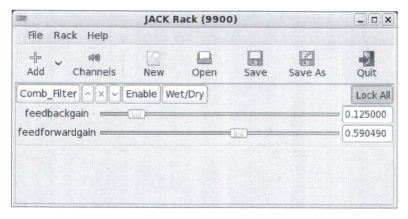

Figure 3.6: JACK Rack screenshot for the example comb filter.

At the risk of belaboring this mini-tour of filter embodiments in common use, Fig. 3.7 shows a screenshot of a PD test patch for the PD plugin generated from the Faust code in Fig. 3.4.

By the way, to change the Faust example of Fig. 3.4 to include its own driving noise, as in the STK example of Fig. 3.3, we need only add the line

```
import("music.lib");
```

at the top to define the **noise** signal (itself only two lines of Faust code), and change the **process** definition as follows:

```
process = noise : firpart : + ~ feedback
```

In summary, the Faust language provides a compact representation for many digital filters, as well as more general digital signal processing, and it is especially useful for quickly generating real-time implementations in various alternative formats. Appendix K gives a number of examples.

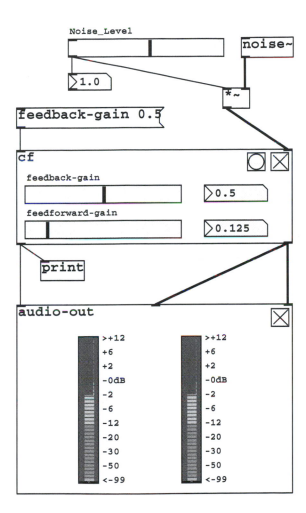

Figure 3.7: Pure Data (PD) screenshot for a test patch exercising a PD plugin named cf.pd that was generated automatically from the Faust code in Fig. 3.4 using the faust program and faust2pd script (see Appendix K for details).

3.6 Impulse Response

Figure 3.8 plots the *impulse response* of the example filter, as computed by
the matlab script shown in Fig. 3.9. (The plot-related commands are also
included for completeness.[5]) The *impulse signal* consists of a single sample
at time 0 having amplitude 1, preceded and followed by zeros (an ideal
"click" at time 0). Linear, time-invariant filters are fully characterized by
their response to this simple signal, as we will show in Chapter 4.

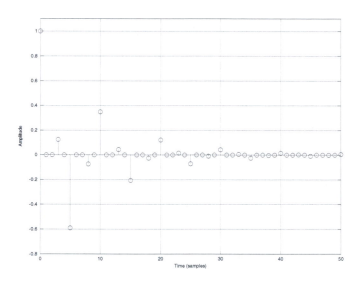

Figure 3.8: Impulse response of the example filter $y(n) = x(n) + 0.5^3 x(n-3) - 0.9^5 y(n-5)$.

The impulse response of this filter is also easy to compute by hand.
Referring to the difference equation

$$y(n) = x(n) + 0.5^3 x(n-3) - 0.9^5 y(n-5)$$

and setting the input $x(n)$ to $\delta(n) = [1, 0, 0, \ldots]$, we compute, for $n =$

---

[5]Most plots in this book are optimized for Matlab. Octave uses `gnuplot` which is quite
different from Matlab's handle-oriented graphics. In Octave, the plots will typically be
visible, but the titles and axis labels may be incorrect due to the different semantics
associated with statement ordering in the two cases.

```
% Example comb filter:
g1 = 0.5^3;   B = [1 0 0 g1];        % Feedforward coeffs
g2 = 0.9^5;   A = [1 0 0 0 0 g2];  % Feedback coefficients

h = filter(B,A,[1,zeros(1,50)]);  % Impulse response
% h = impz(B,A,50); % alternative in octave-forge or MSPTB

% Matlab-compatible plot:
clf; figure(1); stem([0:50],h,'-k'); axis([0 50 -0.8 1.1]);
ylabel('Amplitude'); xlabel('Time (samples)'); grid;
cmd = 'print -deps ../eps/eir.eps'; disp(cmd); eval(cmd);
```

Figure 3.9: Matlab script for computing and plotting the impulse response of the example digital filter.

$0, 1, 2, \ldots$,

$$
\begin{aligned}
y(0) &= 1 \\
y(1) &= 0 \\
y(2) &= 0 \\
y(3) &= 0.5^3 = 0.125 \\
y(4) &= 0 \\
y(5) &= -0.9^5 = -0.59049 \\
y(6) &= 0 \\
y(7) &= 0 \\
y(8) &= -0.9^5 \cdot 0.5^3 = -0.07381125 \\
y(9) &= 0 \\
y(10) &= (-0.9^5)^2 = 0.9^{10} = 0.3486784401 \\
y(11) &= 0 \\
y(12) &= 0 \\
y(13) &= 0.9^{10} \cdot 0.5^3 = 0.043584805 \\
y(14) &= 0 \\
y(15) &= (-0.9^5)^3 = -0.9^{15} = -0.205891132094649 \\
&\vdots \quad\quad \vdots
\end{aligned}
$$

3.7   Transfer Function

As we cover in Chapter 6, the transfer function of a digital filter is defined as $H(z) = Y(z)/X(z)$ where $X(z)$ is the z transform of the input signal $x(n)$, and $Y(z)$ is the z transform of the output signal $y(n)$. We may find $H(z)$ from Eq. (3.1) by taking the z transform of both sides and solving for $Y(z)/X(z)$:

$$
\begin{aligned}
\mathcal{Z}\{y(n)\} &= \mathcal{Z}\{x(n) + g_1 x(n - M_1) - g_2 y(n - M_2)\} \\
&= \mathcal{Z}\{x(n)\} + g_1 \mathcal{Z}\{x(n - M_1)\} \\
&\quad - g_2 \mathcal{Z}\{y(n - M_2)\} \\
\implies \quad Y(z) &= X(z) + g_1 z^{-M_1} X(z) - g_2 z^{-M_2} Y(z) \\
\implies \quad Y(z) + g_2 z^{-M_2} Y(z) &= X(z) + g_1 z^{-M_1} X(z) \\
\implies \quad H(z) \triangleq \frac{Y(z)}{X(z)} &= \frac{1 + g_1 z^{-M_1}}{1 + g_2 z^{-M_2}} \qquad \text{(Transfer Function)}
\end{aligned}
$$

Some principles of this analysis are as follows:

1. The z transform $\mathcal{Z}\{\cdot\}$ is a *linear operator* which means, by definition,

$$\mathcal{Z}\{\alpha x_1(n) + \beta x_2(n)\} = \alpha \mathcal{Z}\{x_1(n)\} + \beta \mathcal{Z}\{x_2(n)\} \triangleq \alpha X_1(z) + \beta X_2(z).$$

2. $\mathcal{Z}\{x(n - M)\} = z^{-M} X(z)$. That is, the z transform of a signal $x(n)$ *delayed* by M samples, $x(n-M)$, $n = 0, 1, 2, \ldots$, is $z^{-M} X(z)$. This is the *shift theorem* for z transforms, which can be immediately derived from the definition of the z transform, as shown in §6.3.

Note that these two properties of the z transform are all we really need to find the transfer function of any linear, time-invariant digital filter from its difference equation (its implementation formula in the time domain).

In matlab, difference-equation coefficients are specified as transfer-function coefficients (vectors B and A in Fig. 3.9). This is why a minus sign is needed in Eq. (3.3) on page 49.

Ok, so finding the transfer function is not too much work. Now, what can we do with it? There are two main avenues of analysis from here: (1) finding the *frequency response* by setting $z = e^{j\omega T}$, and (2) *factoring* the transfer function to find the *poles and zeros* of the filter. One also uses the transfer function to generate different implementation forms such as cascade or parallel combinations of smaller filters to achieve the same overall filter. The following sections will illustrate these uses of the transfer function on the example filter of this chapter.

3.8   Frequency Response

Given the transfer function $H(z)$, the *frequency response* is obtained by evaluating it on the unit circle in the complex plane, *i.e.*, by setting $z = e^{j\omega T}$, where T is the sampling interval in seconds, and ω is *radian frequency*:[6]

$$H(e^{j\omega T}) \triangleq \frac{1 + g_1 e^{-jM_1\omega T}}{1 + g_2 e^{-jM_2\omega T}}, \qquad -\pi \leq \omega T < \pi \qquad \text{(Frequency Response)}$$

(3.4)

In the special case $g_1 = g_2 = 1$, we obtain

$$
\begin{aligned}
H(e^{j\omega T}) &= \frac{1 + e^{-jM_1\omega T}}{1 + e^{-jM_2\omega T}} \\
&= \frac{e^{-jM_1\omega T/2}\left(e^{jM_1\omega T/2} + e^{-jM_1\omega T/2}\right)}{e^{-jM_2\omega T/2}\left(e^{jM_2\omega T/2} + e^{-jM_2\omega T/2}\right)} \\
&= e^{j(M_2-M_1)\omega T/2}\frac{\cos\left(M_1\omega T/2\right)}{\cos\left(M_2\omega T/2\right)}.
\end{aligned}
$$

When $M_1 \neq M_2$, the frequency response is a ratio of cosines in ω times a linear phase term $e^{j(M_2-M_1)\omega T/2}$ (which corresponds to a pure delay of $M_1 - M_2$ samples). This special case gives insight into the behavior of the filter as its coefficients g_1 and g_2 approach 1.

When $M_1 = M_2 \triangleq M$, the filter degenerates to $H(z) = 1$ which corresponds to $y(n) = x(n)$; in this case, the delayed input and output signals cancel each other out. As a check, let's verify this in the time domain:

$$
\begin{aligned}
y(n) &= x(n) + x(n-M) - y(n-M) \\
&= x(n) + x(n-M) - [x(n-M) - y(n-2M)] \\
&= x(n) + y(n-2M) \\
&= x(n) + x(n-2M) - [x(n-2M) - y(n-3M)] \\
&= x(n) + y(n-3M) \\
&= \cdots \\
&= x(n).
\end{aligned}
$$

---

[6]As always, radian frequency ω is related to frequency f in Hz by the relation $\omega = 2\pi f$. Also as always in this book, the sampling rate is denoted by $f_s = 1/T$. Since the frequency axis for digital signals goes from $-f_s/2$ to $f_s/2$ (non-inclusive), we have $\omega T \in [-\pi, \pi)$, where $[\ )$ denotes a half-open interval. Since the frequency $f = \pm f_s/2$ is usually rejected in applications, it is more practical to take $\omega T \in (-\pi, \pi)$.

3.9   Amplitude Response

Since the frequency response is a complex-valued function, it has a *magnitude* and *phase angle* for each frequency. The magnitude of the frequency response is called the *amplitude response* (or *magnitude frequency response*), and it gives the filter *gain* at each frequency ω.

In this example, the amplitude response is

$$\left|H(e^{j\omega T})\right| = \left|\frac{1 + g_1 e^{-jM_1\omega T}}{1 + g_2 e^{-jM_2\omega T}}\right| \tag{3.5}$$

which, for $g_1 = g_2 = 1$, reduces to

$$\left|H(e^{j\omega T})\right| = \frac{|\cos(M_1\omega T/2)|}{|\cos(M_2\omega T/2)|}.$$

Figure 3.10a shows a graph of the amplitude response of one case of this filter, obtained by plotting Eq. (3.5) for $\omega T \in [-\pi, \pi]$, and using the example settings $g_1 = 0.5^3$, $g_2 = 0.9^5$, $M_1 = 3$, and $M_2 = 5$.

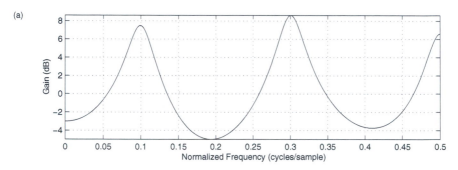

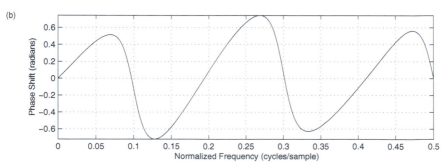

Figure 3.10: Frequency response of the example filter $y(n) = x(n) + 0.5^3 x(n-3) - 0.9^5 y(n-5)$. (a) Amplitude response. (b) Phase response.

3.10 Phase Response

The phase of the frequency response is called the *phase response*. Like the phase of any complex number, it is given by the arctangent of the imaginary part of $H(e^{j\omega T})$ divided by its real part, and it specifies the *delay* of the filter at each frequency. The phase response is a good way to look at short filter delays which are not directly perceivable as causing an "echo".[7] For longer delays in audio, it is usually best to study the filter *impulse response*, which is output of the filter when its input is $[1,0,0,0,\ldots]$ (an "impulse"). We will show later that the impulse response is also given by the inverse z transform of the filter transfer function (or, equivalently, the inverse Fourier transform of the filter frequency response).

In this example, the phase response is

$$\angle H(e^{j\omega T}) = \angle\left(1 + g_1 e^{-jM_1\omega T}\right) - \angle\left(1 + g_2 e^{-jM_2\omega T}\right).$$

A specific case is plotted in Fig. 3.10b, corresponding to the amplitude response in Fig. 3.10a. The impulse response is plotted in Fig. 3.8 on page 56. The matlab code for producing these figures is shown in Fig. 3.11. (The plotting utility `plotfr` is given in §J.4 on page 401.) In Octave or the Matlab Signal Processing Toolbox, a figure similar to Fig. 3.10 can be produced by typing simply `freqz(B,A,Nspec)`.

---

[7]The minimum perceivable delay in audio work depends very much on how the filter is being used and also on what signals are being filtered. A few milliseconds of delay is usually not perceivable in the monaural case. Note, however, that delay perception is a function of frequency. One rule of thumb is that, to be perceived as instantaneous, a filter's delay should be kept below a few cycles at each frequency. A near-worst-case test signal for monaural filter-delay perception is an impulse (pure click). (A worst-case test would require some weighting vs. frequency.) Delay distortion is less noticeable if all frequencies in a signal are delayed by the same amount of time, since that preserves the original waveshape exactly and delays it as a whole. Otherwise *transient smearing* occurs, and the ear is fairly sensitive to onset synchrony across different frequency bands.

```
% efr.m - frequency response computation in Matlab/Octave

% Example filter:
g1 = 0.5^3; B = [1 0 0 g1];        % Feedforward coeffs
g2 = 0.9^5; A = [1 0 0 0 0 g2];    % Feedback coefficients


Nfft = 1024;            % FFT size
Nspec = 1+Nfft/2;       % Show only positive frequencies
f=[0:Nspec-1]/Nfft;     % Frequency axis
Xnum = fft(B,Nfft);     % Frequency response of FIR part
Xden = fft(A,Nfft);     % Frequency response, feedback part
X = Xnum ./ Xden;       % Should check for divide by zero!


clf; figure(1);         % Matlab-compatible plot
plotfr(X(1:Nspec),f);%  Plot frequency response
cmd = 'print -deps ../eps/efr.eps'; disp(cmd); eval(cmd);
```

Figure 3.11: Matlab script for computing and displaying the frequency response of the example filter $y(n) = x(n) + 0.5^3 x(n-3) - 0.9^5 y(n-5)$.

3.11   Pole-Zero Analysis

Since our example transfer function

$$H(z) = \frac{1 + g_1 z^{-M_1}}{1 + g_2 z^{-M_2}}$$

(from Eq. (3.4) on page 58) is a ratio of polynomials in z, and since every polynomial can be characterized by its roots plus a scale factor, we may characterize any transfer function by its numerator roots (called the *zeros* of the filter), its denominator roots (filter *poles*), and a constant gain factor:

$$H(z) = g \frac{(1 - q_1 z^{-1})(1 - q_2 z^{-1}) \cdots (1 - q_{M_1} z^{-1})}{(1 - p_1 z^{-1})(1 - p_2 z^{-1}) \cdots (1 - p_{M_2} z^{-1})}$$

The poles and zeros for this simple example are easy to work out by hand. The zeros are located in the z plane at

$$q_k = -g_1^{\frac{1}{M_1}} e^{j 2\pi \frac{k}{M_1}}, \quad k = 0, 2, \ldots, M_1 - 1$$

where we assume $g_1 > 0$, and the poles are similarly given by

$$p_k = -g_2^{\frac{1}{M_2}} e^{j 2\pi \frac{k}{M_2}}, \quad k = 0, 2, \ldots, M_2 - 1.$$

Figure 3.12 gives the pole-zero diagram of the specific example filter $y(n) = x(n) + 0.5^3 x(n-3) - 0.9^5 y(n-5)$. There are three zeros, marked by '0' in the figure, and five poles, marked by 'X'. Because of the simple form of digital comb filters, the zeros (roots of $z^3 + 0.5^3$) are located at 0.5 times the three cube roots of -1 ($-e^{2k\pi/3}, k = 0, 1, 2$), and similarly the poles (roots of $z^5 + 0.9^5$) are located at 0.9 times the five 5th roots of -1 ($-e^{k2\pi/5}, k = 0, \ldots, 4$). (Technically, there are also two more zeros at $z = 0$.) The matlab code for producing this figure is simply

```
[zeros, poles, gain] = tf2zp(B,A); % Matlab or Octave
zplane(zeros,poles); % Matlab Signal Processing Toolbox
                     % or Octave Forge
```

where B and A are as given in Fig. 3.11. The pole-zero plot utility **zplane** is contained in the Matlab Signal Processing Toolbox, and in the Octave Forge collection. A similar plot is produced by

```
sys = tf2sys(B,A,1);
pzmap(sys);
```

where these functions are both in the Matlab Control Toolbox and in Octave. (Octave includes its own control-systems tool-box functions in the base Octave distribution.)

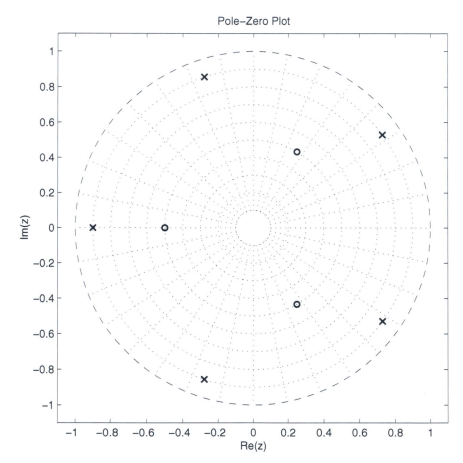

Figure 3.12: Pole-Zero diagram of the example filter $y(n) = x(n) + 0.5^3 x(n-3) - 0.9^5 y(n-5)$.

3.12   Alternative Realizations

For actually implementing the example digital filter, we have only seen the difference equation

$$y(n) = x(n) + g_1 \, x(n - M_1) - g_2 \, y(n - M_2)$$

(from Eq. (3.1) on page 48, diagrammed in Fig. 3.1 on page 48). While this structure, formally known as "direct form I", happens to be a good choice for digital comb filters, there are many other structures to consider in other situations. For example, it is often desirable, for numerical reasons, to implement *low-pass*, *high-pass*, and *band-pass* filters as *series second-order sections*. On the other hand, digital filters for simulating the *vocal tract* (for synthesized voice applications) are typically implemented as *parallel second-order sections*. (When the order is odd, there is one first-order section as well.) The coefficients of the first- and second-order filter sections may be calculated from the poles and zeros of the filter.

We will now illustrate the computation of a parallel second-order realization of our example filter $y(n) = x(n) + 0.5^3 x(n - 3) - 0.9^5 y(n - 5)$. As discussed above in §3.11, this filter has five poles and three zeros. We can use the *partial fraction expansion* (PFE), described in §6.8, to expand the transfer function into a sum of five first-order terms:

$$
\begin{aligned}
H(z) \;&=\; \frac{1 + 0.5^3 z^{-3}}{1 + 0.9^5 z^{-5}} = \sum_{i=1}^{5} \frac{r_i}{1 - p_i z^{-1}} \\[2mm]
&\approx\; \frac{0.1657}{1 + 0.9 z^{-1}} + \frac{0.1894 - j0.0326}{1 - (0.7281 + j0.5290) z^{-1}} + \frac{0.1894 + j0.0326}{1 - (0.7281 - j0.5290) z^{-1}} \\[2mm]
&\qquad + \frac{0.2277 + j0.0202}{1 - (-0.2781 + j0.8560) z^{-1}} + \frac{0.2277 - j0.0202}{1 - (-0.2781 - j0.8560) z^{-1}} \\[2mm]
&=\; \frac{0.1657}{1 + 0.9000 z^{-1}} + \frac{0.3788 - 0.2413 z^{-1}}{1 - 1.4562 z^{-1} + 0.8100 z^{-2}} \\[2mm]
&\qquad + \frac{0.4555 + 0.0922 z^{-1}}{1 + 0.5562 z^{-1} + 0.8100 z^{-2}},
\end{aligned}
$$

where, in the last step, complex-conjugate one-pole sections are combined into real second-order sections. Also, numerical values are given to four decimal places (so '=' is replaced by '≈' in the second line). In the following subsections, we will plot the impulse responses and frequency responses of the first- and second-order filter sections above.

3.12.1   First-Order Parallel Sections

Figure 3.13 shows the impulse response of the real one-pole section

$$H_1(z) = \frac{0.1657}{1 + 0.9z^{-1}},$$

and Fig. 3.14 shows its frequency response, computed using the matlab utility `myfreqz` listed in §7.5.1 on page 154. (Both Matlab and Octave have compatible utilities `freqz`, which serve the same purpose.) Note that the sampling rate is set to 1, and the frequency axis goes from 0 Hz all the way to the sampling rate, which is appropriate for complex filters (as we will soon see). Since real filters have *Hermitian* frequency responses (*i.e.*, an *even* amplitude response and *odd* phase response), they may be plotted from 0 Hz to half the sampling rate without loss of information.

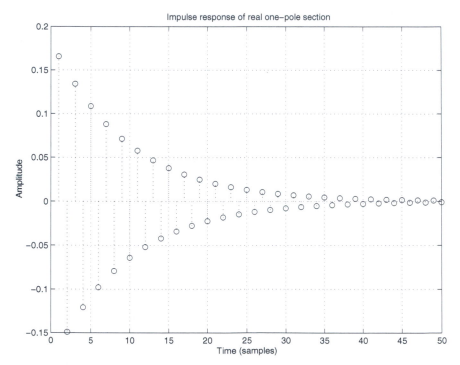

Figure 3.13: Impulse response of section 1 of the example filter.

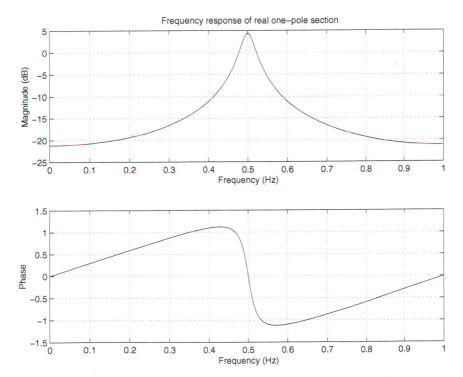

Figure 3.14: Frequency response of section 1 of the example filter.

Figure 3.15 shows the impulse response of the *complex* one-pole section

$$H_2(z) = \frac{0.1894 - j0.0326}{1 - (0.7281 + j0.5290)z^{-1}},$$

and Fig. 3.16 shows the corresponding frequency response.

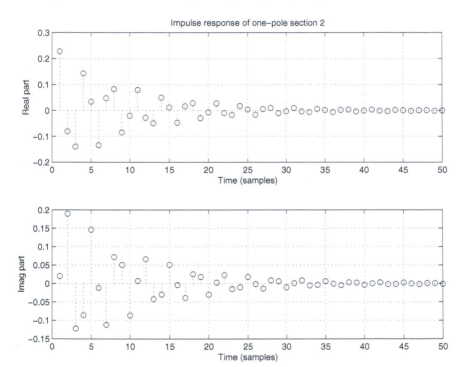

Figure 3.15: Impulse response of complex one-pole section 2 of the full partial-fraction-expansion of the example filter.

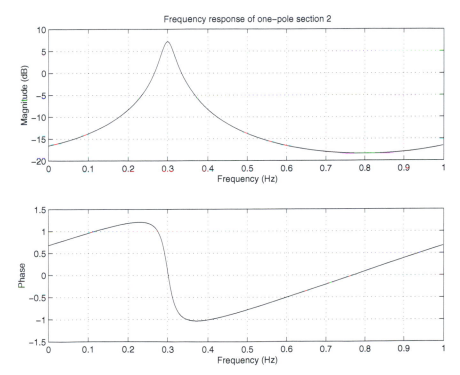

Figure 3.16: Frequency response of complex one-pole section 2.

The complex-conjugate section,

$$H_3(z) = \frac{0.1894 + j0.0326}{1 - (0.7281 - j0.5290)z^{-1}},$$

is of course quite similar, and is shown in Figures 3.17 and 3.18.

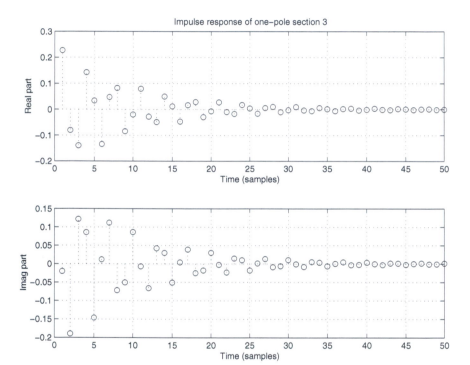

Figure 3.17: Impulse response of complex one-pole section 3 of the full partial-fraction-expansion of the example filter.

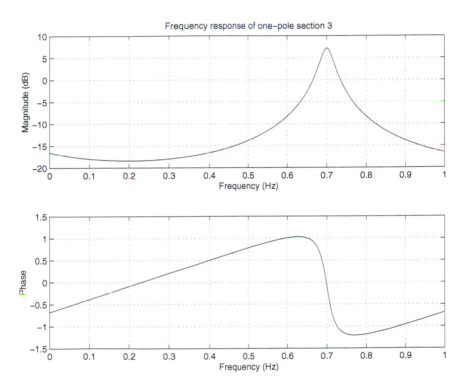

Figure 3.18: Frequency response of complex one-pole section 3.

Figure 3.19 shows the impulse response of the complex one-pole section

$$H_4(z) = \frac{0.2277 + j0.0202}{1 + (0.2781 + j0.8560)z^{-1}},$$

and Fig. 3.20 shows its frequency response. Its complex-conjugate counterpart, $H_5(z)$, is not shown since it is analogous to $H_4(z)$ in relation to
$H_3(z)$.

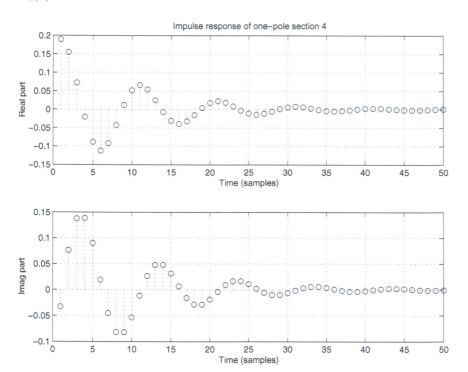

Figure 3.19: Impulse response of complex one-pole section 4 of the full
partial-fraction-expansion of the example filter.

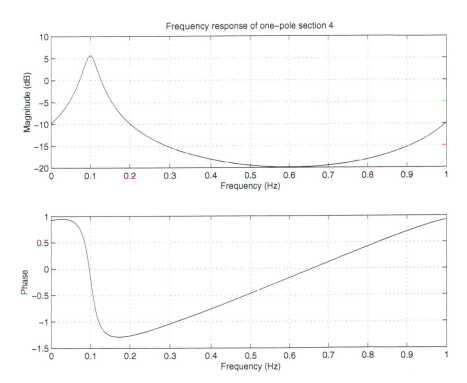

Figure 3.20: Frequency response of complex one-pole section 4.

3.12.2   Parallel, Real, Second-Order Sections

Figure 3.21 shows the impulse response of the real two-pole section

$$H_2^r(z) \triangleq H_2(z) + H_3(z) = \frac{0.3788 - 0.2413z^{-1}}{1 - 1.4562z^{-1} + 0.8100z^{-2}},$$

and Fig. 3.22 shows its frequency response. The frequency axis unnecessarily extends all the way to the sampling rate ($f_s = 1$).

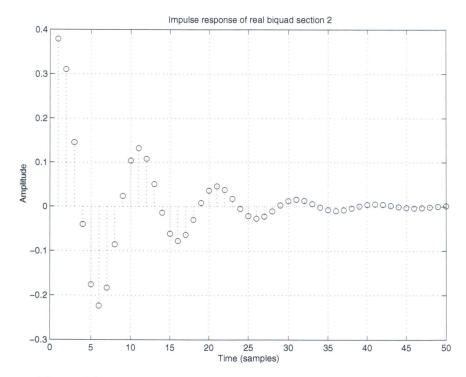

Figure 3.21: Impulse response of real two-pole section $H_2^r(z)$ of the real partial-fraction-expansion of the example filter.

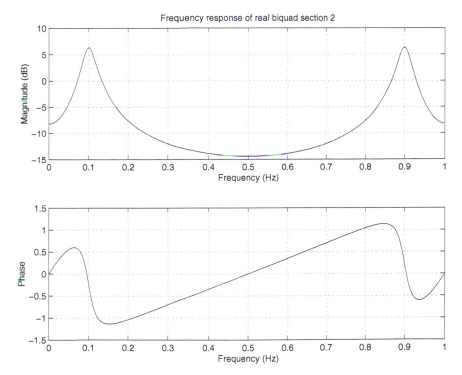

Figure 3.22: Frequency response of real two-pole section $H_2^r(z)$.

Finally, Fig. 3.23 gives the impulse response of the real two-pole section

$$H_3^r(z) \triangleq H_4(z) + H_5(z) = \frac{0.4555 + 0.0922z^{-1}}{1 + 0.5562z^{-1} + 0.8100z^{-2}},$$

and Fig. 3.24 its frequency response.

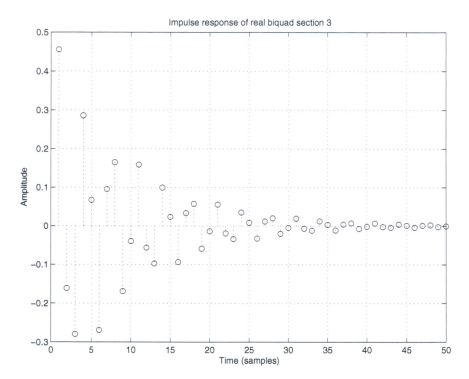

Figure 3.23: Impulse response of real two-pole section $H_3^r(z)$ of the real partial-fraction-expansion of the example filter.

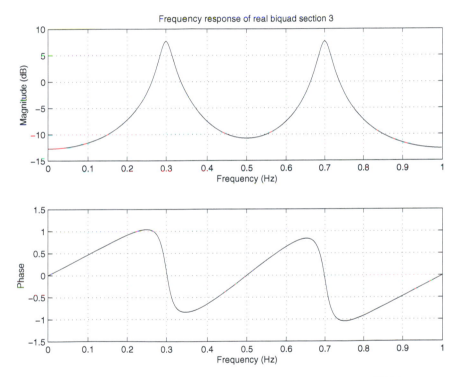

Figure 3.24: Frequency response of real two-pole section $H_3^r(z)$.

3.12.3   Parallel Second-Order Signal Flow Graph

Figure 3.25 shows the signal flow graph for the implementation of our example filter using parallel second-order sections (with one first-order section since the number of poles is odd). This is the same filter as that shown in Fig. 3.1 with $g_1 = 0.5^3$, $g_2 = 0.9^5$, $M_1 = 3$, and $M_2 = 5$. The second-order sections are special cases of the "biquad" filter section, which is often implemented in software (and chip) libraries. Any digital filter can be implemented as a sum of parallel biquads by finding its transfer function and computing the partial fraction expansion.

The two second-order biquad sections in Fig. 3.25 are in so-called "Direct-Form II" (DF-II) form. In Chapter 9, a total of four direct-form filter implementations will be discussed, along with some other commonly used implementation structures. In particular, it is explained there why *Transposed* Direct-Form II (TDF-II) is usually a better choice of implementation structure for IIR filters when numerical dynamic range is limited (as it is in fixed-point "DSP chips"). Figure 3.26 shows how our example looks using TDF-II biquads in place of the DF-II biquads of Fig. 3.25.

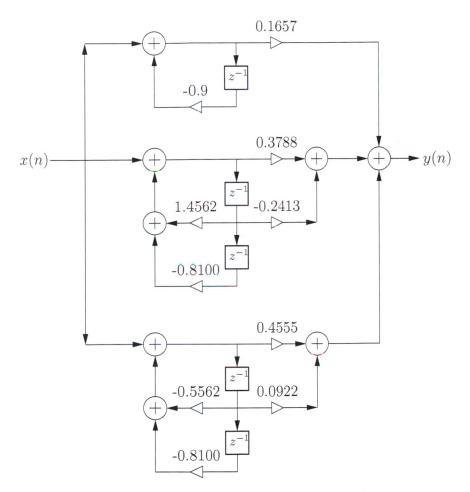

Figure 3.25: Signal flow graph for the re-implementation of the example filter $y(n) = x(n) + 0.5^3 x(n-3) - 0.9^5 y(n-5)$ as a parallel bank of real first- and second-order digital filter sections.

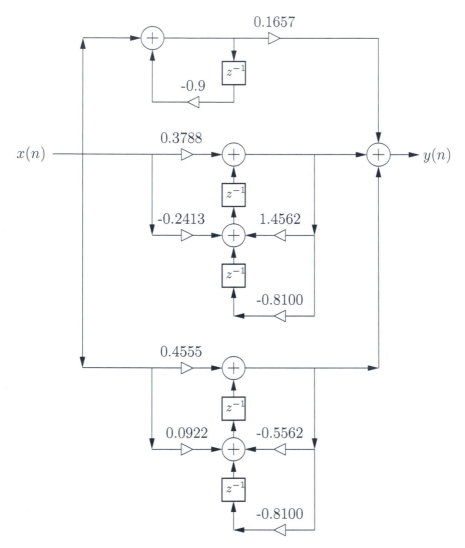

Figure 3.26: Same as Fig. 3.25 except using transposed direct-form-II biquad sections in place of direct-form-II biquad sections.

3.12.4   Series, Real, Second-Order Sections

Converting the difference equation $y(n) = x(n) + 0.5^3 x(n-3) - 0.9^5 y(n-5)$ to a *series* bank of real first- and second-order sections is comparatively easy. In this case, we do not need a full blown partial fraction expansion. Instead, we need only factor the numerator and denominator of the transfer function into first- and/or second-order terms. Since a second-order section can accommodate up to two poles and two zeros, we must decide how to group pairs of poles with pairs of zeros. Furthermore, since the series sections can be implemented in any order, we must choose the section ordering. Both of these choices are normally driven in practice by numerical considerations. In fixed-point implementations, the poles and zeros are grouped such that dynamic range requirements are minimized. Similarly, the section order is chosen so that the intermediate signals are well scaled. For example, internal overflow is more likely if all of the large-gain sections appear before the low-gain sections. On the other hand, the signal-to-quantization-noise ratio will deteriorate if all of the low-gain sections are placed before the higher-gain sections. For further reading on numerical considerations for digital filter sections, see, *e.g.*, [103].

3.13   Summary

This chapter has provided an overview of practical digital filter implementation, analysis, transformation, and display. The principal time-domain views were the difference equation and the impulse response. The signal flow graph applies to either time- or frequency-domain signals. The frequency-domain analyses were derived from the z transform of the difference equation, yielding the transfer function, frequency response, amplitude response, phase response, pole-zero analysis, alternate realizations, and related topics. We will take up these topics and more in the following chapters.

In the next chapter, we begin a more systematic presentation of the main concepts of *linear systems theory*. After that, we will return to practical digital filter analysis, implementation, and (elementary) design.

Chapter 4

Linear Time-Invariant Digital Filters

In this chapter, the important concepts of *linearity* and *time-invariance* (LTI) are discussed. Only LTI filters can be subjected to frequency-domain analysis as illustrated in the preceding chapters. After studying this chapter, you should be able to classify any filter as linear or nonlinear, and time-invariant or time-varying.

The great majority of *audio* filters are LTI, for several reasons: First, *no new spectral components* are introduced by LTI filters. Time-*varying* filters, on the other hand, can generate audible *sideband images* of the frequencies present in the input signal (when the filter changes at audio rates). Time-invariance is not overly restrictive, however, because the static analysis holds very well for filters that change slowly with time. (One rule of thumb is that the coefficients of a quasi-time-invariant filter should be substantially constant over its impulse-response duration.) *Nonlinear* filters generally create new sinusoidal components at all sums and differences of the frequencies present in the input signal.[1] This includes both *harmonic distortion* (when the input signal is periodic) and *intermodulation distortion* (when at least two inharmonically related tones are present). A truly linear filter does not cause harmonic or intermodulation distortion.

---

[1] One might argue that nonlinear filters must be considered a special case of time-varying filters, because any variation in the filter coefficients must occur over time, and in the nonlinear case, this variation simply happens to occur in a manner that depends on the input signal sample values. However, since a constant signal (dc) does not vary over time, a nonlinear filter may also be time-invariant. As we will see in this chapter, the key test for nonlinearity is whether the filter coefficients change as a function of the input signal. A *linear* time-varying filter, on the other hand, must exhibit the *same* coefficient variation over time for *all* input signals.

All the examples of filters mentioned in Chapter 1 were LTI, or approximately LTI. In addition, the z transform and all forms of the Fourier transform are linear operators, and these operators can be viewed as *LTI filter banks*, or as a single LTI filter having multiple outputs.

In the following sections, linearity and time-invariance will be formally introduced, together with some elementary mathematical aspects of signals.

4.1   Definition of a Signal

> **Definition.** A *real discrete-time signal* is defined as any time-ordered sequence of real numbers. Similarly, a *complex discrete-time signal* is any time-ordered sequence of complex numbers.

Mathematically, we typically denote a signal as a real- or complex-valued function of an integer, *e.g.*, $x(n)$, $n = 0, 1, 2, \ldots$. Thus, $x(n)$ is the nth real (or complex) number in the signal, and n represents time as an integer *sample number*.

Using the *set notation* $\mathbf{Z}, \mathbf{R}$, and $\mathbf{C}$ to denote the set of all integers, real numbers, and complex numbers, respectively, we can express that x is a real, discrete-time signal by expressing it as a function mapping every integer (optionally in a restricted range) to a real number:

$$x : \mathbf{Z} \to \mathbf{R}$$

Alternatively, we can write $x(n) \in \mathbf{R}$ for all $n \in \mathbf{Z}$.

Similarly, a discrete-time *complex* signal is a mapping from each integer to a complex number:

$$w : \mathbf{Z} \to \mathbf{C}$$

i.e., $w(n) \in \mathbf{C}, \forall n \in \mathbf{Z}$ ($w(n)$ is a complex number for every integer n).

It is useful to define $\mathcal{S}$ as the *signal space* consisting of all complex signals $x(n) \in \mathbf{C}$, $n \in \mathbf{Z}$.

We may expand these definitions slightly to include functions of the form $x(nT)$, $w(nT)$, where $T \in \mathbf{R}$ denotes the sampling interval in seconds. In this case, the time index has physical units of seconds, but it is isomorphic to the integers. For finite-duration signals, we may prepend and append zeros to extend its domain to all integers $\mathbf{Z}$.

Mathematically, the set of all signals x can be regarded a *vector space*[2] $\mathcal{S}$ in which every signal x is a vector in the space ($x \in \mathcal{S}$). The nth sample of x, $x(n)$, is regarded as the nth *vector coordinate*. Since signals as we

---

[2] A set of vectors $\mathcal{S} \in \mathbf{R}^N$ (or $\mathbf{C}^N$) is said to form a *vector space* if $x + y \in \mathcal{S}$ and $\alpha x \in \mathcal{S}$ for all $x \in \mathcal{S}$, $y \in \mathcal{S}$, and for all scalars $\alpha \in \mathbf{R}$ (or $\mathbf{C}$) [84, 73].

have defined them are infinitely long (being defined over all integers), the corresponding vector space $\mathcal{S}$ is *infinite-dimensional*. Every vector space comes with a field of *scalars* which we may think of as *constant gain factors* that can be applied to any signal in the space. For purposes of this book, "signal" and "vector" mean the same thing, as do "constant gain factor" and "scalar". The signals and gain factors (vectors and scalars) may be either real or complex, as applications may require.

By definition, a vector space is *closed under linear combinations*. That is, given any two vectors $x_1 \in \mathcal{S}$ and $x_2 \in \mathcal{S}$, and any two scalars α and β, there exists a vector $y \in \mathcal{S}$ which satisfies $y = \alpha x_1 + \beta x_2$, *i.e.*,

$$y(n) = \alpha x_1(n) + \beta x_2(n)$$

for all $n \in \mathbf{Z}$.

A linear combination is what we might call a *mix* of two signals x_1 and x_2 using mixing gains α and β ($y = \alpha x_1 + \beta x_2$). Thus, a *signal mix* is represented mathematically as a *linear combination of vectors*. Since signals in practice can overflow the available dynamic range, resulting in *clipping* (or "wrap-around"), it is not normally true that the space of signals used in practice is closed under linear combinations (mixing). However, in floating-point numerical simulations, closure is true for most practical purposes.[3]

4.2   Definition of a Filter

> **Definition.** A *real digital filter* $\mathcal{T}_n$ is defined as any real-valued function of a real signal for each integer $n \in \mathbf{Z}$.

Thus, a real digital filter maps every real, discrete-time signal to a real, discrete-time signal. A *complex* filter, on the other hand, may produce a complex output signal even when its input signal is real.

We may express the input-output relation of a digital filter by the notation

$$y(n) = \mathcal{T}_n\{x(\cdot)\} \qquad (4.1)$$

---

[3] For more about the mathematics of linear vector spaces, look into *linear algebra* [58] (which covers finite-dimensional linear vector spaces) and/or *operator theory* [56] (which treats the infinite-dimensional case). The mathematical treatments used in this book will be closer to *complex analysis* [14, 43], but with some linear algebra concepts popping up from time to time, especially in the context of matlab examples. (The name "matlab" derives from "matrix laboratory," and it was originally written by Cleve Moler to be an interactive desk-calculator front end for a library of numerical linear algebra subroutines (`LINPACK` and `EISPACK`). As a result, matlab syntax is designed to follow linear algebra notation as closely as possible.)

where $x(\cdot)$ denotes the entire input signal, and $y(n)$ is the output signal at time n. (We will also refer to $x(\cdot)$ as simply x.) The general filter is denoted by $\mathcal{T}_n\{x\}$, which stands for any transformation from a signal x to a sample value at time n. The filter $\mathcal{T}$ can also be called an *operator* on the space of signals $\mathcal{S}$. The operator $\mathcal{T}$ maps every signal $x \in \mathcal{S}$ to some new signal $y \in \mathcal{S}$. (For simplicity, we take $\mathcal{S}$ to be the space of complex signals whenever $\mathcal{T}$ is complex.) If $\mathcal{T}$ is linear, it can be called a *linear operator* on $\mathcal{S}$. If, additionally, the signal space $\mathcal{S}$ consists only of finite-length signals, all N samples long, *i.e.*, $\mathcal{S} \subset \mathbf{R}^N$ or $\mathcal{S} \subset \mathbf{C}^N$, then every linear filter $\mathcal{T}$ may be called a *linear transformation*, which is representable by constant $N \times N$ *matrix*.

In this book, we are concerned primarily with *single-input, single-output (SISO) digital filters*. For this reason, the input and output signals of a digital filter are defined as real or complex numbers for each time index n (as opposed to vectors). When both the input and output signals are vector-valued, we have what is called a *multi-input, multi-out (MIMO) digital filter*. We look at MIMO allpass filters in §C.3 and MIMO state-space filter forms in Appendix G, but we will not cover transfer-function analysis of MIMO filters using *matrix fraction descriptions* [37].

4.3   Examples of Digital Filters

While any mapping from signals to real numbers can be called a filter, we normally work with filters which have more structure than that. Some of the main structural features are illustrated in the following examples.

The filter analyzed in Chapter 1 was specified by

$$y(n) = x(n) + x(n-1).$$

Such a specification is known as a *difference equation*. This simple filter is a special case of an important class of filters called *linear time-invariant (LTI) filters*. LTI filters are important in audio engineering because they are the *only* filters that preserve signal frequencies.

The above example remains a real LTI filter if we scale the input samples by any real *coefficients*:

$$y(n) = 2\,x(n) - 3.1\,x(n-1)$$

If we use complex coefficients, the filter remains LTI, but it becomes a *complex filter*:

$$y(n) = (2+j)\,x(n) + 5j\,x(n-1)$$

The filter also remains LTI if we use more input samples in a shift-invariant way:

$$y(n) = x(n) + x(n-1) + x(n+1) + \cdots$$

The use of "future" samples, such as $x(n+1)$ in this difference equation, makes this a *non-causal* filter example. Causal filters may compute $y(n)$ using only *present and/or past input samples* $x(n)$, $x(n-1)$, $x(n-2)$, and so on.

Another class of causal LTI filters involves using *past output samples* in addition to present and/or past input samples. The past-output terms are called *feedback*, and digital filters employing feedback are called *recursive digital filters*:

$$y(n) = x(n) - x(n-1) + 0.1\, y(n-1) + \cdots$$

An example *multi-input, multi-output* (MIMO) digital filter is

$$\left[\begin{array}{c} y_1(n) \\ y_2(n) \end{array} \right] = \left[\begin{array}{cc} a & b \\ c & d \end{array} \right] \left[\begin{array}{c} x_1(n) \\ x_2(n) \end{array} \right] + \left[\begin{array}{cc} e & f \\ g & h \end{array} \right] \left[\begin{array}{c} x_1(n-1) \\ x_2(n-1) \end{array} \right],$$

where we have introduced vectors and matrices inside square brackets. This is the 2D generalization of the SISO filter $y(n) = a\,x(n) + b\,x(n-1)$.

The simplest *nonlinear* digital filter is

$$y(n) = x^2(n),$$

i.e., it squares each sample of the input signal to produce the output signal. This example is also a *memoryless nonlinearity* because the output at time n is not dependent on past inputs or outputs. The nonlinear filter

$$y(n) = x(n) - y^2(n-1)$$

is not memoryless.

Another nonlinear filter example is the *median smoother* of order N which assigns the middle value of N input samples centered about time n to the output at time n. It is useful for "outlier" elimination. For example, it will reject isolated noise spikes, and preserve steps.

An example of a linear *time-varying* filter is

$$y(n) = x(n) + \cos(2\pi n/10)\, x(n-1).$$

It is time-varying because the coefficient of $x(n-1)$ changes over time. It is linear because no coefficients depend on x or y.

These examples provide a kind of "bottom up" look at some of the major types of digital filters. We will now take a "top down" approach and characterize *all* linear, time-invariant filters mathematically. This characterization will enable us to specify frequency-domain analysis tools that work for *any* LTI digital filter.

4.4   Linear Filters

In everyday terms, the fact that a filter is linear means simply that the following two properties hold:

Scaling:

> The amplitude of the output is proportional to the amplitude of the input (the *scaling property*).

Superposition:

> When two signals are added together and fed to the filter, the filter output is the same as if one had put each signal through the filter separately and then added the outputs (the *superposition property*).

While the implications of linearity are far-reaching, the mathematical definition is simple. Let us represent the general *linear* (but possibly *time-varying*) filter as a *signal operator*:

$$y(n) = \mathcal{L}_n\{x(\cdot)\} \qquad\qquad (4.2)$$

where $x(\cdot)$ is the entire input signal, $y(n)$ is the output at time n, and $\mathcal{L}_n\{\}$ is the filter expressed as a *real-valued function of a signal* for each n. Think of the subscript n on $\mathcal{L}_n\{\}$ as selecting the nth output sample of the filter. In general, *each* output sample can be a function of several or even *all* input samples, and this is why we write $x(\cdot)$ as the filter input.

Definition. A filter $\mathcal{L}_n$ is said to be *linear* if for any pair of signals $x_1(\cdot), x_2(\cdot)$ and for all constant gains g, we have the following relation for each sample time $n \in \mathbf{Z}$:

$$\text{Scaling:} \quad \mathcal{L}_n\{g\,x(\cdot)\} = g\,\mathcal{L}_n\{x(\cdot)\}, \quad \forall g \in \mathbf{C},\ \forall x \in \mathcal{S} \quad (4.3)$$

$$\text{Superposition:} \quad \mathcal{L}_n\{x_1(\cdot) + x_2(\cdot)\} = \mathcal{L}_n\{x_1(\cdot)\} + \mathcal{L}_n\{x_2(\cdot)\} \quad (4.4)$$
$$\forall x_1, x_2 \in \mathcal{S},$$

where $\mathcal{S}$ denotes the signal space (complex-valued sequences, in general). These two conditions are simply a mathematical restatement of the previous descriptive definition.

The *scaling* property of linear systems states that scaling the input of a linear system (multiplying it by a constant gain factor) scales the output by the same factor. The *superposition* property of linear systems states that the response of a linear system to a sum of signals is the sum of the responses to each individual input signal. Another view is that the individual signals which have been summed at the input are processed independently inside the filter—they superimpose and do not interact. (The addition of two signals, sample by sample, is like converting stereo to mono by mixing the two channels together equally.)

Another example of a linear signal medium is the earth's atmosphere. When two sounds are in the air at once, the air pressure fluctuations that convey them simply add (unless they are extremely loud). Since any finite continuous signal can be represented as a sum (*i.e.*, superposition) of sinusoids, we can predict the filter response to any input signal just by knowing the response for all sinusoids. Without superposition, we have no such general description and it may be impossible to do any better than to catalog the filter output for each possible input.

Linear operators distribute over linear combinations, *i.e.*,

$$\boxed{\mathcal{L}\{\alpha x_1 + \beta x_2\} = \alpha \mathcal{L}\{x_1\} + \beta \mathcal{L}\{x_2\}}$$

for any linear operator $\mathcal{L}\{\}$, any real or complex signals $x_1, x_2 \in \mathcal{S}$, and any real or complex constant gain factors α, β.

Real Linear Filtering of Complex Signals

When a filter $\mathcal{L}_n\{x\}$ is a linear filter (but not necessarily time-invariant), and its input is a complex signal $w \triangleq x + jy$, then, by linearity,

$$\mathcal{L}_n\{w\} \triangleq \mathcal{L}_n\{x + jy\} = \mathcal{L}_n\{x\} + j\mathcal{L}_n\{y\}.$$

This means every linear filter maps complex signals to complex signals in a manner equivalent to applying the filter separately to the real and imaginary parts (which are each real). In other words, there is no "interaction" between the real and imaginary parts of a complex input signal when passed through a linear filter. If the filter is real, then filtering of complex signals can be carried out by simply performing real filtering on the real and imaginary parts separately (thereby avoiding complex arithmetic).

Appendix H presents a linear-algebraic view of linear filters that can be useful in certain applications.

4.5   Time-Invariant Filters

In plain terms, a *time-invariant filter* (or *shift-invariant filter*) is one which performs the *same operation at all times*. It is awkward to express this mathematically by restrictions on Eq. (4.2) because of the use of $x(\cdot)$ as the symbol for the filter input. What we want to say is that if the input signal is delayed (shifted) by, say, N samples, then the output waveform is simply delayed by N samples and unchanged otherwise. Thus $y(\cdot)$, the output waveform from a time-invariant filter, merely *shifts* forward or backward in time as the input waveform $x(\cdot)$ is shifted forward or backward in time.

Definition. A digital filter $\mathcal{L}_n$ is said to be *time-invariant* if, for every input signal x, we have

$$
\begin{aligned}
\mathcal{L}_n\{\text{SHIFT}_N\{x\}\} &= \mathcal{L}_{n-N}\{x(\cdot)\} = y(n-N) \\
&= \text{SHIFT}_{N,n}\{y\},
\end{aligned}
\tag{4.5}
$$

where the N-sample *shift operator* is defined by

$$
\text{SHIFT}_{N,n}\{x\} \triangleq x(n-N).
$$

On the signal level, we can write

$$
\text{SHIFT}_N\{x\} \triangleq x(\cdot - N).
$$

Thus, $\text{SHIFT}_N\{x\}$ denotes the waveform $x(\cdot)$ shifted right (delayed) by N samples. The most common notation in the literature for $\text{SHIFT}_N\{x\}$ is $x(n-N)$, but this can be misunderstood (if n is not interpreted as '$\cdot$'), so it will be avoided here. Note that Eq. (4.5) can be written on the waveform level instead of the sample level as

$$
\mathcal{L}\{\text{SHIFT}_N\{x\}\} = \text{SHIFT}_N\{\mathcal{L}\{x\}\} = \text{SHIFT}_N\{y\}.
\tag{4.6}
$$

4.6   Showing Linearity and Time Invariance, or Not

The filter $y(n) = 2x^2(n)$ is nonlinear and time invariant. The scaling property of linearity clearly fails since, scaling $x(n)$ by g gives the output signal $2[gx(n)]^2 = 2g^2x^2(n)$, while $gy(n) = 2gx^2(n)$. The filter is time invariant, however, because delaying x by m samples gives $2x^2(n-m)$ which is the same as $y(n-m)$.

The filter $y(n) = nx(n) + x(n-1)$ is linear and *time varying*. We can show linearity by setting the input to a linear combination of two signals

$x(n) = \alpha x_1(n) + \beta x_2(n)$, where α and β are constants:

$$
\begin{aligned}
n[\alpha x_1(n) + \beta x_2(n)] \quad &+ \quad [\alpha x_1(n-1) + \beta x_2(n-1)] \\
&= \quad \alpha n x_1(n) + \alpha x_1(n-1) + \beta n x_2(n) + \beta x_2(n-1) \\
&= \quad \alpha[n x_1(n) + x_1(n-1)] + \beta[n x_2(n) + x_2(n-1)] \\
&\triangleq \quad \alpha y_1(n) + \beta y_2(n)
\end{aligned}
$$

Thus, scaling and superposition are verified. The filter is time-varying, however, since the time-shifted output is $y(n-m) = (n-m)x(n-m) + x(n-m-1)$ which is not the same as the filter applied to a time-shifted input $(nx(n-m)+x(n-m-1))$. Note that in applying the time-invariance test, we time-shift the input signal only, not the coefficients.

The filter $y(n) = c$, where c is any constant, is *nonlinear* and time-invariant, in general. The condition for time invariance is satisfied (in a degenerate way) because a constant signal equals all shifts of itself. The constant filter *is* technically linear, however, for $c = 0$, since $0 \cdot (\alpha x_1 + \beta x_2) = \alpha(0 \cdot x_1) + \beta(0 \cdot x_2) = 0$, even though the input signal has no effect on the output signal at all.

Any filter of the form $y(n) = b_0 x(n) + b_1 x(n-1)$ is linear and time-invariant. This is a special case of a *sliding linear combination* (also called a *running weighted sum*, or *moving average* when $b_0 = b_1 = 1/2$). All sliding linear combinations are linear, and they are time-invariant as well when the coefficients $(b_0, b_1, \ldots)$ are constant with respect to time.

Sliding linear combinations may also include past *output* samples as well (feedback terms). A simple example is any filter of the form

$$y(n) = b_0 x(n) + b_1 x(n-1) - a_1 y(n-1). \tag{4.7}$$

Since linear combinations of linear combinations are linear combinations, we can use *induction* to show linearity and time invariance of a constant sliding linear combination including feedback terms. In the case of this example, we have, for an input signal $x(n)$ starting at time zero,

$$
\begin{aligned}
y(0) &= b_0 x(0) \\
y(1) &= b_0 x(1) + b_1 x(0) - a_1 y(0) = b_0 x(1) + (b_1 - a_1 b_0)x(0) \\
y(2) &= b_0 x(2) + b_1 x(1) - a_1 y(1) \\
&= b_0 x(2) + b_1 x(1) - a_1 [b_0 x(1) + b_1 x(0) - a_1 b_0 x(0)] \\
&= b_0 x(2) + (b_1 - a_1 b_0)x(1) - (a_1 b_1 - a_1^2 b_0)x(0) \\
&= \cdots.
\end{aligned}
$$

If the input signal is now replaced by $x_2(n) \triangleq x(n-m)$, which is $x(n)$ delayed by m samples, then the output $y_2(n)$ is $y_2(n) = 0$ for $n < m$, followed by

$$
\begin{aligned}
y_2(m) &= b_0 x(0) \\
y_2(m+1) &= b_0 x(1) + b_1 x(0) - a_1 y(m) = b_0 x(1) + (b_1 - a_1 b_0) x(0) \\
y_2(m+2) &= b_0 x(2) + b_1 x(1) - a_1 y(m+1) \\
&= b_0 x(2) + b_1 x(1) - a_1 \left[b_0 x(1) + b_1 x(0) - a_1 b_0 x(0) \right] \\
&= b_0 x(2) + (b_1 - a_1 b_0) x(1) - (a_1 b_1 - a_1^2 b_0) x(0) \\
&= \cdots,
\end{aligned}
$$

or $y_2(n) = y(n-m)$ for all $n \geq m$ and $m \geq 0$. This establishes that each output sample from the filter of Eq. (4.7) can be expressed as a time-invariant linear combination of present and past samples.

4.7 Nonlinear Filter Example: Dynamic Range Compression

A simple practical example of a *nonlinear* filtering operation is *dynamic range compression*, such as occurs in Dolby or DBX noise reduction when recording to magnetic tape (which, believe it or not, still happens once in a while). The purpose of dynamic range compression is to map the natural dynamic range of a signal to a smaller range. For example, audio signals can easily span a range of 100 dB or more, while magnetic tape has a linear range on the order of only 55 dB. It is therefore important to compress the dynamic range when making analog recordings to magnetic tape. Compressing the dynamic range of a signal for recording and then expanding it on playback may be called *companding*[4] (compression/expansion).

Recording engineers often compress the dynamic range of individual tracks to intentionally "flatten" their audio dynamic range for greater musical uniformity. Compression is also often applied to a final mix.

Another type of dynamic-range compressor is called a *limiter*, which is used in recording studios to "soft limit" a signal when it begins to exceed the available dynamic range. A limiter may be implemented as a very high compression ratio above some amplitude threshold. This replaces "hard clipping" by "soft limiting," which sounds less harsh and may even go unnoticed if there were no indicator.

The preceding examples can be modeled as a variable *gain* that automatically "turns up the volume" (increases the gain) when the signal level is low, and turns it down when the level is high. The signal level is normally measured over a short time interval that includes at least one period of the

---

[4]http://en.wikipedia.org/wiki/Compander

lowest frequency allowed, and typically several periods of any pitched signal present. The gain normally reacts faster to attacks than to decays in audio compressors.

Why Dynamic Range Compression is Nonlinear

We can model dynamic range compression as a *level-dependent gain*. Multiplying a signal by a constant gain ("volume control"), on the other hand, is a linear operation. Let's check that the scaling and superposition properties of linear systems are satisfied by a constant gain: For any signals x_1, x_2, and for any constants α, β, we must have

$$g \cdot [\alpha \cdot x_1(n) + \beta \cdot x_2(n)] = \alpha \cdot [g \cdot x_1(n)] + \beta \cdot [g \cdot x_2(n)].$$

Since this is obviously true from the algebraic properties of real or complex numbers, both scaling and superposition have been verified. (For clarity, an explicit "·" is used to indicate multiplication.)

Dynamic range compression can also be seen as a *time-varying gain* factor, so one might be tempted to classify it as a linear, time-varying filter. However, this would be incorrect because the gain g, which multiplies the input, *depends on the input signal* $x(n)$. This happens because the compressor must estimate the current signal level in order to normalize it. Dynamic range compression can be expressed symbolically as a filter of the form

$$y(n) = g_n(x) \cdot x(n)$$

where $g_n(x)$ denotes a gain that depends on the "current level" of $x(\cdot)$ at time n. A common definition of signal level is *rms level* (the "root mean square" [84, p. 75] computed over a sliding time-window). Since many successive samples of x are needed to estimate the current level, we cannot correctly write $g[x(n)]$ for the gain function, although we could write something like $g[x(n - M : n)]$ (borrowing matlab syntax), where M is the number of past samples needed to estimate the current amplitude level. In general,

$$g(x_1 + x_2) \cdot [x_1(n) + x_2(n)] \neq g(x_1) \cdot x_1(n) + g(x_2) \cdot x_2(n).$$

That is, the compression of the sum of two signals is not generally the same as the addition of the two signals compressed individually. Therefore, the superposition condition of linearity fails. It is also clear that the scaling condition fails.

In general, any signal operation that includes a multiplication in which both multiplicands depend on the input signal can be shown to be nonlinear.

4.8   A Musical Time-Varying Filter Example

Note, however, that a gain g may vary with time *independently* of x to yield a linear *time-varying* filter. In this case, linearity may be demonstrated by verifying

$$g(n)\left[\alpha \cdot x_1(n) + \beta \cdot x_2(n)\right] = \alpha \cdot [g(n) \cdot x_1(n)] + \beta \cdot [g(n) \cdot x_2(n)]$$

to show that both scaling and superposition hold. A simple example of a linear time-varying filter is a *tremolo* function, which can be written as a time-varying gain, $y(n) = g(n)x(n)$. For example, $g(n) = 1 + \cos[2\pi(4)nT]$ would give a maximally deep tremolo with 4 swells per second.

4.9   Analysis of Nonlinear Filters

There is no general theory of nonlinear systems. A nonlinear system with memory can be quite surprising. In particular, it can emit any output signal in response to any input signal. For example, it could replace all music by Beethoven with something by Mozart, etc. That said, many subclasses of nonlinear filters can be successfully analyzed:

- A nonlinear, memoryless, time-invariant "black box" can be "mapped out" by measuring its response to a scaled impulse $\alpha\delta(n)$ at each amplitude α, where $\delta(n)$ denotes the impulse signal ($[1, 0, 0, \ldots]$).

- A memoryless nonlinearity followed by an LTI filter can similarly be characterized by a stack of impulse-responses indexed by amplitude (look up *dynamic convolution* on the Web).

One often-used tool for nonlinear systems analysis is Volterra series [4]. A Volterra series expansion represents a nonlinear system as a sum of iterated convolutions:

$$y = h_0 + h_1 * x + ((h_{2,n} * x)_n * x) + \cdots$$

Here $x(n)$ is the input signal, $y(n)$ is the output signal, and the impulse-response replacements $h_i(n)$ are called *Volterra kernels*. The special notation $((h_{2,n} * x)_n * x)$ indicates that the second-order kernel h_2 is fundamentally two-dimensional, meaning that the third term above (the first nonlinear term) is written out explicitly as

$$((h_{2,n} * x)_n * x) \triangleq \sum_{l=0}^{\infty} \sum_{m=0}^{\infty} h_2(l, m)x(n - l)x(n - m).$$

Similarly, the third-order kernel h_3 is three-dimensional, in general. In principle, every nonlinear system can be represented by its (typically infinite) Volterra series expansion. The method is most successful when the kernels rapidly approach zero as order increases.

In the special case for which the Volterra expansion reduces to

$$y = h_0 + h_1 * x + h_2 * x * x + \cdots,$$

we have an immediate frequency-domain interpretation in which the output spectrum is expressed as a power series in the input spectrum:

$$Y = H_0 + H_1 X + H_2 X^2 + \cdots.$$

4.10   Conclusions

This chapter has discussed the concepts of linearity and time-invariance in some detail, with various examples considered. In the rest of this book, all filters discussed will be linear and (at least approximately) time-invariant. For brevity, these will be referred to as *LTI filters*.

4.11   Linearity and Time-Invariance Problems

1. Label each of the following filters as either linear (L) or nonlinear (NL), and time-inviariant (TI) or time varying (TV). When in doubt, apply the test!

   (a) $y[n] = |x[n]|e^{-\pi n}$

   (b) $y[n] = \sqrt{x^2[n] + 2x[n-1] + x[n-2]}$

   (c) $y[n] = x[n] + 2\cos(2\pi n)y[n-1]$

   (d) $y[n] = \max\{x[n], x[n-1], x[n-2]\}$

   (e) $y[n] = 0$

   (f) $y[n] = 1$

   (g) $y[n] = \begin{cases} x[n], & x[n] \geq 0 \\ 2x[n], & x[n] < 0 \end{cases}$

   (h) $y[n] = \cos(x[n]) + \sin(x[n-1])\cos(100n)$

   (i) $y[n] = x[n] + x[n-1]y[n-1]$

   (j) $y[n] = x[n] + y[n-1]/n$

   (k) $y[n] = \sum_{m=-\infty}^{\infty} h[m](x[n+m] + x[n-m])$

2. Show that the z-transform is a *linear* operator. Specifically, show that $\mathcal{Z}_z\{\alpha x_1(\cdot) + \beta x_2(\cdot)\} = \alpha X_1(z) + \beta X_2(z)$ for any two (real or complex) signals x_1 and x_2, and any two (real or complex) scalars (constant gains) α, β.

3. Recall that an operator $\mathcal{L}$ is said to be *linear* when it exhibits both superposition $\mathcal{L}\{x + y\} = \mathcal{L}\{x\} + \mathcal{L}\{y\}$ and scaling $\mathcal{L}\{\alpha x\} = \alpha \mathcal{L}\{x\}$, where x and y are arbitrary signals (vectors), and α is any scalar. Show that superposition implies scaling for rational scalars. Under what conditions does superposition imply scaling for real scalars?

4. *Musical Time-Varying Filter.* With a time-varying gain $g(n)$, we can create a *tremolo* effect, which can be written as

$$y(n) = g(n)x(n)$$

   (a) Show that the filter is linear.

   (b) State conditions under which the filter is time-invariant, if any.

5. A system consists of the cascade combination of a memoryless non-linearity (such as a soft-clipper) followed by a two-pole, two-zero, LTI filter.

   (a) Can we commute the nonlinearity with the LTI filter and obtain the same input-output behavior? If so, prove it. If not, find a counterexample.

   (b) Describe how we can determine the frequency response of the LTI filter by choosing known input signals and measuring the resulting response, or show that this is impossible. [Assume we can choose the input to the nonlinearity and observe the LTI filter output, with no input/output access to the signal leaving the nonlinearity and entering the LTI filter.]

   (c) Under the same conditions as the previous problem, describe what signals we can use to determine the memoryless nonlinearity, or show that this cannot be done.

Chapter 5

Time Domain Digital Filter Representations

This chapter discusses several time-domain representations for digital filters, including the *difference equation, system diagram,* and *impulse response.* Additionally, the *convolution representation* for LTI filters is derived, and the special case of FIR filters is considered. The *transient response, steady-state response,* and *decay response* are examined for FIR and IIR digital filters.

5.1 Difference Equation

The *difference equation* is a formula for computing an output sample at time n based on past and present input samples and past output samples in the time domain.[1] We may write the general, causal, LTI difference equation as follows:

$$
\begin{aligned}
y(n) &= b_0\, x(n) + b_1\, x(n-1) + \cdots + b_M\, x(n-M) \\
&\qquad -a_1\, y(n-1) - \cdots - a_N\, y(n-N)
\end{aligned}
$$

$$
= \sum_{i=0}^{M} b_i\, x(n-i) - \sum_{j=1}^{N} a_j\, y(n-j) \tag{5.1}
$$

---

[1]The term "difference equation" is a discrete-time counterpart to the term "differential equation" in continuous time. LTI difference equations in discrete time correspond to *linear* differential equations with *constant coefficients* in continuous time. The subject of *finite differences* is devoted to "discretizing" differential equations to obtain difference equations [96, 3].

where x is the input signal, y is the output signal, and the constants $b_i, i = 0, 1, 2, \ldots, M$, $a_i, i = 1, 2, \ldots, N$ are called the *coefficients*

As a specific example, the difference equation

$$y(n) = 0.01\, x(n) + 0.002\, x(n-1) + 0.99\, y(n-1)$$

specifies a digital filtering operation, and the coefficient sets $(0.01, 0.002)$ and (0.99) fully characterize the filter. In this example, we have $M = N = 1$.

When the coefficients are real numbers, as in the above example, the filter is said to be *real*. Otherwise, it may be *complex*.

Notice that a filter of the form of Eq. (5.1) can use "past" output samples (such as $y(n-1)$) in the calculation of the "present" output $y(n)$. This use of past output samples is called *feedback*. Any filter having one or more feedback paths ($N > 0$) is called *recursive*. (By the way, the minus signs for the feedback in Eq. (5.1) will be explained when we get to transfer functions in §6.1.)

More specifically, the b_i coefficients are called the *feedforward coefficients* and the a_i coefficients are called the *feedback coefficients*.

A filter is said to be *recursive* if and only if $a_i \neq 0$ for some $i > 0$. Recursive filters are also called *infinite-impulse-response (IIR)* filters. When there is no feedback ($a_i = 0, \forall i > 0$), the filter is said to be a *nonrecursive* or *finite-impulse-response (FIR)* digital filter.

When used for discrete-time physical modeling, the difference equation may be referred to as an *explicit finite difference scheme*.[2]

Showing that a recursive filter is LTI (Chapter 4) is easy by considering its *impulse-response representation* (discussed in §5.6 on page 100). For example, the recursive filter

$$\begin{aligned} y(n) &= x(n) + \frac{1}{2}y(n-1) \\ &= x(n) + \frac{1}{2}x(n-1) + \frac{1}{4}x(n-2) + \frac{1}{8}x(n-3) + \cdots, \end{aligned}$$

has impulse response $h(m) = 2^{-m}$, $m = 0, 1, 2, \ldots$. It is now straightforward to apply the analysis of the previous chapter to find that time-invariance, superposition, and the scaling property hold.

---

[2]The term "explicit" in this context means that the output $y(n)$ at time n can be computed using only *past* output samples $y(n-1)$, $y(n-2)$, etc. When solving *partial* differential equations numerically on a grid in 2 or more dimensions, it is possible to derive finite difference schemes which cannot be computed recursively, and these are termed *implicit finite difference schemes* [96, 3]. Implicit schemes can often be converted to explicit schemes by a change of coordinates (*e.g.*, to *modal coordinates* [86]).

5.2   Signal Flow Graph

One possible *signal flow graph* (or *system diagram*) for Eq. (5.1) is given in Fig. 5.1a for the case of $M = 2$ and $N = 2$. Hopefully, it is easy to see how this diagram represents the difference equation (a box labeled "z^{-1}" denotes a one-sample delay in time). The diagram remains true if it is converted to the *frequency domain* by replacing all time-domain signals by their respective z transforms (or Fourier transforms); that is, we may replace $x(n)$ by $X(z)$ and $y(n)$ by $Y(z)$. Z transforms and their usage will be discussed in Chapter 6.

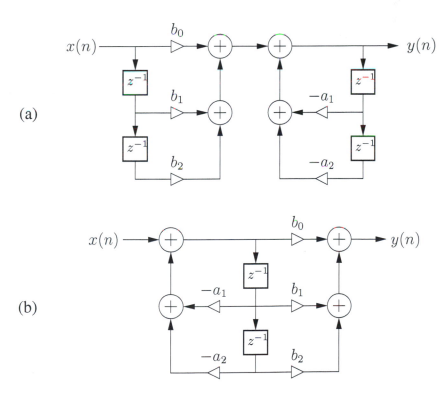

Figure 5.1: Signal flow graph for the filter difference equation
$$y(n) = b_0 x(n) + b_1 x(n-1) + b_2 x(n-2) - a_1 y(n-1) - a_2 y(n-2).$$
(a) Direct form I. (b) Direct form II.

5.3 Causal Recursive Filters

Equation (5.1) does not cover all LTI filters, for it represents only *causal* LTI filters. A filter is said to be causal when its output does not depend on any "future" inputs. (In more colorful terms, a filter is causal if it does not "laugh" before it is "tickled.") For example, $y(n) = x(n+1)$ is a non-causal filter because the output anticipates the input one sample into the future. Restriction to causal filters is quite natural when the filter operates in real time. Many digital filters, on the other hand, are implemented on a computer where time is artificially represented by an array index. Thus, noncausal filters present no difficulty in such an "off-line" situation. It happens that the analysis for noncausal filters is pretty much the same as that for causal filters, so we can easily relax this restriction.

5.4 Filter Order

The maximum delay, in samples, used in creating each output sample is called the *order* of the filter. In the difference-equation representation, the order is the larger of M and N in Eq. (5.1). For example, $y(n) = x(n) - x(n-1) - 2y(n-1) + y(n-2)$ specifies a particular second-order filter. If M and N in Eq. (5.1) are constrained to be finite (which is, of course, necessary in practice), then Eq. (5.1) represents the class of all *finite-order causal LTI digital filters*.

5.5 Direct-Form-I Implementation

The difference equation (Eq. (5.1)) is often used as the recipe for numerical implementation in software or hardware. As such, it specifies the *direct-form I* (DF-I) implementation of a digital filter, one of four direct-form structures to choose from. The DF-I signal flow graph for the second-order case is shown in Fig. 5.1a. The direct-form II structure, another common choice, is depicted in Fig. 5.1b. The other two direct forms are obtained by *transposing* direct forms I and II. Chapter 9 discusses all four direct-form structures.

5.6 Impulse-Response Representation

In addition to difference-equation coefficients, any LTI filter may be represented in the time domain by its response to a specific signal called the *impulse*. This response is called, naturally enough, the *impulse response* of the filter. Any LTI filter can be implemented by *convolving* the input signal with the filter impulse response, as we will see.

> **Definition.** The *impulse signal* is denoted $\delta(n)$ and defined by

$$\delta(n) \triangleq \begin{cases} 1, & n = 0 \\ 0, & n \neq 0. \end{cases}$$

We may also write $\delta = [1, 0, 0, \ldots]$.

A plot of $\delta(n)$ is given in Fig. 5.2a. In the physical world, an impulse may be approximated by a swift hammer blow (in the mechanical case) or balloon pop (acoustic case). We also have a special notation for the impulse *response* of a filter:

> **Definition.** The *impulse response* of a filter is the response of the filter to $\delta(n)$ and is most often denoted $h(n)$:

$$h(n) \triangleq \mathcal{L}_n\{\delta(\cdot)\}$$

The impulse response $h(n)$ is the response of the filter $\mathcal{L}$ at time n to a unit impulse occurring at time 0. We will see that $h(n)$ fully describes any LTI filter.[3]

We normally require that the impulse response decay to zero over time; otherwise, we say the filter is *unstable*. The next section formalizes this notion as a definition.

5.7   Filter Stability

> **Definition.** An LTI filter is said to be *stable* if the impulse response $h(n)$ approaches zero as n goes to infinity.

In this context, we may say that an impulse response "approaches zero" by definition if there exists a finite integer n_f, and real numbers $A \geq 0$ and $\alpha > 0$, such that $|h(n)| < A\exp(-\alpha n)$ for all $n \geq n_f$. In other terms, the impulse response is *asymptotically bounded* by a *decaying* exponential.

Every finite-order nonrecursive filter is stable. Only the feedback coefficients a_i in Eq. (5.1) can cause instability. Filter stability will be discussed

---

[3]Instead of defining the impulse response as the response of the filter to $\delta(n)$, a unit-amplitude impulse arriving at time zero, we could equally well choose our "standard impulse" to be $A\delta(n - n_0)$, an amplitude-A impulse arriving at time n_0. However, setting $n_0 = 0$ and $A = 1$ makes the math simpler to write, as we will see.

further in §8.4 after poles and zeros have been introduced. Suffice it to say for now that, for stability, the feedback coefficients must be restricted so that the feedback gain is less than 1 at every frequency. (We'll learn in §8.4 that stability is guaranteed when all filter poles have magnitude less than 1.) In practice, the stability of a recursive filter is usually checked by computing the filter *reflection coefficients*, as described in §8.4.1.

5.8   Impulse Response Example

An example impulse response for the first-order recursive filter

$$
\begin{aligned}
y(n) &= x(n) + 0.9y(n-1) & (5.2) \\
&= x(n) + 0.9x(n-1) + 0.9^2 x(n-2) + \cdots & (5.3)
\end{aligned}
$$

is shown in Fig. 5.2b. The impulse response is a *sampled exponential decay*, $(1, 0.9, 0.81, 0.73, \ldots)$, or, more formally,

$$
h(n) = \begin{cases} (0.9)^n, & n \geq 0 \\ 0, & n < 0. \end{cases}
$$

We can more compactly represent this by means of the *unit step function*,

$$
u(n) \triangleq \begin{cases} 1, & n \geq 0 \\ 0, & n < 0 \end{cases} ,
$$

so that

$$
h(n) = u(n)(0.9)^n, \quad n \in \mathbf{Z}
$$

where $n \in \mathbf{Z}$ means n is any integer.

5.9   Implications of Linear-Time-Invariance

Using the basic properties of linearity and time-invariance, we will derive the *convolution representation* which gives an algorithm for implementing the filter directly in terms of its impulse response. In other words,

> *the output y(n) of any LTI filter (including recursive LTI filters) may be computed by convolving the input signal with the filter impulse response.*

The convolution formula plays the role of the difference equation when the impulse response is used in place of the difference-equation coefficients

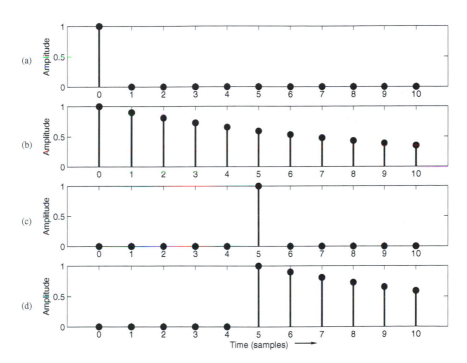

Figure 5.2: Input and output signals for the filter $y(n) = x(n) + 0.9\,y(n-1)$. (a) Input impulse $\delta(n)$. (b) Output impulse response $h(n) = u(n)\,0.9^n$. (c) Input delayed-impulse $\delta(n-5)$. (d) Output delayed-impulse response $h(n-5)$.

as a filter representation. In fact, we will find that, for FIR filters (non-recursive, *i.e.*, no feedback), the difference equation and convolution representation are essentially the same thing. For recursive filters, one can think of the convolution representation as the difference equation with all feedback terms "expanded" to an infinite number of feedforward terms.

An outline of the derivation of the convolution formula is as follows: Any signal $x(n)$ may be regarded as a superposition of impulses at various amplitudes and arrival times, *i.e.*, each sample of $x(n)$ is regarded as an impulse with amplitude $x(n)$ and delay n. We can write this mathematically as $x(n)\delta(\cdot - n)$. By the *superposition principle* for LTI filters, the filter output is simply the superposition of impulse *responses* $h(\cdot)$, each having a scale factor and time-shift given by the amplitude and time-shift of the corresponding input impulse. Thus, the sample $x(n)$ contributes the signal $x(n)h(\cdot - n)$ to the convolution output, and the total output is the sum of such contributions, by superposition. This is the heart of LTI filtering.

Before proceeding to the general case, let's look at a simple example with pictures. If an impulse strikes at time $n = 5$ rather than at time $n = 0$, this is represented by writing $\delta(n-5)$. A picture of this delayed impulse is given in Fig. 5.2c. When $\delta(n-5)$ is fed to a time-invariant filter, the output will be the impulse response $h(n)$ delayed by 5 samples, or $h(n-5)$. Figure 5.2d shows the response of the example filter of Eq. (5.3) to the delayed impulse $\delta(n - 5)$.

In the general case, for time-invariant filters we may write

$$\mathcal{L}_n\{\text{SHIFT}_K\{\delta\}\} \triangleq \mathcal{L}_n\{\delta(\cdot - K)\} = \mathcal{L}_{n-K}\{\delta(\cdot)\} = h(n - K)$$

where K is the number of samples delay. This equation states that right-shifting the input impulse by K points merely right-shifts the output (impulse response) by K points. Note that this is just a special case of the definition of time-invariance, Eq. (4.5).

If *two* impulses arrive at the filter input, the first at time $n = 0$, say, and the second at time $n = 5$, then this input may be expressed as $\delta(n)+\delta(n-5)$. If, in addition, the amplitude of the first impulse is 2, while the second impulse has an amplitude of 1, then the input may be written as $2\delta(n) + \delta(n - 5)$. In this case, using *linearity* as well as time-invariance, the response of the general LTI filter to this input may be expressed as

$$\begin{aligned}
\mathcal{L}_n\{2\delta(\cdot) + \delta(\cdot - 5)\} &= \mathcal{L}_n\{2\delta(\cdot)\} + \mathcal{L}_n\{\delta(\cdot - 5)\} \\
&= 2\mathcal{L}_n\{\delta(\cdot)\} + \mathcal{L}_{n-5}\{\delta(\cdot)\} \\
&= 2h(n) + h(n - 5).
\end{aligned}$$

For the example filter of Eq. (5.3), given the input $2\delta(n) + \delta(n - 5)$ (pictured in Fig. 5.3a), the output may be computed by scaling, shifting, and adding together copies of the impulse response $h(n)$. That is, taking the impulse response in Fig. 5.2b, multiplying it by 2, and adding it to the delayed impulse response in Fig. 5.2d, we obtain the output shown in Fig. 5.3b. Thus, a weighted sum of impulses produces the *same* weighted sum of impulse *responses*.

$$2h(n) + h(n-5) = \begin{cases} 2(0.9)^n + (0.9)^{n-5}, & n \geq 5 \\ 2(0.9)^n, & 0 \leq n < 5 \\ 0, & n < 0 \end{cases}$$

$$= 2u(n)0.9^n + u(n-5)0.9^{n-5}$$

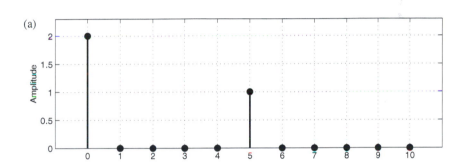

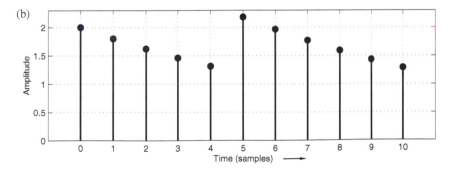

Figure 5.3: Input impulse pair and corresponding output for the filter $y(n) = x(n) + 0.9y(n-1)$. (a) Input: impulse of amplitude 2 plus delayed-impulse $2\delta(n) + \delta(n-5)$. (b) Output: $2h(n) + h(n-5)$.

5.10   Convolution Representation

We will now derive the convolution representation for LTI filters in its full generality. The first step is to express an arbitrary signal $x(\cdot)$ as a linear combination of shifted impulses, $i.e.,$

$$x(n) = \sum_{i=0}^{n} x(i)\delta(n - i) \triangleq (x * \delta)(n), \quad n \in \mathbf{Z} \tag{5.4}$$

where "$*$" denotes the convolution operator. (See [84][4] for an elementary introduction to convolution.)

If the above equation is not obvious, here is how it is built up intuitively. Imagine $\delta(\cdot)$ as a 1 in the midst of an infinite string of 0s. Now think of $\delta(\cdot - i)$ as the same pattern shifted over to the right by i samples. Next multiply $\delta(\cdot - i)$ by $x(\cdot)$, which plucks out the sample $x(i)$ and surrounds it on both sides by 0's. An example collection of waveforms $x(i)\delta(\cdot - i)$ for the case $x(i) = i, i = -2, -1, 0, 1, 2$ is shown in Fig. 5.4a. Now, sum over all i, bringing together the samples of x, to obtain $x(\cdot)$. Figure 5.4b shows the result of this addition for the sequences in Fig. 5.4a. Thus, any signal $x(\cdot)$ may be expressed as a weighted sum of shifted impulses.

Equation (5.4) expresses a signal as a linear combination (or weighted sum) of impulses. That is, each sample may be viewed as an impulse at some amplitude and time. As we have already seen, each impulse (sample) arriving at the filter's input will cause the filter to produce an impulse response. If another impulse arrives at the filter's input before the first impulse response has died away, then the impulse response for both impulses will *superimpose* (add together sample by sample). More generally, since the input is a linear combination of impulses, the output is the *same* linear combination of impulse responses. This is a direct consequence of the *superposition principle* which holds for any LTI filter.

We repeat this in more precise terms. First linearity is used and then time-invariance is invoked. Using the form of the general linear filter in Eq. (4.2), and the definition of linearity, Eq. (4.3) and Eq. (4.5) on page 88, we can express the output of any linear (and possibly time-varying) filter

---

[4]http://ccrma.stanford.edu/~jos/mdft/Convolution.html

(a)

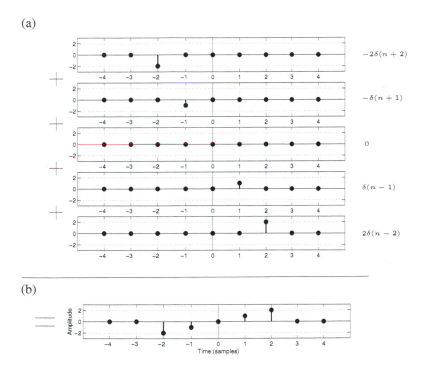

(b)

Figure 5.4: Any signal may be considered to be a sum of impulses. (a) Family of impulses at various amplitudes and time shifts. (b) Addition of impulses in (a), giving part of a ramp signal $x(i) = i$.

by

$$
\begin{aligned}
y(n) &= \mathcal{L}_n\{x(\cdot)\} \\
&= \mathcal{L}_n\{(x * \delta)(\cdot)\} \\
&\triangleq \mathcal{L}_n\left\{ \sum_{i=-\infty}^{\infty} x(i)\delta(\cdot - i) \right\} \\
&= \sum_{i=-\infty}^{\infty} x(i)\mathcal{L}_n\{\delta(\cdot - i)\} \\
&\triangleq \sum_{i=-\infty}^{\infty} x(i)h(n,i)
\end{aligned}
$$

where we have written $h(n,i) \triangleq \mathcal{L}_n\{\delta(\cdot - i)\}$ to denote the filter response at time n to an impulse which occurred at time i. If we are to be completely rigorous mathematically, certain "smoothness" restrictions must be placed on the linear operator $\mathcal{L}$ in order that it may be distributed inside the infinite summation [37]. However, practically useful filters of the form of Eq. (5.1) satisfy these restrictions. If in addition to being linear, the filter is time-invariant, then $h(n,i) = h(n-i)$, which allows us to write

$$
y(n) = \sum_{i=-\infty}^{\infty} x(i)h(n-i) \triangleq (x * h)(n), \ n \in \mathbf{Z}. \tag{5.5}
$$

This states that the filter output y is the *convolution* of the input x with the filter impulse response h.

The infinite sum in Eq. (5.5) can be replaced by more typical practical limits. By choosing time 0 as the beginning of the signal, we may define $x(n)$ to be 0 for $n < 0$ so that the lower summation limit of $-\infty$ can be replaced by 0. Also, if the filter is causal, we have $h(n) = 0$ for $n < 0$, so the upper summation limit can be written as n instead of ∞. Thus, the *convolution representation of a linear, time-invariant, causal digital filter* is given by

$$
\boxed{y(n) = \sum_{i=0}^{n} x(i)h(n-i) = (x * h)(n), \ n = 0, 1, 2, \ldots,}
$$

for causal input signals (*i.e.*, $x(n) = 0$ for $n < 0$).

Since the above equation is a convolution, and since convolution is commutative (*i.e.*, $(x * h)(n) = (h * x)(n)$ [84]), we can rewrite it as

$$
\boxed{y(n) = \sum_{i=0}^{n} h(i)x(n-i) = (h * x)(n), \ n \geq 0}
$$

or

$$y(n) = h(0)x(n) + h(1)x(n-1) + h(2)x(n-2) + \cdots + h(n)x(0).$$

This latter form looks more like the general difference equation presented in Eq. (5.1). In this form one can see that $h(i)$ may be identified with the b_i coefficients in Eq. (5.1). It is also evident that the filter operates by summing *weighted echoes* of the input signal together. At time n, the weight of the echo from i samples ago $[x(n-i)]$ is $h(i)$.

Convolution Representation Summary

We have shown that the output y of any LTI filter may be calculated by convolving the input x with the impulse response h. It is instructive to compare this method of filter implementation to the use of difference equations, Eq. (5.1). If there is no feedback (no a_j coefficients in Eq. (5.1)), then the difference equation and the convolution formula are essentially *identical*, as shown in the next section. For recursive filters, we can convert the difference equation into a convolution by calculating the filter impulse response. However, this can be rather tedious, since with nonzero feedback coefficients the impulse response generally lasts forever. Of course, for stable filters the response is infinite only in theory; in practice, one may truncate the response after an appropriate length of time, such as after it falls below the quantization noise level due to round-off error.

5.11   Finite Impulse Response Digital Filters

In §5.1 we defined the general difference equation for IIR filters, and a couple of second-order examples were diagrammed in Fig. 5.1 on page 99. In this section, we take a more detailed look at the special case of Finite Impulse Response (FIR) digital filters. In addition to introducing various terminology and practical considerations associated with FIR filters, we'll look at a preview of transfer-function analysis (Chapter 6) for this simple special case.

Figure 5.5 gives the signal flow graph for a general causal FIR filter Such a filter is also called a *transversal filter*, or a *tapped delay line*. The implementation shown is classified as a *direct-form* implementation.

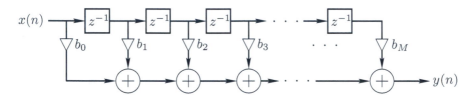

Figure 5.5: The general, causal, length $N = M + 1$, finite-impulse-response (FIR) digital filter. For FIR filters, direct-form I and direct-form II are the same (see Chapter 9).

5.11.1   FIR impulse response

The *impulse response* $h(n)$ is obtained at the output when the input signal is the *impulse signal* $\delta = [1,0,0,0,\ldots]$ (§5.6 on page 100). If the kth tap is denoted b_k, then it is obvious from Fig. 5.5 that the impulse response *signal* is given by

$$h(n) \triangleq \begin{cases} 0, & n < 0 \\ b_n, & 0 \leq n \leq M \\ 0, & n > M \end{cases} \tag{5.6}$$

In other words, the impulse response simply consists of the tap coefficients, prepended and appended by zeros.

5.11.2   Convolution Representation of FIR Filters

Notice that the output of the kth delay element in Fig. 5.5 is $x(n-k)$, $k = 0,1,2,\ldots,M$, where $x(n)$ is the input signal amplitude at time n. The output signal $y(n)$ is therefore

$$\begin{aligned} y(n) &= b_0 x(n) + b_1 x(n-1) + b_2 x(n-2) + \cdots + b_M x(n-M) \\ &= \sum_{m=0}^{M} b_m x(n-m) \\ &= \sum_{m=-\infty}^{\infty} h(m)x(n-m) \\ &\triangleq (h * x)(n) \end{aligned} \tag{5.7}$$

where we have used the *convolution operator* "$*$" to denote the convolution of h and x, as defined in Eq. (5.4) on page 106. An FIR filter thus operates by convolving the input signal x with the filter's *impulse response h*.

The "Finite" in FIR

From Eq. (5.7), we can see that the impulse response becomes zero after time $M = N - 1$. Therefore, a tapped delay line (Fig. 5.5 on page 110) can only implement *finite-duration* impulse responses in the sense that the non-zero portion of the impulse response must be finite. This is what is meant by the term *finite impulse response* (FIR). We may say that the impulse response has *finite support* [52].

Causal FIR Filters

From Eq. (5.6), we see also that the impulse response $h(n)$ is always *zero* for $n < 0$. Recall from §5.3 on page 100 that any LTI filter having a zero impulse response prior to time 0 is said to be *causal*. Thus, a tapped delay line such as that depicted in Fig. 5.5 can *only* implement causal FIR filters. In software, on the other hand, we may easily implement non-causal FIR filters as well, based simply on the definition of convolution.

5.11.3   FIR Transfer Function

The *transfer function* of an FIR filter is given by the z transform of its impulse response. This is true for any LTI filter, as discussed in Chapter 6. For FIR filters in particular, we have, from Eq. (5.6),

$$H(z) \triangleq \sum_{n=-\infty}^{\infty} h_n z^{-n} = \sum_{n=0}^{M} b_n z^{-n} \tag{5.8}$$

Thus, the transfer function of every length $N = M + 1$ FIR filter is an Mth-order *polynomial* in z^{-1}.

FIR Order

The *order* of a filter is defined as the order of its transfer function, as discussed in Chapter 6. For FIR filters, this is just the order of the transfer-function polynomial. Thus, from Equation (5.8), the order of the general, causal, length $N = M + 1$ FIR filter is M (provided $b_M \neq 0$).

Note from Fig. 5.5 that the order M is also the *total number of delay elements* in the filter. This is typical of practical digital filter implementations. When the number of delay elements in the implementation (Fig. 5.5) is equal to the filter order, the filter implementation is said to be *canonical with respect to delay*. It is not possible to implement a given transfer function in fewer delays than the transfer function order, but it is possible (and sometimes even desirable) to have extra delays.

5.11.4   FIR Software Implementations

In matlab, an efficient FIR filter is implemented by calling

$$\texttt{outputsignal = filter(B,1,inputsignal);}$$

where

$$\texttt{B} = [b_0, b_1, \ldots, b_M].$$

It is relatively efficient because `filter` is a built-in function (compiled C code in most matlab implementations). However, for FIR filters longer than a hundred or so taps, *FFT convolution* should be used for maximum speed. In Octave and the Matlab Signal Processing Toolbox, `fftfilt` implements FIR filters using FFT convolution (say "`help fftfilt`").

Figure 5.6 lists a second-order FIR filter implementation in the C programming language.

```
typedef double *pp;  // pointer to array of length NTICK
typedef double word; // signal and coefficient data type

typedef struct _fir3Vars {
    pp outputAout;
    pp inputAinp;
    word b0;
    word b1;
    word b2;
    word s1;
    word s2;
} fir3Vars;

void fir3(fir3Vars *a)
{
    int i;
    word input;
    for (i=0; i<NTICK; i++) {
        input = a->inputAinp[i];
        a->outputAout[i] = a->b0 * input
                + a->b1 * a->s1  +  a->b2 * a->s2;
        a->s2 = a->s1;
        a->s1 = input;
    }
}
```

Figure 5.6: C code for implementing a length 3 FIR filter.

5.12   Transient Response, Steady State, and Decay

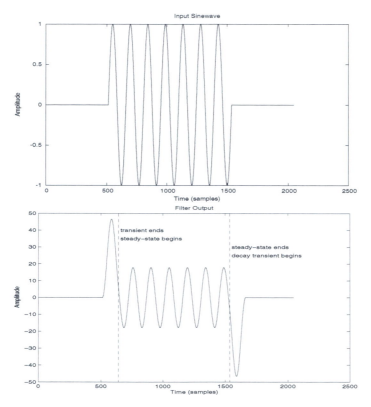

Figure 5.7: Example transient, steady-state, and decay responses for an FIR "running sum" filter driven by a gated sinusoid.

The terms *transient response* and *steady state response* arise naturally in the context of sinewave analysis (*e.g.*, §2.2 on page 30). When the input sinewave is switched on, the filter takes a while to "settle down" to a perfect sinewave at the same frequency, as illustrated in Fig. 5.12. The filter response during this "settling" period is called the *transient response* of the filter. The response of the filter *after* the transient response, provided the filter is linear and time-invariant, is called the *steady-state response*, and it consists of a pure sinewave at the same frequency as the input sinewave, but with amplitude and phase determined by the filter's *frequency response* at that frequency. In other words, the steady-state response begins when the LTI filter is fully "warmed up" by the input signal. More precisely, the filter output is the same as if the input signal had been applied since time minus infinity. Length N FIR filters only "remember" $N - 1$ samples into the past. Thus, for length N FIR filters, the duration of the transient response is $N - 1$ samples.

To show this, (it may help to refer to the general FIR filter implementation in Fig. 5.5 on page 110), consider that a length $N = 1$ (zero-order) FIR filter (a simple gain), has no state memory at all, and thus it is in "steady state" immediately when the input sinewave is switched on. A length $N = 2$ FIR filter, on the other hand, reaches steady state one sample after the input sinewave is switched on, because it has one sample of delay. At the switch-on time instant, the length 2 FIR filter has a single sample of state that is still zero (instead of its steady-state value which is the previous input sinewave sample).

In general, a length N FIR filter is fully "warmed up" after $N - 1$ samples of input; that is, for an input starting at time $n = 0$, by time $n = N - 1$, all internal state delays of the filter contain delayed input samples instead of their initial zeros. When the input signal is a unit step $u(n)$ times a sinusoid (or, by superposition, any linear combination of sinusoids), we may say that the filter output reaches *steady state* at time $n = N - 1$.

5.12.1   FIR Example

An example sinewave input signal is shown in Fig. 5.12, and the output of a length $N = 128$ FIR "running sum" filter is shown in Fig. 5.12. These signals were computed by the following matlab code:

```
Nx = 1024; % input signal length (nonzero portion)
Nh = 128;  % FIR filter length
A = 1; B = ones(1,Nh); % FIR "running sum" filter
n = 0:Nx-1;
x = sin(n*2*pi*7/Nx);  % input sinusoid - zero-pad it:
zp=zeros(1,Nx/2); xzp=[zp,x,zp]; nzp=[0:length(xzp)-1];
y = filter(B,A,xzp);   % filtered output signal
```

We know that the transient response must end $Nh - 1 = 127$ samples after the input sinewave switches on, and the decay-time lasts the same amount of time after the input signal switches back to zero.

Since the coefficients of an FIR filter are also its nonzero impulse response samples, we can say that the duration of the transient response equals the length of the impulse response minus one.

For Infinite Impulse Response (IIR) filters, such as the recursive comb filter analyzed in Chapter 3, the transient response decays *exponentially*.

This means it is never really completely finished. In other terms, since its impulse response is infinitely long, so is its transient response, in principle. However, in practice, we treat it as finished for all practical purposes after several time constants of decay. For example, seven time-constants of decay correspond to more than 60 dB of decay, and is a common cut-off used for audio purposes. Therefore, we can adopt t_{60} as the definition of *decay time* (or "*ring time*") for typical audio filters. See [84][5] for a detailed derivation of t_{60} and related topics. In summary, we can say that the transient response of an audio filter is over after t_{60} seconds, where t_{60} is the time it takes the filter impulse response to decay by 60 dB.

5.12.2   IIR Example

Figure 5.8 plots an IIR filter example for the filter

$$y(n) = x(n) + 0.99\, y(n-1).$$

The previous matlab is modified as follows:

```
Nh = 300; % APPROXIMATE filter length (visually in plot)
B = 1; A = [1 -0.99]; % One-pole recursive example
...        % otherwise as above for the FIR example
```

The decay time for this recursive filter was arbitrarily marked at 300 samples (about three time-constants of decay).

5.12.3   Transient and Steady-State Signals

Loosely speaking, any sudden change in a signal is regarded as a *transient*, and transients in an input signal disturb the steady-state operation of a filter, resulting in a transient response at the filter output. This leads us to ask how do we define "transient" in a precise way? This turns out to be difficult in practice.

A mathematically convenient definition is as follows: A signal is said to contain a *transient* whenever its Fourier expansion [84] requires an *infinite* number of sinusoids. Conversely, any signal expressible as a *finite* number of sinusoids can be defined as a *steady-state signal*. Thus, waveform discontinuities are transients, as are discontinuities in the waveform slope, curvature, etc. Any fixed sum of sinusoids, on the other hand, is a steady-state signal.

In practical audio signal processing, defining transients is more difficult. In particular, since hearing is bandlimited, all audible signals are

---

[5]http://ccrma.stanford.edu/~jos/mdft/

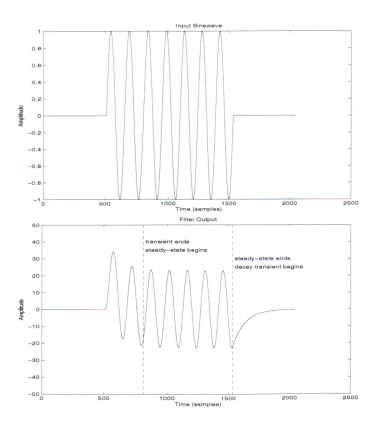

Figure 5.8: Example transient, steady-state, and decay responses for an IIR "one-pole" filter driven by a gated sinusoid.

technically steady-state signals under the above definition. One way to pose the question is to ask which sounds should be "stretched" and which should be translated in time when a signal is "slowed down"? In the case of speech, for example, short consonants would be considered transients, while vowels and sibilants such as "ssss" would be considered steady-state signals. Percussion hits are generally considered transients, as are the "attacks" of plucked and struck strings (such as piano). More generally, almost any "attack" is considered a transient, but a slow fade-in of a string section, *e.g.*, might not be. In sum, musical discrimination between "transient" and "steady state" signals depends on our perception, and on our learned classifications of sounds. However, to first order, transient sounds can be defined practically as sudden "wideband events" in an otherwise steady-state signal. This is at least similar in spirit to the mathematical definition given above.

In summary, a filter transient response is caused by suddenly switching on a filter input signal, or otherwise disturbing a steady-state input signal away from its steady-state form. After the transient response has died out, we see the steady-state response, provided that the input signal itself is a steady-state signal (a fixed linear combination of sinusoids) and given that the filter is LTI.

5.12.4   Decay Response, Initial Conditions Response

If a filter is in steady state and we switch *off* the input signal, we see its *decay response*. This response is identical (but for a time shift) to the filter's *response to initial conditions*. In other words, when the input signal is switched off (becomes zero), the future output signal is computed entirely from the filter's internal state, because the input signal remains zero.

5.12.5   Complete Response

In general, the so-called *complete response* of a linear, time-invariant filter is given by the *superposition* of its

- *zero-state response* and
- *initial-condition response*.

"Zero-state response" simply means the response of the filter to an input signal when the initial state of the filter (all its memory cells) are zeroed to begin with. The initial-condition response is of course the response of the filter to its own initial state, with the input signal being zero. This clean superposition of the zero-state and initial-condition responses only holds in general for linear filters. In §G.3 on page 349, this superposition will be considered for state-space filter representations.

5.13   Summary and Conclusions

This concludes the discussion of time-domain filter descriptions, including difference equations, signal flow graphs, and impulse-response representations. More time-domain forms (alternative digital filter implementations) will be described in Chapter 9. A tour of elementary digital filter sections used often in audio applications is presented in Appendix B. Beyond that, some matrix-based representations are included in Appendix F, and the state-space formulation is discussed in Appendix G.

Time-domain forms are typically used to implement recursive filters in software or hardware, and they generalize readily to nonlinear and/or time-varying cases. For an understanding of the effects of an LTI filter on a sound, however, it is usually more appropriate to consider a *frequency-domain* picture, to which we now turn in the next chapter.

5.14   Time-Domain Representation Problems

1. From the definition of order given in the discussion after Eq. (5.1), determine the order of the following filter:

$$y(n) = x(n-1) + x(n-2) + y(n-1)$$

2. What is the order of the filter below?

$$y(n) = x(n) + x(n-1) + y(n-1)$$

3. State a difference equation for the tremolo filter using a sinusoidally varying gain, maximum "depth", and a "rate" of 6 pulsations per second.

4. Consider the difference equation for the recursive integrator,

$$y(n) = x(n) + y(n-1).$$

Find its impulse response and write down its convolution representation. Why can you not program this form? How might the recursive form develop trouble even though you can program it?

5. Show that there is no upper bound on the maximum gain of a stable filter. [Hint: Consider the first-order recursive filter $y(n) = x(n) + g\,y(n-1)$, where $|g| < 1$, and consider a dc input signal.]

6. Given the impulse response of an FIR digital filter $h(n)$, $n = 0:L-1$, find the input signal $x(n)$ which satisfies $|x(n)| \leq 1$ and which results in the *maximum amplitude* in the output signal. Find the time(s) that the maximum amplitude is achieved.

7. Show that the *maximum amplitude* of the output of a digital filter is given by the *L1 norm* of its impulse response, where the input signal is confined to the interval $|x(n)| \leq 1$, and the L^1 norm of a signal $x(n)$ is defined as the sum of the absolute values of its samples:

$$\| x \|_1 \triangleq \sum_{n=-\infty}^{\infty} |x(n)|$$

Chapter 6

Transfer Function Analysis

This chapter discusses filter *transfer functions* and associated analysis. The transfer function provides an algebraic representation of a linear, time-invariant (LTI) filter in the frequency domain:

> The *transfer function* of a linear time-invariant discrete-time filter is defined as $Y(z)/X(z)$, where $Y(z)$ denotes the z transform of the filter output signal $y(n)$, and $X(z)$ denotes the z transform of the filter input signal $x(n)$.

The transfer function is also called the *system function* [60].

Let $h(n)$ denote the *impulse response* of the filter. It turns out (as we will show) that *the transfer function is equal to the z transform of the impulse response $h(n)$:*

$$H(z) = \frac{Y(z)}{X(z)}$$

Since multiplying the input transform $X(z)$ by the transfer function $H(z)$ gives the output transform $Y(z)$, we see that $H(z)$ embodies the *transfer characteristics* of the filter—hence the name.

It remains to define "z transform", and to prove that the z transform of the impulse response always gives the transfer function, which we will do by proving the *convolution theorem* for z transforms.

121

6.1   The Z Transform

The *bilateral z transform* of the discrete-time signal $x(n)$ is defined to be

$$X(z) \triangleq \sum_{n=-\infty}^{\infty} x(n)z^{-n} \qquad \text{(bilateral z transform)} \qquad (6.1)$$

where z is a complex variable. Since signals are typically defined to begin (become nonzero) at time $n = 0$, and since filters are often assumed to be causal,[1] the lower summation limit given above may be written as 0 rather than $-\infty$ to yield the *unilateral z transform*:

$$X(z) \triangleq \sum_{n=0}^{\infty} x(n)z^{-n} \qquad \text{(unilateral z transform)} \qquad (6.2)$$

The unilateral z transform is most commonly used. For inverting z transforms, see §6.8 on page 129.

Recall (§4.1) that the mathematical representation of a discrete-time signal $x(n)$ maps each integer $n \in \mathbf{Z}$ to a complex number $(x(n) \in \mathbf{C})$ or real number $(x(n) \in \mathbf{R})$. The z transform of x, on the other hand, $X(z)$, maps every complex number $z \in \mathbf{C}$ to a new complex number $X(z) \in \mathbf{C}$. On a higher level, the z transform, viewed as a *linear operator*, maps an entire signal x to its z transform X. We think of this as a "function to function" mapping. We may say X is the z transform of x by writing

$$\boxed{X \leftrightarrow x}$$

or, using operator notation,

$$X(z) = \mathcal{Z}_z\{x(\cdot)\}$$

which can be abbreviated as

$$X = \mathcal{Z}\{x\}.$$

One also sees the convenient but possibly misleading notation $X(z) \leftrightarrow x(n)$, in which n and z must be understood as standing for the entire domains $n \in \mathbf{Z}$ and $z \in \mathbf{C}$, as opposed to denoting particular fixed values.

The z transform of a signal x can be regarded as a *polynomial* in z^{-1}, with coefficients given by the signal samples. For example, the signal

$$x(n) = \begin{cases} n+1, & 0 \leq n \leq 2 \\ 0, & \text{otherwise} \end{cases}$$

---

[1]In a causal filter (§5.3), each output sample is computed using only current and past input samples—no future samples. A *causal signal* is similarly zero before time zero $(x(n) = 0, \forall n < 0)$. An LTI filter is causal if and only if its impulse response is a causal signal.

has the z transform $X(z) = 1 + 2z^{-1} + 3z^{-2} = 1 + 2z^{-1} + 3(z^{-1})^2$.

6.2   Existence of the Z Transform

The z transform of a finite-amplitude signal x will always *exist* provided (1) the signal starts at a finite time and (2) it is *asymptotically exponentially bounded*, i.e., there exists a finite integer n_f, and finite real numbers $A \geq 0$ and σ, such that $|x(n)| < A \exp(\sigma n)$ for all $n \geq n_f$. The bounding exponential may even be growing with n ($\sigma > 0$). These are not the most general conditions for existence of the z transform, but they suffice for most practical purposes.

For a signal $x(n)$ growing as $\exp(\sigma n)$, for $\sigma > 0$, one would naturally expect the z transform $X(z)$ to be defined only in the region $|z| > \exp(\sigma)$ of the complex plane. This is expected because the infinite series

$$\sum_{n=0}^{\infty} e^{\sigma n} z^{-n} = \sum_{n=0}^{\infty} \left(\frac{e^{\sigma}}{z}\right)^n$$

requires $|z| > \exp(\sigma)$ to ensure convergence. Since $\sigma < 0 \Leftrightarrow \exp(\sigma) < 1$ for a decaying exponential, we see that *the region of convergence of the z transform of a decaying exponential always includes the unit circle of the z plane.*

More generally, it turns out that, in all cases of practical interest, the domain of $X(z)$ can be *extended* to include the *entire complex plane*, except at isolated "singular" points[2] at which $|X(z)|$ approaches infinity (such as at $z = \exp(\sigma)$ when $x(n) = \exp(\sigma n)$). The mathematical technique for doing this is called *analytic continuation*, and it is described in §D.1 on page 310 as applied to the *Laplace transform* (the continuous-time counterpart of the z transform). A point to note, however, is that in the extension region (all points z such that $|z| < \exp(\sigma)$ in the above example), the signal component corresponding to each singularity inside the extension region is "flipped" in the time domain. That is, "causal" exponentials become "anticausal" exponentials, as discussed in §8.7 on page 190.

The z transform is discussed more fully elsewhere [52, 60], and we will derive below only what we will need.

---

[2] When $X(z)$ is a filter transfer function (*i.e.*, $x(n)$ is a filter impulse response), these singularities are called *poles* of the transfer function, as will be defined in §6.6 below. Analogously, one can speak of "poles" in the z transform of a signal containing exponential components of the form $\exp \sigma n \cos(\omega n + \phi)$.

6.3   Shift and Convolution Theorems

In this section, we prove the highly useful *shift theorem* and *convolution theorem* for unilateral z transforms. We consider the space of infinitely long, causal, complex sequences $x(n) \in \mathbf{C}$, $n \in \mathbf{Z}$, with $x(n) = 0$ for $n < 0$.

Shift Theorem

The *shift theorem* says that a *delay* of Δ samples in the time domain corresponds to a *multiplication by* $z^{-\Delta}$ in the frequency domain:

$$\mathcal{Z}_z\{\text{SHIFT}_\Delta\{x\}\} \;=\; z^{-\Delta}X(z), \; \Delta \geq 0,$$

or, using more common notation,

$$\boxed{x(n - \Delta) \;\leftrightarrow\; z^{-\Delta}X(z), \; \Delta \geq 0.}$$

Thus, $x(\cdot - \Delta)$, which is the waveform $x(\cdot)$ delayed by Δ samples, has the z transform $z^{-\Delta}X(z)$.

Proof:

$$
\begin{aligned}
\mathcal{Z}_z\{\text{SHIFT}_\Delta\{x\}\} \;&\triangleq\; \sum_{n=0}^{\infty} x(n - \Delta)z^{-n} \\[2mm]
&=\; \sum_{m=-\Delta}^{\infty} x(m)z^{-(m+\Delta)} \qquad (m \triangleq n - \Delta) \\[2mm]
&=\; \sum_{m=0}^{\infty} x(m)z^{-m}z^{-\Delta} \qquad (\Delta \geq 0,\; x(n) = 0 \text{ for } n < 0) \\[2mm]
&=\; z^{-\Delta} \sum_{m=0}^{\infty} x(m)z^{-m} \\[2mm]
&\triangleq\; z^{-\Delta}X(z),
\end{aligned}
$$

where we used the causality assumption $x(m) = 0$ for $m < 0$.

Convolution Theorem

The *convolution theorem for z transforms* states that for any (real or) complex causal signals x and y, *convolution in the time domain is multiplication in the z domain*, i.e.,

$$\boxed{x * y \;\leftrightarrow\; X \cdot Y}$$

or, using operator notation,

$$\mathcal{Z}_z\{x * y\} = X(z)Y(z),$$

where $X(z) \triangleq \mathcal{Z}_z(x)$, and $Y(z) \triangleq \mathcal{Z}_z(y)$. (See [84] for a development of the convolution theorem for discrete Fourier transforms.)

Proof:

$$\mathcal{Z}_z(x * y) \triangleq \sum_{n=0}^{\infty} (x * y)_n z^{-n}$$

$$\triangleq \sum_{n=0}^{\infty} \sum_{m=0}^{\infty} x(m) y(n - m) z^{-n}$$

$$= \sum_{m=0}^{\infty} x(m) \underbrace{\sum_{n=0}^{\infty} y(n - m) z^{-n}}_{z^{-m} Y(z)}$$

$$= \left(\sum_{m=0}^{\infty} x(m) z^{-m} \right) Y(z) \quad \text{(by the Shift Theorem)}$$

$$\triangleq X(z)Y(z)$$

The convolution theorem provides a major cornerstone of linear systems theory. It implies, for example, that any stable causal LTI filter (recursive or nonrecursive) can be implemented by convolving the input signal with the impulse response of the filter, as shown in the next section.

6.4   *Z* Transform of Convolution

From Eq. (5.5) on page 108, we have that the output y from a linear time-invariant filter with input x and impulse response h is given by the *convolution* of h and x, *i.e.*,

$$y(n) = (h * x)(n) \tag{6.3}$$

where "*" means convolution as before. Taking the z transform of both sides of Eq. (6.3) and applying the convolution theorem from the preceding section gives

$$Y(z) = H(z)X(z) \tag{6.4}$$

where H(z) is the z transform of the filter impulse response. We may divide Eq. (6.4) by $X(z)$ to obtain

$$H(z) = \frac{Y(z)}{X(z)} \triangleq \text{transfer function.}$$

This shows that, as a direct result of the convolution theorem, the z transform of an impulse response $h(n)$ is equal to the transfer function $H(z) = Y(z)/X(z)$ of the filter, provided the filter is linear and time invariant.

6.5   Z Transform of Difference Equations

Since z transforming the convolution representation for digital filters was so fruitful, let's apply it now to the general difference equation, Eq. (5.1) on page 97. To do this requires two properties of the z transform, *linearity* (easy to show) and the *shift theorem* (derived in §6.3 above). Using these two properties, we can write down the z transform of any difference equation by inspection, as we now show. In §6.8.2 on page 132, we'll show how to *invert* by inspection as well.

Repeating the general difference equation for LTI filters, we have (from Eq. (5.1))

$$y(n) = b_0 x(n) + b_1 x(n-1) + \cdots + b_M x(n-M)$$
$$- a_1 y(n-1) - \cdots - a_N y(n-N).$$

Let's take the z transform of both sides, denoting the transform by $\mathcal{Z}\{\}$. Because $\mathcal{Z}\{\}$ is a linear operator, it may be distributed through the terms on the right-hand side as follows:[3]

$$\mathcal{Z}_z\{y(\cdot)\} = \mathcal{Z}\{b_0 x(n) + b_1 x(n-1) + \cdots + b_M x(n-M)$$
$$- a_1 y(n-1) - \cdots - a_N (n-N)\}$$
$$= \mathcal{Z}\{b_0 x(n)\} + \mathcal{Z}\{b_1 x(n-1)\} + \cdots + \mathcal{Z}\{b_M x(n-M)\}$$
$$- \mathcal{Z}\{a_1 y(n-1)\} - \cdots - \mathcal{Z}\{a_N y(n-N)\}$$
$$= b_0 \mathcal{Z}\{x(n)\} + b_1 \mathcal{Z}\{x(n-1)\} + \cdots + b_M \mathcal{Z}\{x(n-M)\}$$
$$- a_1 \mathcal{Z}\{y(n-1)\} - \cdots - a_N \mathcal{Z}\{y(n-N)\}$$
$$= b_0 X(z) + b_1 z^{-1} X(z) + \cdots + b_M z^{-M} X(z)$$
$$- a_1 z^{-1} Y(z) - \cdots - a_N z^{-N} Y(z),$$

where we used the superposition and scaling properties of linearity given on page 88, followed by use of the shift theorem, in that order. The terms in $Y(z)$ may be grouped together on the left-hand side to get

$$Y(z) + a_1 z^{-1} Y(z) + \cdots + a_N z^{-N} Y(z) =$$
$$b_0 X(z) + b_1 z^{-1} X(z) + \cdots + b_M z^{-M} X(z).$$

Factoring out the common terms $Y(z)$ and $X(z)$ gives

$$Y(z) \left[1 + a_1 z^{-1} + \cdots + a_N z^{-N}\right] = X(z) \left[b_0 + b_1 z^{-1} + \cdots + b_M z^{-M}\right].$$

---

[3] Each 'n' in these equations should be interpreted as '$\cdot$'.

Defining the polynomials

$$A(z) \quad \triangleq \quad 1 + a_1\,z^{-1} + \cdots + a_N\,z^{-N}$$
$$B(z) \quad \triangleq \quad b_0 + b_1\,z^{-1} + \cdots + b_M\,z^{-M},$$

the z transform of the difference equation yields

$$A(z)\,Y(z) = B(z)\,X(z).$$

Finally, solving for $Y(z)/X(z)$, which is by definition the transfer function $H(z)$, gives

$$H(z) \triangleq \frac{Y(z)}{X(z)} = \frac{b_0 + b_1 z^{-1} + \cdots + b_M z^{-M}}{1 + a_1 z^{-1} + \cdots + a_N z^{-N}} \triangleq \frac{B(z)}{A(z)}. \qquad (6.5)$$

Thus, taking the z transform of the general difference equation led to a new formula for the transfer function in terms of the difference equation coefficients. (Now the minus signs for the feedback coefficients in the difference equation Eq. (5.1) on page 97 are explained.)

6.6   Factored Form

By the fundamental theorem of algebra, every Nth order polynomial can be *factored* into a product of N first-order polynomials. Therefore, Eq. (6.5) above can be written in *factored form* as

$$H(z) = b_0 \frac{(1 - q_1 z^{-1})(1 - q_2 z^{-1}) \cdots (1 - q_M z^{-1})}{(1 - p_1 z^{-1})(1 - p_2 z^{-1}) \cdots (1 - p_N z^{-1})}. \qquad (6.6)$$

The numerator roots $\{q_1, \ldots, q_M\}$ are called the *zeros* of the transfer function, and the denominator roots $\{p_1, \ldots, p_N\}$ are called the *poles* of the filter. Poles and zeros are discussed further in Chapter 8.

6.7   Series and Parallel Transfer Functions

The transfer function conveniently captures the *algebraic structure* of a filtering operation with respect to *series or parallel combination*. Specifically, we have the following cases:

1. *Transfer functions of filters in series multiply together.*

2. *Transfer functions of filters in parallel sum together.*

$$v(n)$$

$$x(n) \longrightarrow \boxed{H_1(z)} \longrightarrow \boxed{H_2(z)} \longrightarrow y(n)$$

Figure 6.1: Series combination of transfer functions $H_1(z)$ and $H_2(z)$ to produce the combined transfer function $H(z) = H_1(z)H_2(z)$.

Series Case

Figure 6.1 illustrates the *series connection* of two filters $H_1(z) = V(z)/X(z)$ and $H_2(z) = Y(z)/V(z)$. The output $v(n)$ from filter 1 is used as the input to filter 2. Therefore, the overall transfer function is

$$H(z) \triangleq \frac{Y(z)}{X(z)} = \frac{H_2(z)V(z)}{X(z)} = H_2(z)H_1(z).$$

In summary, if the output of filter $H_1(z)$ is given as input to filter $H_2(z)$ (a series combination), as shown in Fig. 6.1, the overall transfer function is $H(z) = H_1(z)H_2(z)$—transfer functions of filters connected in series *multiply* together.

Parallel Case

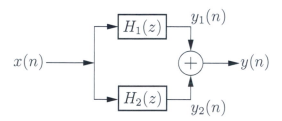

Figure 6.2: Parallel combination of transfer functions $H_1(z)$ and $H_2(z)$, yielding $H(z) = H_1(z) + H_2(z)$.

Figure 6.2 illustrates the *parallel combination* of two filters. The filters $H_1(z)$ and $H_2(z)$ are driven by the *same* input signal $x(n)$, and their respective outputs $y_1(n)$ and $y_2(n)$ are *summed*. The transfer function of the parallel combination is therefore

$$H(z) \triangleq \frac{Y(z)}{X(z)} = \frac{Y_1(z) + Y_2(z)}{X(z)} = \frac{Y_1(z)}{X(z)} + \frac{Y_2(z)}{X(z)} \triangleq H_1(z) + H_2(z).$$

where we needed only linearity of the z transform to have that $\mathcal{Z}\{y_1 + y_2\} = \mathcal{Z}\{y_1\} + \mathcal{Z}\{y_2\}$.

Series Combination is Commutative

Since multiplication of complex numbers is commutative, we have

$$H_1(z)H_2(z) = H_2(z)H_1(z),$$

which implies that any ordering of filters in series results in the same overall transfer function. Note, however, that the *numerical* performance of the overall filter is usually affected by the ordering of filter stages in a series combination [103]. Chapter 9 further considers numerical performance of filter implementation structures.

By the convolution theorem for z transforms, commutativity of a product of transfer functions implies that *convolution is commutative*:

$$h_1 * h_2 \;\leftrightarrow\; H_1 \cdot H_2 \;=\; H_2 \cdot H_1 \;\leftrightarrow\; h_2 * h_1$$

6.8 Partial Fraction Expansion

An important tool for inverting the z transform and converting among digital filter implementation structures is the *partial fraction expansion* (PFE). The term "partial fraction expansion" refers to the expansion of a rational transfer function into a sum of first and/or second-order terms. The case of first-order terms is the simplest and most fundamental:

$$H(z) \;\triangleq\; \frac{B(z)}{A(z)} \;=\; \sum_{i=1}^{N} \frac{r_i}{1 - p_i z^{-1}} \tag{6.7}$$

where

$$
\begin{aligned}
B(z) &= b_0 + b_1 z^{-1} + b_2 z^{-2} + \cdots + b_M z^{-M} \\
A(z) &= 1 + a_1 z^{-1} + a_2 z^{-2} + \cdots + a_N z^{-N}
\end{aligned}
$$

and $M < N$. (The case $M \geq N$ is addressed in the next section.) The denominator coefficients p_i are called the *poles* of the transfer function, and each numerator r_i is called the *residue* of pole p_i. Equation (6.7) is general only if the poles p_i are *distinct*. (Repeated poles are addressed in §6.8.5 below.) Both the poles and their residues may be complex. The poles may be found by factoring the polynomial $A(z)$ into first-order terms,[4] *e.g.*, using the roots function in matlab. The residue r_i corresponding to pole p_i may be found analytically as

$$r_i \;=\; \left. (1 - p_i z^{-1}) H(z) \right|_{z=p_i} \tag{6.8}$$

---

[4]By the fundamental theorem of algebra, a polynomial $A(z)$ of any degree can be completely factored as a product of first-order polynomials, where the zeros may be complex.

when the poles p_i are distinct. The matlab function `residuez`[5] will find poles and residues computationally, given the difference-equation (transfer-function) coefficients.

Note that in Eq. (6.8), there is always a pole-zero cancellation at $z = p_i$. That is, the term $(1 - p_i z^{-1})$ is always cancelled by an identical term in the denominator of $H(z)$, which must exist because $H(z)$ has a pole at $z = p_i$. The residue r_i is simply the *coefficient* of the one-pole term $1/(1 - p_i z^{-1})$ in the partial fraction expansion of $H(z)$ at $z = p_i$. The transfer function is $r_i/(1 - p_i z^{-1})$, in the limit, as $z \to p_i$.

Example

Consider the two-pole filter

$$H(z) = \frac{1}{(1 - z^{-1})(1 - 0.5z^{-1})}.$$

The poles are $p_1 = 1$ and $p_2 = 0.5$. The corresponding residues are then

$$
\begin{aligned}
r_1 &= (1 - z^{-1})H(z)\big|_{z=1} = \frac{1 - z^{-1}}{(1 - z^{-1})(1 - 0.5z^{-1})}\bigg|_{z=1} \\
&= \frac{1}{1 - 0.5z^{-1}}\bigg|_{z=1} = 2, \text{ and}
\end{aligned}
$$

$$
\begin{aligned}
r_2 &= (1 - 0.5z^{-1})H(z)\big|_{z=0.5} = \frac{1 - 0.5z^{-1}}{(1 - z^{-1})(1 - 0.5z^{-1})}\bigg|_{z=0.5} \\
&= \frac{1}{1 - z^{-1}}\bigg|_{z=0.5} = -1.
\end{aligned}
$$

We thus conclude that

$$H(z) = \frac{2}{1 - z^{-1}} - \frac{1}{1 - 0.5z^{-1}}.$$

As a check, we can add the two one-pole terms above to get

$$\frac{2}{1 - z^{-1}} - \frac{1}{1 - 0.5z^{-1}} = \frac{2 - z^{-1} - 1 + z^{-1}}{(1 - z^{-1})(1 - 0.5z^{-1})} = \frac{1}{(1 - z^{-1})(1 - 0.5z^{-1})}$$

as expected.

---

[5]Matlab Signal Processing Toolbox or Octave Forge collection—see also §J.5 (p. 403).

Complex Example

To illustrate an example involving complex poles, consider the filter

$$H(z) = \frac{g}{1 + z^{-2}},$$

where g can be any real or complex value. (When g is real, the filter as a whole is real also.) The poles are then $p_1 = j$ and $p_2 = -j$ (or vice versa), and the factored form can be written as

$$H(z) = \frac{g}{(1 - jz^{-1})(1 + jz^{-1})}.$$

Using Eq. (6.8), the residues are found to be

$$r_1 = (1 - jz^{-1})H(z)\big|_{z=j} = \frac{g}{1 + jz^{-1}}\bigg|_{z=j} = \frac{g}{2}, \text{ and}$$

$$r_2 = (1 + jz^{-1})H(z)\big|_{z=-j} = \frac{g}{1 - jz^{-1}}\bigg|_{z=-j} = \frac{g}{2}.$$

Thus,

$$H(z) = \frac{g/2}{1 - jz^{-1}} + \frac{g/2}{1 + jz^{-1}}.$$

A more elaborate example of a partial fraction expansion into complex one-pole sections is given in §3.12.1 on page 66.

6.8.1   PFE to Real, Second-Order Sections

When all coefficients of $A(z)$ and $B(z)$ are real (implying that $H(z) = B(z)/A(z)$ is the transfer function of a *real* filter), it will always happen that the complex one-pole filters will occur in *complex conjugate pairs*. Let (r, p) denote any one-pole section in the PFE of Eq. (6.7). Then if p is complex and $H(z)$ describes a real filter, we will also find $(\bar{r}, \bar{p})$ somewhere among the terms in the one-pole expansion. These two terms can be paired to form a *real second-order section* as follows:

$$H(z) = \frac{r}{1 - pz^{-1}} + \frac{\bar{r}}{1 - \bar{p}z^{-1}}$$

$$= \frac{r - r\bar{p}z^{-1} + \bar{r} - \bar{r}pz^{-1}}{(1 - pz^{-1})(1 - \bar{p}z^{-1})}$$

$$= \frac{2\mathrm{re}\{r\} - 2\mathrm{re}\{r\bar{p}\}z^{-1}}{1 - 2\mathrm{re}\{p\}z^{-1} + |p|^2 z^{-2}}$$

Expressing the pole p in *polar form* as $p = Re^{j\theta}$, and the residue as $r = Ge^{j\phi}$, the last expression above can be rewritten as

$$H(z) = 2G \frac{\cos(\phi) - \cos(\phi - \theta)z^{-1}}{1 - 2R\,\cos(\theta)z^{-1} + R^2 z^{-2}}.$$

The use of polar-form coefficients is discussed further in the section on two-pole filters (§B.1.3 on page 258).

Expanding a transfer function into a sum of second-order terms with real coefficients gives us the filter coefficients for a parallel bank of real second-order filter sections. (Of course, each real pole can be implemented in its own real one-pole section in parallel with the other sections.) In view of the foregoing, we may conclude that every real filter with $M < N$ can be implemented as a parallel bank of *biquads*.[6] However, the full generality of a biquad section (two poles and two zeros) is not needed because the PFE requires only one zero per second-order term.

To see why we must stipulate $M < N$ in Eq. (6.7) on page 129, consider the sum of two first-order terms by direct calculation:

$$H_2(z) = \frac{r_1}{1 - p_1 z^{-1}} + \frac{r_2}{1 - p_2 z^{-1}} = \frac{(r_1 + r_2) - (r_1 p_2 + r_2 p_1)z^{-1}}{(1 - p_1 z^{-1})(1 - p_2 z^{-1})} \quad (6.9)$$

Notice that the numerator order, viewed as a polynomial in z^{-1}, is one less than the denominator order. In the same way, it is easily shown by mathematical induction that the sum of N one-pole terms $r_i/(1 - p_i z^{-1})$ can produce a numerator order of at most $M = N - 1$ (while the denominator order is N if there are no pole-zero cancellations). Following terminology used for analog filters, we call the case $M < N$ a *strictly proper transfer function*.[7] Thus, every strictly proper transfer function (with distinct poles) can be implemented using a parallel bank of two-pole, one-zero filter sections.

6.8.2   Inverting the Z Transform

The partial fraction expansion (PFE) provides a simple means for inverting the z transform of rational transfer functions. The PFE provides a sum of first-order terms of the form

$$H_i(z) = \frac{r_i}{1 - p_i z^{-1}}.$$

It is easily verified that such a term is the z transform of

$$h_i(n) = r_i p_i^n, \quad n = 0, 1, 2, \ldots .$$

---

[6] A *biquad* is simply a second-order filter section—see §B.1.6 on page 269 for details.
[7] The case $M = N$ is called a *proper transfer function*, and $M > N$ is termed *improper*.

Thus, the inverse z transform of $H(z)$ is simply

$$h(n) \;=\; \sum_{i=1}^{N} h_i(n) \;=\; \sum_{i=1}^{N} r_i p_i^n, \quad n = 0, 1, 2, \ldots .$$

Thus, the impulse response of every strictly proper LTI filter (with distinct poles) can be interpreted as a *linear combination of sampled complex exponentials*. Recall that a uniformly sampled exponential is the same thing as a *geometric sequence*. Thus, h is a linear combination of N geometric sequences. The *term ratio* of the ith geometric sequence is the ith pole, p_i, and the *coefficient* of the ith sequence is the ith residue, r_i.

In the *improper* case, discussed in the next section, we additionally obtain an *FIR part* in the z transform to be inverted:

$$F(z) \;=\; f_0 + f_1 z^{-1} + f_2 z^{-2} + \cdots + f_K z^{-K} \;\longleftrightarrow\; [f_0, f_1, \ldots, f_K, 0, 0, \ldots].$$

The FIR part (a finite-order polynomial in z^{-1}) is also easily inverted by inspection.

The case of repeated poles is addressed in §6.8.5 below.

6.8.3   FIR Part of a PFE

When $M \geq N$ in Eq. (6.7), we may perform a step of *long division* of $B(z)/A(z)$ to produce an *FIR part* in parallel with a strictly proper IIR part:

$$H(z) \;\triangleq\; \frac{B(z)}{A(z)} \;=\; F(z) + \sum_{i=1}^{N} \frac{r_i}{1 - p_i z^{-1}} \qquad (6.10)$$

where

$$
\begin{aligned}
B(z) &= b_0 + b_1 z^{-1} + b_2 z^{-2} + \cdots + b_M z^{-M} \\
A(z) &= 1 + a_1 z^{-1} + a_2 z^{-2} + \cdots + a_N z^{-N} \\
F(z) &= f_0 + f_1 z^{-1} + f_2 z^{-2} + \cdots + f_K z^{-K}, \quad K = M - N.
\end{aligned}
$$

When $M < N$, we define $F(z) = 0$. This type of decomposition is computed by the **residuez** function (a matlab function for computing a complete partial fraction expansion, as illustrated in §6.8.8 on page 142 below).

An alternate FIR part is obtained by performing long division on the *reversed* polynomial coefficients to obtain

$$H(z) \;=\; F(z) + z^{-(K+1)} \sum_{i=1}^{N} \frac{r_i}{1 - p_i z^{-1}}, \qquad (6.11)$$

where $K = M - N \geq 0$ is again the order of the FIR part. This type of decomposition is computed (as part of the PFE) by `residued`, described in §J.6 on page 406 and illustrated numerically in §6.8.8 below.

We may compare these two PFE alternatives as follows: Let A_N denote $A(z)$, $F_K \triangleq F(z)$, and $B_M \triangleq B(z)$. (*I.e.*, we use a subscript to indicate polynomial order, and '(z)' is omitted for notational simplicity.) Then for $K = M - N \geq 0$ we have two cases:

$$(1) \qquad H(z) \;=\; F_K + \frac{B'_{N-1}}{A_N} \;=\; \frac{F_K A_N + B'_{N-1}}{A_N}$$

$$(2) \qquad H(z) \;=\; F_K + z^{-(K+1)}\frac{B''_{N-1}}{A_N} \;=\; \frac{F_K A_N + z^{-(K+1)} B''_{N-1}}{A_N}$$

In the first form, the B'_{N-1} coefficients are "left justified" in the reconstructed numerator, while in the second form they are "right justified". The second form is generally more efficient for *modeling* purposes, since the numerator of the IIR part ($B''_{N-1}(z)$) can be used to match additional terms in the impulse response after the FIR part $F_K(z)$ has "died out".

In summary, an arbitrary digital filter transfer function $H(z)$ with N distinct poles can always be expressed as a parallel combination of *complex one-pole filters*, together with a parallel FIR part when $M \geq N$. When there is an FIR part, the strictly proper IIR part may be delayed such that its impulse response begins where that of the FIR part leaves off.

In artificial reverberation applications, the FIR part may correspond to the *early reflections*, while the IIR part provides the *late reverb*, which is typically dense, smooth, and exponentially decaying [86]. The *predelay* ("pre-delay") control in some commercial reverberators is the amount of pure delay at the beginning of the reverberator's impulse response. Thus, neglecting the early reflections, the order of the FIR part can be viewed as the amount of predelay for the IIR part.

Example: The General Biquad PFE

The general second-order case with $M = N = 2$ (the so-called *biquad* section) can be written when $b_0 \neq 0$ as

$$H(z) \;=\; g\frac{1 + b_1 z^{-1} + b_2 z^{-2}}{1 + a_1 z^{-1} + a_2 z^{-2}}.$$

To perform a partial fraction expansion, we need to extract an order 0 (length 1) FIR part via long division. Let $d = z^{-1}$ and rewrite $H(z)$ as a ratio of polynomials in d:

$$H(d^{-1}) \;=\; g\frac{b_2 d^2 + b_1 d + 1}{a_2 d^2 + a_1 d + 1}$$

Then long division gives

$$
\begin{array}{r}
\frac{b_2}{a_2} \\[4pt]
a_2 \quad a_1 \quad 1 \;\overline{\Big)\; b_2 \qquad b_1 \qquad\quad 1\;} \\[4pt]
b_2 \qquad \frac{b_2}{a_2}a_1 \qquad \frac{b_2}{a_2} \\[4pt]
\hline
b_1 - \frac{b_2}{a_2}a_1 \quad 1 - \frac{b_2}{a_2}
\end{array}
$$

yielding

$$
H(d^{-1}) \;=\; g\frac{b_2}{a_2} + g\frac{\left(b_1 - \frac{b_2}{a_2}a_1\right)d + \left(1 - \frac{b_2}{a_2}\right)}{a_2 d^2 + a_1 d + 1}
$$

or

$$
H(z) \;=\; g\frac{b_2}{a_2} + g\frac{\left(1 - \frac{b_2}{a_2}\right) + \left(b_1 - \frac{b_2}{a_2}a_1\right)z^{-1}}{1 + a_1 z^{-1} + a_2 z^{-2}}.
$$

The delayed form of the partial fraction expansion is obtained by leaving the coefficients in their original order. This corresponds to writing $H(z)$ as a ratio of polynomials in z:

$$
H(z) \;=\; g\frac{z^2 + b_1 z + b_2}{z^2 + a_1 z + a_2}
$$

Long division now looks like

$$
\begin{array}{r}
1 \\[4pt]
1 \quad a_1 \quad a_2 \;\overline{\Big)\; 1 \qquad b_1 \qquad\quad b_2\;} \\[4pt]
1 \qquad a_1 \qquad\quad a_2 \\[4pt]
\hline
b_1 - a_1 \quad b_2 - a_2
\end{array}
$$

giving

$$
H(z) \;=\; g + z^{-1}g\frac{(b_1 - a_1) + (b_2 - a_2)z^{-1}}{1 + a_1 z^{-1} + a_2 z^{-2}}.
$$

Numerical examples of partial fraction expansions are given in §6.8.8 on page 142 below. Another worked example, in which the filter $y(n) = x(n) + 0.5^3 x(n-3) - 0.9^5 y(n-5)$ is converted to a set of parallel, second-order sections is given in §3.12 on page 65. See also §9.2 on page 207 regarding conversion to second-order sections in general, and §G.9.1 (especially Eq. (G.22) on page 366) regarding a state-space approach to partial fraction expansion.

6.8.4 Alternate PFE Methods

Another method for finding the pole residues is to write down the general form of the PFE, obtain a common denominator, expand the numerator terms to obtain a single polynomial, and equate like powers of z^{-1}. This gives a linear system of N equations in N unknowns r_i, $i = 1, \ldots, N$.

Yet another method for finding residues is by means of Taylor series expansions of the numerator $B(z)$ and denominator $A(z)$ about each pole p_i, using l'Hôpital's rule.[8].

Finally, one can alternatively construct a *state space realization* of a strictly proper transfer function (using, *e.g.*, tf2ss in matlab) and then *diagonalize* it via a *similarity transformation*. (See Appendix G for an introduction to state-space models and diagonalizing them via similarity transformations.) The transfer function of the diagonalized state-space model is trivially obtained as a sum of one-pole terms—*i.e.*, the PFE. In other words, diagonalizing a state-space filter realization implicitly performs a partial fraction expansion of the filter's transfer function. When the poles are distinct, the state-space model can be diagonalized; when there are repeated poles, it can be block-diagonalized instead, as discussed further in §G.10 on page 370.

6.8.5 Repeated Poles

When poles are repeated, an interesting new phenomenon emerges. To see what's going on, let's consider two identical poles arranged in parallel and in series. In the parallel case, we have

$$H_1(z) \;=\; \frac{r_1}{1 - pz^{-1}} + \frac{r_2}{1 - pz^{-1}} \;=\; \frac{r_1 + r_2}{1 - pz^{-1}} \;\triangleq\; \frac{r_3}{1 - pz^{-1}}.$$

In the series case, we get

$$H_2(z) \;=\; \frac{r_1}{1 - pz^{-1}} \cdot \frac{r_2}{1 - pz^{-1}} \;=\; \frac{r_1 r_2}{(1 - pz^{-1})^2} \;\triangleq\; \frac{r_3}{(1 - pz^{-1})^2}.$$

Thus, two one-pole filters in *parallel* are equivalent to a new one-pole filter[9] (when the poles are identical), while the same two filters in *series* give a *two-pole* filter with a repeated pole. To accommodate both possibilities, the general partial fraction expansion must include the terms

$$\frac{r_{1,1}}{(1 - pz^{-1})^2} + \frac{r_{1,2}}{(1 - pz^{-1})}$$

for a pole p having multiplicity 2.

---

[8]http://en.wikipedia.org/wiki/L'Hopital's_rule

[9]In physical models, such a superposition of identical resonances is often called *degeneracy* [86].

Dealing with Repeated Poles Analytically

A pole of *multiplicity* m_i has m_i residues associated with it. For example,

$$H(z) \quad \triangleq \quad \frac{7 - 5z^{-1} + z^{-2}}{\left(1 - \frac{1}{2}z^{-1}\right)^3}$$

$$= \quad \frac{1}{\left(1 - \frac{1}{2}z^{-1}\right)^3} + \frac{2}{\left(1 - \frac{1}{2}z^{-1}\right)^2} + \frac{4}{\left(1 - \frac{1}{2}z^{-1}\right)} \qquad (6.12)$$

and the three residues associated with the pole $z = 1/2$ are 1, 2, and 4.

Let r_{ij} denote the jth residue associated with the pole p_i, $j = 1, \ldots, m_i$. Successively differentiating $(1 - p_i z^{-1})^{m_i} H(z)$ $k - 1$ times with respect to z^{-1} and setting $z = p_i$ isolates the residue r_{ik}:

$$r_{i1} \quad = \quad \left.(1 - p_i z^{-1})^{m_i} H(z)\right|_{z=p_i}$$

$$r_{i2} \quad = \quad \frac{1}{-p_i} \frac{d}{dz^{-1}} (1 - p_i z^{-1})^{m_i} H(z) \bigg|_{z=p_i}$$

$$r_{i3} \quad = \quad \frac{1}{2(-p_i)^2} \frac{d^2}{d(z^{-1})^2} (1 - p_i z^{-1})^{m_i} H(z) \bigg|_{z=p_i}$$

$$r_{i4} \quad = \quad \frac{1}{3 \cdot 2(-p_i)^3} \frac{d^3}{d(z^{-1})^3} (1 - p_i z^{-1})^{m_i} H(z) \bigg|_{z=p_i}$$

or

$$r_{ik} = \frac{1}{(k-1)!(-p_i)^{k-1}} \frac{d^{k-1}}{d(z^{-1})^{k-1}} (1 - p_i z^{-1})^{m_i} H(z) \bigg|_{z=p_i}$$

Example

For the example of Eq. (6.12), we obtain

$$r_{11} = \left(1 - \frac{1}{2}z^{-1}\right)^3 H(z)\Bigg|_{z=\frac{1}{2}}$$

$$= 7 - 5z^{-1} + z^{-2}\big|_{z=\frac{1}{2}} = 7 - 5\cdot 2 + 2^2 = 1$$

$$r_{12} = -2\frac{d}{dz^{-1}}(7 - 5z^{-1} + z^{-2})\Bigg|_{z^{-1}=2}$$

$$= -2(-5 + 2z^{-1})\big|_{z^{-1}=2} = 2$$

$$r_{13} = \frac{1}{2\left(-\frac{1}{2}\right)^2}\frac{d}{dz^{-1}}(-5 + 2z^{-1})\Bigg|_{z^{-1}=2} = 2\cdot 2 = 4.$$

Impulse Response of Repeated Poles

In the time domain, repeated poles give rise to *polynomial amplitude envelopes* on the decaying exponentials corresponding to the (stable) poles. For example, in the case of a single pole repeated twice, we have

$$\boxed{\frac{1}{(1 - pz^{-1})^2} \longleftrightarrow (n+1)p^n, \quad n = 0, 1, 2, \ldots .}$$

Proof: First note that

$$\frac{d}{dz^{-1}}\left(\frac{1}{1 - pz^{-1}}\right) = (-1)(1 - pz^{-1})^{-2}(-p) = \frac{p}{(1 - pz^{-1})^2}.$$

Therefore,

$$\frac{1}{(1 - pz^{-1})^2} = \frac{1}{p}\frac{d}{dz^{-1}}\left(\frac{1}{1 - pz^{-1}}\right)$$

$$= \frac{1}{p}\frac{d}{dz^{-1}}\left(1 + pz^{-1} + p^2z^{-2} + p^3z^{-3} + \cdots\right)$$

$$= \frac{1}{p}\left(0 + p + 2p^2z^{-1} + 3p^3z^{-2} + \cdots\right)$$

$$= 1 + 2pz^{-1} + 3p^2z^{-2} + \cdots$$

$$= \sum_{n=0}^{\infty}(n+1)p^n z^{-n}$$

$$\triangleq \mathcal{Z}\{(n+1)p^n\} \longleftrightarrow (n+1)p^n. \tag{6.13}$$

Note that $n + 1$ is a first-order polynomial in n. Similarly, a pole repeated three times corresponds to an impulse-response component that is an exponential decay multiplied by a *quadratic* polynomial in n, and so on. As long as $|p| < 1$, the impulse response will eventually decay to zero, because exponential decay always overtakes polynomial growth in the limit as n goes to infinity.

So What's Up with Repeated Poles?

In the previous section, we found that repeated poles give rise to polynomial amplitude-envelopes multiplying the exponential decay due to the pole. On the other hand, two *different* poles can only yield a convolution (or sum) of two different exponential decays, with no polynomial envelope allowed. This is true no matter how closely the poles come together; the polynomial envelope can occur only when the poles merge exactly. This might violate one's intuitive expectation of a continuous change when passing from two closely spaced poles to a repeated pole.

To study this phenomenon further, consider the convolution of two one-pole impulse-responses $h_1(n) = p_1^n$ and $h_2(n) = p_2^n$:

$$h(n) \triangleq (h_1 * h_2)(n) = \sum_{m=0}^{n} h_1(m) h_2(n-m) = \sum_{m=0}^{n} p_1^m p_2^{n-m} = p_2^n \sum_{m=0}^{n} \left(\frac{p_1}{p_2}\right)^m$$
$$(6.14)$$

The finite limits on the summation result from the fact that both h_1 and h_2 are causal. Recall the closed-form sum of a truncated geometric series:

$$\sum_{m=0}^{n} r^m = \frac{1 - r^{n+1}}{1 - r}$$

Applying this to Eq. (6.14) yields

$$h(n) = p_2^n \frac{1 - (p_1/p_2)^{n+1}}{1 - (p_1/p_2)} = \frac{p_2^{n+1} - p_1^{n+1}}{p_2 - p_1} = \frac{p_1^{n+1} - p_2^{n+1}}{p_1 - p_2}.$$

Note that the result is symmetric in p_1 and p_2. If $|p_1| > |p_2|$, then $h(n)$ becomes proportional to p_1^n for large n, while if $|p_2| > |p_1|$, it becomes instead proportional to p_2^n.

Going back to Eq. (6.14), we have

$$h(n) = p_2^n \sum_{m=0}^{n} \left(\frac{p_1}{p_2}\right)^m = p_1^n \sum_{m=0}^{n} \left(\frac{p_2}{p_1}\right)^m. \qquad (6.15)$$

Setting $p_1 = p_2 = p$ yields

$$h(n) = (n+1) p^n \qquad (6.16)$$

which is the first-order polynomial amplitude-envelope case for a repeated pole. We can see that the transition from "two convolved exponentials" to "single exponential with a polynomial amplitude envelope" is perfectly continuous, as we would expect.

We also see that the polynomial amplitude-envelopes fundamentally arise from *iterated convolutions*. This corresponds to the repeated poles being arranged in *series*, rather than in parallel. The simplest case is when the repeated pole is at $p = 1$, in which case its impulse response is a constant:

$$\frac{1}{1 - z^{-1}} = 1 + z^{-1} + z^{-2} + \cdots \longleftrightarrow [1, 1, 1, \ldots]$$

The convolution of a constant with itself is a ramp:

$$h_1(n) = \sum_{m=0}^{n} 1 \cdot 1 = n + 1$$

The convolution of a constant and a ramp is a quadratic, and so on:[10]

$$h_2(n) = \sum_{m=0}^{n} (m+1) \cdot 1 = \frac{(n+1)(n+2)}{2}$$

$$h_3(n) = \sum_{m=0}^{n} \frac{(m+1)(m+2)}{2} \cdot 1 = \frac{(n+1)(n+2)(n+3)}{3!}$$

$$\cdots$$

6.8.6 Alternate Stability Criterion

In §5.6 (page 101), a filter was defined to be *stable* if its impulse response $h(n)$ decays to 0 in magnitude as time n goes to infinity. In §6.8.5, we saw that the impulse response of every finite-order LTI filter can be expressed as a possible FIR part (which is always stable) plus a linear combination of terms of the form $a_i(n)p_i^n$, where $a_i(n)$ is some finite-order polynomial in n, and p_i is the ith pole of the filter. In this form, it is clear that the impulse response always decays to zero when each pole is strictly inside the unit circle of the z plane, *i.e.*, when $|p_i| < 1$. Thus, having all poles strictly inside the unit circle is a *sufficient* criterion for filter stability. If the filter is *observable* (meaning that there are no pole-zero cancellations

---

[10]These closed-form sums were quickly computed using the free symbolic mathematics program called `maxima` running under Linux, specifically by typing `factor(ev(sum(m+1,m,0,n),simpsum));` followed by `factor(ev(sum(%,n,0,m),simpsum));`.

in the transfer function from input to output), then this is also a *necessary* criterion.

A transfer function with no pole-zero cancellations is said to be *irreducible*. For example, $H(z) = (1 + z^{-1})/(1 - z^{-1})$ is irreducible, while $H(z) = (1 - z^{-2})/(1 - 2z^{-2} + z^{-2})$ is reducible, since there is the common factor of $(1 - z^{-1})$ in the numerator and denominator. Using this terminology, we may state the following stability criterion:

> *An irreducible transfer function $H(z)$ is stable if and only if its poles have magnitude less than one.*

This characterization of stability is pursued further in §8.4 on page 184, and yet another stability test (most often used in practice) is given in §8.4.1.

6.8.7   Summary of the Partial Fraction Expansion

In summary, the partial fraction expansion can be used to expand any rational z transform

$$H(z) = \frac{B(z)}{A(z)} = \frac{b_0 + b_1 z^{-1} + \cdots + b_M z^{-M}}{1 + a_1 z^{-1} + \cdots + a_N z^{-N}}$$

as a sum of first-order terms

$$H(z) \triangleq \frac{B(z)}{A(z)} = \sum_{i=1}^{N} \frac{r_i}{1 - p_i z^{-1}} \qquad (6.17)$$

for $M < N$, and

$$H(z) = F(z) + z^{-(K+1)} \sum_{i=1}^{N} \frac{r_i}{1 - p_i z^{-1}} \qquad (6.18)$$

for $M \geq N$, where the term $z^{-(K+1)}$ is optional, but often preferred. For real filters, the complex one-pole terms may be paired up to obtain second-order terms with real coefficients. The PFE procedure occurs in two or three steps:

1. When $M \geq N$, perform a step of long division to obtain an FIR part $F(z)$ and a strictly proper IIR part $B'(z)/A(z)$.

2. Find the N poles p_i, $i = 1, \ldots, N$ (roots of $A(z)$).

3. If the poles are distinct, find the N residues r_i, $i = 1, \ldots, N$ from

$$r_i = (1 - p_i z^{-1}) \frac{B(z)}{A(z)} \bigg|_{z = p_i}$$

4. If there are repeated poles, find the additional residues via the method of §6.8.5 on page 137, and the general form of the PFE is

$$H(z) = F(z) + z^{-(K+1)} \sum_{i=1}^{N_p} \sum_{k=1}^{m_i} \frac{r_{i,k}}{(1 - p_i z^{-1})^k} \qquad (6.19)$$

where N_p denotes the number of distinct poles, and $m_i \geq 1$ denotes the multiplicity of the ith pole.

In step 2, the poles are typically found by *factoring* the denominator polynomial $A(z)$. This is a dangerous step numerically which may fail when there are many poles, especially when many poles are clustered close together in the z plane.

The following matlab code illustrates factoring $A(z) = 1 - z^{-3}$ to obtain the three roots, $p_k = e^{jk2\pi/3}$, $k = 0, 1, 2$:

```
A = [1 0 0 -1];  % Filter denominator polynomial
poles = roots(A) % Filter poles
```

See Chapter 9 for additional discussion regarding digital filters implemented as parallel sections (especially §9.2.2 on page 209).

6.8.8   Software for Partial Fraction Expansion

Figure 6.3 illustrates the use of **residuez** (§J.5) for performing a partial fraction expansion on the transfer function

$$H(z) = \frac{1 + 0.5^3 z^{-3}}{1 + 0.9^5 z^{-5}}$$

The complex-conjugate terms can be combined to obtain two real second-order sections, giving a total of one real first-order section in parallel with two real second-order sections, as discussed and depicted in §3.12 on page 65.

Example 2

For the filter

$$H(z) \triangleq \frac{2 + 6z^{-1} + 6z^{-2} + 2z^{-3}}{1 - 2z^{-1} + z^{-2}} \qquad (6.20)$$

$$= (2 + 10z^{-1}) + z^{-2} \left[\frac{8}{1 - z^{-1}} + \frac{16}{(1 - z^{-1})^2} \right] \qquad (6.21)$$

we obtain the output of **residued** (§J.6 on page 406) shown in Fig. 6.4. In contrast to **residuez**, **residued** delays the IIR part until after the FIR part.

```
B = [1 0 0 0.125];
A = [1 0 0 0 0 0.9^5];
[r,p,f] = residuez(B,A)
% r =
%    0.16571
%    0.22774 - 0.02016i
%    0.22774 + 0.02016i
%    0.18940 + 0.03262i
%    0.18940 - 0.03262i
%
% p =
%   -0.90000
%   -0.27812 - 0.85595i
%   -0.27812 + 0.85595i
%    0.72812 - 0.52901i
%    0.72812 + 0.52901i
%
% f = [] (0x0)
```

Figure 6.3: Use of `residuez` to perform a partial fraction expansion of an IIR filter transfer function $H(z) = B(z)/A(z)$.

In contrast to this result, `residuez` returns r=[-24;16] and f=[10;2], corresponding to the PFE

$$H(z) = 10 + 2z^{-1} - \frac{24}{1 - z^{-1}} + \frac{16}{(1 - z^{-1})^2}, \qquad (6.22)$$

in which the FIR and IIR parts have overlapping impulse responses.

See Sections J.5 and J.6 starting on page 403 for listings of `residuez`, `residued` and related discussion.

Polynomial Multiplication in Matlab

The matlab function `conv` (*convolution*) can be used to perform *polynomial multiplication*. For example:

```
B1 = [1 1];    % 1st row of Pascal's triangle
B2 = [1 2 1];  % 2nd row of Pascal's triangle
B3 = conv(B1,B2) % 3rd row
% B3 = 1   3   3   1
B4 = conv(B1,B3) % 4th row
% B4 = 1   4   6   4   1
% ...
```

```
B=[2 6 6 2]; A=[1 -2 1];
[r,p,f,m] = residued(B,A)
% r =
%     8
%    16
%
% p =
%    1
%    1
%
% f =
%     2   10
%
% m =
%    1
%    2
```

Figure 6.4: Use of **residued** to perform a partial fraction expansion of an IIR filter transfer function $H(z) = B(z)/A(z)$.

The matlab `conv(B1,B2)` is identical to `filter(B1,1,B2)`, except that `conv` returns the *complete* convolution of its two input vectors, while `filter` truncates the result to the length of the "input signal" B2.[11] Thus, if B2 is zero-padded with `length(B1)-1` zeros, it will return the complete convolution:

```
B1 = [1 2 3];
B2 = [4 5 6 7];
conv(B1,B2)
% ans = 4   13   28   34   32   21
filter(B1,1,B2)
% ans = 4   13   28   34
filter(B1,1,[B2,zeros(1,length(B1)-1)])
% ans = 4   13   28   34   32   21
```

---

[11]Since convolution is *commutative*, either operand to a convolution can be interpreted as the filter impulse-response while the other is interpreted as the input signal. However, in the matlab `filter` function, the operand designated as the input signal (3rd argument) determines the length to which the output signal is truncated.

Polynomial Division in Matlab

The matlab function `deconv` (*deconvolution*) can be used to perform *polynomial long division* in order to split an improper transfer function into its FIR and strictly proper parts:

```
B = [ 2 6 6 2]; % 2*(1+1/z)^3
A = [ 1 -2 1];  % (1-1/z)^2
[firpart,remainder] = deconv(B,A)
% firpart =
%   2   10
% remainder =
%   0   0   24   -8
```

Thus, this example finds that $H(z)$ is as written in Eq. (6.21) on page 142. This result can be checked by obtaining a common denominator in order to recalculate the direct-form numerator:

```
Bh = remainder + conv(firpart,A)
%  = 2 6 6 2
```

The operation `deconv(B,A)` can be implemented using `filter` in a manner analogous to the polynomial multiplication case (see §6.8.8 above):

```
firpart = filter(B,A,[1,zeros(1,length(B)-length(A))])
%        = 2 10
remainder = B - conv(firpart,A)
%          =  0 0 24 -8
```

That this must work can be seen by looking at Eq. (6.21) on page 142 and noting that the impulse-response of the remainder (the strictly proper part) does not begin until time $n = 2$, so that the first two samples of the impulse-response come only from the FIR part.

In summary, we may conveniently use convolution and deconvolution to perform polynomial multiplication and division, respectively, such as when converting transfer functions to various alternate forms.

6.9   Transfer Function Analysis Problems

1. Show that
$$\mathrm{FLIP}(h * \mathrm{FLIP}(x)) = \mathrm{FLIP}(h) * x,$$
where $\mathrm{FLIP}_n(x) \triangleq x(-n)$. That is, show that time reversing a signal x, applying a filter h and reversing the resulting output y is equivalent to convolving the unflipped signal x with the flipped impulse response $h(-n)$. [Hint: Use the convolution theorem for z transforms.]

2. For the filter
$$H(z) = \frac{1}{1 - \frac{1}{10}z^{-1}}$$

   (a) Find the impulse response.

   (b) Find the step response.

   (c) Sketch the pole-zero diagram.

   (d) Find the frequency of maximum gain.

   (e) Find the maximum gain.

   (f) Find the frequency of minimum gain.

   (g) Find the minimum gain.

   (h) Find the phase delay in samples at half the sampling rate. Explain this result in terms of the pole-zero diagram.

3. Prove that a stable, causal, recursive digital filter cannot have a symmetric impulse response $h(n)$. [Hint: Use the fact that $h(n)$ is an IIR which must asymptotically approach 0 as $n \to \infty$.]

4. *Canceling Nonlinear Phase:* A recording has been made from a condenser microphone and digitized into a disk file. The microphone introduced a wandering dc bias (a wandering average value that should be 0) which you removed with a high-order recursive highpass filter. The producer has found out and threatens to wring your neck because he is fashionably afraid of nonlinear phase for reasons he does not understand. You claim that you can perfectly undo the nonlinear phase effects while making your highpass filtering job twice as good in terms of the amplitude response (reverse-time filtering). (a) Prove that your method works by deriving the frequency response for a general filter used in the same way as your highpass filter. (b) Derive another way to accomplish the same thing without having to filter the data backward in time. (Hint: Apply the substitution $z \leftarrow z^{-1}$.) Is there anything "fishy" about this method? Pick an example recursive filter (such as Eq. (5.3)) and compute the impulse response for both the original filter and the transformed filter.

5. *Interchanging Sections:* Since the transfer functions of series-connected filter stages just multiply, the transfer function is unaffected if we permute the order of the sections. Use this fact to show that Fig. 5.1a is equivalent to Fig. 5.1b. (Hint: Find a way to share delays.)

6. *Convolving Noncausal Signals:* Work out the shift and convolution theorems for the case of noncausal signals and the bilateral z transform. State any needed conditions to ensure existence of the convolution and z transforms.

Partial Fraction Expansion Problems

7. Given

$$H(z) = \frac{b_0 + b_1 z^{-1} + b_2 z^{-2}}{1 + a_1 z^{-1}},$$

perform each of the two types of partial fraction expansion to show

$$H(z) = \left(\frac{b_1}{a_1} - \frac{b_2}{a_1^2}\right) + \frac{b_2}{a_1} z^{-1} + \frac{b_0 - \frac{b_1}{a_1} + \frac{b_2}{a_1^2}}{1 + a_1 z^{-1}}$$

$$= b_0 + (b_1 - b_0 a_1) z^{-1} + z^{-2} \frac{b_0 - a_1 b_1 + a_1^2 b_0}{1 + a_1 z^{-1}}$$

8. [Adapted from [60]] For the z transform

$$X(z) = \frac{1}{(1 - az^{-1})(1 - bz^{-1})}$$

$$= \frac{a^{-1}b^{-1}}{(z^{-1} - a^{-1})(z^{-1} - b^{-1})} = \frac{z^2}{(z - a)(z - b)}$$

(a) Find the partial fraction expansion, viewing $X(z)$ as a ratio of polynomials in z^{-1}.

(b) Find a different partial fraction expansion, viewing $X(z)$ as a polynomial in z. [Hint: this one starts out "improper".]

(c) Find the inverse z transform from the partial fraction expansion of the previous problem, and verify it gives the same numbers for $n = 0, 1, 2, \ldots$.

9. *Partial Fraction Expansion in Matlab:* Given

$$H(z) = \frac{0.5 + 0.5z^{-1} + 0.25z^{-2}}{1 + 0.5z^{-1} + 0.5z^{-2} + 0.75z^{-3}},$$

verify that the partial fraction expansion of the filter has the same frequency response by following the steps below:

(a) (5 points) Find the residues and poles using the **residuez** function in Matlab.

(b) (10 points) Obtain the frequency responses of three one-pole filters using the residues and the poles found in the previous problem, and sum them to get the total frequency response of the filter (in Matlab).

(c) (10 points) Plot the amplitude response in dB and the phase response in degrees of the filter using **subplot** to align them vertically.

(d) (10 points) Plot the frequency response of the original filter using **freqz** function, and compare it with that obtained in the previous problem.

Chapter 7

Frequency Response Analysis

This chapter discusses *frequency-response analysis* of digital filters. The frequency response is a complex function which yields the gain and phase-shift as a function of frequency. Useful variants such as *phase delay* and *group delay* are defined, and examples and applications are considered.

7.1 Frequency Response

The *frequency response* of an LTI filter may be defined as the spectrum of the output signal divided by the spectrum of the input signal. In this section, we show that the frequency response of any LTI filter is given by its transfer function $H(z)$ evaluated on the unit circle, *i.e.*, $H(e^{j\omega T})$. We then show that this is the same result we got using sine-wave analysis in Chapter 1.

Beginning with Eq. (6.4) on page 125, we have

$$Y(z) = H(z)X(z)$$

where X(z) is the z transform of the filter input signal $x(n)$, $Y(z)$ is the z transform of the output signal $y(n)$, and $H(z)$ is the filter transfer function.

A basic property of the z transform is that, over the unit circle $z = e^{j\omega T}$, we find the *spectrum* [84].[1] To show this, we set $z = e^{j\omega T}$ in the

---

[1]Some elementary review regarding signals and spectra is given in Appendix A.

definition of the z transform, Eq. (6.1), to obtain

$$X(e^{j\omega T}) = \sum_{n=-\infty}^{\infty} x(n)e^{-j\omega T n}$$

which may be recognized as the definition of the *bilateral discrete time Fourier transform (DTFT)* when T is normalized to 1 [59, 84]. When x is causal, this definition reduces to the usual (unilateral) DTFT definition:

$$\text{DTFT}_\omega(x) \triangleq \sum_{n=0}^{\infty} x(n)e^{-j\omega n} \tag{7.1}$$

Applying this relation to $Y(z) = H(z)X(z)$ gives

$$Y(e^{j\omega T}) = H(e^{j\omega T})X(e^{j\omega T}). \tag{7.2}$$

Thus, the spectrum of the filter output is just the input spectrum times the spectrum of the impulse response. We have therefore shown the following:

> The frequency response of a linear time-invariant filter equals the transfer function $H(z)$ evaluated on the unit circle in the z plane, i.e., $H(e^{j\omega T})$.

This immediately implies the following:

> The frequency response of an LTI filter equals the discrete-time Fourier transform of the impulse response.

We can express this mathematically by writing

$$\boxed{H(e^{j\omega T}) = \text{DTFT}_{\omega T}(h).}$$

By Eq. (7.2), the frequency response specifies the *gain* and *phase shift* applied by the filter at each frequency. Since e, j, and T are constants, the frequency response $H(e^{j\omega T})$ is only a function of radian frequency ω. Since ω is real, the frequency response may be considered a *complex-valued function of a real variable*. The response at frequency f Hz, for example, is $H(e^{j2\pi f T})$, where T is the sampling period in seconds. It might be more convenient to define new functions such as $H'(\omega) \triangleq H(e^{j\omega T})$ and write simply $Y'(\omega) = H'(\omega)X'(\omega)$ instead of having to write $e^{j\omega T}$ so often, but doing so would add a lot of new functions to an already notation-rich scenario. Furthermore, writing $H(e^{j\omega T})$ makes explicit the connection between the transfer function and the frequency response.

Notice that defining the frequency response as a function of $e^{j\omega T}$ places the frequency "axis" on the *unit circle* in the complex z plane, since $\left|e^{j\omega T}\right| = 1$. As a result, adding multiples of the sampling frequency to ω corresponds to traversing whole cycles around the unit circle, since

$$e^{j(\omega + k2\pi f_s)T} = e^{j(\omega T + k2\pi)} = e^{j\omega T},$$

whenever k is an integer. Since every discrete-time spectrum repeats in frequency with a "period" equal to the sampling rate, we may restrict ωT to one traversal of the unit circle; a typical choice is $-\pi \leq \omega T < \pi$ $[\omega T \in [-\pi, \pi)]$. For convenience, $\omega T \in [-\pi, \pi]$ is often allowed.

We have seen that the spectrum is a particular slice through the transfer function. It is also possible to go the other way and generalize the spectrum (defined only over the unit circle) to the entire z plane by means of *analytic continuation* (§D.2). Since analytic continuation is unique (for all filters encountered in practice), we get the same result going either direction.

Because every complex number z can be represented as a magnitude $r = |z|$ and angle $\theta = \angle z$, *viz.*, $z = r\exp(j\theta)$, the frequency response $H(e^{j\omega T})$ may be decomposed into two real-valued functions, the *amplitude response* $|H(e^{j\omega T})|$ and the *phase response* $\angle H(e^{j\omega T})$. Formally, we may define them as follows:

7.2 Amplitude Response

Definition. The *amplitude response* $G(\omega)$ of an LTI filter is defined as the *magnitude* (or modulus) of the (complex) filter frequency response $H(e^{j\omega T})$, *i.e.*,

$$\boxed{G(\omega) \triangleq \left|H(e^{j\omega T})\right|.}$$

Another common name for the amplitude response is *magnitude frequency response*.

The real-valued amplitude response $G(\omega)$ specifies the amplitude *gain* that the filter provides at each frequency $\omega T \in [-\pi, \pi]$.

7.3   Phase Response

Definition. The *phase response* $\Theta(\omega)$ of an LTI filter is defined as the phase (or angle) of the frequency response $H(e^{j\omega T})$:

$$\Theta(\omega) \triangleq \angle H(e^{j\omega T})$$

The phase response is often referred to as the "phase" of the filter. For real filters (filters with real coefficients), the *filter phase* can be defined unambiguously as the phase of its frequency response.

The real-valued phase response $\Theta(\omega)$ gives the *phase shift* in radians that each input component sinusoid will undergo.

7.4   Polar Form of the Frequency Response

When the complex-valued frequency response is expressed in *polar form*, the amplitude response and phase response explicitly appear:

$$H(e^{j\omega T}) = G(\omega)e^{j\Theta(\omega)} \qquad (7.3)$$

Writing the basic frequency response description

$$Y(e^{j\omega T}) = H(e^{j\omega T})X(e^{j\omega T})$$

(from Eq. (7.2)) in polar form gives

$$
\begin{aligned}
Y(e^{j\omega T}) &= \left|Y(e^{j\omega T})\right| e^{j\angle Y(e^{j\omega T})} = \left|H(e^{j\omega T})X(e^{j\omega T})\right| e^{j\angle H(e^{j\omega T})X(e^{j\omega T})} \\
&= \left[G(\omega)\left|X(e^{j\omega T})\right|\right] e^{j[\angle X(e^{j\omega T})+\Theta(\omega)]}
\end{aligned}
$$

which implies

$$
\begin{aligned}
\left|Y(e^{j\omega T})\right| &= G(\omega)\left|X(e^{j\omega T})\right| \\
\angle Y(e^{j\omega T}) &= \Theta(\omega) + \angle X(e^{j\omega T}).
\end{aligned}
$$

This states explicitly that the output magnitude spectrum equals the input magnitude spectrum *times* the filter amplitude response, and the output phase equals the input phase *plus* the filter phase at each frequency ω.

Equation (7.3) gives the frequency response in polar form. For completeness, recall the transformations between polar and rectangular forms (*i.e.*, for converting real and imaginary parts to magnitude and angle, and vice versa):

$$G(\omega) \triangleq \left|H(e^{j\omega T})\right| = \sqrt{\text{re}^2\left\{H(e^{j\omega T})\right\} + \text{im}^2\left\{H(e^{j\omega T})\right\}}$$

$$\Theta(\omega) \triangleq \angle H(e^{j\omega T}) = \tan^{-1}\left[\frac{\text{im}\left\{H(e^{j\omega T})\right\}}{\text{re}\left\{H(e^{j\omega T})\right\}}\right]$$

Going the other way from polar to rectangular (using Euler's formula),

$$\text{re}\left\{H(e^{j\omega T})\right\} = G(\omega)\cos[\Theta(\omega)]$$
$$\text{im}\left\{H(e^{j\omega T})\right\} = G(\omega)\sin[\Theta(\omega)].$$

Application of these formulas to some basic example filters are carried out in Appendix B. Some useful trig identities are summarized in Appendix A. A matlab listing for computing the frequency response of any IIR filter is given in §7.5.1 below.

Separating the Transfer Function Numerator and Denominator

From Eq. (6.5) on page 127 we have that the transfer function of a recursive filter is a ratio of polynomials in z:

$$H(z) = \frac{B(z)}{A(z)} \qquad (7.4)$$

where

$$B(z) = b_0 + b_1 z^{-1} + \cdots + b_M z^{-M}$$
$$A(z) = 1 + a_1 z^{-1} + \cdots + a_N z^{-N}.$$

By elementary properties of complex numbers, we have

$$G(\omega) = \frac{\left|B(e^{j\omega T})\right|}{\left|A(e^{j\omega T})\right|}$$
$$\Theta(\omega) = \angle B(e^{j\omega T}) - \angle A(e^{j\omega T}).$$

These relations can be used to simplify calculations by hand, allowing the numerator and denominator of the transfer function to be handled separately.

7.5 Frequency Response as a Ratio of DTFTs

From Eq. (6.5) on page 127, we have $H(z) = B(z)/A(z)$, so that the frequency response is

$$H(e^{j\omega T}) = \frac{B(e^{j\omega T})}{A(e^{j\omega T})},$$

and

$$
\begin{aligned}
B(e^{j\omega T}) &= \mathrm{DTFT}_{\omega T}(\underline{b}) \\
A(e^{j\omega T}) &= \mathrm{DTFT}_{\omega T}(\underline{a}),
\end{aligned}
$$

where

$$
\begin{aligned}
\underline{b} &\triangleq [b_0, b_1, \ldots, b_M, 0, \ldots] \\
\underline{a} &\triangleq [1, a_1, \ldots, a_N, 0, \ldots],
\end{aligned}
$$

and the DTFT is as defined in Eq. (7.1) on page 150.

From the above relations, we may express the frequency response of any IIR filter as a ratio of two finite DTFTs:

$$
H(e^{j\omega T}) = \frac{\mathrm{DTFT}_{\omega T}(\underline{b})}{\mathrm{DTFT}_{\omega T}(\underline{a})} \triangleq \frac{\displaystyle\sum_{m=0}^{M} b_m e^{-j\omega m T}}{\displaystyle\sum_{n=0}^{N} a_n e^{-j\omega n T}} \tag{7.5}
$$

This expression provides a convenient basis for the computation of an IIR frequency response in software, as we pursue further in the next section.

7.5.1   Frequency Response in Matlab

In practice, we usually work with a *sampled* frequency axis. That is, instead of evaluating the transfer function $H(z) = B(z)/A(z)$ at $z = e^{j\omega T}$ to obtain the frequency response $H(e^{j\omega T})$, where ω is *continuous* radian frequency, we compute instead

$$
H(e^{j\omega_k T}) = \frac{B(e^{j\omega_k T})}{A(e^{j\omega_k T})}, \quad e^{j\omega_k T} \triangleq e^{j 2\pi k/N_s}, \quad k = 0, 1, 2, \ldots, N_s - 1,
$$

where N_s is the desired number of spectral samples around the unit circle in the z plane. From Eq. (7.5) we have that this is the same thing as the *sampled DTFT* of $\underline{b}$ divided by the *sampled DTFT* of $\underline{a}$:

$$
H(e^{j\omega_k T}) = \frac{\mathrm{DTFT}_{\omega_k T}(\underline{b})}{\mathrm{DTFT}_{\omega_k T}(\underline{a})}
$$

The uniformly sampled DTFT has its own name: the *discrete Fourier transform (DFT)* [84]. Thus, we can write

$$
H(e^{j\omega_k T}) = \frac{\mathrm{DFT}_{\omega_k T}(\underline{b})}{\mathrm{DFT}_{\omega_k T}(\underline{a})}, \quad k = 0, 1, 2, \ldots, N_s - 1
$$

where

$$\mathrm{DFT}_{\omega_k T}(x) \triangleq \sum_{n=0}^{N_s-1} x(n) e^{-j\omega_k nT}$$

and $\omega_k \triangleq 2\pi f_s k/N_s$, where $f_s = 1/T$ denotes the sampling rate in Hz.

To avoid undersampling $B(e^{j\omega T})$, we must have $N_s \geq M$, and to avoid undersampling $A(e^{j\omega T})$, we must have $N_s \geq N$. In general, $H(e^{j\omega T})$ *will be undersampled* (when $N > 0$), because it is the quotient of $B(e^{j\omega T})$ over $A(e^{j\omega T})$. This means, for example, that computing the impulse response $h(n)$ from the sampled frequency response $H(e^{j\omega_k T})$ will be *time aliased* in general. *I.e.*,

$$h(n) = \mathrm{IDFT}_n(H) \triangleq \frac{1}{N_s} \sum_{k=0}^{N_s-1} H(e^{j\omega_k T}) e^{j\omega_k nT}$$

will be time-aliased in the IIR case. In other words, an infinitely long impulse response cannot be Fourier transformed using a finite-length DFT, and this corresponds to not being able to sample the frequency response of an IIR filter without some loss of information. In practice, we simply choose N_s sufficiently large so that the sampled frequency response is accurate enough for our needs. A conservative practical rule of thumb when analyzing stable digital filters is to choose $N_s > 7/(1 - R_{\max})$, where $R_{\max}$ denotes the maximum pole magnitude. This choice provides more than 60 dB of decay in the impulse response over a duration of N_s samples, which is the time-aliasing block size. (The time to decay 60 dB, or "t_{60}", is a little less than 7 time constants [84], and the time-constant of decay for a single pole at radius R can be approximated by $1/(1 - R)$ samples, when R is close to 1, as derived in §8.6 on page 189.)

As is well known, when the DFT length N_s is a power of 2, *e.g.*, $N_s = 2^{10} = 1024$, the DFT can be computed extremely efficiently using the *Fast Fourier Transform (FFT)*. Figure 7.1 gives an example matlab script for computing the frequency response of an IIR digital filter using two FFTs. The Matlab function `freqz` also uses this method when possible (*e.g.*, when N_s is a power of 2).

```
function [H,w] = myfreqz(B,A,N,whole,fs)
%MYFREQZ Frequency response of IIR filter B(z)/A(z).
%    N = number of uniform frequency-samples desired
%    H = returned frequency-response samples (length N)
%    w = frequency axis for H (length N) in radians/sec
%    Compatible with simple usages of FREQZ in Matlab.
%    FREQZ(B,A,N,whole) uses N points around the whole
%    unit circle, where 'whole' is any nonzero value.
%    If whole=0, points go from theta=0 to pi*(N-1)/N.
%    FREQZ(B,A,N,whole,fs) sets the assumed sampling
%    rate to fs Hz instead of the default value of 1.
%    If there are no output arguments, the amplitude and
%    phase responses are displayed.  Poles cannot be
%    on the unit circle.

A = A(:).'; na = length(A); % normalize to row vectors
B = B(:).'; nb = length(B);
if nargin < 3, N = 1024; end
if nargin < 4, if isreal(b) & isreal(a), whole=0;
                else whole=1; end; end
if nargin < 5, fs = 1; end
Nf = 2*N; if whole, Nf = N; end
w = (2*pi*fs*(0:Nf-1)/Nf)';

H = fft([B zeros(1,Nf-nb)]) ./ fft([A zeros(1,Nf-na)]);

if whole==0, w = w(1:N); H = H(1:N); end

if nargout==0 % Display frequency response
  if fs==1, flab = 'Frequency (cyles/sample)';
  else, flab = 'Frequency (Hz)'; end
  subplot(2,1,1); % In octave, labels go before plot:
  plot([0:N-1]*fs/N,20*log10(abs(H)),'-k'); grid('on');
  xlabel(flab'); ylabel('Magnitude (dB)');
  subplot(2,1,2);
  plot([0:N-1]*fs/N,angle(H),'-k'); grid('on');
  xlabel(flab); ylabel('Phase');
end
```

Figure 7.1: Matlab function for computing and optionally plotting the frequency response of an IIR digital filter.

7.5.2   Example LPF Frequency Response Using `freqz`

Figure 7.2 lists a short matlab program illustrating usage of `freqz` in Octave (as found in the `octave-forge` package). The same code should also run in Matlab, provided the Signal Processing Toolbox is available. The lines of code not pertaining to plots are the following:

```
[B,A] = ellip(4,1,20,0.5); % Design lowpass filter B(z)/A(z)
[H,w] = freqz(B,A);        % Compute frequency response H(w)
```

The filter example is a recursive fourth-order elliptic function lowpass filter cutting off at half the Nyquist limit ("0.5π" in the fourth argument to `ellip`). The maximum passband ripple[2] is 1 dB (2nd argument), and the maximum stopband ripple is 20 dB (3rd arg). The sampled frequency response is returned in the H array, and the specific radian frequency samples corresponding to H are returned in the w ("omega") array. An immediate plot can be obtained in either Matlab or Octave by simply typing

```
plot(w,abs(H));
plot(w,angle(H));
```

However, the example of Fig. 7.2 uses more detailed "compatibility" functions listed in Appendix J. In particular, the `freqplot` utility is a simple compatibility wrapper for `plot` with label and title support (see §J.2 on page 399 for Octave and Matlab version listings), and `saveplot` is a trivial compatibility wrapper for the `print` function, which saves the current plot to a disk file (§J.3 on page 400). The saved `freqplot` plots are shown in Fig. 7.3(a) and Fig. 7.3(b).[3]

---

[2] A *passband* may be defined as any frequency band that the filter is trying to "pass"— *i.e.*, not trying to suppress. For example, in a lowpass filter with cut-off frequency ω_c, the passband is the interval $[-\omega_c, \omega]$. A lowpass filter typically also has a *stopband* that the filter *is* designed to suppress. For practical realizability, there should be a *transition band* between a passband and stopband. In some simple filters, such as Butterworth filters introduced in §7.6.4 below, there are passbands but no stopbands; instead, the stopband is replaced by a *roll-off*, typically specifiable in dB/octave. (The rolloff region can be viewed as a transition band between a passband and a "stop point" such as some number of zeros at $\omega = \infty$ for lowpass filters, or $\omega = 0$ for highpass filters. Within a passband or stopband, the amplitude response may exhibit *ripple*, that is, it may oscillate about the desired band gain, as discussed further in §7.6.4 below. A *ripple specification* sets a maximum deviation limit on the ripple.

[3] The "multiplot" created by the `plotfr` utility (§J.4 on page 401) cannot be saved to disk in Octave, although it looks fine on screen. In Matlab, there is no problem saving multiplots to disk.

```
[B,A] = ellip(4,1,20,0.5); % Design the lowpass filter
[H,w] = freqz(B,A);        % Compute its frequency response

% Plot the frequency response H(w):
%
figure(1);
freqplot(w,abs(H),'-k','Amplitude Response',...
         'Frequency (rad/sample)', 'Gain');
saveplot('../eps/freqzdemo1.eps');

figure(2);
freqplot(w,angle(H),'-k','Phase Response',...
         'Frequency (rad/sample)', 'Phase (rad)');
saveplot('../eps/freqzdemo2.eps');

% Plot frequency response in a "multiplot" like Matlab uses:
%
figure(3);
plotfr(H,w/(2*pi));
if exist('OCTAVE_VERSION')
  disp('Cannot save multiplots to disk in Octave')
else
  saveplot('../eps/freqzdemo3.eps');
end
```

Figure 7.2: Illustration of using freqz from octave-forge (version 2006-07-09) to produce Fig. 7.3 (using Octave version = 2.9.7). Also illustrated are a few plotting and plot-saving utilities from Appendix J.

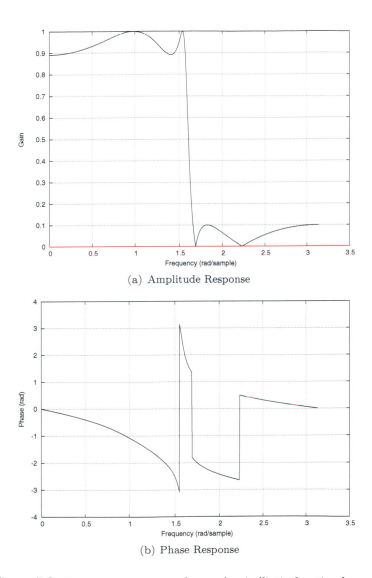

(a) Amplitude Response

(b) Phase Response

Figure 7.3: Frequency response of an order 4 elliptic function lowpass filter computed using the matlab listing in Fig. 7.2.

7.6   Phase and Group Delay

In the previous sections we looked at the two most important frequency-domain representations for LTI digital filters, the transfer function $H(z)$ and the frequency response:

$$H(e^{j\omega T}) \triangleq H(z)|_{z=e^{j\omega T}}$$

We looked further at the polar form of the frequency response $H(e^{j\omega T}) = G(\omega)e^{j\Theta(\omega)}$, thereby breaking it down into the amplitude response $G(\omega)$ times the phase-response term $e^{j\Theta(\omega)}$.

In the next two sections we look at two alternative forms of the phase response: *phase delay* and *group delay*. After considering some examples and special cases, *poles* and *zeros* of the transfer function are discussed in the next chapter.

7.6.1   Phase Delay

The phase response $\Theta(\omega)$ of an LTI filter gives the radian phase shift added to the phase of each sinusoidal component of the input signal. It is often more intuitive to consider instead the *phase delay*, defined as

$$\boxed{P(\omega) \triangleq -\frac{\Theta(\omega)}{\omega}.}\qquad \text{(Phase Delay)}$$

The phase delay gives the *time delay* in seconds experienced by each sinusoidal component of the input signal. For example, in the simplest lowpass filter of Chapter 1, we found that the phase response was $\Theta(\omega) = -\omega T/2$, which corresponds to a phase delay $P(\omega) = T/2$, or one-half sample. Thus, we can say precisely that the filter $y(n) = x(n) + x(n-1)$ exhibits half a sample of time delay at every frequency. (Regarding the discussion in §1.3.2 on page 8, it is now obvious how we should define the filter phase response at frequencies 0 and $f_s/2$.)

From a sinewave-analysis point of view, if the input to a filter with frequency response $H(e^{j\omega T}) = G(\omega)e^{j\Theta(\omega)}$ is

$$x(n) = \cos(\omega nT)$$

then the output is

$$\begin{aligned} y(n) &= G(\omega)\cos[\omega nT + \Theta(\omega)]\\ &= G(\omega)\cos\{\omega[nT - P(\omega)]\} \end{aligned}$$

and it can be clearly seen in this form that the phase delay expresses the phase response as a time delay in seconds.

7.6.2 Phase Unwrapping

In working with phase delay, it is often necessary to "unwrap" the phase response $\Theta(\omega)$. Phase unwrapping ensures that all appropriate multiples of 2π have been included in $\Theta(\omega)$. We defined $\Theta(\omega)$ simply as the complex angle of the frequency response $H(e^{j\omega T})$, and this is not sufficient for obtaining a phase response which can be converted to true time delay. If multiples of 2π are discarded, as is done in the definition of complex angle, the phase delay is modified by multiples of the sinusoidal period. Since LTI filter analysis is based on sinusoids without beginning or end, one cannot in principle distinguish between "true" phase delay and a phase delay with discarded sinusoidal periods when looking at a sinusoidal output at any given frequency. Nevertheless, it is often useful to define the filter phase response as a *continuous* function of frequency with the property that $\Theta(0) = 0$ or π (for real filters). This specifies how to *unwrap* the phase response at all frequencies where the amplitude response is finite and nonzero. When the amplitude response goes to zero or infinity at some frequency, we can try to take a limit from below and above that frequency.

Matlab and Octave have a function called unwrap() which implements a numerical algorithm for phase unwrapping. Figures 7.6.2 and 7.6.2 show the effect of the unwrap function on the phase response of the example elliptic lowpass filter of §7.5.2 on page 157, modified to contract the zeros from the unit circle to a circle of radius 0.95 in the z plane:

```
[B,A] = ellip(4,1,20,0.5); % design lowpass filter
 B = B .* (0.95).^[1:length(B)]; % contract zeros by 0.95
[H,w] = freqz(B,A);      % frequency response
theta = angle(H);        % phase response
thetauw = unwrap(theta); % unwrapped phase response
```

In Fig. 7.6.2, the phase-response minimum has "wrapped around" to the top of the plot. In Fig. 7.6.2, the phase response is continuous. We have contracted the zeros away from the unit circle in this example, because the phase response really does switch discontinuously by π radians when frequency passes through a point where the phases crosses zero along the unit circle (see Fig. 7.3(b) on page 159). The unwrap function need not modify these discontinuities, but it is free to add or subtract any integer multiple of 2π in order to obtain the "best looking" discontinuity. Typically, for best results, such discontinuities should *alternate* between $+\pi$ and $-\pi$, making the phase response resemble a distorted "square wave", as in Fig. 7.3(b). A more precise example appears in Fig. 10.2 on page 223.

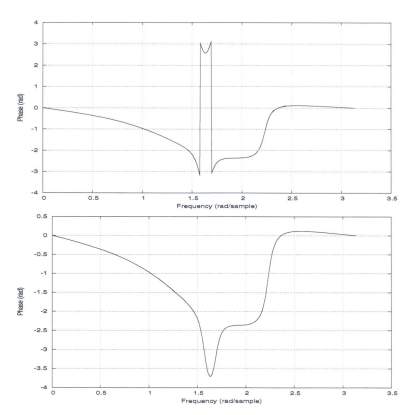

Figure 7.4: Phase response of a modified order 4 elliptic function lowpass filter cutting off at $f_s/4$.

7.6.3   Group Delay

A more commonly encountered representation of filter phase response is called the *group delay*, defined by

$$\boxed{D(\omega) \;\stackrel{\Delta}{=}\; -\frac{d}{d\omega}\Theta(\omega).}\qquad \text{(Group Delay)}$$

For linear phase responses, *i.e.*, $\Theta(\omega) = -\alpha\omega$ for some constant α, the group delay and the phase delay are identical, and each may be interpreted as time delay (equal to α samples when $\omega \in [-\pi, \pi]$). If the phase response is nonlinear, then the relative phases of the sinusoidal signal components are generally altered by the filter. A nonlinear phase response normally causes a "smearing" of attack transients such as in percussive sounds. Another term for this type of phase distortion is *phase dispersion*. This can be seen below in §7.6.5.

An example of a linear phase response is that of the simplest lowpass filter, $\Theta(\omega) = -\omega T/2 \;\Rightarrow\; P(\omega) = D(\omega) = T/2$. Thus, both the phase delay and the group delay of the simplest lowpass filter are equal to half a sample at every frequency.

For any reasonably smooth phase function, the group delay $D(\omega)$ may be interpreted as the *time delay of the amplitude envelope* of a sinusoid at frequency ω [63]. The bandwidth of the amplitude envelope in this interpretation must be restricted to a frequency interval over which the phase response is approximately linear. We derive this result in the next subsection.

Thus, the name "group delay" for $D(\omega)$ refers to the fact that it specifies the delay experienced by a narrow-band "group" of sinusoidal components which have frequencies within a narrow frequency interval about ω. The width of this interval is limited to that over which $D(\omega)$ is approximately constant.

Derivation of Group Delay as Modulation Delay

Suppose we write a narrowband signal centered at frequency ω_c as

$$x(n) = a_m(n)e^{j\omega_c n} \qquad (7.6)$$

where ω_c is defined as the *carrier frequency* (in radians per sample), and $a_m(n)$ is some "lowpass" *amplitude modulation* signal. The modulation a_m can be complex-valued to represent either phase or amplitude modulation or both. By "lowpass," we mean that the spectrum of a_m is concentrated near dc, *i.e.*,

$$a_m(n) \;\stackrel{\Delta}{=}\; \frac{1}{2\pi}\int_{-\pi}^{\pi} A_m(\omega)e^{j\omega n}d\omega \;\approx\; \frac{1}{2\pi}\int_{-\epsilon}^{\epsilon} A_m(\omega)e^{j\omega n}d\omega,$$

for some $|\epsilon| \ll \pi$. The modulation bandwidth is thus bounded by $2\epsilon \ll \pi$.

Using the above frequency-domain expansion of $a_m(n)$, $x(n)$ can be written as

$$x(n) = a_m(n)e^{j\omega_c n} = \left[\frac{1}{2\pi}\int_{-\epsilon}^{\epsilon} A_m(\omega)e^{j\omega n}d\omega\right]e^{j\omega_c n},$$

which we may view as a scaled superposition of sinusoidal components of the form

$$x_\omega(n) \triangleq A_m(\omega)e^{j\omega n}e^{j\omega_c n} = A_m(\omega)e^{j(\omega+\omega_c)n}$$

with ω near 0. Let us now pass the frequency component $x_\omega(n)$ through an LTI filter $H(z)$ having frequency response

$$H(e^{j\omega}) = G(\omega)e^{j\Theta(\omega)}$$

to get

$$y_\omega(n) = [G(\omega_c + \omega)A_m(\omega)]\, e^{j[(\omega_c+\omega)n+\Theta(\omega_c+\omega)]}. \qquad (7.7)$$

Assuming the phase response $\Theta(\omega)$ is approximately linear over the narrow frequency interval $\omega \in [\omega_c - \epsilon, \omega_c + \epsilon]$, we can write

$$\Theta(\omega_c + \omega) \approx \Theta(\omega_c) + \Theta'(\omega_c)\omega \triangleq \Theta(\omega_c) - D(\omega_c)\omega,$$

where $D(\omega_c)$ is the filter group delay at ω_c. Making this substitution in Eq. (7.7) gives

$$\begin{aligned}
y_\omega(n) &= [G(\omega_c + \omega)A_m(\omega)]\, e^{j[(\omega_c+\omega)n+\Theta(\omega_c)-D(\omega_c)\omega]}\\
&= [G(\omega_c + \omega)A_m(\omega)]\, e^{j\{[\omega_c n+\Theta(\omega_c)]+\omega[n-D(\omega_c)]\}}\\
&= [G(\omega_c + \omega)A_m(\omega)]\, e^{j\omega[n-D(\omega_c)]}e^{j\omega_c[n-P(\omega_c)]},
\end{aligned}$$

where we also used the definition of phase delay, $P(\omega_c) = -\Theta(\omega_c)/\omega_c$, in the last step. In this expression we can already see that the carrier sinusoid is delayed by the phase delay, while the amplitude-envelope frequency-component is delayed by the group delay. Integrating over ω to recombine the sinusoidal components (*i.e.*, using a Fourier superposition integral for y) gives

$$\begin{aligned}
y(n) &= \frac{1}{2\pi}\int_\omega y_\omega(n)d\omega\\
&= \left\{\frac{1}{2\pi}\int_{-\pi}^{\pi} [G(\omega_c + \omega)A_m(\omega)]\, e^{j\omega[n-D(\omega_c)]}d\omega\right\} e^{j\omega_c[n-P(\omega_c)]}\\
&= a^f[n - D(\omega_c)] \cdot e^{j\omega_c[n-P(\omega_c)]}
\end{aligned}$$

where $a^f(n)$ denotes a zero-phase filtering of the amplitude envelope $a(n)$ by $G(\omega + \omega_c)$. We see that the amplitude modulation is delayed by $D(\omega_c)$ while the carrier wave is delayed by $P(\omega_c)$.

We have shown that, for narrowband signals expressed as in Eq. (7.6) as a modulation envelope times a sinusoidal carrier, the carrier wave is delayed by the filter phase delay, while the modulation is delayed by the filter group delay, provided that the filter phase response is approximately linear over the narrowband frequency interval.

7.6.4   Group Delay Examples in Matlab

Figure 7.6 on page 167 compares the group delay responses for a number of classic lowpass filters, including the example of Fig. 7.2 on page 158. The matlab code is listed in Fig. 7.5. See, *e.g.*, Parks and Burrus [64] for a discussion of Butterworth, Chebyshev, and Elliptic Function digital filter design. See also §I.2 on page 384 for details on the Butterworth case. The various types may be summarized as follows:

- Butterworth filters are maximally flat in middle of the passband.

- Chebyshev Type I filters are "equiripple" in the passband and "Butterworth" in the stopband.

- Chebyshev Type II filters are "Butterworth" in the passband and equiripple in the stopband.

- Elliptic function filters are equiripple in both the passband and stopband.

Here, *"equiripple"* means "equal ripple"; that is, the error oscillates with equal peak magnitudes across the band. An equiripple error characterizes *optimality in the Chebyshev sense* [64, 78].

As Fig. 7.6.4 indicates, and as is well known, the Butterworth filter has the flattest group delay curve (and most gentle transition from passband to stopband) for the four types compared. The elliptic function filter has the largest amount of "delay distortion" near the cut-off frequency (passband edge frequency). Fundamentally, the more abrupt the transition from passband to stopband, the greater the delay-distortion across that transition, for any minimum-phase filter. (Minimum-phase filters are introduced in Chapter 11.) The delay-distortion can be compensated by *delay equalization*, *i.e.*, adding delay at other frequencies in order approach an overall constant group delay versus frequency. Delay equalization is typically carried out using an allpass filter (defined in §B.2 on page 272) in series with the filter to be delay-equalized [1].

```
[Bb,Ab] = butter(4,0.5); % order 4, cutoff at 0.5 * pi
Hb=freqz(Bb,Ab);
Db=grpdelay(Bb,Ab);

[Bc1,Ac1] = cheby1(4,1,0.5); % 1 dB passband ripple
Hc1=freqz(Bc1,Ac1);
Dc1=grpdelay(Bc1,Ac1);

[Bc2,Ac2] = cheby2(4,20,0.5); % 20 dB stopband attenuation
Hc2=freqz(Bc2,Ac2);
Dc2=grpdelay(Bc2,Ac2);

[Be,Ae] = ellip(4,1,20,0.5);  % like cheby1 + cheby2
He=freqz(Be,Ae);
[De,w]=grpdelay(Be,Ae);

figure(1); plot(w,abs([Hb,Hc1,Hc2,He])); grid('on');
xlabel('Frequency (rad/sample)'); ylabel('Gain');
legend('butter','cheby1','cheby2','ellip');
saveplot('../eps/grpdelaydemo1.eps');

figure(2); plot(w,[Db,Dc1,Dc2,De]); grid('on');
xlabel('Frequency (rad/sample)'); ylabel('Delay (samples)');
legend('butter','cheby1','cheby2','ellip');
saveplot('../eps/grpdelaydemo2.eps');
```

Figure 7.5: Program (matlab) for comparing the amplitude and group-delay responses of four classic lowpass filter types: Butterworth, Chebyshev Type I, Chebyshev Type II, and Elliptic Function.

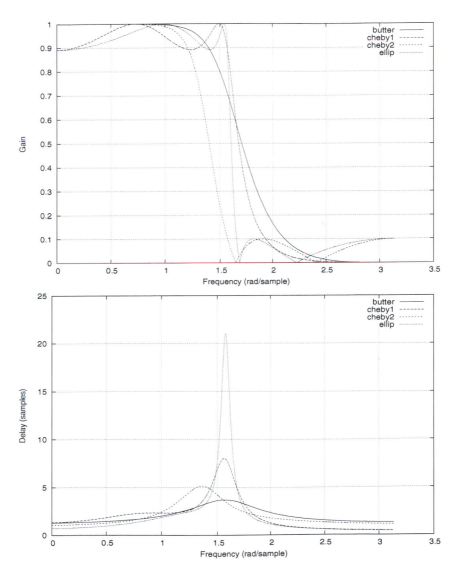

Figure 7.6: Comparison of amplitude and group-delay responses for classic lowpass-filter types Butterworth, Chebyshev Type I, Chebyshev Type II, and Elliptic Function. Plots generated by Octave 2.9.7 and octave-forge 2006-07-09.

7.6.5 Vocoder Analysis

The definitions of phase delay and group delay apply quite naturally to the analysis of the *vocoder* ("voice coder") [21, 26, 54, 76]. The vocoder provides a bank of bandpass filters which decompose the input signal into narrow spectral "slices." This is the analysis step. For synthesis (often called *additive synthesis*), a bank of sinusoidal oscillators is provided, having amplitude and frequency control inputs. The oscillator frequencies are tuned to the filter center frequencies, and the amplitude controls are driven by the amplitude envelopes measured in the filter-bank analysis. (Typically, some data reduction or envelope modification has taken place in the amplitude envelope set.) With these oscillators, the band slices are independently regenerated and summed together to resynthesize the signal.

Suppose we excite only channel k of the vocoder with the input signal

$$a(nT)\cos(\omega_k nT), \qquad n = 0, 1, 2, \dots$$

where ω_k is the center frequency of the channel in radians per second, T is the sampling interval in seconds, and the bandwidth of $a(nT)$ is smaller than the channel bandwidth. We may regard this input signal as an *amplitude modulated sinusoid*. The component $\cos(\omega_k nT)$ can be called the *carrier wave*, while $a(nT) \geq 0$ is the *amplitude envelope*.

If the phase of each channel filter is linear in frequency within the passband (or at least across the width of the spectrum $A(e^{j\omega T})$ of $a(nT)$), and if each channel filter has a flat amplitude response in its passband, then the filter output will be, by the analysis of the previous section,

$$y_k(n) \approx a[nT - D(\omega_k)]\cos\{\omega_k[nT - P(\omega_k)]\} \qquad (7.8)$$

where $P(\omega_k)$ is the phase delay of the channel filter at frequency ω_k, and $D(\omega_k)$ is the group delay at that frequency. Thus, in vocoder analysis for additive synthesis, the phase delay of the analysis filter bank gives the time delay experienced by the oscillator carrier waves, while the group delay of the analysis filter bank gives the time delay imposed on the estimated oscillator amplitude-envelope functions.

Note that a nonlinear phase response generally results in $D(\omega_k) \neq P(\omega_k)$, and $D(\omega_k) \neq D(\omega_l)$ for $k \neq l$. As a result, the *dispersive* nature of additive synthesis reconstruction in this case can be seen in Eq. (7.8).

7.6.6   Numerical Computation of Group Delay

The definition of group delay,

$$D(\omega) \triangleq -\frac{d}{d\omega}\Theta(\omega) \triangleq -\frac{d}{d\omega}\angle H(e^{j\omega T}),$$

does not give an immediately useful recipe for computing group delay numerically. In this section, we describe the theory of operation behind the matlab function for group-delay computation given in §J.8 on page 408.

A more useful form of the group delay arises from the *logarithmic derivative* of the frequency response. Expressing the frequency response $H(e^{j\omega T})$ in polar form as

$$H(e^{j\omega T}) \triangleq G(\omega)e^{j\Theta(\omega)}$$

yields the following logarithmic decomposition of magnitude and phase:

$$\ln H(e^{j\omega T}) = \ln G(\omega) + j\Theta(\omega)$$

Thus, the real part of the logarithm of the frequency response equals the log amplitude response, while the imaginary part equals the phase response.

Since differentiation is linear, the logarithmic derivative becomes

$$\frac{d}{d\omega}\ln H(e^{j\omega T}) = \frac{G'(\omega)}{G(\omega)} + j\Theta'(\omega),$$

where $G'(\omega)$ and $\Theta'(\omega)$ denote the derivatives of $G(\omega)$ and $\Theta(\omega)$, respectively, with respect to ω. We may therefore express the group delay as

$$D(\omega) \triangleq -\frac{d}{d\omega}\Theta(\omega) = -\mathrm{im}\left\{\frac{d}{d\omega}\ln H(e^{j\omega T})\right\} = -\mathrm{im}\left\{\frac{H'(e^{j\omega T})}{H(e^{j\omega T})}\right\}.$$

Consider first the FIR case in which $H(z) = B(z)$, with

$$B(z) \triangleq b_0 + b_1 z^{-1} + b_2 z^{-2} + \cdots + b_M z^{-M}. \tag{7.9}$$

In this case, the derivative is simply

$$
\begin{aligned}
B'(e^{j\omega T}) &\triangleq \frac{d}{d\omega}\left[b_0 + b_1 e^{-j\omega T} + b_2 e^{-j2\omega T} + \cdots + b_M e^{-jM\omega T}\right] \\
&= -jT\left[b_1 e^{-j\omega T} + 2\,b_2 e^{-j2\omega T} + \cdots + M\,b_M e^{-jM\omega T}\right] \\
&\triangleq -jT\,B_r(e^{j\omega T}),
\end{aligned}
$$

where $B_r(z)$ denotes "B ramped", *i.e.*, the ith coefficient of the polynomial B_r is $i\,b_i$, for $i = 0, 1, 2, \ldots, M$. In matlab, we may compute Br from B via the following statement:

```
Br = B .* [0:M]; % Compute ramped B polynomial
```

The group delay of an FIR filter $B(z)$ can now be written as

$$D(\omega) = -\text{im}\left\{\frac{B'(e^{j\omega T})}{B(e^{j\omega T})}\right\} = -\text{im}\left\{-jT\frac{B_r(e^{j\omega T})}{B(e^{j\omega T})}\right\} = T\,\text{re}\left\{\frac{B_r(e^{j\omega T})}{B(e^{j\omega T})}\right\}$$

In matlab, the group delay, in samples, can be computed simply as

```
D = real(fft(Br) ./ fft(B))
```

where the `fft`, of course, approximates the Discrete Time Fourier Transform (DTFT). Such sampling of the frequency axis by this approximation is information-preserving whenever the number of samples (FFT length) exceeds the polynomial order M. The *ratio* of sampled DTFTs, however, is *undersampled*, in general. In fact, we may have $B(e^{j\omega T}) = 0$ at some frequencies ("zeros on the unit circle"). The `grpdelay` matlab utility in §J.8 watches out for division by zero, and simply sets the group delay to zero at such frequencies. Note that the true group delay approaches infinite magnitude as either a zero or pole approaches the unit circle.

Finally, when there are both poles and zeros, we have

$$H(e^{j\omega T}) = \frac{B(e^{j\omega T})}{A(e^{j\omega T})},$$

where $B(e^{j\omega T})$ is given in Eq. (7.9), and

$$A(z) \triangleq 1 + a_1 z^{-1} + a_2 z^{-2} + \cdots + a_N z^{-N}. \qquad (7.10)$$

Straightforward differentiation yields

$$\frac{H'}{H} = \frac{(B/A)'}{(B/A)} = \frac{B'A - BA'}{BA}, \qquad (7.11)$$

and this can be implemented analogous to the FIR case discussed above. However, a faster algorithm (usually) results from converting the IIR case to the FIR case:

$$C(z) \triangleq B(z)\left[z^{-N}\overline{A}(1/z)\right] \triangleq B(z)\tilde{A}(z) \qquad (7.12)$$

where

$$\tilde{A}(z) \triangleq z^{-N}\overline{A}(1/z) = [\overline{a}_N, \overline{a}_{N-1}z^{-1}, \overline{a}_{N-2}z^{-2}, \ldots, \overline{a}_1 z^{-(N-1)} + z^{-N}]$$

may be called the "flip-conjugate" or "Hermitian conjugate" of the polynomial $A(z)$.[4] In matlab, the C polynomial is given by

---

[4]The quantity $\overline{A}(1/z)$ is known as the *para-Hermitian conjugate* of the polynomial $A(z)$. It coincides with the ordinary complex conjugate along the unit circle, while elsewhere in the z-plane, z is replaced by $1/z$ and only the coefficients of A are conjugated. A mathematical feature of the para-Hermitian conjugate is that $\overline{A}(1/z)$ is an *analytic* function of z while $\overline{A(z)}$ is not.

```
C = conv(B,fliplr(conj(A)));
```

It is straightforward to show (Problem 11) that

$$\angle\tilde{A}(e^{j\omega T}) = -\angle A(e^{j\omega T}) - N\omega T.$$

The phase of the IIR filter $H(z) = B(z)/A(z)$ is therefore

$$\begin{aligned}
\angle H(e^{j\omega T}) &= \angle B(e^{j\omega T}) - \angle A(e^{j\omega T}) \\
&= \angle B(e^{j\omega T}) + \angle\tilde{A}(e^{j\omega T}) + N\omega T \\
&= \angle C(e^{j\omega T}) + N\omega T,
\end{aligned}$$

and the group delay computation thus reduces to the FIR case:

$$D(\omega) = -\frac{d}{d\omega}\angle C(e^{j\omega T}) - NT = T\,\mathrm{re}\left\{\frac{C_r(e^{j\omega T})}{C(e^{j\omega T})}\right\} - NT.$$

This method is implemented in §J.8 on page 408.

7.7 Frequency Response Analysis Problems

1. Derive the frequency response for the two digital filters below:

   (a) $y(n) = x(n-1) + x(n-2) + y(n-1)$
   (b) $y(n) = x(n) + x(n-1) + y(n-1)$

   In what ways are these filters identical? How are they different?

2. Prove that the frequency response

   $$H(e^{j\omega T}) = e^{-16.5 j\omega T}$$

   does not correspond to a finite impulse response.

3. *Symmetric FIR Filter:* Consider the impulse response $h(n) = \delta(n) + \delta(n-1)$. Find the

   (a) phase delay $P(\omega)$
   (b) group delay $D(\omega)$

   Explain how they differ and why.

4. *Antisymmetric FIR Filter:* Consider the antisymmetric impulse response $h(n) = \delta(n) - \delta(n-1)$. Find the

   (a) phase delay $P(\omega)$

(b) group delay $D(\omega)$

Explain how they differ and why, comparing with your results for Problem 3.

5. *Zero-Phase Filter:* A *zero-phase filter* is a special case of a linear-phase filter in which the phase slope is 0. The real impulse response $h(n)$ of a zero-phase filter is *even*. That is, if $h(n) = h(-n)$ (zero-phase condition), the filter is zero-phase. Verify this by showing the impulse response

$$h(n) = b_1\delta(n+1) + b_0\delta(n) + b_1\delta(n-1)$$

has a zero phase response when b_0, b_1 are real.

6. *Exponential Decay:* This problem is concerned with verifying the accuracy of the rule of §E.7.1 which states that a second-order resonator impulse-response decays 96 percent in Q periods. Prepare a table of actual decays (in percent) for $Q = 0.5, 1, 2, 4, 8$. Add a column giving the difference between this amount of decay and that predicted by the rule of thumb (`1-exp(-pi`) $= 0.0432139182637723$).

7. *Complex Resonator:* There is nothing mandatory about real coefficients (a_i, b_i) in Eq. (5.1). Write a program to implement a filter which has the frequency response

$$H(e^{j\omega T}) = \frac{1}{1 - (Re^{j\theta_c})e^{-j\omega T}}$$

8. *Graphic Equalizer:* Use the trigonometric identity

$$\cos^2(\theta) + \sin^2(\theta) = 1$$

to design a two-band graphic equalizer which is transparent ($G(\omega) = 1$) when the two slide pots are even with each other. Is there any phase distortion caused by this equalizer?

9. *Two Types of Comb Filter:* Find the frequency response of

$$y(n) = b_0 x(n) + b_M x(n - M)$$

where $M > 1$ is some integer. (If M varies with time, we get a popular device known as *flanger*.) For $b_0 = b_M = b$, find a general formula for the number of notches and the notch frequencies as a function of M. Next try the following filter:

$$y(n) = b_0 x(n) - a_M y(n - M)$$

For $b_0 = -a_M = a$, find an expression for the number of peaks and the peak frequencies as a function of M. How does this all-pole comb filter compare to the all-zero comb filter above? How do the peak gains compare when $a = b$? (The peak gain is defined as the maximum value assumed by the amplitude response $G(\omega)$ over all $\omega \in [-\pi, \pi]$.)

10. *Allpass Filter:* Give the conditions necessary on $\{b_0, b_M, a_M\}$ in the previous problem such that the cascade combination of an all-pole and all-zero comb filter will have an amplitude response $G(\omega) = 1$, but a nontrivial phase response. Where are the poles and zeros for this case? What is the simple "all-pass rule" for b_M given a particular a_M and b_0? Check your rule by applying it to the numerator coefficients versus the denominator coefficients of a general transfer function and seeing if the transfer function is all-pass. Can you also find the general all-pass rule which specifies the zeroes given the poles or vice versa?

11. Show that
$$\angle \tilde{A}(e^{j\omega T}) = -\angle A(e^{j\omega T}) - N\omega.$$
where $\tilde{A}(z) \triangleq z^{-N} A(1/z)$ is the polynomial obtained by reversing ("flipping") the coefficients of $A(z)$.

12. Determine the conditions under which Eq. (7.11) on page 170 gives a faster group-delay algorithm than Eq. (7.12)

Chapter 8

Pole-Zero Analysis

This chapter discusses *pole-zero analysis* of digital filters. Every digital filter can be specified by its poles and zeros (together with a gain factor). Poles and zeros give useful insights into a filter's response, and can be used as the basis for digital filter design. This chapter additionally presents the Durbin step-down recursion for checking filter stability by finding the reflection coefficients, including matlab code.

Going back to Eq. (6.5) on page 127, we can write the general transfer function for the recursive LTI digital filter as

$$H(z) = g \frac{1 + \beta_1 z^{-1} + \cdots + \beta_M z^{-M}}{1 + a_1 z^{-1} + \cdots + a_N z^{-N}} \tag{8.1}$$

which is the same as Eq. (6.5) except that we have factored out the leading coefficient b_0 in the numerator (assumed to be nonzero) and called it g. (Here $\beta_i \triangleq b_i/b_0$.) In the same way that $z^2 + 3z + 2$ can be factored into $(z + 1)(z + 2)$, we can factor the numerator and denominator to obtain

$$H(z) = g \frac{(1 - q_1 z^{-1})(1 - q_2 z^{-1}) \cdots (1 - q_M z^{-1})}{(1 - p_1 z^{-1})(1 - p_2 z^{-1}) \cdots (1 - p_N z^{-1})}. \tag{8.2}$$

Assume, for simplicity, that none of the factors cancel out. The (possibly complex) numbers $\{q_1, \ldots, q_M\}$ are the *roots*, or *zeros*, of the numerator polynomial. When z is set to any of these values, the transfer function evaluates to 0. For this reason, the numerator roots q_i are called the *zeros* of the filter. In other words, the zeros of the numerator of an irreducible transfer-function are called the zeros of the transfer-function. Similarly, when z approaches any root of the denominator polynomial, the magnitude of the transfer function approaches infinity. Consequently, the *denominator* roots $\{p_1, \ldots, p_N\}$ are called the *poles* of the filter.

The term "pole" makes sense when one plots the magnitude of $H(z)$ as a function of z. Since z is complex, it may be taken to lie in a plane (the z plane). The magnitude of $H(z)$ is real and therefore can be represented by distance above the z plane. The plot appears as an infinitely thin surface spanning in all directions over the z plane. The zeros are the points where the surface dips down to touch the z plane. At high altitude, the poles look like thin, well, "poles" that go straight up forever, getting thinner the higher they go.

Notice that the $M + 1$ feedforward coefficients from the general difference quation, Eq. (5.1) on page 97, give rise to M zeros. Similarly, the N feedback coefficients in Eq. (5.1) give rise to N poles. Recall that we defined the filter order as the maximum of N and M in Eq. (6.5). Therefore, *the filter order equals the number of poles or zeros, whichever is greater.*

8.1   Filter Order = Transfer Function Order

Recall that the *order of a polynomial* is defined as the highest power of the polynomial variable. For example, the order of the polynomial $p(x) = 1 + 2x + 3x^2$ is 2. From Eq. (8.1), we see that M is the order of the transfer-function numerator polynomial in z^{-1}. Similarly, N is the order of the denominator polynomial in z^{-1}.

A *rational function* is any ratio of polynomials. That is, $R(z)$ is a rational function if it can be written as

$$R(z) = \frac{P(z)}{Q(z)}$$

for finite-order polynomials $P(z)$ and $Q(z)$. The *order of a rational function* is defined as the maximum of its numerator and denominator polynomial orders. As a result, we have the following simple rule:

The order of an LTI filter is the order of its transfer function.

It turns out the transfer function can be viewed as a rational function of either z^{-1} or z without affecting order. Let $K = \max\{M, N\}$ denote the order of a general LTI filter with transfer function $H(z)$ expressible as in Eq. (8.1). Then multiplying $H(z)$ by z^K/z^K gives a rational function of z (as opposed to z^{-1}) that is also order K when viewed as a ratio of polynomials in z. Another way to reach this conclusion is to consider that replacing z by z^{-1} is a *conformal map* [57] that inverts the z-plane with respect to the unit circle. Such a transformation clearly preserves the number of poles and zeros, provided poles and zeros at $z = \infty$ and $z = 0$ are either both counted or both not counted.

8.2 Graphical Computation of Amplitude Response from Poles and Zeros

Now consider what happens when we take the factored form of the general transfer function, Eq. (8.2), and set z to $e^{j\omega T}$ to get the frequency response in factored form:

$$H(e^{j\omega T}) = g\frac{(1 - q_1e^{-j\omega T})(1 - q_2e^{-j\omega T})\cdots(1 - q_Me^{-j\omega T})}{(1 - p_1e^{-j\omega T})(1 - p_2e^{-j\omega T})\cdots(1 - p_Ne^{-j\omega T})}$$

As usual for the frequency response, we prefer the polar form for this expression. Consider first the amplitude response $G(\omega) \triangleq \left|H(e^{j\omega T})\right|$.

$$
\begin{aligned}
G(\omega) &= |g|\frac{\left|1 - q_1e^{-j\omega T}\right| \cdot \left|1 - q_2e^{-j\omega T}\right| \cdots \left|1 - q_Me^{-j\omega T}\right|}{\left|1 - p_1e^{-j\omega T}\right| \cdot \left|1 - p_2e^{-j\omega T}\right| \cdots \left|1 - p_Ne^{-j\omega T}\right|} \\
&= |g|\frac{\left|e^{-jM\omega T}\right| \cdot \left|e^{j\omega T} - q_1\right| \cdot \left|e^{j\omega T} - q_2\right| \cdots \left|e^{j\omega T} - q_M\right|}{\left|e^{-jN\omega T}\right| \cdot \left|e^{j\omega T} - p_1\right| \cdot \left|e^{j\omega T} - p_2\right| \cdots \left|e^{j\omega T} - p_N\right|} \\
&= |g|\frac{\left|e^{j\omega T} - q_1\right| \cdot \left|e^{j\omega T} - q_2\right| \cdots \left|e^{j\omega T} - q_M\right|}{\left|e^{j\omega T} - p_1\right| \cdot \left|e^{j\omega T} - p_2\right| \cdots \left|e^{j\omega T} - p_N\right|} \qquad (8.3)
\end{aligned}
$$

In the complex plane, the number $z = x + jy$ is plotted at the coordinates (x, y) [84]. The difference of two vectors $u = x_1 + jy_1$ and $v = x_2 + jy_2$ is $u - v = (x_1 - x_2) + j(y_1 - y_2)$, as shown in Fig. 8.1. Translating the origin of the vector $u - v$ to the tip of v shows that $u - v$ is an arrow drawn from the tip of v to the tip of u. The length of a vector is unaffected by translation away from the origin. However, the angle of a translated vector must be measured relative to a translated copy of the real axis. Thus the term $e^{j\omega T} - q_i$ may be drawn as an arrow from the ith zero to the point $e^{j\omega T}$ on the unit circle, and $e^{j\omega T} - p_i$ is an arrow from the ith pole. Therefore, *each term in Eq. (8.3) is the length of a vector drawn from a pole or zero to a single point on the unit circle*, as shown in Fig. 8.2 for two poles and two zeros. In summary:

> The frequency response magnitude (amplitude response) at frequency ω is given by the product of the lengths of vectors drawn from the zeros to the point $e^{j\omega T}$ divided by the product of lengths of vectors drawn from the poles to $e^{j\omega T}$.

For example, the dc gain is obtained by multiplying the lengths of the lines drawn from all poles and zeros to the point $z = 1$. The filter gain at half the sampling rate is the product of the lengths of these lines

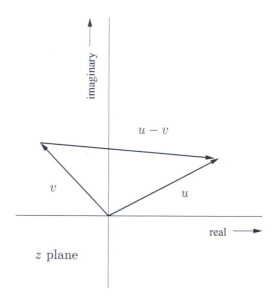

Figure 8.1: Treatment of complex numbers as vectors in a plane.

when drawn to the point $z = -1$. For an arbitrary frequency f Hz, we draw arrows from the poles and zeros to the point $z = e^{j2\pi fT}$. Thus, at the frequency where the arrows in Fig. 8.2 join, (which is slightly less than one-eighth the sampling rate) the gain of this two-pole two-zero filter is $G(\omega) = (d_1 d_2)/(d_3 d_4)$. Figure 8.3 gives the complete amplitude response for the poles and zeros shown in Fig. 8.2. Before looking at that, it is a good exercise to try sketching it by inspection of the pole-zero diagram. It is usually easy to sketch a qualitatively accurate amplitude-response directly from the poles and zeros (to within a scale factor).

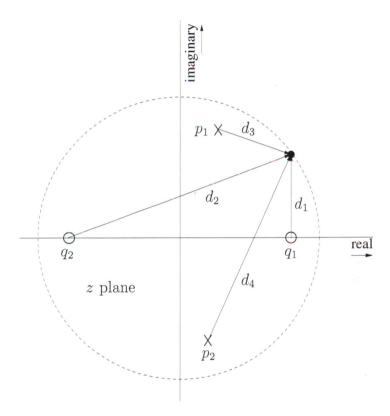

Figure 8.2: Measurement of amplitude response from a pole-zero diagram. Poles are represented in the complex plane by 'X'; zeros by 'O'.

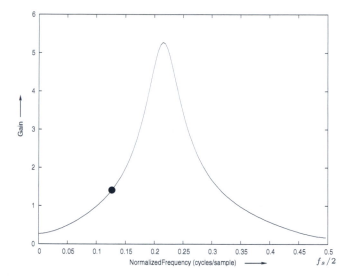

Figure 8.3: Amplitude response obtained by traversing the entire upper semicircle in Fig. 8.2 with the point $e^{j\omega T}$. The point of the amplitude obtained in that figure is marked by a heavy dot. For real filters, precisely the same curve is obtained if the lower half of the unit circle is traversed, since $G(\omega) = G(-\omega)$. Thus, plotting the response over positive frequencies only is sufficient for real filters.

8.3   Graphical Phase Response Calculation

The phase response is almost as easy to evaluate graphically as is the amplitude response:

$$
\begin{aligned}
\Theta(\omega) \;\triangleq\;& \angle\left\{ g \frac{(1 - q_1 e^{-j\omega T})(1 - q_2 e^{-j\omega T}) \cdots (1 - q_M e^{-j\omega T})}{(1 - p_1 e^{-j\omega T})(1 - p_2 e^{-j\omega T}) \cdots (1 - p_N e^{-j\omega T})} \right\} \\
=\;& \angle g + \angle e^{j(N-M)\omega T} \frac{(e^{j\omega T} - q_1)(e^{j\omega T} - q_2) \cdots (e^{j\omega T} - q_M)}{(e^{j\omega T} - p_1)(e^{j\omega T} - p_2) \cdots (e^{j\omega T} - p_N)} \\
=\;& \angle g + (N - M)\omega T \\
& + \angle(e^{j\omega T} - q_1) + \angle(e^{j\omega T} - q_2) + \cdots + \angle(e^{j\omega T} - q_M) \\
& - \angle(e^{j\omega T} - p_1) - \angle(e^{j\omega T} - p_2) - \cdots - \angle(e^{j\omega T} - p_N)
\end{aligned}
$$

If g is real, then $\angle g$ is either 0 or π. Terms of the form $e^{j\omega T} - z$ can be interpreted as a vector drawn from the point z to the point $e^{j\omega T}$ in the complex plane. The angle of $e^{j\omega T} - z$ is the angle of the constructed vector (where a vector pointing horizontally to the right has an angle of 0). Therefore, the phase response at frequency f Hz is again obtained by drawing lines from all the poles and zeros to the point $e^{j2\pi fT}$, as shown in Fig. 8.4. The angles of the lines from the zeros are added, and the angles of the lines from the poles are subtracted. Thus, at the frequency ω the phase response of the two-pole two-zero filter in the figure is $\Theta(\omega) = \theta_1 + \theta_2 - \theta_3 - \theta_4$.

Note that an additional phase of $(N - M)2\pi fT$ radians appears when the number of poles is not equal to the number of zeros. This factor comes from writing the transfer function as

$$
H(z) = g z^{(N-M)} \frac{(z - q_1)(z - q_2) \cdots (z - q_M)}{(z - p_1)(z - p_2) \cdots (z - p_N)}
$$

and may be thought of as arising from $N - M$ additional zeros at $z = 0$ when $N > M$, or $M - N$ poles at $z = 0$ when $M > N$. Strictly speaking, every digital filter has an equal number of poles and zeros when those at $z = 0$ and $z = \infty$ are counted. It is customary, however, when discussing the number of poles and zeros a filter has, to neglect these, since they correspond to pure delay and do not affect the amplitude response. Figure 8.5 gives the phase response for this two-pole two-zero example.

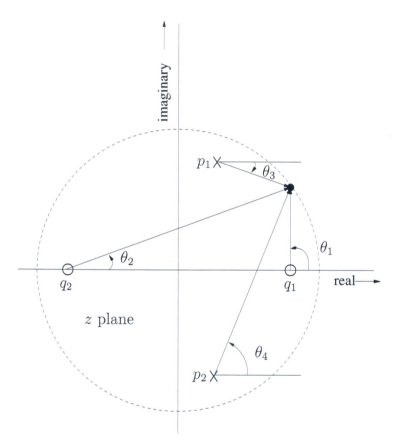

Figure 8.4: Measurement of phase response from a pole-zero diagram.

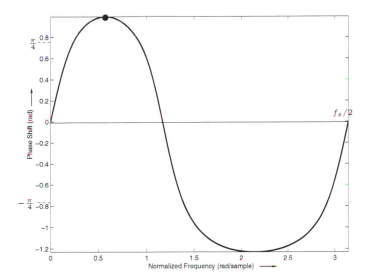

Figure 8.5: Phase response obtained from Fig. 8.4 for positive frequencies. The point of the phase response corresponding to the arrows in that figure is marked by a heavy dot. For real filters, the phase response is *odd* ($\Theta(-\omega) = -\Theta(\omega)$), so the curve shown here may be reflected through 0 and negated to obtain the plot for negative frequencies.

8.4   Stability Revisited

As defined earlier in §5.6 (page 101), a filter is said to be *stable* if its impulse response $h(n)$ decays to 0 as n goes to infinity. In terms of poles and zeros, an irreducible filter transfer function is stable if and only if all its poles are inside the unit circle in the z plane (as first discussed in §6.8.6 on page 140). This is because the transfer function is the z transform of the impulse response, and if there is an observable (non-canceled) pole outside the unit circle, then there is an exponentially increasing component of the impulse response. To see this, consider a causal impulse response of the form

$$h(n) = R^n e^{j\omega nT}, \qquad n = 0, 1, 2, \dots .$$

This signal is a damped complex sinusoid when $0 < R < 1$. It oscillates with zero-crossing rate $2\omega/2\pi = \omega/\pi$ zeros per second, and it has an exponentially decaying amplitude envelope. If $R > 1$, then the amplitude envelope increases exponentially as R^n.

The signal $h(n) = R^n e^{j\omega nT}$ has the z transform

$$
\begin{aligned}
H(z) &= \sum_{n=0}^{\infty} R^n e^{j\omega nT} z^{-n} \\
&= \sum_{n=0}^{\infty} \left(R e^{j\omega T} z^{-1} \right)^n \\
&= \frac{1}{1 - R e^{j\omega T} z^{-1}},
\end{aligned}
$$

where the last step holds for $\left| R e^{j\omega T} z^{-1} \right| < 1$, which is true whenever $R < |z|$. Thus, the transfer function consists of a single pole at $z = R e^{j\omega T}$, and it exists for $|z| > R$.[1] Now consider what happens when we let R become greater than 1. The pole of $H(z)$ moves outside the unit circle, and the impulse response has an exponentially *increasing* amplitude. (Note $|h(n)| = R^n$.) Thus, the definition of stability is violated. Since the z transform exists only for $|z| > R$, we see that $R \geq 1$ implies that the z transform no longer exists on the unit circle, so that the frequency response becomes undefined!

The above one-pole analysis shows that a one-pole filter is stable if and only if its pole is inside the unit circle. In the case of an arbitrary transfer function, inspection of its partial fraction expansion (§6.8) shows that the behavior near any pole approaches that of a one-pole filter consisting of only that pole. Therefore, *all* poles must be inside the unit circle for stability.

In summary, we can state the following:

---

[1] See §6.2 on page 123 and §8.7 on page 190 for related discussion.

> A necessary and sufficient condition for the *stability* of a finite-order causal LTI digital filter is that all poles of its irreducible transfer function lie strictly inside the unit circle.

Isolated poles *on* the unit circle may be called *marginally stable*. The impulse response component corresponding to a single pole on the unit circle never decays, but neither does it grow.[2] In physical modeling applications, marginally stable poles occur often in *lossless* systems, such as ideal vibrating string models [86].

8.4.1   Computing Reflection Coefficients to Check Filter Stability

Since we know that a recursive filter is stable if and only if all its poles have magnitude less than 1, an obvious method for checking stability is to find the roots of the denominator polynomial $A(z)$ in the filter transfer function [Eq. (7.4) on page 153]. If the moduli of all roots are less than 1, the filter is stable. This test works fine for low-order filters (*e.g.*, on the order of 100 poles or less), but it may fail numerically at higher orders because the roots of a polynomial are very sensitive to round-off error in the polynomial coefficients [62]. It is therefore of interest to use a stability test that is faster and more reliable numerically than polynomial root-finding. Fortunately, such a test exists based on the filter *reflection coefficients*.

It is a mathematical fact [48] that all poles of a recursive filter are inside the unit circle if and only if all its reflection coefficients (which are always real) are strictly between -1 and 1. The full theory associated with reflection coefficients is beyond the scope of this book, but can be found in most modern treatments of *linear prediction* [48, 47] or *speech modeling* [92, 19, 69]. An online derivation appears in [86].[3] Here, we will settle for a simple recipe for computing the reflection coefficients from the transfer-function denominator polynomial $A(z)$. This recipe is called the *step-down procedure*, *Schur-Cohn stability test*, or *Durbin recursion* [48], and it is essentially the same thing as the *Schur recursion* (for allpass filters) or *Levinson algorithm* (for autocorrelation functions of autoregressive stochastic processes) [38].

---

[2] As discussed in §6.8.5 on page 138, the impulse response of a *repeated* pole of multiplicity k at a point on the unit circle may grow with amplitude envelope proportional to n^{k-1}.

[3] See, *e.g.*, `http://ccrma.stanford.edu/~jos/pasp/Passive_Reflectances.html`[4] .

8.4.2   Step-Down Procedure

Let $A_N(z)$ denote the Nth-order denominator polynomial of the recursive filter transfer function $H(z) = B(z)/A_N(z)$:

$$A_N(z) \triangleq 1 + a_{N,1}\, z^{-1} + a_{N,2}\, z^{-2} + \cdots + a_{N,N-1}\, z^{-(N-1)} + a_{N,N}\, z^{-N} \quad (8.4)$$

We have introduced the new subscript N because the step-down procedure is defined recursively in polynomial order. We will need to keep track of polynomials orders between 1 and N.

In addition to the denominator polynomial $A_N(z)$, we need its *flip*:

$$\begin{aligned}
\tilde{A}_N(z) \;\triangleq\;& z^{-N} A_N(1/z) \\
=\;& a_{N,N} + a_{N,N-1}\, z^{-1} + a_{N,N-2}\, z^{-2} + \cdots \\
& + a_{N,2}\, z^{-(N-2)} + a_{N,1}\, z^{-(N-1)} + z^{-N} \quad (8.5)
\end{aligned}$$

The recursion begins by setting the Nth reflection coefficient to $k_N = a_{N,N}$. If $|k_N| \geq 1$, the recursion halts prematurely, and the filter is declared unstable. (Equivalently, the polynomial $A_N(z)$ is declared non-minimum phase, as defined in Chapter 11.)

Otherwise, if $|k_N| < 1$, the polynomial order is decremented by 1 to yield $A_{N-1}(z)$ as follows (recall that $A_N(z)$ is *monic*):

$$A_{N-1}(z) = \frac{A_N(z) - k_N \tilde{A}_N(z)}{1 - k_N^2} = \frac{A_N(z) - z^{-N} k_N A_N(1/z)}{1 - k_N^2} \quad (8.6)$$

Next k_{N-1} is set to $a_{N-1,N-1}$, and the recursion continues until $k_1 = a_{1,1}$ is reached, or $|k_i| \geq 1$ is found for some i.

Whenever $|k_m| = 1$, the recursion halts prematurely, and the filter is usually declared unstable (at best it is *marginally stable*, meaning that it has at least one pole on the unit circle).

Note that the reflection coefficients can also be used to *implement* the digital filter in what are called *lattice* or *ladder* structures [48]. Lattice/ladder filters have superior numerical properties relative to direct-form filter structures based on the difference equation. As a result, they can be very important for fixed-point implementations such as in custom VLSI or low-cost (fixed-point) signal processing chips. Lattice/ladder structures are also a good point of departure for *computational physical models* of acoustic systems such as vibrating strings, wind instrument bores, and the human vocal tract [81, 16, 48].

8.4.3   Testing Filter Stability in Matlab

Figure 8.6 gives a listing of a matlab function `stabilitycheck` for testing the stability of a digital filter using the Durbin step-down recursion. Figure 8.7 lists a main program for testing `stabilitycheck` against the more prosaic method of factoring the transfer-function denominator and measuring the pole radii. The Durbin recursion is far faster than the method based on root-finding.

```
function [stable] = stabilitycheck(A);

N = length(A)-1; % Order of A(z)
stable = 1;      % stable unless shown otherwise
A = A(:);        % make sure it's a column vector
for i=N:-1:1
  rci=A(i+1);
  if abs(rci) >= 1
    stable=0;
    return;
  end
  A = (A(1:i) - rci * A(i+1:-1:2))/(1-rci^2);
% disp(sprintf('A[%d]=',i)); A(1:i)'
end
```

Figure 8.6: Matlab function for testing digital filter stability by computing its reflection coefficients.

When run in Octave over Linux 2.4 on a 2.8 GHz Pentium PC, the Durbin recursion is approximately 140 times faster than brute-force root-finding, as measured by the program listed in Fig. 8.7.

```
% TSC - test function stabilitycheck, comparing against
%        pole radius computation

N = 200; % polynomial order
M = 20; % number of random polynomials to generate
disp('Random polynomial test');
nunstp = 0; % count of unstable A polynomials
sctime = 0; % total time in stabilitycheck()
rftime = 0; % total time computing pole radii
for pol=1:M
  A = [1; rand(N,1)]'; % random polynomial
  tic;
  stable = stabilitycheck(A);
  et=toc;  % Typ. 0.02 sec Octave/Linux, 2.8GHz Pentium
  sctime = sctime + et;
  % Now do it the old fashioned way
  tic;
  poles = roots(A); % system poles
  pr = abs(poles);  % pole radii
  unst = (pr >= 1); % bit vector
  nunst = sum(unst);% number of unstable poles
  et=toc; % Typ. 2.9 sec Octave/Linux, 2.8GHz Pentium
  rftime = rftime + et;
  if stable, nunstp = nunstp + 1; end
  if (stable & nunst>0) | (~stable & nunst==0)
    error('*** stabilitycheck() and poles DISAGREE ***');
  end
end
disp(sprintf(...
      ['Out of %d random polynomials of order %d,',...
        ' %d were unstable'], M,N,nunstp));
```

Figure 8.7: Test program (matlab) for function stabilitycheck.

8.5 Bandwidth of One Pole

A typical formula relating *3-dB bandwidth* B (in Hz) to the pole radius $R \in [0, 1)$ is

$$\boxed{R = e^{-\pi B T}} \tag{8.7}$$

where T denotes the sampling interval as usual. Solving for B gives

$$B = -\frac{\ln(R)}{\pi T}.$$

In §E.6 on page 326 (see also §B.1.3 on page 261), it is shown that B is the *3-dB bandwidth* or *half-power bandwidth*, in the limit, as the sampling rate goes to infinity.

8.6 Time Constant of One Pole

A useful approximate formula giving the *decay time-constant*[5] τ (in seconds) in terms of a pole radius $R \in [0, 1)$ is

$$\boxed{\tau \approx \frac{T}{1 - R}} \tag{8.8}$$

where T denotes the sampling interval in seconds, and we assume $T \ll \tau$.

The exact relation between τ and R is obtained by sampling an exponential decay:

$$e^{-t/\tau} \;\rightarrow\; e^{-nT/\tau} \;\overset{\Delta}{=}\; R^n$$

Thus, setting $n = 1$ yields

$$R = e^{-T/\tau}.$$

Expanding the right-hand side in a Taylor series and neglecting terms higher than first order gives

$$e^{-\frac{T}{\tau}} = 1 - \frac{T}{\tau} + \frac{1}{2!}\left(\frac{T}{\tau}\right)^2 - +\frac{1}{3!}\left(\frac{T}{\tau}\right)^3 + \cdots \approx 1 - \frac{T}{\tau},$$

which derives $R \approx 1 - T/\tau$. Solving for τ then gives Eq. (8.8). From its derivation, we see that the approximation is valid for $T \ll \tau$. Thus, as long as the impulse response of a pole p "rings" for many samples, the

---

[5]Decay time constants were introduced in Book I [84] of this series ("Exponentials"). The *time constant* τ is formally defined for exponential decays as the time it takes to decay by the factor $1/e$. In audio signal processing, exponential decay times are normally defined instead as t_{60} or t_{40}, etc., where t_{60}, *e.g.*, is the time to decay by 60 dB. A quick calculation reveals that t_{60} is a little less than seven time constants ($t_{60} \approx 6.91\tau$).

formula $\tau \approx T/(1 - |p|)$ should well estimate the time-constant of decay in seconds. The time-constant estimate in *samples* is of course $1/(1 - |p|)$. For higher-order systems, the approximate decay time is $1/(1 - R_{\max})$, where $R_{\max}$ is the largest pole magnitude (closest to the unit circle) in the (stable) system.

8.7   Unstable Poles—Unit Circle Viewpoint

We saw in §8.4 on page 184 that an LTI filter is stable if and only if all of its poles are strictly inside the unit circle ($|z| = 1$) in the complex z plane. In particular, a pole p outside the unit circle ($|p| > 1$) gives rise to an impulse-response component proportional to p^n which grows exponentially over time n. We also saw in §6.2 on page 123 that the z transform of a growing exponential does not not converge on the unit circle in the z plane. However, this was the case for a *causal* exponential $u(n)p^n$, where $u(n)$ is the unit-step function (which switches from 0 to 1 at time 0). If the same exponential is instead *anticausal*, *i.e.*, of the form $u(-n)p^n$, then, as we'll see in this section, its z transform does exist on the unit circle, and the pole is in exactly the same place as in the causal case. Therefore,to unambiguously invert a z transform, we must know its *region of convergence*. The critical question is whether the region of convergence includes the unit circle: If it does, then each pole outside the unit circle corresponds to an anticausal, finite energy, exponential, while each pole inside corresponds to the usual causal decaying exponential.

8.7.1   Geometric Series

The essence of the situation can be illustrated using a simple geometric series. Let R be any real (or complex) number. Then we have

$$\frac{1}{1 - R} = 1 + R + R^2 + R^3 + \cdots \quad < \infty \quad \text{when} \quad |R| < 1.$$

In other words, the geometric series $1 + R + R^2 + R^3 + \cdots$ is guaranteed to be summable when $|R| < 1$, and in that case, the sum is given by $1/(1 - R)$. On the other hand, if $|R| > 1$, we can rewrite $1/(1 - R)$ as $-R^{-1}/(1 - R^{-1})$ to obtain

$$\frac{1}{1 - R} = \frac{-R^{-1}}{1 - R^{-1}} = -R^{-1}\left[1 + R^{-1} + R^{-2} + R^{-3} + \cdots\right]$$

which is summable when $|R| > 1$. Thus, $1/(1 - R)$ is a valid closed-form sum whether or not $|R|$ is less than or greater than 1. When $|R| < 1$, it is the sum of the causal geometric series in powers of R. When $|R| > 1$, it is the sum of the causal geometric series in powers of R^{-1}, *or*, an anticausal geometric series in (negative) powers of R.

8.7.2 One-Pole Transfer Functions

We can apply the same analysis to a one-pole transfer function. Let $p \in \mathbf{C}$ denote any real or complex number:

$$H(z) = \frac{1}{1 - pz^{-1}} = 1 + pz^{-1} + pz^{-2} + pz^{-3} + \cdots$$

The convergence criterion is now $|pz^{-1}| < 1$, or $|z| > |p|$. For the region of convergence to include the unit circle (our frequency axis), we must have $|p| < 1$, which is our usual stability criterion for a pole at $z = p$. The inverse z transform is then the causal decaying sampled exponential

$$H(z) \longleftrightarrow h(n) = u(n)p^n$$

Now consider the rewritten case:

$$
\begin{aligned}
\frac{1}{1 - pz^{-1}} &= \frac{-p^{-1}z}{1 - p^{-1}z} \\
&= -p^{-1}z \left[1 + p^{-1}z + p^{-2}z^2 + p^{-3}z^3 + \cdots\right] \\
&= -\left[p^{-1}z + p^{-2}z^2 + p^{-3}z^3 + p^{-4}z^4 + \cdots\right] \\
&\leftrightarrow -u(-n-1)p^n, \quad n \in \mathbf{Z}
\end{aligned}
$$

where the inverse z transform is the inverse *bilateral* z transform. In this case, the convergence criterion is $|p^{-1}z| < 1$, or $|z| < |p|$, and this region includes the unit circle when $|p| > 1$.

In summary, when the region-of-convergence of the z transform is assumed to include the unit circle of the z plane, poles inside the unit circle correspond to stable, causal, decaying exponentials, while poles outside the unit circle correspond to anticausal exponentials that decay toward time $-\infty$, and stop before time zero.

Figure 8.8 illustrates the two types of exponentials (causal and anticausal) that correspond to poles (inside and outside the unit circle) when the z transform region of convergence is defined to include the unit circle.

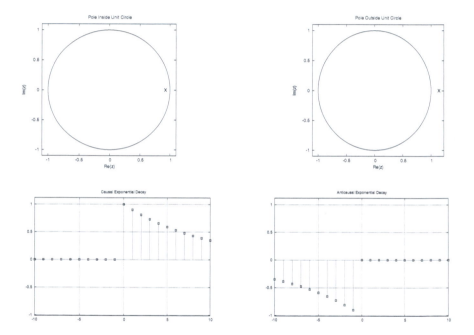

Figure 8.8: Left column: Causal exponential decay, pole at $p = 0.9$. Right column: Anticausal exponential decay, pole at $p = 1/0.9$. Top: Pole-zero diagram. Bottom: Corresponding impulse response, assuming the region of convergence includes the unit circle in the z plane.

8.8   Poles and Zeros of the Cepstrum

The *complex cepstrum* of a sequence $h(n)$ is typically defined as the inverse Fourier transform of its log spectrum [60]

$$\tilde{h}(n) \triangleq \frac{1}{2\pi} \int_{-\pi}^{\pi} \ln[H(e^{j\omega})]e^{j\omega n} d\omega,$$

where $\ln(x)$ denotes the natural logarithm (base e) of x, and $H(e^{j\omega})$ denotes the Fourier transform (DTFT) of $h(n)$,

$$H(e^{j\omega}) \triangleq \sum_{n=-\infty}^{\infty} h(n)e^{-j\omega n}.$$

(The *real cepstrum*, in contrast, is the inverse Fourier transform of the log-*magnitude* spectrum.) An equivalent definition (when the DTFT exists) is to define the complex cepstrum of h as the inverse z transform of $\ln H(z)$. The cepstrum has numerous applications in digital signal processing including speech modeling [60] and pitch detection [34]. In §11.7 on page 240, we use the cepstrum to compute minimum-phase spectra corresponding to a given spectral magnitude—an important tool in digital filter design.

From Eq. (8.2) on page 175, the log z transform can be written in terms of the factored form as

$$
\begin{aligned}
\ln H(z) &= \ln(g) \\
&\quad + \ln(1 - q_1 z^{-1}) + \ln(1 - q_2 z^{-1}) + \cdots + \ln(1 - q_M z^{-1}) \\
&\quad - \ln(1 - p_1 z^{-1}) - \ln(1 - p_2 z^{-1}) - \cdots - \ln(1 - p_N z^{-1}) \\
&= \ln(g) + \sum_{m=1}^{M} \ln(1 - q_m z^{-1}) - \sum_{n=1}^{N} \ln(1 - p_n z^{-1}) \\
&= \ln(g) - \sum_{m=1}^{M} \ln\left(\frac{1}{1 - q_m z^{-1}}\right) + \sum_{n=1}^{N} \ln\left(\frac{1}{1 - p_n z^{-1}}\right), \quad (8.9)
\end{aligned}
$$

where q_m denotes the mth zero and p_n denotes the nth pole of the z transform $H(z)$. Applying the Maclaurin series expansion

$$\ln\left(\frac{1}{1-x}\right) = x + \frac{x^2}{2} + \frac{x^3}{3} + \cdots + \frac{x^k}{k} + \cdots, \qquad |x| < 1,$$

we have that each pole and zero term in Eq. (8.9) may be expanded as

$$\ln\left(\frac{1}{1 - q_i z^{-1}}\right) = \sum_{n=1}^{\infty} \frac{q_i^n}{n} z^{-n}, \qquad |z| > |q_i|$$

$$\ln\left(\frac{1}{1 - p_i z^{-1}}\right) = \sum_{n=1}^{\infty} \frac{p_i^n}{n} z^{-n}, \qquad |z| > |p_i|.$$

Since the region of convergence of the z transform must include the unit circle (where the spectrum (DTFT) is defined), we see that the Maclaurin expansion gives us the inverse z transform of all terms of Eq. (8.9) corresponding to poles and zeros *inside* the unit circle of the z plane. Since the poles must be inside the unit circle anyway for stability, this restriction is normally not binding for the poles. However, zeros outside the unit circle— so-called "non-minimum-phase zeros"—are used quite often in practice.

For a zero (or pole) outside the unit circle, we may rewrite the corresponding term of Eq. (8.9) as

$$\ln\left(\frac{1}{1 - q_i z^{-1}}\right) = \ln\left(\frac{q_i^{-1} z}{q_i^{-1} z - 1}\right) = \ln\left(\frac{-z}{q_i}\right) + \ln\left(\frac{1}{1 - q_i^{-1} z}\right)$$

$$= \ln\left(\frac{-z}{q_i}\right) + \sum_{n=1}^{\infty} \frac{q_i^{-n}}{n} z^n, \qquad |z| < |q_i^{-1}|,$$

where we used the Maclaurin series expansion for $\ln(1/(1 - x))$ once again with the region of convergence including the unit circle. The infinite sum in this expansion is now the bilateral z transform of an *anticausal* sequence, as discussed in §8.7. That is, the time-domain sequence is zero for nonnegative times ($n \geq 0$) and the sequence decays in the direction of time minus-infinity. The factored-out terms $-z/q_i$ and $-z/p_i$, for all poles and zeros outside the unit circle, can be collected together and associated with the overall gain factor g in Eq. (8.9), resulting in a modified scaling and time-shift for the original sequence $h(n)$ which can be dealt with separately [60].

When all poles and zeros are inside the unit circle, the complex cepstrum is *causal* and can be expressed simply in terms of the filter poles and zeros as

$$\tilde{h}(n) = \begin{cases} \ln(g), & n = 0 \\ \displaystyle\sum_{i=1}^{N} \frac{p_i^n}{n} - \sum_{k=1}^{M} \frac{q_k^n}{n}, & n = 1, 2, 3, \ldots, \end{cases}$$

where N is the number of poles and M is the number of zeros. Note that when $N > M$, there are really $N - M$ additional zeros at $z = 0$, but these contribute zero to the complex cepstrum (since $q_i = 0$). Similarly, when

$M > N$, there are $M - N$ additional poles at $z = 0$ which also contribute zero (since $p_i = 0$).

In summary, each stable pole contributes a *positive* decaying exponential (weighted by $1/n$) to the complex cepstrum, while each zero inside the unit circle contributes a *negative* weighted-exponential of the same type. The decaying exponentials start at time 1 and have unit amplitude (ignoring the $1/n$ weighting) in the sense that extrapolating them to time 0 (without the $1/n$ weighting) would use the values $p_i^0 = 1$ and $-q_i^0 = -1$. The decay rates are faster when the poles and zeros are well inside the unit circle, but cannot decay slower than $1/n$.

On the other hand, poles and zeros *outside* the unit circle contribute *anticausal* exponentials to the complex cepstrum, negative for the poles and positive for the zeros (see Problem 10 on page 197).

8.9   Conversion to Minimum Phase

As discussed in §11.7 on page 240, any spectrum can be converted to minimum-phase form (without affecting the spectral magnitude) by computing its cepstrum and replacing any anticausal components with corresponding causal components. In other words, the anticausal part of the cepstrum, if any, is "flipped" about time zero so that it adds to the causal part. Doing this corresponds to *reflecting* non-minimum phase zeros (and any unstable poles) inside the unit circle in a manner that preserves spectral magnitude. The original spectral phase is then replaced by the unique minimum phase corresponding to the given spectral magnitude.

A matlab listing for computing a minimum-phase spectrum from the magnitude spectrum is given in §J.11 on page 412.

8.10   Hilbert Transform Relations

Closely related to the cepstrum are the so-called *Hilbert transform relations* that relate the real and imaginary parts of the spectra of causal signals. In particular, for minimum-phase spectra, the cepstrum is causal, and this means that the log-magnitude and phase form a Hilbert-transform pair. Methods for designing allpass filters have been based on this relationship (see §B.2.2 on page 273). For more about cepstra and Hilbert transform relations, see [60].

8.11   Pole-Zero Analysis Problems

1. *Hum Cancellation:* Design a second-order filter which will completely reject 60 Hz hum, given a sampling rate of 40 KHz. How is the frequency response not ideal? What is a simple way to obtain a better frequency response at the price of higher filter order? (Hint: Consider $\lim_{M \to \infty} |\cos(\theta_c)|^M$.)

2. *Graphical Phase-Response Calculation:* Define

$$H_p(z) = -p \frac{1 - \frac{1}{p}z^{-1}}{1 - pz^{-1}}$$

   where p is a real number.

   (a) Find the *amplitude response* $G_p(\omega) \triangleq |H_p(e^{j\omega T})|$ as a function of ω and p.

   (b) Find the *phase response* $\Theta_p(\omega) \triangleq \angle H_p(e^{j\omega T})$ as a function of ω and p.

   (c) List all poles and zeros of $H_p(z)$.

   (d) Find the phase response of $H_p(z)$ *graphically* using its poles and zeros.

   (e) Find $H_0(z) = \lim_{p \to 0} H_p(z)$.

   (f) Find $\Theta_0(\omega) = \lim_{p \to 0} \Theta_p(\omega)$, assuming p approaches zero from the negative real axis, i.e., $p < 0$. Do this for both the analytical and graphical methods.

   (g) Find $\Theta_0(\omega) = \lim_{p \to 0} \Theta_p(\omega)$, assuming p approaches zero from the positive real axis, i.e., $p > 0$. Do this for both the analytical and graphical methods.

   (h) Explain why zeros at infinity can be ignored when computing the phase response of a digital filter using the graphical method.

3. *Direct-Form Coefficient-Stability Region:* For the two-pole filter $H(z) = 1/(1 + a_1 z^{-1} + a_2 z^{-2})$, find the set of direct-form coefficients a_1 and a_2 that yield a stable filter, and indicate this set the (a_1, a_2) plane. [Hint: One closed curve bounds the stability region.]

4. *Stability of Linearly Interpolated Direct-Form Filters:* For the two-pole filter $H(z) = 1/(1 + a_1 z^{-1} + a_2 z^{-2})$, when linearly interpolating the direct-form coefficients a_1 and a_2 from one stable setting to another, determine whether the intermediate filters are stable as well. [Hint: The result of the previous problem can be helpful here.]

5. Repeat the previous problem for the three-pole filter $H(z) = 1/(1 + a_1 z^{-1} + a_2 z^{-2} + a_3 z^{-3})$.

6. *Step-Down Recursion:* Derive the *step-down recursion* of Eq. (8.6) in detail, clearly showing all intermediate steps.

7. *Schur Recursion:* Define an Nth order allpass filter

$$S_N(z) \triangleq \frac{\tilde{A}_N(z)}{A_N(z)}$$

where $\tilde{A}_N(z)$ is defined in Eq. (8.5), and $A_N(z)$ is defined in Eq. (8.4). Find the analog of the *step-down recursion* (Eq. (8.6)) for producing an order $N - 1$ allpass filter, $S_{N-1}(z)$, given $S_N(z)$ and k_N.

8. *Allpass Nesting = Inverse Schur Recursion:* (a) Find the *inverse* of the Schur recursion found in the previous problem. (b) Show that it can be interpreted as *nesting allpass filters.* That is, show that $S_{m+1}(z)$ is created from $S_m(z)$ by taking the first-order allpass filter determined by the coefficient k_{m+1} and replacing its unit-sample delay(s) by $S_m(z)$. (c) Show that $S_{m+1}(z)$ is always a stable allpass filter, provided $S_m(z)$ is a stable allpass and $|k_{m+1}| < 1$.

9. In §8.5 on page 189, the bandwidth of a one-pole filter section (in Hz) was defined as $B = -\ln(R)/(\pi T)$, where R is the pole radius and T is the sampling interval in seconds. In §8.6, the time-constant of decay (in seconds) for the impulse-response of a one-pole filter was estimated to be $\tau \approx T/(1 - R)$. Using these formulas, find a formula giving τ in terms of B and a formula giving B in terms of τ.

10. *Complex Cepstrum:* For each of the z transforms below, find the corresponding complex cepstrum:

   (a) $H(z) = \frac{1 - \frac{1}{2} z^{-1}}{1 - \frac{1}{3} z^{-1}}$

   (b) $H(z) = -z^{-1}$

   (c) $H(z) = \frac{1 - 2z^{-1}}{1 - 3z^{-1}}$

   (d) $H(z) = \frac{\left(1 - \frac{1}{2} z^{-1}\right)\left(1 - 2z^{-1}\right)}{\left(1 - \frac{1}{3} z^{-1}\right)(1 - 3z^{-1})}$

Chapter 9

Implementation Structures for Recursive Digital Filters

This chapter introduces the four direct-form filter implementations, and discusses implementation of filters as parallel or series combinations of smaller filter sections. A careful study of filter forms can be important when *numerical issues* arise, such as when implementing a digital filter in a *fixed-point* processor. (The least expensive "DSP chips" use fixed-point numerical processing, sometimes with only a 16-bit word length in low-cost audio applications.) For implementations in floating-point arithmetic, especially at 32-bit word-lengths or greater, the choice of filter implementation structure is usually not critical. In matlab software, for example, one rarely uses anything but the `filter` function, which is implemented in double-precision floating point (typically 64 bits at the time of this writing, and more bits internally in the floating-point unit).

9.1   The Four Direct Forms

9.1.1   Direct-Form I

As mentioned in §5.5 on page 100, the difference equation

$$y(n) \;=\; b_0 x(n) + b_1 x(n-1) + \cdots + b_M x(n-M)$$
$$-a_1 y(n-1) - \cdots - a_N y(n-N)$$

$$= \sum_{i=0}^{M} b_i x(n-i) - \sum_{j=1}^{N} a_j y(n-j) \qquad (9.1)$$

specifies the *Direct-Form I* (DF-I) implementation of a digital filter [60]. The DF-I signal flow graph for the second-order case is shown in Fig. 9.1.

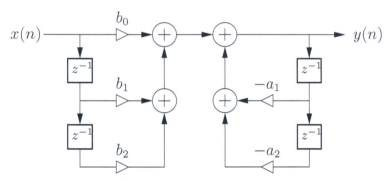

Figure 9.1: Direct-Form-I implementation of a 2nd-order digital filter.

The DF-I structure has the following properties:

1. It can be regarded as a two-zero filter section followed in series by a two-pole filter section.

2. In most *fixed-point* arithmetic schemes (such as two's complement, the most commonly used [84][1]) there is *no possibility of internal filter overflow*. That is, since there is fundamentally only one summation point in the filter, and since fixed-point overflow naturally "wraps around" from the largest positive to the largest negative number and vice versa, then as long as the final result $y(n)$ is "in range", overflow is avoided, even when there is overflow of intermediate results in the sum (see below for an example). This is an important, valuable, and unusual property of the DF-I filter structure.

[1]http://ccrma.stanford.edu/~jos/mdft/Two_s_Complement_Fixed_Point_Format.html

3. There are twice as many delays as are necessary. As a result, the DF-I structure is *not canonical with respect to delay*. In general, it is always possible to implement an Nth-order filter using only N delay elements.

4. As is the case with all direct-form filter structures (those which have coefficients given by the transfer-function coefficients), the filter poles and zeros can be very sensitive to round-off errors in the filter coefficients. This is usually not a problem for a simple second-order section, such as in Fig. 9.1, but it can become a problem for higher order direct-form filters. This is the same numerical sensitivity that polynomial roots have with respect to polynomial-coefficient round-off. As is well known, the sensitivity tends to be larger when the roots are clustered closely together, as opposed to being well spread out in the complex plane [18, p. 246]. To minimize this sensitivity, it is common to factor filter transfer functions into series and/or parallel second-order sections, as discussed in §9.2 below.

It is a very useful property of the direct-form I implementation that it cannot overflow internally in two's complement fixed-point arithmetic: As long as the output signal is in range, the filter will be free of numerical overflow. Most IIR filter implementations do not have this property. While DF-I is immune to internal overflow, it should not be concluded that it is always the best choice of implementation. Other forms to consider include *parallel and series second-order sections* (§9.2 below), and *normalized ladder forms* [32, 48, 86].[2] Also, we'll see that the *transposed direct-form II* (Fig. 9.4 on page 205 below) is a strong contender as well.

Two's Complement Wrap-Around

In this section, we give an example showing how *temporary* overflow in two's complement fixed-point causes no ill effects.

In 3-bit signed fixed-point arithmetic, the available numbers are as shown in Table 9.1.

Let's perform the sum $3 + 3 - 4 = 2$, which gives a temporary overflow ($3 + 3 = 6$, which wraps around to -2), but a final result (2) which is in

---

[2]http://ccrma.stanford.edu/~jos/pasp/Conventional_Ladder_Filters.html

Decimal	Binary
-4	100
-3	101
-2	110
-1	111
0	000
1	001
2	010
3	011

Table 9.1: Three-bit two's-complement binary fixed-point numbers.

the allowed range $[-4, 3]$:[3]

$$011 + 011 \quad = \quad 110 \qquad (3 + 3 = -2 \ (\text{mod } 8))$$
$$110 + 100 \quad = \quad 010 \qquad (-2 - 4 = 2 \ (\text{mod } 8))$$

Now let's do $1 + 3 - 2 = 2$ in three-bit two's complement:

$$001 + 011 \quad = \quad 100 \qquad (1 + 3 = -4 \ (\text{mod } 8))$$
$$100 + 110 \quad = \quad 010 \qquad (-4 - 2 = 2 \ (\text{mod } 8))$$

In both examples, the intermediate result overflows, but the final result is correct. Another way to state what happened is that a *positive* wrap-around in the first addition is canceled by a *negative* wrap-around in the second addition.

9.1.2   Direct Form II

The signal flow graph for the Direct-Form-II (DF-II) realization of the second-order IIR filter section is shown in Fig. 9.2.

The difference equation for the second-order DF-II structure can be written as

$$v(n) \quad = \quad x(n) - a_1 v(n-1) - a_2 v(n-2)$$
$$y(n) \quad = \quad b_0 v(n) + b_1 v(n-1) + b_2 v(n-2)$$

which can be interpreted as a two-pole filter followed in series by a two-zero filter. This contrasts with the DF-I structure of the previous section

---

[3]The notation "(mod 8)" is an abbreviation for "modulo 8" commonly used in the branch of mathematics known as *number theory.*. Two integers m and n are said to be equal modulo M if there exists an integer k such that $m = n + kM$. Thus, 6 is equal to -2 modulo 8 because $6 = -2 + 8$. These integers are also equal (mod 8) to 14, -10, 22, -18, and so on.

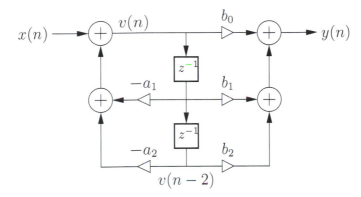

Figure 9.2: Direct-Form-II implementation of a 2nd-order digital filter.

(diagrammed in Fig. 9.1 on page 200) in which the two-zero FIR section precedes the two-pole recursive section in series. Since LTI filters in series *commute* (§6.7 on page 129), we may reverse this ordering and implement an all-pole filter followed by an FIR filter in series. In other words, the zeros may come first, followed by the poles, without changing the transfer function. When this is done, it is easy to see that the delay elements in the two filter sections contain the same numbers (see Fig. 5.1 on page 99). As a result, a single delay line can be *shared* between the all-pole and all-zero (FIR) sections. This new combined structure is called "direct form II" [60, p. 153–155]. The second-order case is shown in Fig. 9.2. It specifies exactly the same digital filter as shown in Fig. 9.1 in the case of infinite-precision numerical computations.

In summary, the DF-II structure has the following properties:

1. It can be regarded as a two-pole filter section followed by a two-zero filter section.

2. It is *canonical with respect to delay*. This happens because delay elements associated with the two-pole and two-zero sections are *shared*.

3. In fixed-point arithmetic, overflow can occur at the delay-line input (output of the leftmost summer in Fig. 9.2), unlike in the DF-I implementation.

4. As with all direct-form filter structures, the poles and zeros are sensitive to round-off errors in the coefficients a_i and b_i, especially for high transfer-function orders. Lower sensitivity is obtained using series low-order sections (*e.g.*, second order), or by using ladder or lattice filter structures [86].

More about Potential Internal Overflow of DF-II

Since the poles come first in the DF-II realization of an IIR filter, the signal entering the state delay-line (see Fig. 9.2) typically requires a larger dynamic range than the output signal $y(n)$. In other words, it is common for the feedback portion of a DF-II IIR filter to provide a large signal *boost* which is then compensated by *attenuation* in the feedforward portion (the zeros). As a result, if the input dynamic range is to remain unrestricted, the two delay elements may need to be implemented with high-order *guard bits* to accommodate an extended dynamic range. If the number of bits in the delay elements is doubled (which still does not guarantee impossibility of internal overflow), the benefit of halving the number of delays relative to the DF-I structure is approximately canceled. In other words, the DF-II structure, which is canonical with respect to delay, may require just as much or more memory as the DF-I structure, even though the DF-I uses twice as many addressable delay elements for the filter state memory.

9.1.3   Transposed Direct-Forms

The remaining two direct forms are obtained by formally *transposing* direct-forms I and II [60, p. 155]. Filter transposition may also be called *flow graph reversal*, and transposing a Single-Input, Single-Output (SISO) filter does not alter its transfer function. This fact can be derived as a consequence of *Mason's gain formula* for signal flow graphs [49, 50] or *Tellegen's theorem* (which implies that an LTI signal flow graph is *interreciprocal* with its transpose) [60, pp. 176–177]. Transposition of filters in state-space form is discussed in §G.5 on page 351.

The *transpose* of a SISO digital filter is quite straightforward to find: *Reverse the direction of all signal paths, and make obviously necessary accommodations.* "Obviously necessary accommodations" include changing signal branch-points to summers, and summers to branch-points. Also, after this operation, the input signal, normally drawn on the left of the signal flow graph, will be on the right, and the output on the left. To renormalize the layout, the whole diagram is usually left-right flipped.

Figure 9.3 shows the *Transposed-Direct-Form-I* (TDF-I) structure for the general second-order IIR digital filter, and Fig. 9.4 shows the *Transposed-Direct-Form-II* (TDF-II) structure. To facilitate comparison of the transposed with the original, the inputs and output signals remain "switched", so that signals generally flow right-to-left instead of the usual left-to-right. (**Exercise:** Derive forms TDF-I/II by transposing the DF-I/II structures shown in Figures 9.1 and 9.2.)

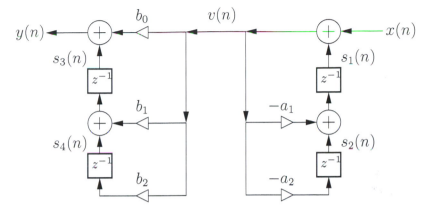

Figure 9.3: Transposed-Direct-Form-I implementation of a second-order IIR digital filter. Note that the input signal comes in from the right, and the output is on the left. Compare to Fig. 9.1 on page 200. The four "state variable" signals are labeled arbitrarily as $s_1(n)$ through $s_4(n)$.

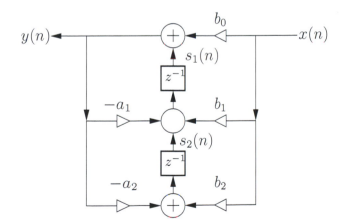

Figure 9.4: Transposed-Direct-Form-II implementation of a second-order IIR digital filter (input on the right, output on the left). Compare to Fig. 9.2 on page 203.

9.1.4   Numerical Robustness of TDF-II

An advantage of the transposed direct-form II structure (depicted in Fig. 9.4) is that the zeros effectively precede the poles in series order. As mentioned above, in many digital filters design, the poles by themselves give a large gain at some frequencies, and the zeros often provide compensating attenuation. This is especially true of filters with sharp transitions in their frequency response, such as the elliptic-function-filter example on page 157; in such filters, the sharp transitions are achieved using near pole-zero cancellations close to the unit circle in the z plane.[4]

---

[4]To plot the poles and zeros for the example of §7.5.2 on page 157, one can say (in matlab) `plot(roots(B),'o',roots(A),'x')` — or say `help zplane`.

9.2   Series and Parallel Filter Sections

In many situations it is better to implement a digital filter $H(z)$ in terms of first- and/or second-order *elementary sections*, either in *series* or in *parallel*. In particular, such an implementation may have numerical advantages. In the time-varying case, it is easier to control fundamental parameters of small sections, such as pole frequencies, by means of coefficient variations.

9.2.1   Series Second-Order Sections

For many filter types, such as lowpass, highpass, and bandpass filters, a good choice of implementation structure is often *series second-order sections*. In fixed-point applications, the ordering of the sections can be important.

The matlab function `tf2sos`[5] converts from "transfer function form", $H(z) = B(z)/A(z)$, to series "second-order-section" form. For example, the line

```
BAMatrix = tf2sos(B,A);
```

converts the real filter specified by polynomial vectors `B` and `A` to a series of second-order sections (biquads) specified by the rows of `BAMatrix`. Each row of `BAMatrix` is of the form $[b_0, b_1, b_2, 1, a_1, a_2]$. The function `tf2sos` may be implemented simply as a call to `tf2zp` followed by a call to `zp2sos`, where the `zp` form of a digital filter consists of its (possibly complex) zeros, poles, and an overall gain factor:

```
function [sos,g] = tf2sos(B,A)
[z,p,g]=tf2zp(B(:)',A(:)'); % Direct form to (zeros,poles,gain)
sos=zp2sos(z,p,g); % (z,p,g) to series second-order sections
```

Matlab Example

The following matlab example expands the filter

$$H(z) = \frac{B(z)}{A(z)} = \frac{1 + z^{-5}}{1 + 0.9z^{-5}}$$

---

[5]In Matlab, the Signal Processing Toolbox is required for second-order section support. In Octave, the free Octave-Forge add-on collection is required.

into a series of second order sections:

```
B=[1 0 0 0 0 1];
A=[1 0 0 0 0 .9];
[sos,g] = tf2sos(B,A)
sos =
     1.00000    0.61803    1.00000    1.00000    0.60515    0.95873
     1.00000   -1.61803    1.00000    1.00000   -1.58430    0.95873
     1.00000    1.00000   -0.00000    1.00000    0.97915   -0.00000

g = 1
```

The g parameter is an input (or output) scale factor; for this filter, it was not needed. Thus, in this example we obtained the following filter factorization:

$$
\begin{aligned}
H(z) &\triangleq \frac{1 + z^{-5}}{1 + 0.9z^{-5}} \\
&= \left(\frac{1 + 0.61803z^{-1} + z^{-2}}{1 + 0.60515z^{-1} + 0.95873z^{-2}} \right) \left(\frac{1 - 1.61803z^{-1} + z^{-2}}{1 - 1.58430z^{-1} + 0.95873z^{-2}} \right) \\
&\quad \left(\frac{1 + z^{-1}}{1 + 0.97915z^{-1}} \right)
\end{aligned}
$$

Note that the first two sections are second-order, while the third is first-order (when coefficients are rounded to five digits of precision after the decimal point).

In addition to tf2sos, tf2zp, and zp2sos discussed above, there are also functions sos2zp and sos2tf, which do the obvious conversion in both Matlab and Octave.[6] The sos2tf function can be used to check that the second-order factorization is accurate:

```
% Numerically challenging "clustered roots" example:
[B,A] = zp2tf(ones(10,1),0.9*ones(10,1),1);
[sos,g] = tf2sos(B,A);
[Bh,Ah] = sos2tf(sos,g);
format long;
disp(sprintf('Relative L2 numerator error: %g',...
norm(Bh-B)/norm(B)));
% Relative L2 numerator error: 1.26558e-15
disp(sprintf('Relative L2 denominator error: %g',...
norm(Ah-A)/norm(A)));
% Relative L2 denominator error: 1.65594e-15
```

---

[6]The Matlab Signal Processing Toolbox has even more sos functions—say "lookfor sos" in Matlab to find them all.

Thus, in this test, the original direct-form filter is compared with one created from the second-order sections. Such checking should be done for high-order filters, or filters having many poles and/or zeros close together, because the polynomial factorization used to find the poles and zeros can fail numerically. Moreover, the stability of the factors should be checked individually.

9.2.2   Parallel First and/or Second-Order Sections

Instead of breaking up a filter into a *series* of second-order sections, as discussed in the previous section, we can break the filter up into a *parallel sum* of first and/or second-order sections. Parallel sections are based directly on the *partial fraction expansion* (PFE) of the filter transfer function discussed in §6.8 on page 129. As discussed in §6.8.3, there is additionally an *FIR part* when the order of the transfer-function denominator does not exceed that of the numerator (*i.e.*, when the transfer function is not *strictly proper*). The most general case of a PFE, valid for any finite-order transfer function, was given by Eq. (6.19) on page 142, repeated here for convenience:

$$H(z) = F(z) + z^{-(K+1)} \sum_{i=1}^{N_p} \sum_{k=1}^{m_k} \frac{r_{i,k}}{(1 - p_i z^{-1})^k} \tag{9.2}$$

where N_p denotes the number of distinct poles, and $m_i \geq 1$ denotes the multiplicity of the ith pole. The polynomial $F(z)$ is the transfer function of the FIR part, as discussed in §6.8.3.

The FIR part $F(z)$ is typically realized as a tapped delay line, as shown in Fig. 5.5 on page 110.

First-Order Complex Resonators

For distinct poles, the recursive terms in the complete partial fraction expansion of Eq. (9.2) can be realized as a parallel sum of *complex* one-pole filter sections, thereby producing a *parallel complex resonator* filter bank. Complex resonators are efficient for processing complex input signals, and they are especially easy to work with. Note that a complex resonator bank is similarly obtained by implementing a diagonalized state-space model [Eq. (G.22) on page 366].

Real Second-Order Sections

In practice, however, signals are typically real-valued functions of time. As a result, for real filters (§5.1), it is typically more efficient computationally to combine complex-conjugate one-pole sections together to form real second-order sections (two poles and one zero each, in general). This process was discussed in §6.8.1 on page 131, and the resulting transfer function of each second-order section becomes

$$\frac{r}{1 - pz^{-1}} + \frac{\bar{r}}{1 - \bar{p}z^{-1}} = \frac{r - r\bar{p}z^{-1} + \bar{r} - \bar{r}pz^{-1}}{(1 - pz^{-1})(1 - \bar{p}z^{-1})}$$

$$= \frac{2\text{re}\{r\} - 2\text{re}\{r\bar{p}\}z^{-1}}{1 - 2\text{re}\{p\}z^{-1} + |p|^2 z^{-2}}, \qquad (9.3)$$

where p is one of the poles, and r is its corresponding residue. This is a special case of the *biquad section* discussed in §B.1.6 on page 269.

When the two poles of a real second-order section are complex, they form a complex-conjugate pair, *i.e.*, they are located at $z = R\exp(\pm j\theta)$ in the z plane, where $R = |p|$ is the modulus of either pole, and θ is the angle of either pole. In this case, the "resonance-tuning coefficient" in Eq. (9.3) can be expressed as

$$2\text{re}\{p\} = 2R\cos(\theta)$$

which is often more convenient for real-time control of resonance tuning and/or bandwidth. A more detailed derivation appears in §B.1.3 on page 258.

Figures 3.25 and 3.26 (p. 79) illustrate filter realizations consisting of one first-order and two second-order filter sections in parallel.

Implementation of Repeated Poles

Fig. 9.5 illustrates an efficient implementation of terms due to a repeated pole with multiplicity three, contributing the additive terms

$$\frac{r_1}{1 - pz^{-1}} + \frac{r_2}{(1 - pz^{-1})^2} + \frac{r_3}{(1 - pz^{-1})^3}$$

to the transfer function. Note that, using this approach, the total number of poles implemented equals the total number of poles of the system. For clarity, a single real (or complex) pole is shown. Implementing a repeated complex-conjugate pair as a repeated real second-order section is analogous.

9.2.3   Formant Filtering Example

In *speech synthesis* [27, 39], digital filters are often used to simulate *formant filtering* by the vocal tract. It is well known [23] that the different *vowel sounds* of speech can be simulated by passing a "buzz source" through a only two or three formant filters. As a result, speech is fully intelligible through the telephone bandwidth (nominally only 200-3200 Hz).

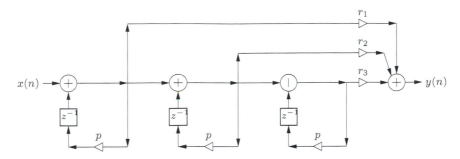

Figure 9.5: Implementation of a pole p repeated three times.

A *formant* is a *resonance* in the voice spectrum. A single formant may thus be modeled using one *biquad* (second-order filter section). For example, in the vowel [a] as in "father," the first three formant center-frequencies have been measured near 700, 1220, and 2600 Hz, with half-power bandwidths[7] 130, 70, and 160 Hz [40].

In principle, the formant filter sections are in *series*, as can be found by deriving the transfer function of an acoustic tube [48]. As a consequence, the vocal-tract transfer function is an all-pole filter (provided that the nasal tract is closed off or negligible). As a result, there is no need to specify *gains* for the formant resonators—only center-frequency and bandwidth are necessary to specify each formant, leaving only an overall scale factor unspecified in a cascade (series) formant filter bank.

Numerically, however, it makes more sense to implement disjoint resonances in *parallel* rather than in series.[8] This is because when one formant filter is resonating, the others will be attenuating, so that to achieve a particular peak-gain at resonance, the resonating filter must overcome all combined attenuations as well as applying its own gain. In fixed-point arithmetic, this can result in large quantization-noise gains, especially for the last resonator in the chain. As a result of these considerations, our example will implement the formant sections in parallel. This means we must find the appropriate biquad *numerators* so that when added together, the overall transfer-function numerator is a constant. This will be accomplished using the *partial fraction expansion* (§6.8).[9]

---

[7]See §E.6 on page 326 for a definition of half-power bandwidth.

[8]In this particular case, there is an even better structure known as a *ladder filter* that can be interpreted as a *physical model* of the vocal tract [48, 86].

[9]In practice, it is not critical to get the biquad numerators exactly right. In fact, the vowel still sounds ok if all the biquad numerators are set to 1, in which case, nulls are introduced between the formant resonances in the spectrum. The ear is not nearly as sensitive to spectral nulls as it is to spectral peaks. Furthermore, natural listening

The matlab below illustrates the construction of a parallel formant filter bank for simulating the vowel [a]. For completeness, it is used to filter a bandlimited impulse train, in order to synthesize the vowel sound.

```
F =   [700, 1220, 2600]; % Formant frequencies (Hz)
BW = [130,  70,  160];  % Formant bandwidths (Hz)
fs = 8192;              % Sampling rate (Hz)

nsecs = length(F);
R = exp(-pi*BW/fs);       % Pole radii
theta = 2*pi*F/fs;        % Pole angles
poles = R .* exp(j*theta); % Complex poles
B = 1;  A = real(poly([poles,conj(poles)]));
% freqz(B,A); % View frequency response:

% Convert to parallel complex one-poles (PFE):
[r,p,f] = residuez(B,A);
As = zeros(nsecs,3);
Bs = zeros(nsecs,3);
% complex-conjugate pairs are adjacent in r and p:
for i=1:2:2*nsecs
    k = 1+(i-1)/2;
    Bs(k,:) = [r(i)+r(i+1),  -(r(i)*p(i+1)+r(i+1)*p(i)), 0];
    As(k,:) = [1, -(p(i)+p(i+1)), p(i)*p(i+1)];
end
sos = [Bs,As]; % standard second-order-section form
iperr = norm(imag(sos))/norm(sos); % make sure sos is ~real
disp(sprintf('||imag(sos)||/||sos|| = %g',iperr)); % 1.6e-16
sos = real(sos) % and make it exactly real

% Reconstruct original numerator and denominator as a check:
[Bh,Ah] = psos2tf(sos); % parallel sos to transfer function
% psos2tf appears in the matlab-utilities appendix
disp(sprintf('||A-Ah|| = %g',norm(A-Ah))); % 5.77423e-15
% Bh has trailing epsilons, so we'll zero-pad B:
disp(sprintf('||B-Bh|| = %g',...
            norm([B,zeros(1,length(Bh)-length(B))] - Bh)));
% 1.25116e-15

% Plot overlay and sum of all three
% resonator amplitude responses:
```

environments introduce nulls quite often, such as when a direct signal is mixed with its own reflection from a flat surface (such as a wall or floor).

```
nfft=512;
H = zeros(nsecs+1,nfft);
for i=1:nsecs
  [Hiw,w] = freqz(Bs(i,:),As(i,:));
  H(1+i,:) = Hiw(:).';
end
H(1,:) = sum(H(2:nsecs+1,:));
ttl = 'Amplitude Response';
xlab = 'Frequency (Hz)';
ylab = 'Magnitude (dB)';
sym = '';
lgnd = {'sum','sec 1','sec 2', 'sec 3'};
np=nfft/2; % Only plot for positive frequencies
wp = w(1:np); Hp=H(:,1:np);
figure(1); clf;
myplot(wp,20*log10(abs(Hp)),sym,ttl,xlab,ylab,1,lgnd);
disp('PAUSING'); pause;
saveplot('../eps/lpcexovl.eps');

% Now synthesize the vowel [a]:
nsamps = 256;
f0 = 200; % Pitch in Hz
w0T = 2*pi*f0/fs; % radians per sample

nharm = floor((fs/2)/f0); % number of harmonics
sig = zeros(1,nsamps);
n = 0:(nsamps-1);
% Synthesize bandlimited impulse train
for i=1:nharm,
    sig = sig + cos(i*w0T*n);
end;
sig = sig/max(sig);
speech = filter(1,A,sig);
soundsc([sig,speech]); % hear buzz, then 'ah'
```

Notes:

- The sampling rate was chosen to be $f_s = 8192$ Hz because that is the default Matlab sampling rate, and because that is a typical value used for "telephone quality" speech synthesis.

- The **psos2tf** utility is listed in §J.7 on page 407.

- The overlay of the amplitude responses are shown in Fig. 9.6.

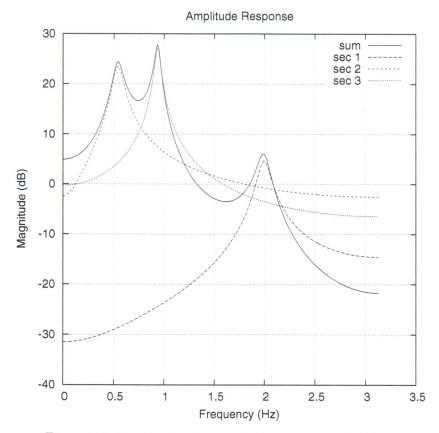

Figure 9.6: Overlay of section amplitude responses and their sum.

9.2.4   Butterworth Lowpass Filter Example

This example illustrates the design of a 5th-order Butterworth lowpass filter, implementing it using second-order sections. Since all three sections contribute to the same passband and stopband, it is numerically advisable to choose a *series* second-order-section implementation, so that their passbands and stopbands will multiply together instead of add.

```
fc = 1000; % Cut-off frequency (Hz)
fs = 8192; % Sampling rate (Hz)
order = 5; % Filter order
[B,A] = butter(order,2*fc/fs); % [0:pi] maps to [0:1] here
[sos,g] = tf2sos(B,A)
% sos =
%   1.00000   2.00080   1.00080   1.00000  -0.92223   0.28087
%   1.00000   1.99791   0.99791   1.00000  -1.18573   0.64684
%   1.00000   1.00129  -0.00000   1.00000  -0.42504   0.00000
%
% g = 0.0029714
%
% Compute and display the amplitude response
Bs = sos(:,1:3); % Section numerator polynomials
As = sos(:,4:6); % Section denominator polynomials
[nsec,temp] = size(sos);
nsamps = 256; % Number of impulse-response samples
% Note use of input scale-factor g here:
x = g*[1,zeros(1,nsamps-1)]; % SCALED impulse signal
for i=1:nsec
  x = filter(Bs(i,:),As(i,:),x); % Series sections
end
%
%plot(x); % Plot impulse response to make sure
          % it has decayed to zero (numerically)
%
% Plot amplitude response
% (in Octave - Matlab slightly different):
figure(2);
X=fft(x); % sampled frequency response
f = [0:nsamps-1]*fs/nsamps; grid('on');
axis([0 fs/2 -100 5]); legend('off');
plot(f(1:nsamps/2),20*log10(X(1:nsamps/2)));
```

The final plot appears in Fig. 9.7. A Matlab function for frequency response plots is given in §J.4 on page 401. (Of course, one can also use **freqz** in either Matlab or Octave, but that function uses subplots which are not easily printable in Octave.)

Note that the Matlab Signal Processing Toolbox has a function called `sosfilt` so that "`y=sosfilt(sos,x)`" will implement an array of second-order sections without having to unpack them first as in the example above.

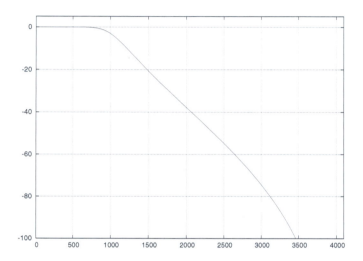

Figure 9.7: Measured amplitude response of three second-order sections (in series) implementing a 5th order Butterworth lowpass filter with half-power point at $f_c = 1$ kHz.

9.2.5   Summary of Series/Parallel Filter Sections

In summary, we noted above the following general guidelines regarding series vs. parallel elementary-section implementations:

- Series sections are preferred when all sections contribute to the *same passband*, such as in a lowpass, highpass, bandpass, or bandstop filter.

- Parallel sections are usually preferred when the sections have *disjoint passbands*, such as a formant filter bank used in voice models. Another example would be the *phase vocoder* filter bank [21].

9.3   Filter Structure Problems

1. (a) Draw the general first-order IIR digital filter in *direct-form II*.

   (b) Derive the *transpose* of this filter by reversing all the arrows and interchanging summers and branch-points as needed.

   (c) Derive the *transfer function* of the transposed DF-II first-order filter (show your work).

2. Draw the general TDF-I filter structure.

3. Derive the *difference equation* for the second-order TDF-I structure depicted in Fig. 9.3, using the signal labels shown in the figure.

4. Derive the *difference equation* for the second-order TDF-II structure depicted in Fig. 9.4, using the signal labels shown in the figure.

5. Derive the *difference equation* for the second-order TDF-I structure depicted in Fig. 9.3, using the signal labels shown in the figure.

6. Consider the following 9th-order digital filter having all nine zeros at $z = 1$ and all nine poles at $z = 0.9$:

   ```
   [B,A] = zp2tf(ones(10,1),0.9*ones(10,1),1);
   ```

   (a) Write matlab code to find the maximum relative error in the magnitudes of the zeros and poles:

   ```
   [z,p,g] = tf2zp(B,A);
   ```

   (b) Write matlab code to find the maximum relative error in the filter coefficients reconstructed from a series second-order factorization:

   ```
   [sos,g] = tf2sos(B,A);
   [Bh,Ah] = sos2tf(sos,g);
   ```

7. Find an example first-order real IIR digital filter having at least one coefficient with a nonzero imaginary part. In other words, find a filter transfer function having at least one necessarily complex coefficient that behaves as a real filter.

8. Consider a second-order digital allpass filter with poles located at $z = \pm g\, j$, $0 < g < 1$:

$$H(z) = \frac{g^2 + z^{-2}}{1 + g^2 z^{-2}}$$

   (a) Draw a realization of this filter in direct-form II (DF-II).

(b) Draw a realization of this filter in transposed DF-II (TDF-II).

(c) For a unit amplitude dc input signal (*i.e.*, the input signal is a constant, $x(n) = 1$ for all $n > 0$), Find the maximum internal amplitude in the DF-II structure (in the limit as $n \to \infty$).

(d) Repeat the previous problem for the TDF-II structure.

(e) Briefly discuss the meaning and implications of your results.

Chapter 10

Filters Preserving Phase

In this chapter, *linear phase* and *zero phase* filters are defined and discussed.

10.1 Linear-Phase Filters (Symmetric Impulse Responses)

A *linear-phase filter* is typically used when a *causal* filter is needed to modify a signal's magnitude-spectrum while preserving the signal's time-domain waveform as much as possible. Linear-phase filters have a *symmetric impulse response*, *e.g.*,

$$h(n) = h(N - 1 - n), \quad n = 0, 1, 2, \ldots, N - 1.$$

The symmetric-impulse-response constraint means that *linear-phase filters must be FIR filters*, because a causal recursive filter cannot have a symmetric impulse response (see Problem 3 on page 146).

We will show that every real symmetric impulse response corresponds to a *real* frequency response times a *linear phase term* $e^{-j\alpha\omega T}$, where $\alpha = (N-1)/2$ is the *slope* of the linear phase. Linear phase is often ideal because a filter phase of the form $\Theta(\omega) = -\alpha\omega T$ corresponds to phase delay

$$P(\omega) \triangleq -\frac{\Theta(\omega)}{\omega} = -\frac{-\alpha\omega T}{\omega} = \alpha T = \frac{(N - 1)T}{2}$$

and group delay

$$D(\omega) \triangleq -\frac{\partial}{\partial\omega}\Theta(\omega) = -\frac{\partial}{\partial\omega}\left(-\alpha\omega T\right) = \alpha T = \frac{(N - 1)T}{2}.$$

That is, both the phase and group delay of a linear-phase filter are equal to $(N - 1)/2$ samples of plain delay *at every frequency*. Since a length N FIR

filter implements $N - 1$ samples of delay, the value $(N - 1)/2$ is exactly
half the total filter delay. Delaying all frequency components by the same
amount *preserves the waveshape* as much as possible for a given amplitude
response.

10.2   Zero-Phase Filters
(Even Impulse Responses)

A *zero-phase filter* is a special case of a linear-phase filter in which the
phase slope is $\alpha = 0$. The real impulse response $h(n)$ of a zero-phase filter
is *even*.[1] That is, it satisfies

$$h(n) = h(-n), \quad n \in \mathbf{Z}$$

Note that every even signal is symmetric, but not every symmetric signal
is even. To be even, it must be symmetric about time 0.

A *zero-phase filter cannot be causal* (except in the trivial case when
the filter is a constant scale factor $h(n) = g\delta(n)$). However, in many "off-
line" applications, such as when filtering a sound file on a computer disk,
causality is not a requirement, and zero-phase filters are often preferred.

It is a well known Fourier symmetry that *real, even signals have real,
even Fourier transforms* [84]. Therefore,

> a real, even impulse response corresponds to a real,
> even frequency response.

This follows immediately from writing the DTFT of h in terms of a cosine
and sine transform:

$$H(e^{j\omega T}) = \text{DTFT}_{\omega T}(h) = \sum_{n=-\infty}^{\infty} h(n)\cos(\omega nT) - j \sum_{n=-\infty}^{\infty} h(n)\sin(\omega nT)$$

Since h is even, cosine is even, and sine is odd; and since even times even
is even, and even times odd is odd; and since the sum over an odd function
is zero, we have that

$$H(e^{j\omega T}) = \sum_{n=-\infty}^{\infty} h(n)\cos(\omega nT)$$

for any real, even impulse-response h. Thus, the frequency response $H(e^{j\omega T})$
is a real, even function of ω.

---

[1]In the complex case, the zero-phase impulse response is *Hermitian*, *i.e.*,
$h(n) = \overline{h(-n)}$.

A real frequency response has phase zero when it is positive, and phase π when it is negative. Therefore, we define a *zero-phase filter* as follows:

> A filter is said to be *zero phase* when its frequency response $H(e^{j\omega T})$ is a real and even function of radian frequency ω, and when $H(e^{j\omega T}) > 0$ in the filter passband(s).

Recall from §7.5.2 on page 157 that a *passband* is defined as a frequency band that is "passed" by the filter, *i.e.*, the filter is not designed to minimize signal amplitude in the band. For example, in a lowpass filter with cut-off frequency ω_c rad/s, the passband is $\omega \in [-\omega_c, \omega_c]$.

π-Phase Filters

Under our definition, a zero-phase filter always has a real, even impulse response $[h(n) = h(-n)]$, but not every real, even, impulse response is a zero-phase filter. For example, if $h(n)$ is zero phase, then $-h(n)$ is not; however, we could call $-h(n)$ a "π-phase filter" if we like (a zero-phase filter in series with a sign inversion).

Phase π in the Stopband

Practical zero-phase filters are zero-phase in their passbands, but may switch between 0 and π in their stopbands (as illustrated in the upcoming example of Fig. 10.2 on page 223). Thus, typical zero-phase filters are more precisely described as *piecewise constant-phase filters*, where the constant phase is 0 in all passbands, and π over various intervals within stopbands. Similarly, practical "linear phase" filters are typically truly linear phase across their passbands, but typically exhibit discontinuities by π radians in their stopband(s). As long as the stopbands are negligible, which is the goal by definition, the π-phase regions can be neglected completely.

10.2.1   Example Zero-Phase Filter Design

Figure 10.1 shows the impulse response and frequency response of a length 11 zero-phase FIR lowpass filter designed using the Remez exchange algorithm.[2] The matlab code for designing this filter is as follows:

```
N = 11;                    % filter length - must be odd
b = [0 0.1 0.2 0.5]*2;     % band edges
M = [1  1   0   0 ];       % desired band values
h = remez(N-1,b,M);        % Remez multiple exchange design
```

The impulse response h is returned in linear-phase form, so it must be left-shifted $(N - 1)/2 = 5$ samples to make it zero phase.

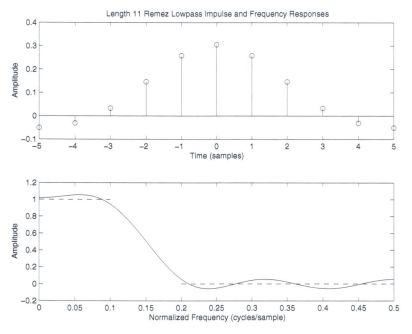

Figure 10.1: Impulse response and frequency response of a length 11 zero-phase FIR lowpass filter. Note that the frequency response is real because the filter is zero phase. Also plotted (in dashed lines) are the desired passband and stopband gains.

---

[2]The **remez** function is implemented in the Matlab Signal Processing Toolbox and in the Octave Forge collection.

Figure 10.2 shows the amplitude and phase responses of the FIR filter designed by remez. The phase response is zero throughout the passband and transition band. However, each zero-crossing in the stopband results in a phase jump of π radians, so that the phase alternates between zero and π in the stopband. This is typical of practical zero-phase filters.

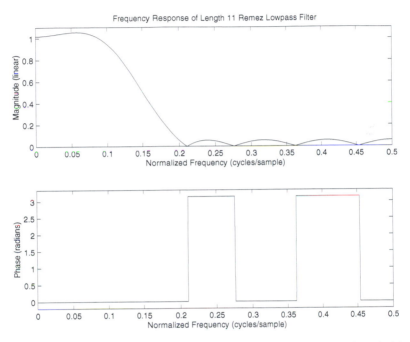

Figure 10.2: Amplitude response and phase response of the length 11 zero-phase FIR lowpass filter in Fig. 10.1.

10.2.2   Elementary Zero-Phase Filter Examples

A practical zero-phase filter was illustrated in Figures 10.1 and 10.2. Some simple general cases are as follows:

- The trivial (non-)filter $h(n) = \delta(n)$ has frequency response $H(e^{j\omega T}) = 1$, which is zero phase for all ω.

- Every second-order zero-phase FIR filter has an impulse response of the form

$$h(n) \;=\; b_1 \delta(n+1) + b_0 \delta(n) + b_1 \delta(n-1),$$

  where the coefficients b_i are assumed real. The transfer function of the general, second-order, real, zero-phase filter is

$$H(z) \;=\; b_1 z + b_0 + b_1 z^{-1}$$

  and the frequency response is

$$H(e^{j\omega T}) \;=\; b_1 e^{j\omega T} + b_0 + b_1 e^{-j\omega T} \;=\; b_0 + 2b_1 \cos(\omega T)$$

  which is real for all ω.

- Extending the previous example, every order $2N$ zero-phase real FIR filter has an impulse response of the form

$$
\begin{aligned}
h(n) \;=\;\; & b_N \delta(n+N) \;+\; \cdots \;+\; b_1 \delta(n+1) \;+\; b_0 \delta(n) \\
& + \, b_1 \delta(n-1) \;+\; \cdots \;+\; b_N \delta(n-N)
\end{aligned}
$$

  and frequency response

$$H(e^{j\omega T}) \;=\; b_0 \;+\; 2 \sum_{k=1}^{N} b_k \cos(k\omega T)$$

  which is clearly real whenever the coefficients b_k are real.

- There is no first-order (length 2) zero-phase filter, because, to be even, its impulse response would have to be proportional to $h(n) = \delta(n+1/2) + \delta(n-1/2)$. Since the bandlimited digital impulse signal $\delta(n)$ is ideally interpolated using bandlimited interpolation [91, 84], giving samples of $\operatorname{sinc}(n) \triangleq \sin(\pi n)/(\pi n)$—the unit-amplitude *sinc function* having zero-crossings on the integers, we see that sampling h on the integers yields an *IIR* filter:

$$h(n) = \sum_{m=-\infty}^{\infty} \operatorname{sinc}(n-m-1/2) + \operatorname{sinc}(n-m+1/2)$$

- Similarly, there are no odd-order (even-length) zero-phase filters.

10.3   Odd Impulse Reponses

Note that *odd impulse responses* of the form $h(n) = -h(-n)$ are closely related to zero-phase filters (even impulse responses). This is because another Fourier symmetry relation is that the DTFT of an odd sequence is purely *imaginary* [84]. In practice, *Hilbert transform filters* and *differentiators* are often implemented as odd FIR filters [68]. A purely imaginary frequency response can be divided by j to give a real frequency response. As a result, filter-design software for one case is easily adapted to the other [68].

Equivalently, an odd impulse response can be multiplied by j in the time domain to yield a purely imaginary impulse response that is *Hermitian*. Hermitian signals have real Fourier transforms [84]. Therefore, a Hermitian impulse response gives a filter having a phase response that is either zero or π at each frequency.

10.4   Symmetric Linear-Phase Filters

As stated at the beginning of this chapter, the impulse response of every causal, linear-phase, FIR filter is symmetric:

$$h(n) = h(N - 1 - n), \quad n = 0, 1, 2, \ldots, N - 1.$$

Assume that N is odd. Then the filter

$$h_{\mathrm{zp}}(n) = h\left(n + \frac{N-1}{2}\right), \quad n = -\frac{N-1}{2}, \ldots, \frac{N-1}{2}$$

is a *zero-phase* filter. Thus, every odd-length linear-phase filter can be expressed as a delay of some zero-phase filter,

$$h(n) = h_{\mathrm{zp}}\left(n - \frac{N-1}{2}\right), \quad n = 0, 1, 2, \ldots, N - 1.$$

By the shift theorem for z transforms (§6.3), the transfer function of a linear-phase filter is

$$H(z) = z^{-\frac{N-1}{2}} H_{\mathrm{zp}}(z)$$

and the frequency response is

$$H(e^{j\omega T}) = e^{-j\omega \frac{N-1}{2} T} H_{\mathrm{zp}}(e^{j\omega T})$$

which is a *linear phase term* times $H_{\mathrm{zp}}(e^{j\omega T})$ which is real. Since $H_{\mathrm{zp}}(e^{j\omega T})$ can go negative, the phase response is

$$\Theta(\omega) = \begin{cases} -\dfrac{N-1}{2}\omega T, & H_{\mathrm{zp}}(e^{j\omega T}) \geq 0 \\ -\dfrac{N-1}{2}\omega T + \pi, & H_{\mathrm{zp}}(e^{j\omega T}) < 0 \end{cases}.$$

For frequencies ω at which $H_{zp}(e^{j\omega T})$ is nonnegative, the phase delay and group delay of a linear-phase filter are simply half its length:

$$P(\omega) \triangleq -\frac{\Theta(\omega)}{\omega} = \frac{N-1}{2}T, \qquad H_{zp}(e^{j\omega T}) \geq 0$$

$$D(\omega) \triangleq -\frac{\partial}{\partial \omega}\Theta(\omega) = \frac{N-1}{2}T, \qquad H_{zp}(e^{j\omega T}) \geq 0$$

10.4.1 Simple Linear-Phase Filter Examples

- The example of §10.2.1 on page 222 was in fact a linear-phase FIR filter design example. The resulting causal finite impulse response was left-shifted ("advanced" in time) to make it zero phase.

- While the trivial "bypass filter" $h(n) = \delta(n)$ is zero-phase (§10.2.2), the "bypass filter with a unit delay," $h(n) = \delta(n-1)$ is *linear phase*. It is (trivially) symmetric about time $n = 1$, and the frequency response is $H(z) = e^{-j\omega T}$, which is a pure linear phase term $\Theta(\omega) = -\omega T$ having a slope of -1 samples (radians per radians-per-sample), or $-T$ seconds (radians per radians-per-second). The phase- and group-delays are each 1 sample at every frequency.

- The impulse response of the simplest lowpass filter studied in Chapter 1 was $h = \delta(n)+\delta(n-1)$ $[H(z) = 1+z^{-1}]$. Since this impulse response is symmetric about time $n = 1/2$ samples, it is linear phase, and $\Theta(\omega) = -\omega T/2$, as derived in Chapter 1. The phase delay and group delay are both $1/2$ sample at each frequency. Note that even-length linear-phase filters cannot be time-shifted (without interpolation) to create a corresponding zero-phase filter. However, they can be shifted to make a near-zero-phase filter that has a phase delay and group delay equal to half a sample at all passband frequencies.

10.4.2   Software for Linear-Phase Filter Design

The Matlab Signal Processing Toolbox covers many applications with the following functions:

remez()	(optimal Chebyshev linear-phase FIR filter design),
firls()	(optimal least-squares linear-phase FIR filter design),
fir1()	(window method for linear-phase FIR *lowpass* design),
fir2()	(window method for linear-phase FIR filter design), and
invfreqz()	(weighted least-squares method for general FIR (or IIR) filter design [78, page 50]).

All of these functions except `firls` are implemented in the free, open-source, Octave Forge collection as well.

Methods for *FIR filter design* are discussed in the fourth book of the music signal processing series [87], and classic references include [64, 68]. There is also quite a large research literature on this subject.

10.5   Antisymmetric Linear-Phase Filters

In the same way that odd impulse responses are related to even impulse responses, linear-phase filters are closely related to *antisymmetric impulse responses* of the form $h(n) = -h(N-1-n)$, $n = 0 : N-1$. An antisymmetric impulse response is simply a delayed odd impulse response (usually delayed enough to make it causal). The corresponding frequency response is not strictly linear phase, but the phase is instead linear with a constant offset (by $\pm\pi/2$). Since an *affine function* is any function of the form $f(\omega) = \alpha\omega + \beta$, where α and β are constants, an antisymmetric impulse response can be called an *affine-phase filter*. These same remarks apply to any linear-phase filter that can be expressed as a time-shift of a π-phase filter (*i.e.*, it is inverting in some passband). However, in practice, all such filters may be loosely called "linear-phase" filters, because they are designed and implemented in essentially the same way [68].

Note that truly linear-phase filters have both a constant phase delay and a constant group delay. Affine-phase filters, on the other hand, have a constant group delay, but not a constant phase delay (see Problem 4 on page 171).

10.6   Forward-Backward Filtering

There are no linear-phase recursive filters because a recursive filter cannot generate a symmetric impulse response (see Problem 3 on page 146). However, it *is* possible to implement a zero-phase filter *offline* using a recursive filter twice. That is, if the entire input signal $x(\cdot)$ is stored in a computer memory or hard disk, for example, then we can apply a recursive filter both forward and backward in time. Doing this *squares* the amplitude response of the filter and *zeros* the phase response.

To show this analytically, let $v(n)$ denote the output of the first filtering operation (which we'll take to be "forward" in time in the normal way), and let $h(n)$ be the impulse response of the recursive filter. Then we have

$$v(n) = (h * x)(n),$$

where $x(n)$ is the input signal at sample n. For the second pass, we "flip" $v(n)$ to obtain $v(-n)$ and apply the filter again:

$$w(n) = (h * \text{FLIP}(v))(n)$$

The final output is then this result flipped:

$$y = \text{FLIP}(w) = \text{FLIP}(h * \text{FLIP}(v)) = \text{FLIP}(h) * v,$$

where the last simplification tells us that flipping the input and output signals is equivalent to flipping the impulse response instead (see Problem 1 on page 146). Putting all these operations together, we have

$$y(n) = \text{FLIP}_n(h * \text{FLIP}(h * x)) = (\text{FLIP}(h) * (h * x))(n).$$

By the *flip theorem for z transforms*, we have that the z transform of $\text{FLIP}(x)$ is $X(z^{-1})$:

$$\mathcal{Z}\{\text{FLIP}(x)\} \;\triangleq\; \sum_{n=-\infty}^{\infty} x(-n)z^{-n} = \sum_{m=-\infty}^{\infty} x(m)z^{m}$$

$$= \sum_{m=-\infty}^{\infty} x(m)(z^{-1})^{-m} \triangleq X(z^{-1})$$

Using this result and applying the convolution theorem (§6.3) twice gives the z transform

$$Y(z) = H(z^{-1})[H(z)X(z)].$$

On the unit circle, this reduces to, for real filters h,

$$Y(e^{j\omega T}) \;=\; H(e^{-j\omega T})H(e^{j\omega T})X(e^{j\omega T}) = \left|H(e^{j\omega T})\right|^{2} X(e^{j\omega T})$$

$$\triangleq\; G^{2}(\omega)X(e^{j\omega T}).$$

If the filter were complex, then we would need to conjugate its coefficients when running it backwards.

In summary, we have thus shown that forward-backward filtering *squares* the amplitude response and *zeros* the phase response. Note also that the phase response is truly zero, never alternating between zero and π. No matter what nonlinear phase response $\Theta(\omega)$ a filter may have, this phase is completely canceled out by forward and backward filtering. The amplitude response, on the other hand, is squared. For simple bandpass filters (including lowpass, highpass, etc.), for which the desired gain is 1 in the passband and 0 in the stopband, squaring the amplitude response usually *improves* the response, because the "stopband ripple" (deviation from 0) is squared, thereby *doubling* the stopband attenuation in dB. On the other hand, passband ripple (deviation from 1) is only doubled by the squaring (because $(1 + \epsilon)^2 = 1 + 2\epsilon + \epsilon^2 \approx 1 + 2\epsilon$).

A Matlab example of forward-backward filtering is presented in §11.6 (in Fig. 11.1 on page 237).

10.7   Phase Distortion at Passband Edges

For many applications (such as lowpass, bandpass, or highpass filtering), the most *phase dispersion* occurs at the extreme edge of the passband (*i.e.*, in the vicinity of *cut-off frequencies*). This phenomenon was clearly visible in the example of Fig. 7.6.4 on page 167. Only filters without feedback can have exactly linear phase (unless forward-backward filtering is feasible), and such filters generally need many more multiplies for a given specification on the amplitude response $G(\omega)$ [68]. One should keep in mind that phase dispersion near a cut-off frequency (or any steep transition in the amplitude response) usually appears as *ringing* near that frequency in the time domain. (This can be heard in the upcoming matlab example of §11.6, Fig. 11.1.)

For musical purposes, $G(\omega)$, or the effect that a filter has on the magnitude spectrum of the input signal, is usually of primary interest. This is true for all "instantaneous" filtering operations such as tone controls, graphical equalizers, parametric equalizers, formant filter banks, shelving filters, and the like. (Elementary examples in this category are discussed in Appendix B.) Notable exceptions are echo and reverberation [86], in which delay characteristics are as important as magnitude characteristics.

When designing an "instantaneous" filtering operation, *i.e.*, when not designing a "delay effect" such as an echo unit or reverberator, the amplitude response $G(\omega)$ should be *as smooth as possible as a function of frequency* ω. Smoother amplitude responses correspond to shorter impulse responses (when the phase is zero, linear, or "minimum phase" as discussed in the next chapter). By keeping impulse-responses as short as possible, phase dispersion is minimized, and ideally inaudible. Linearizing the phase response with a delay equalizer (a type of allpass filter) does not eliminate ringing, but merely shifts it in time. A general rule of thumb is to keep the total impulse-response duration below the time-discrimination threshold of hearing in the context of the intended application.

Chapter 11

Minimum-Phase Filters

This chapter discusses minimum-phase signals and filters, the minimum-phase/allpass decomposition, and hybrid minimum-phase/linear-phase audio filters. Matlab code is given for computing minimum-phase spectra from spectral magnitude only.

11.1 Definition of Minimum Phase Filters

In Chapter 10 we looked at linear-phase and zero-phase digital filters. While such filters preserve waveshape to a maximum extent in some sense, there are times when phase linearity is not important. In such cases, it is valuable to allow the phase to be arbitrary, or else to set it in such a way that the amplitude response is easier to match. In many cases, this means specifying *minimum phase*:

> An LTI filter $H(z) = B(z)/A(z)$ is said to be *minimum phase* if all its poles and zeros are inside the unit circle $|z| = 1$ (excluding the unit circle itself).

Note that minimum-phase filters are stable by definition since the poles must be inside the unit circle. In addition, because the zeros must also be inside the unit circle, the inverse filter $1/H(z)$ is also stable when $H(z)$ is minimum phase. One can say that minimum-phase filters form an algebraic *group* in which the group elements are impulse-responses and the group operation is convolution (or, alternatively, the elements are minimum-phase transfer functions, and the group operation is multiplication).

A minimum phase filter is also *causal* since noncausal terms in the impulse response correspond to poles at infinity. The simplest example of this would be the unit-sample *advance*, $H(z) = z$, which consists of a zero at $z = 0$ and a pole at $z = \infty$.[1]

11.2   Minimum-Phase Polynomials

A filter is minimum phase if both the numerator and denominator of its transfer function are *minimum-phase polynomials* in z^{-1}:

A polynomial of the form

$$
\begin{aligned}
B(z) &= b_0 + b_1 z^{-1} + b_2 z^{-2} + \cdots + b_M z^{-M} \\
&= b_0 (1 - \xi_1 z^{-1})(1 - \xi_2 z^{-1}) \cdots (1 - \xi_M z^{-1}),
\end{aligned}
$$

where $b_0 \neq 0$, is said to be *minimum phase* if all of its roots ξ_i are inside the unit circle, *i.e.*, $|\xi_i| < 1$.

The case $b_0 = 0$ is excluded because the polynomial cannot be minimum phase in that case, because then it would have a zero at $z = \infty$ unless all its coefficients were zero.

As usual, definitions for filters generalize to definitions for *signals* by simply treating the signal as an *impulse response*:

A signal $h(n)$, $n \in \mathbf{Z}$, is said to be minimum phase if its z transform $H(z)$ is minimum phase.

Note that *every stable all-pole filter $H(z) = b_0/A(z)$ is minimum phase*, because stability implies that $A(z)$ is minimum phase, and there are "no zeros" (all are at $z = 0$). Thus, minimum phase is the only phase available to a stable all-pole filter.

The contribution of minimum-phase zeros to the *complex cepstrum* was described in §8.8 on page 193.

---

[1]Another way to show that all minimum-phase filters and their inverses are causal, using the Cauchy integral theorem from complex variables [14], is to consider a Laurent series expansion of the transfer function $H(z)$ about any point on the unit circle. Because all poles are inside the unit circle (for either $H(z)$ or $1/H(z)$), the expansion is one-sided (no positive powers of z). A Laurent expansion about a point on the unit circle interprets unstable poles as noncausal exponentials in the time domain, which "decay" in the direction of negative time, as discussed and illustrated in §8.7 on page 190.

11.3   Maximum Phase Filters

The opposite of minimum phase is *maximum phase*:

> A stable LTI filter $H(z) = B(z)/A(z)$ is said to be *maximum phase* if all its zeros are outside the unit circle.

For example, every stable allpass filter (§B.2) is a maximum-phase filter, because its transfer function can be written as

$$H(z) = \frac{z^{-N}A(z^{-1})}{A(z)},$$

where $A(z) = 1 + a_1 z^{-1} + a_2 z^{-2} + \cdots + a_N z^{-N}$ is an Nth-order minimum-phase polynomial in z^{-1} (all roots inside the unit circle). As another example of a maximum-phase filter (a special case of allpass filters, in fact), a pure delay of N samples has the transfer function z^{-N}, which is N poles at $z = 0$ and N zeros at $z = \infty$.

If zeros of $B(z)$ occur both inside and outside the unit circle, the filter is said to be a *mixed-phase filter*. Note that zeros on the unit circle are neither minimum nor maximum phase according to our definitions. Since poles on the unit circle are sometimes called "marginally stable," we could say that zeros on the unit circle are "marginally minimum and/or maximum phase" for consistency. However, such a term does not appear to be very useful. When pursuing *minimum-phase filter design* (see §11.7 on page 240), we will find that zeros on the unit circle must be treated separately.

If $B(z)$ is order M and minimum phase, then $z^{-M}B(z^{-1})$ is maximum phase, and vice versa. To restate this in the time domain, if $b = [b_0, b_1, \ldots, b_M, 0, \ldots]$ is a minimum-phase FIR sequence of length $M + 1$, then $\text{SHIFT}_M(\text{FLIP}(b))$ is a maximum-phase sequence. In other words, *time reversal inverts the locations of all zeros*, thereby "reflecting" them across the unit circle in a manner that does not affect spectral magnitude. Time reversal is followed by a shift in order to obtain a causal result, but this is not required: Adding a pure delay to a maximum-phase filter $(B(z) \to z^{-1}B(z))$ gives a new maximum-phase filter with the same amplitude response (and order increased by 1).

Example

It is easy to classify completely all first-order FIR filters:

$$H(z) = 1 + h_1 z^{-1}$$

where we have normalized h_0 to 1 for simplicity. We have a single zero at $z = -h_1$. If $|h_1| < 1$, the filter is minimum phase. If $|h_1| > 1$, it is maximum phase. Note that the minimum-phase case is the one in which the impulse response $[1, h_1, 0, \ldots]$ *decays* instead of grows. It can be shown that this is a general property of minimum-phase sequences, as elaborated in the next section.

11.4   Minimum Phase Means Fastest Decay

The previous example is an instance of the following general result:

> Among all causal signals $h_i(n)$ having identical magnitude spectra, the minimum-phase signal $h_{\mathrm{mp}}(n)$ has the *fastest decay* in the sense that
>
> $$\sum_{n=0}^{K} |h_{\mathrm{mp}}(n)|^2 \geq \sum_{n=0}^{K} |h_i(n)|^2, \qquad K = 0, 1, 2, \ldots .$$

That is, the signal energy in the first $K+1$ samples of the minimum-phase case is at least as large as any other causal signal having the same magnitude spectrum. (See [60] for a proof outline.) Thus, minimum-phase signals are *maximally concentrated toward time 0* when compared against all causal signals having the same magnitude spectrum. As a result of this property, minimum-phase signals are sometimes called *minimum-delay signals*.

11.5   Minimum-Phase/Allpass Decomposition

Every causal stable filter $H(z)$ with *no zeros on the unit circle* can be factored into a minimum-phase filter in cascade with a causal stable allpass filter:

$$H(z) = H_{\mathrm{mp}}(z)\, S(z) \qquad \text{(Minimum-Phase/Allpass Decomposition)}$$

where $H_{\mathrm{mp}}(z)$ is minimum phase, $S(z)$ is a stable allpass filter:

$$S(z) = \frac{s_L + s_{L-1}z^{-1} + \cdots + s_1 z^{-(L-1)} + z^{-L}}{1 + s_1 z^{-1} + s_2 z^{-2} + \cdots + s_L z^{-L}},$$

and L is the number of maximum-phase zeros of $H(z)$.

This result is easy to show by induction. Consider a single maximum-phase zero ξ of $H(z)$. Then $|\xi| > 1$, and $H(z)$ can be written with the maximum-phase zero factored out as

$$H(z) = H_1(z)(1 - \xi z^{-1}).$$

Now multiply by $1 = (1 - \xi^{-1}z^{-1})/(1 - \xi^{-1}z^{-1})$ to get

$$H(z) = \underbrace{H_1(z)(1 - \xi^{-1}z^{-1})}_{\triangleq H_2(z)} \underbrace{\frac{1 - \xi z^{-1}}{1 - \xi^{-1}z^{-1}}}_{\triangleq S_1(z)}.$$

We have thus factored $H(z)$ into the product of $H_2(z)$, in which the maximum-phase zero has been *reflected inside the unit circle* to become minimum-phase (from $z = \xi$ to $z = 1/\xi$), times a stable allpass filter $S_1(z)$ consisting of the original maximum-phase zero ξ and a new pole at $z = 1/\xi$ (which cancels the reflected zero at $z = 1/\xi$ given to $H_2(z)$).[2] This procedure can now be repeated for each maximum-phase zero in $H(z)$.

In summary, we may factor maximum-phase zeros out of the transfer function and replace them with their minimum-phase counterparts without altering the amplitude response. This modification is equivalent to placing a stable allpass filter in series with the original filter, where the allpass filter cancels the maximum-phase zero and introduces the minimum-phase zero.

A procedure for computing the minimum phase for a given spectral magnitude is discussed in §11.7 below. More theory pertaining to minimum phase sequences may be found in [60].

11.6   Is Linear Phase Really Ideal for Audio?

It is generally accepted that zero or linear phase filters are ideal for audio applications. This is because such filters delay all frequencies by the same amount, thereby maximally preserving waveshape. Mathematically, all Fourier-components passed by the filter remain time-synchronized exactly as they were in the original signal. However, this section will argue that a phase response somewhere between linear- and minimum-phase may be even better in some cases. We show this by means of a Matlab experiment comparing minimum-phase and zero-phase impulse responses.

---

[2] The allpass $S_1(z)$ as defined has magnitude $|\xi| > 1$ over the unit circle instead of 1 as is usually defined for allpass gains. To normalize the allpass gain to 1, we can define $H_2(z) = (\xi - z^{-1})H_1(z)$ instead.

The matlab code is shown in Fig. 11.1. An order 8 elliptic-function low-pass filter [64] is designed with a cut-off frequency at 2 kHz. We choose an elliptic-function filter because it has a highly nonlinear phase response near its cut-off frequency, resulting in extra delay there which can be perceived as "ringing" at that frequency. The cut-off is chosen at 2kHz because this is a highly audible frequency. We want to clearly hear the ringing in this experiment in order to compare the zero-phase and minimum-phase cases.

Let the impulse response of the 8th order lowpass filter be denoted $h(n)$. It is neither minimum nor maximum phase because there are zeros on the unit circle. (An elliptic-function filter has all of its zeros *on* the unit circle.) However, nothing of practical importance changes if we move the zeros from radius 1 to radius $1 - 10^{-12}$, say, which would give a minimum-phase perturbation of the elliptic lowpass.

From $h(n)$ we prepare two impulse responses having the same magnitude spectra but different phase spectra:

$$h_{\mathrm{mp}} \triangleq h * h,$$

which is minimum phase,[3] and

$$h_{\mathrm{zp}} \triangleq h * \mathrm{FLIP}(h),$$

which is zero phase, as discussed in §10.6. In both cases, the magnitude spectrum is

$$\left|H_{\mathrm{mp}}(e^{j\omega T})\right| = \left|H_{\mathrm{zp}}(e^{j\omega T})\right| = \left|H(e^{j\omega T})\right|^2,$$

while the phase spectra are

$$\angle H_{\mathrm{mp}}(e^{j\omega T}) = 2\angle H(e^{j\omega T})$$
$$\angle H_{\mathrm{zp}}(e^{j\omega T}) = 0,$$

again as discussed in §10.6.

Since we are listening to a lowpass-filtered impulse, it is reasonable to define the ideal expected sound as a "lowpass-filtered click," or some kind of "compact thump." We may therefore ask which signal sounds more like a lowpassed click, h_{mp} or h_{zp}? In the minimum-phase case, all filter ringing occurs after the main pulse, while in the zero-phase case, it is equally divided before and after the main pulse (see Fig. 11.2). Listening tests confirm that the "pre-ring" of the zero-phase case is audible before the main click, giving it a kind of "chirp" quality. Most listeners would say the

---

[3]The convolution of two minimum phase sequences is minimum phase, since this just doubles each pole and zero in place, so they remain inside the unit circle.

```
% ellipt.m - Compare minimum-phase and zero-phase
%            lowpass impulse responses.

dosounds = 1;
N = 8;     % filter order
Rp = 0.5;  % passband ripple (dB)
Rs = 60;   % stopband ripple (-dB)
Fs = 8192; % default sampling rate (Windows Matlab)
Fp = 2000; % passband end
Fc = 2200; % stopband begins [gives order 8]
Ns = 4096; % number of samples in impulse responses

[B,A] = nellip(Rp, Rs, Fp/(0.5*Fs), Fc/(0.5*Fs)); % Octave
% [B,A] = ellip(N, Rp, Rs, Fp/(0.5*Fs)); % Matlab

% Minimum phase case:
imp = [1,zeros(1,Ns/2-1)]; % or 'h1=impz(B,A,Ns/2-1)'
h1 = filter(B,A,imp); % min-phase impulse response
hmp = filter(B,A,[h1,zeros(1,Ns/2)]); % apply twice

% Zero phase case:
h1r = fliplr(h1); % maximum-phase impulse response
hzp = filter(B,A,[h1r,zeros(1,Ns/2)]); % min*max=zp
% hzp = fliplr(hzp); % not needed here since symmetric

elliptplots; % plot impulse- and amplitude-responses

% Let's hear them!
while(dosounds)
  sound(hmp,Fs);
  pause(0.5);
  sound(hzp,Fs);
  pause(1);
end
```

Figure 11.1: Matlab script for listening to minimum-phase and zero-phase impulse responses having the same amplitude response.

minimum-phase case is a better "click". Since forward masking is stronger than backward masking in hearing perception, the optimal distribution of ringing is arguably a small amount before the main pulse (however much is inaudible due to backward masking, for example), with the rest occurring after the main pulse.

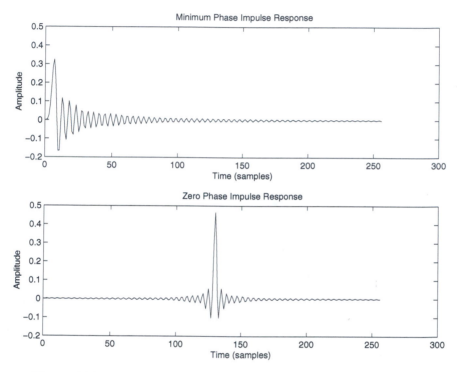

Figure 11.2: Minimum-phase and zero-phase impulse responses derived from two applications of an order 8 elliptic-function lowpass filter.

Figure 11.3 verifies that the magnitude spectra are the same in each case.

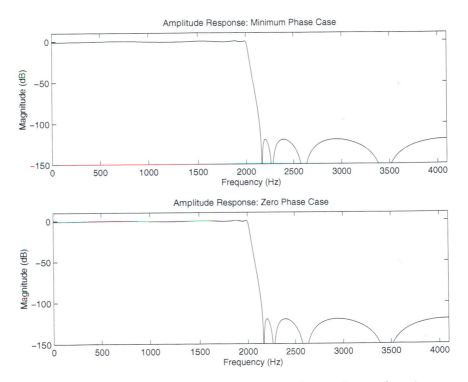

Figure 11.3: Magnitude spectra of minimum-phase and zero-phase impulse responses derived from two passes through an order 8 elliptic-function lowpass filter.

11.7   Creating Minimum Phase Filters and Signals

Minimum-phase filter design often requires creating a minimum-phase desired frequency response $H(e^{j\omega})$ from a given magnitude response $|H(e^{j\omega})|$). As is clear from §11.5 on page 234, any filter transfer function $H(z)$ can be made minimum-phase, in principle, by completely factoring $H(z)$ and "reflecting" all zeros z_i for which $|z_i| > 1$ inside the unit circle, *i.e.*, replacing z_i by $1/z_i$. However, factoring a polynomial this large can be impractical. An approximate "nonparametric" method[4] is based on the property of the *complex cepstrum* (see §8.8 on page 193) that each minimum-phase zero in the spectrum gives rise to a causal exponential in the cepstrum, while each maximum-phase zero corresponds to an anti-causal exponential in the cepstrum [60]. Therefore, by computing the cepstrum and converting anti-causal exponentials to causal exponentials, the corresponding spectrum is converted *nonparametrically* to minimum-phase form.

A matlab function `mps.m` which carries out this method is listed in §J.11 on page 412.[5] It works best for *smooth* desired frequency response curves, but in principle the error can be made arbitrarily small by simply enlarging the FFT sizes used. Specifically, the inverse FFT of the log magnitude frequency response should not "wrap around" in the time domain (negligible "time aliasing").

It is important to use something like `mps` when designing digital filters based on a magnitude frequency-response specification using "phase sensitive" filter-design software (such as `invfreqz` in matlab). In other words, poor results are generally obtained when phase-sensitive filter-design software is asked to design a causal, stable, zero-phase filter. As a general rule, when phase doesn't matter, ask for minimum phase.

A related practical note is that unstable recursive filter designs can often be stabilized by simply adding more delay to the desired impulse response (*i.e.*, adding a negatively sloped linear phase to the desired phase response). For example, the Steiglitz-McBride algorithm in Matlab (`stmcb`) is a phase-sensitive IIR filter-design function that accepts a desired impulse response, while Matlab's `invfreqz` (which can optionally iterate toward the Steiglitz-McBride solution), accepts a complex desired frequency response.

---

[4]We can loosely define *nonparametric signal processing* as performing array operations on signals and spectra, as opposed to working with parametric representations such as poles and zeros. Generally speaking, nonparametric signal processing is typically more robust than parametric signal processing [87].

[5]A Mathematica notebook for this purpose was written by Andrew Simper:

http://www.vellocet.com/dsp/MinimumPhase/MinimumPhase.html

Conclusion

An introduction to digital filters has been presented. The main utility of the analysis methods presented is in ascertaining how a given filter will affect the spectrum of a signal passing through it. Some of the concepts introduced were linearity, time-invariance, filter impulse response, difference equations, transient response, steady-state response, transfer functions, amplitude response, phase response, phase delay, group delay, linear phase, minimum phase, maximum phase, poles and zeros, filter stability, and the general use of complex numbers to represent signals, spectra, and filters. Additionally, practical filtering in matlab has been discussed.

However, this is still only the beginning. With these foundations there is an unlimited number of avenues of investigation into applications of digital filters. Some elementary examples are introduced in Appendix B, such as first- and second-order sections, the dc blocker, shelf equalizer, peaking equalizer, and time-varying resonators. A starting introduction to analog filters appears in Appendix E, and matrix formulations of digital filters are pursued in Appendices F and G. Some methods for digital filter *design* are discussed in Appendix I. Book III [86] of the music signal processing book series further discusses delay lines, comb filters, feedback delay networks, reverberator design, and computational physical modeling for sound synthesis and audio effects using digital filters, among other related topics. The fourth book [87] introduces FFT-based FIR filtering, and psychoacoustically motivated signal processing, with particular emphasis on time-varying spectral modifications in audio signal processing. Book IV also contains more about audio FIR filter design.

Given the immense range of naturally occurring filters in the domain of music, it is reasonable to expect that filter theory will continue to provide valuable tools for the analysis, synthesis, and manipulation of sound.

The following appendices provide elementary background material in support of the preceding chapters, as well as related and more advanced topics for further study.

Appendix A

Background Fundamentals

A.1   Signal Representation and Notation

Below is a summary of various notational conventions used in digital signal processing for representing signals and spectra. For a more detailed presentation, see the elementary introduction to signal representation, sinusoids, and exponentials in [84].[1]

A.1.1   Units

In this book, time t is always in physical units of *seconds* (s), while time n or m is in units of *samples* (counting numbers having no physical units). Time t is a continuous real variable, while discrete-time in samples is integer-valued. The physical time t corresponding to time n in samples is given by

$$t = nT,$$

where T is the *sampling interval* in seconds.

For *frequencies*, we have two physical units: (1) *cycles per second* and (2) *radians per second*. The name for cycles per second is *Hertz (Hz)* (though in the past it was *cps*). One cycle equals 2π radians, which is 360 degrees (°). Therefore, f Hz is the same frequency as $2\pi f$ radians per second (rad/s). It is easy to confuse the two because both radians and cycles are pure numbers, so that both types of frequency are in physical units of inverse seconds (s^{-1}).

For example, a *periodic signal* with a period of P seconds has a frequency of $f = (1/P)$ Hz, and a radian frequency of $\omega = 2\pi/P$ rad/s. The

---

[1]http://ccrma.stanford.edu/~jos/mdft/Sinusoids_Exponentials.html

sampling rate, f_s, is the reciprocal of the sampling period T, *i.e.*,

$$f_s = \frac{1}{T}.$$

Since the sampling period T is in seconds, the sampling rate $f_s = 1/T$ is in Hz. It can be helpful, however, to think "seconds per sample" and "samples per second," where "samples" is a dimensionless quantity (pure number) included for clarity. The *amplitude* of a signal may be in any arbitrary units such as volts, sound pressure (SPL), and so on.

A.1.2   Sinusoids

The term *sinusoid* means a waveform of the type

$$A\cos(2\pi ft + \phi) = A\cos(\omega t + \phi). \tag{A.1}$$

Thus, a sinusoid may be defined as a *cosine* at amplitude A, frequency f, and phase ϕ. (See [84] for a fuller development and discussion.) A sinusoid's *phase* ϕ is in radian units. We may call

$$\theta(t) \triangleq \omega t + \phi$$

the *instantaneous phase*, as distinguished from the *phase offset* ϕ. Thus, the "phase" of a sinusoid typically refers to its phase offset. The *instantaneous frequency* of a sinusoid is defined as the *derivative* of the instantaneous phase with respect to time (see [84] for more):

$$f(t) \triangleq \frac{d}{dt}\theta(t) = \frac{d}{dt}[\omega t + \phi] = \omega$$

A *discrete-time sinusoid* is simply obtained from a continuous-time sinusoid by replacing t by nT in Eq. (A.1):

$$A\cos(2\pi fnT + \phi) = A\cos(\omega nT + \phi).$$

A.1.3   Spectrum

In this book, we think of filters primarily in terms of their effect on the *spectrum* of a signal. This is appropriate because the ear (to a first approximation) converts the time-waveform at the eardrum into a neurologically encoded spectrum. Intuitively, a spectrum (a complex function of frequency ω) gives the amplitude and phase of the sinusoidal signal-component at frequency ω. Mathematically, the spectrum of a signal x is the Fourier transform of its time-waveform. Equivalently, the spectrum is the z transform evaluated on the unit circle $z = e^{j\omega T}$. A detailed introduction to spectrum analysis is given in [84].[2]

We denote both the spectrum and the z transform of a signal by uppercase letters. For example, if the time-waveform is denoted $x(n)$, its z transform is called $X(z)$ and its spectrum is therefore $X(e^{j\omega T})$. The time-waveform $x(n)$ is said to "correspond" to its z transform $X(z)$, meaning they are transform pairs. This correspondence is often denoted $x(n) \leftrightarrow X(z)$, or $x(n) \leftrightarrow X(e^{j\omega T})$. Both the z transform and its special case, the (discrete-time) Fourier transform, are said to transform from the *time domain* to the *frequency domain*.

We deal most often with discrete time nT (or simply n) but continuous frequency f (or $\omega = 2\pi f$). This is because the computer can represent only digital signals, and digital time-waveforms are discrete in time but may have energy at any frequency. On the other hand, if we were going to talk about FFTs (Fast Fourier Transforms—efficient implementations of the Discrete Fourier Transform, or DFT) [84], then we would have to discretize the frequency variable also in order to represent spectra inside the computer. In this book, however, we use spectra only for conceptual insights into the perceptual effects of digital filtering; therefore, we avoid discrete frequency for simplicity.

When we wish to consider an entire signal as a "thing in itself," we write $x(\cdot)$, meaning the whole time-waveform ($x(n)$ for all n), or $X(\cdot)$, to mean the entire spectrum taken as a whole. Imagine, for example, that we have plotted $x(n)$ on a strip of paper that is infinitely long. Then $x(\cdot)$ refers to the complete picture, while $x(n)$ refers to the nth sample point on the plot.

---

[2]http://ccrma.stanford.edu/~jos/mdft/Discrete_Fourier_Transform_DFT.html

A.2   Complex and Trigonometric Identities

This section gives a summary of some of the more useful mathematical identities for complex numbers and trigonometry in the context of digital filter analysis. For many more, see handbooks of mathematical functions such as Abramowitz and Stegun [2].

The symbol $\triangleq$ means "is defined as"; z stands for a complex number; and r, θ, x, and y stand for real numbers. The quantity t is used below to denote $\tan(\theta/2)$.

A.2.1   Complex Numbers

$$j \triangleq \sqrt{-1}$$

$$z \triangleq x + jy \triangleq re^{j\theta}$$

$$x = r\cos(\theta)$$
$$y = r\sin(\theta)$$

$$r = |z| = \sqrt{x^2 + y^2}$$
$$\theta = \angle z = \tan^{-1}(y/x)$$

$$|z_1 z_2| = |z_1|\,|z_2|$$
$$|z_1/z_2| = |z_1|\,/\,|z_2|$$

$$|e^{j\theta}| = 1$$
$$\angle r = 0$$

$$z_1 z_2 = (x_1 x_2 - y_1 y_2) + j(x_1 y_2 + x_2 y_1)$$
$$z_1 z_2 = r_1 r_2 e^{j(\theta_1 + \theta_2)}$$

$$\overline{z} \triangleq x - jy = re^{-j\theta}$$
$$z\overline{z} = |z|^2 = x^2 + y^2 = r^2$$

A.2.2   The Exponential Function

$$e^x \quad \triangleq \quad \lim_{n \to \infty} \left(1 + \frac{x}{n}\right)^n$$

$$e^x \quad = \quad \sum_{n=0}^{\infty} \frac{x^n}{n!}$$

$$e^{j\theta} \quad = \quad \cos(\theta) + j\sin(\theta)$$

$$e^{jn\theta} \quad = \quad \cos(n\theta) + j\sin(n\theta)$$

$$\sin(\theta) \quad = \quad \frac{e^{j\theta} - e^{-j\theta}}{2j}$$

$$\cos(\theta) \quad = \quad \frac{e^{j\theta} + e^{-j\theta}}{2}$$

$$e \quad = \quad 2.7\,1828\,1828\,4590 \ldots$$

A.2.3   Trigonometric Identities

$$\sin(-\theta) = -\sin(\theta)$$
$$\cos(-\theta) = \cos(\theta)$$

$$\sin(A+B) = \sin(A)\cos(B) + \cos(A)\sin(B)$$
$$\cos(A+B) = \cos(A)\cos(B) - \sin(A)\sin(B)$$

$$\sin^2(\theta) = \frac{1 - \cos(2\theta)}{2}$$

$$\cos^2(\theta) = \frac{1 + \cos(2\theta)}{2}$$

$$\sin(A)\sin(B) = \frac{\cos(A-B) - \cos(A+B)}{2}$$

$$\cos(A)\cos(B) = \frac{\cos(A+B) + \cos(A-B)}{2}$$

$$\sin(A)\cos(B) = \frac{\sin(A+B) + \sin(A-B)}{2}$$

$$\cos(A)\sin(B) = \frac{\sin(A+B) - \sin(A-B)}{2}$$

$$\sin(A) + \sin(B) = 2\sin\left(\frac{A+B}{2}\right)\cos\left(\frac{A-B}{2}\right)$$

$$\cos(A) + \cos(B) = -2\cos\left(\frac{A+B}{2}\right)\cos\left(\frac{A-B}{2}\right)$$

Trigonometric Identities, Continued

$$\sin(A) - \sin(B) = 2\cos\left(\frac{A+B}{2}\right)\sin\left(\frac{A-B}{2}\right)$$

$$\cos(A) - \cos(B) = -2\sin\left(\frac{A+B}{2}\right)\sin\left(\frac{A-B}{2}\right)$$

$$\sin^2(A) - \sin^2(B) = \sin(A+B)\sin(A-B)$$

$$\cos^2(A) - \cos^2(B) = -\sin(A+B)\sin(A-B)$$

$$\cos^2(A) - \sin^2(B) = \cos(A+B)\cos(A-B)$$

$$\tan(\theta) \triangleq \frac{\sin(\theta)}{\cos(\theta)}$$

$$\tan(A) + \tan(B) = \frac{\sin(A+B)}{\cos(A)\cos(B)}$$

$$\tan(A+B) = \frac{\tan(A+B)}{1 - \tan(A)\tan(B)}$$

A.2.4   Half-Angle Tangent Identities

$$t \triangleq \tan\left(\frac{\theta}{2}\right) = \frac{\sin(\theta)}{1+\cos(\theta)}$$

$$= \frac{1-\cos(\theta)}{\sin(\theta)}$$

$$t^2 = \frac{1-\cos(\theta)}{1+\cos(\theta)}$$

$$\sin(\theta) = \frac{2t}{1+t^2}$$

$$\cos(\theta) = \frac{1-t^2}{1+t^2}$$

$$\tan(\theta) = \frac{2t}{1-t^2}$$

A.3 A Sum of Sinusoids at the Same Frequency is Another Sinusoid at that Frequency

It is an important and fundamental fact that a sum of sinusoids at the same frequency, but different phase and amplitude, can always be expressed as a *single* sinusoid at that frequency with some resultant phase and amplitude. An important implication, for example, is that

> sinusoids are eigenfunctions of linear time-invariant (LTI) systems.

That is, if a sinusoid is input to an LTI system, the output will be a sinusoid at the same frequency, but possibly altered in amplitude and phase. This follows because the output of every LTI system can be expressed as a linear combination of delayed copies of the input signal. In this section, we derive this important result for the general case of N sinusoids at the same frequency.

A.3.1 Proof Using Trigonometry

We want to show it is always possible to solve

$$A\cos(\omega t + \phi) = A_1\cos(\omega t + \phi_1) + A_2\cos(\omega t + \phi_2) + \cdots + A_N\cos(\omega t + \phi_N)$$
$$\text{(A.2)}$$

for A and ϕ, given A_i, ϕ_i for $i = 1, \ldots, N$. For each component sinusoid, we can write

$$
\begin{aligned}
A_i\cos(\omega t + \phi_i) &= A_i\cos(\omega t)\cos(\phi_i) - A_i\sin(\omega t)\sin(\phi_i) \\
&= [A_i\cos(\phi_i)]\cos(\omega t) - [A_i\sin(\phi_i)]\sin(\omega t) \quad \text{(A.3)}
\end{aligned}
$$

Applying this expansion to Eq. (A.2) yields

$$
\begin{aligned}
[A\cos(\phi)]\cos(\omega t) \quad &- \quad [A\sin(\phi)]\sin(\omega t) \\
&= \left[\sum_{i=1}^{N} A_i\cos(\phi_i)\right]\cos(\omega t) - \left[\sum_{i=1}^{N} A_i\sin(\phi_i)\right]\sin(\omega t).
\end{aligned}
$$

Equating coefficients gives

$$
\begin{aligned}
A\cos(\phi) &= \sum_{i=1}^{N} A_i\cos(\phi_i) \triangleq x \\
A\sin(\phi) &= \sum_{i=1}^{N} A_i\sin(\phi_i) \triangleq y. \quad \text{(A.4)}
\end{aligned}
$$

where x and y are known. We now have two equations in two unknowns which are readily solved by (1) squaring and adding both sides to eliminate ϕ, and (2) forming a ratio of both sides of Eq. (A.4) to eliminate A. The results are

$$
\begin{aligned}
A &= \sqrt{x^2 + y^2} \\
\phi &= \tan^{-1}\left(\frac{y}{x}\right)
\end{aligned}
$$

which has a unique solution for any values of A_i and ϕ_i.

A.3.2   Proof Using Complex Variables

To show by means of *phasor analysis* that Eq. (A.2) always has a solution, we can express each component sinusoid as

$$
A_i \cos(\omega t + \phi_i) = \mathrm{re}\left\{ A_i e^{j(\omega t + \phi_i)} \right\}
$$

Equation (A.2) therefore becomes

$$
\mathrm{re}\left\{ A e^{j(\omega t + \phi)} \right\} = \sum_{i=1}^{N} \mathrm{re}\left\{ A_i e^{j(\omega t + \phi_i)} \right\} = \mathrm{re}\left\{ \sum_{i=1}^{N} A_i e^{j(\omega t + \phi_i)} \right\}
$$

$$
= \mathrm{re}\left\{ \underbrace{\sum_{i=1}^{N} \left(A_i e^{j\phi_i}\right) e^{j(\omega t)}}_{\triangleq A e^{j\phi}} \right\} \triangleq \mathrm{re}\left\{ \left(A e^{j\phi}\right) e^{j(\omega t)} \right\}
$$

$$
= \mathrm{re}\left\{ A e^{j(\omega t + \phi)} \right\}.
$$

Thus, equality holds when we define

$$
A e^{j\phi} \triangleq \sum_{i=1}^{N} A_i e^{j\phi_i}. \tag{A.5}
$$

Since $A e^{j\phi}$ is just the polar representation of a complex number, there is always some value of $A \geq 0$ and $\phi \in [-\pi, \pi)$ such that $A e^{j\phi}$ equals whatever complex number results on the right-hand side of Eq. (A.5).

As is often the case, we see that the use of Euler's identity and complex analysis gives a simplified *algebraic* proof which replaces a proof based on trigonometric identities.

A.3.3 Phasor Analysis: Factoring a Complex Sinusoid into Phasor Times Carrier

The heart of the preceding proof was the algebraic manipulation

$$\sum_{i=1}^{N} A_i e^{j(\omega t + \phi_i)} = e^{j\omega t} \sum_{i=1}^{N} A_i e^{j\phi_i}.$$

The *carrier term* $e^{j\omega t}$ "factors out" of the sum. Inside the sum, each sinusoid is represented by a complex constant $A_i e^{j\phi_i}$, known as the *phasor* associated with that sinusoid.

For an arbitrary sinusoid having amplitude A, phase ϕ, and radian frequency ω, we have

$$A\cos(\omega t + \phi) = \mathrm{re}\left\{ (Ae^{j\phi})e^{j\omega t} \right\}.$$

Thus, a sinusoid is determined by its frequency ω (which specifies the carrier term) and its phasor $\mathcal{A} \triangleq Ae^{j\phi}$, a complex constant. Phasor analysis is discussed further in [84].

Appendix B

Elementary Audio Digital Filters

This appendix is devoted to small but useful digital filters that are commonly used in audio applications. Analytical tools from the main chapters are used to analyze these "audio gems".

B.1 Elementary Filter Sections

This section gives condensed analysis summaries of the four most elementary digital filters: the one-zero, one-pole, two-pole, and two-zero filters. Despite their relative simplicity, they are quite valuable to master in practice. In particular, recall from Chapter 9 that every causal, finite-order, LTI filter (any difference equation of the form Eq. (5.1) on page 97) may be factored into a *series and/or parallel combination* of such sections. Implementing high-order filters as parallel and/or series combinations of low-order sections offers several advantages, such as numerical robustness and easier/safer control in real time.

B.1.1   One-Zero

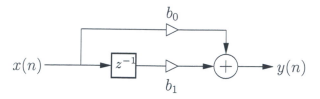

Figure B.1: Signal flow graph for the general one-zero filter
$$y(n) = b_0 x(n) + b_1 x(n-1).$$

Figure B.1 gives the signal flow graph for the general one-zero filter. The frequency response for the one-zero filter may be found by the following steps:

Difference equation:	$y(n) = b_0 x(n) + b_1 x(n-1)$
z transform:	$Y(z) = b_0 X(z) + b_1 z^{-1} X(z)$
Transfer function:	$H(z) = b_0 + b_1 z^{-1}$
Frequency response:	$H(e^{j\omega T}) = b_0 + b_1 e^{-j\omega T}$

By factoring out $e^{-j\omega T/2}$ from the frequency response, to balance the exponents of e, we can get this closer to polar form as follows:

$$
\begin{aligned}
H(e^{j\omega T}) &= b_0 + b_1 e^{-j\omega T} \\
&= (b_0 - b_1) + b_1 + b_1 e^{-j\omega T} \\
&= (b_0 - b_1) + e^{-j\omega T/2}(b_1 e^{j\omega T/2} + b_1 e^{-j\omega T/2}) \\
&= (b_0 - b_1) + e^{-j\omega T/2} 2 b_1 \cos(\omega T/2) \\
&= (b_0 - b_1) + e^{-j\pi fT} 2 b_1 \cos(\pi fT)
\end{aligned}
$$

We now apply the general equations given in Chapter 7 for filter gain $G(\omega)$ and filter phase $\Theta(\omega)$ as a function of frequency:

$$
\begin{aligned}
H(e^{j\omega T}) &= b_0 + b_1 e^{-j\omega T} \\
&= b_0 + b_1 \cos(\omega T) - j b_1 \sin(\omega T)
\end{aligned}
$$

$$
\begin{aligned}
G(\omega) &= \sqrt{[b_0 + b_1 \cos(\omega T)]^2 + [-b_1 \sin(\omega T)]^2} \\
&= \sqrt{b_0^2 + b_1^2 + 2 b_0 b_1 \cos(\omega T)}
\end{aligned}
$$

$$
\Theta(\omega) = \tan^{-1}\left[\frac{-b_1 \sin(\omega T)}{b_0 + b_1 \cos(\omega T)}\right]
$$

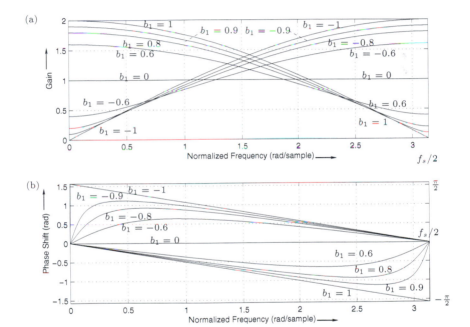

Figure B.2: Family of frequency responses of the one-zero filter
$$y(n) = x(n) + b_1 x(n-1)$$
for various values of b_1. (a) Amplitude response. (b) Phase response.

A plot of $G(\omega)$ and $\Theta(\omega)$ for $b_0 = 1$ and various real values of b_1, is given in Fig. B.2. The filter has a zero at $z = -b_1/b_0 = -b_1$ in the z plane, which is always on the real axis. When a point on the unit circle comes close to the zero of the transfer function the filter gain at that frequency is low. Notice that one real zero can basically make either a highpass $(b_1/b_0 < 0)$ or a lowpass filter $(b_1/b_0 > 0)$. For the phase response calculation using the graphical method, it is necessary to include the pole at $z = 0$.

B.1.2   One-Pole

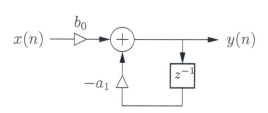

$$x(n) \xrightarrow{b_0} (+) \xrightarrow{\quad} y(n)$$

$$-a_1$$

$$z^{-1}$$

Figure B.3: Signal flow graph for the general one-pole filter
$$y(n) = b_0 x(n) - a_1 y(n-1).$$

Fig. B.3 gives the signal flow graph for the general one-pole filter. The road to the frequency response goes as follows:

Difference equation:	$y(n) = b_0 x(n) - a_1 y(n-1)$
z transform:	$Y(z) = b_0 X(z) - a_1 z^{-1} Y(z)$
Transfer function:	$H(z) = \dfrac{b_0}{1 + a_1 z^{-1}}$
Frequency response:	$H(e^{j\omega T}) = \dfrac{b_0}{1 + a_1 e^{-j\omega T}}$

The one-pole filter has a transfer function (hence frequency response) which is the reciprocal of that of a one-zero. The analysis is thus quite analogous. The frequency response in polar form is given by

$$
\begin{aligned}
G(\omega) &= \frac{|b_0|}{\sqrt{[1 + a_1 \cos(\omega T)]^2 + [-a_1 \sin(\omega T)]^2}} \\
&= \frac{|b_0|}{\sqrt{1 + a_1^2 + 2a_1 \cos(\omega T)}}
\end{aligned}
$$

$$
\Theta(\omega) = \begin{cases}
-\tan^{-1}\left[\frac{-a_1 \sin(\omega T)}{1 + a_1 \cos(\omega T)}\right], & b_0 > 0 \\[2mm]
\pi - \tan^{-1}\left[\frac{-a_1 \sin(\omega T)}{1 + a_1 \cos(\omega T)}\right], & b_0 < 0
\end{cases}.
$$

(a)

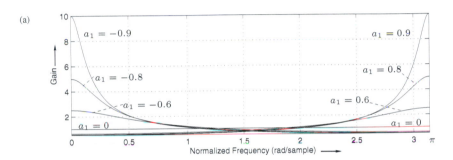

(b)

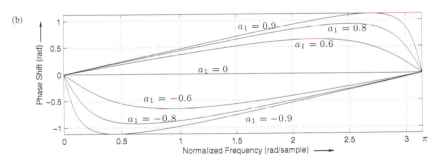

Figure B.4: Family of frequency responses of the one-pole filter
$$y(n) = x(n) - a_1 y(n-1)$$
for various real values of a_1. (a) Amplitude response. (b) Phase response.

A plot of the frequency response in polar form for $b_0 = 1$ and various values of a_1 is given in Fig. B.4.

The filter has a pole at $z = -a_1$, in the z plane (and a zero at $z = 0$). Notice that the one-pole exhibits either a lowpass or a highpass frequency response, like the one-zero. The lowpass character occurs when the pole is near the point $z = 1$ (dc), which happens when a_1 approaches -1. Conversely, the highpass nature occurs when a_1 is positive.

The one-pole filter section can achieve much more drastic differences between the gain at high frequencies and the gain at low frequencies than can the one-zero filter. This difference is achieved in the one-pole by gain *boost* in the passband rather than *attenuation* in the stopband; thus it is usually desirable when using a one-pole filter to set b_0 to a small value, such as $1 - |a_1|$, so that the peak gain is 1 or so. When the peak gain is 1, the filter is unlikely to overflow.[1]

Finally, note that the one-pole filter is stable if and only if $|a_1| < 1$.

B.1.3   Two-Pole

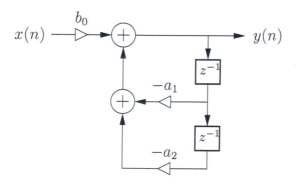

Figure B.5: Signal flow graph for the general two-pole filter
$$y(n) = b_0 x(n) - a_1 y(n-1) - a_2 y(n-2).$$

The signal flow graph for the general two-pole filter is given in Fig. B.5. We proceed as usual with the general analysis steps to obtain the following:

---

[1] A small chance of overflow remains because sinusoids at different frequencies can be delayed differently by the filter, causing an increased peak amplitude in the output due to phase realignment.

$$\boxed{\begin{aligned}
\text{Difference equation:} &\quad y(n) = b_0 x(n) - a_1 y(n-1) - a_2 y(n-2) \\[4pt]
\text{z transform:} &\quad Y(z) = b_0 X(z) - a_1 z^{-1} Y(z) - a_2 z^{-2} Y(z) \\[4pt]
\text{Transfer function:} &\quad H(z) = \frac{b_0}{1 + a_1 z^{-1} + a_2 z^{-2}} \\[4pt]
\text{Frequency response:} &\quad H(e^{j\omega T}) = \frac{b_0}{1 + a_1 e^{-j\omega T} + a_2 e^{-j2\omega T}}
\end{aligned}}$$

The numerator of $H(z)$ is a constant, so there are no zeros other than two at the origin of the z plane.

The coefficients a_1 and a_2 are called the *denominator coefficients*, and they determine the two *poles* of $H(z)$. Using the quadratic formula, the poles are found to be located at

$$z = -\frac{a_1}{2} \pm \sqrt{\left(\frac{a_1}{2}\right)^2 - a_2}.$$

When the coefficients a_1 and a_2 are real (as we typically assume), the poles must be either real (when $(a_1/2)^2 \geq a_2$) or form a complex conjugate pair (when $(a_1/2)^2 < a_2$).

When both poles are real, the two-pole can be analyzed simply as a cascade of two one-pole sections, as in the previous section. That is, one can *multiply pointwise* two magnitude plots such as Fig. B.4a, and *add pointwise* two phase plots such as Fig. B.4b.

When the poles are complex, they can be written as

$$\begin{aligned}
p_1 &= x_p + j y_p \\
p_2 &= x_p - j y_p = \bar{p}_1
\end{aligned}$$

since they must form a complex-conjugate pair when a_1 and a_2 are real. We may express them in *polar form* as

$$\begin{aligned}
p_1 &= R e^{j\theta_c} \\
p_2 &= R e^{-j\theta_c}
\end{aligned}$$

where

$$\begin{aligned}
R &= \sqrt{x_p^2 + y_p^2} > 0 \\
\theta_c &= \tan^{-1}\left(\frac{y_p}{x_p}\right).
\end{aligned}$$

R is the pole *radius*, or distance from the origin in the z-plane. As discussed in Chapter 8, we must have $R < 1$ for stability of the two-pole filter. The angles $\pm\theta_c$ are the poles' respective *angles* in the z plane. The pole angle θ_c corresponds to the *pole frequency* ω_c via the relation

$$\theta_c = \omega_c T = 2\pi f_c T$$

where T denotes the sampling interval. See Chapter 8 for a discussion and examples of pole-zero plots in the complex z-plane.

If R is sufficiently large (but less than 1 for stability), the filter exhibits a *resonance*[2] at radian frequency $\omega_c = 2\pi f_c = \theta_c/T$. We may call ω_c or f_c the *center frequency* of the resonator. Note, however, that the resonance frequency is not usually the precise frequency of *peak-gain* in a two-pole resonator (see Fig. B.9 on page 268). The peak of the amplitude response is usually a little different because each pole sits on the other's "skirt," which is slanted. (See §B.1.5 and §B.6 for an elaboration of this point.)

Using polar form for the (complex) poles, the two-pole transfer function can be expressed as

$$H(z) \quad = \quad \frac{b_0}{(1 - Re^{j\theta_c}z^{-1})(1 - Re^{-j\theta_c}z^{-1})}$$

$$= \quad \frac{b_0}{1 - 2R\cos(\theta_c)z^{-1} + R^2 z^{-2}} \tag{B.1}$$

Comparing this to the transfer function derived from the difference equation, we may identify

$$a_1 \quad = \quad -2R\cos(\theta_c)$$
$$a_2 \quad = \quad R^2.$$

The difference equation can thus be rewritten as

$$y(n) = b_0 x(n) + [2R\cos(\theta_c)]y(n-1) - R^2 y(n-2). \tag{B.2}$$

Note that coefficient a_2 depends only on the pole radius R (which determines damping) and is independent of the resonance frequency, while a_1 is a function of both. As a result, we may *retune* the resonance frequency of the two-pole filter section by modifying a_1 only.

The gain at the resonant frequency $\omega = \omega_c$, is found by substituting $z = e^{j\theta_c} = e^{j\omega_c T}$ into Eq. (B.1) to get

$$G(\omega_c) \triangleq |H(e^{j\theta_c})| \quad = \quad \left| \frac{b_0}{(1-R)(1-Re^{-j2\theta_c})} \right|$$

$$= \quad \frac{|b_0|}{(1-R)\sqrt{1-2R\cos(2\theta_c)+R^2}} \tag{B.3}$$

---

[2] A *resonance* may be defined as a local peak in the amplitude response of a filter, caused by a pole close to the unit circle.

See §B.6 for details on how the resonance gain (and peak gain) can be normalized as the tuning of ω_c is varied in real time.

Since the radius of both poles is R, we must have $R < 1$ for filter stability (§8.4). The closer R is to 1, the higher the gain at the resonant frequency $\omega_c = 2\pi f_c$. If $R = 0$, the filter degenerates to the form $H(z) = b_0$, which is a nothing but a scale factor. We can say that when the two poles move to the origin of the z plane, they are canceled by the two zeros there.

Resonator Bandwidth in Terms of Pole Radius

The *magnitude* R of a complex pole determines the *damping* or *bandwidth* of the resonator. (Damping may be defined as the reciprocal of the bandwidth.)

As derived in §8.5 on page 189, when R is close to 1, a reasonable definition of 3dB-bandwidth B is provided by

$$B \triangleq -\frac{\ln(R)}{\pi T} \tag{B.4}$$

$$R = e^{-\pi B T} \tag{B.5}$$

where R is the pole radius, B is the bandwidth in Hertz (cycles per second), and T is the sampling interval in seconds.

Figure B.6 shows a family of frequency responses for the two-pole resonator obtained by setting $b_0 = 1$ and varying R. The value of θ_c in all cases is $\pi/4$, corresponding to $f_c = f_s/8$. The analytic expressions for amplitude and phase response are

$$G(\omega) = \frac{b_0}{\sqrt{[1 + a_1 \cos(\omega T) + a_2 \cos(2\omega T)]^2 + [-a_1 \sin(\omega T) - a_2 \sin(2\omega T)]^2}}$$

$$\Theta(\omega) = -\tan^{-1}\left[\frac{-a_1 \sin(\omega T) - a_2 \sin(2\omega T)}{1 + a_1 \cos(\omega T) + a_2 \cos(2\omega T)}\right] \qquad (b_0 > 0)$$

where $a_1 = -2R\cos(\theta_c)$ and $a_2 = R^2$.

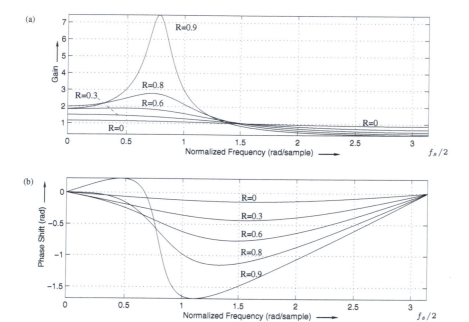

Figure B.6: Frequency response of the two-pole filter
$$y(n) = x(n) + 2R\cos(\theta_c)y(n-1) - R^2 y(n-2)$$
with θ_c fixed at $\pi/4$ and for various values of R. (a) Amplitude response.
(b) Phase response.

B.1.4   Two-Zero

The signal flow graph for the general two-zero filter is given in Fig. B.7, and the derivation of frequency response is as follows:

Difference equation:	$y(n) = b_0 x(n) + b_1 x(n-1) + b_2 x(n-2)$
z transform:	$Y(z) = b_0 X(z) + b_1 z^{-1} X(z) + b_2 z^{-2} X(z)$
Transfer function:	$H(z) = b_0 + b_1 z^{-1} + b_2 z^{-2}$
Frequency response:	$H(e^{j\omega T}) = b_0 + b_1 e^{-j\omega T} + b_2 e^{-j2\omega T}$
Amplitude response:	$G^2(\omega) = [b_0 + b_1 \cos(\omega T) + b_2 \cos(2\omega T)]^2$
	$\quad + [-b_1 \sin(\omega T) - b_2 \sin(2\omega T)]^2$
Phase response:	$\Theta(\omega) = \tan^{-1}\left[\dfrac{-b_1 \sin(\omega T) - b_2 \sin(2\omega T)}{b_0 + b_1 \cos(\omega T) + b_2 \cos(2\omega T)}\right]$

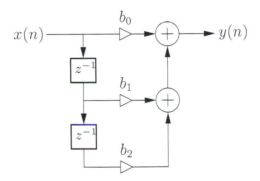

Figure B.7: Signal flow graph for the general two-zero filter
$$y(n) = b_0 x(n) + b_1 x(n-1) + b_2 x(n-2).$$

As discussed in §5.1, the parameters b_1 and b_2 are called the *numerator coefficients*, and they determine the two *zeros*. Using the quadratic formula for finding the roots of a second-order polynomial, we find that the zeros are located at

$$z = \frac{-b_1 \pm \sqrt{b_1^2 - 4b_0 b_2}}{2b_0}$$

If the zeros are real $[(b_1/2)^2 \geq b_2]$, then the two-zero case reduces to two instances of our earlier analysis for the one-zero. Assuming the zeros to be complex, we may express the zeros in polar form as $Re^{j\theta_c}$ and $Re^{-j\theta_c}$, where $\theta_c = \omega_c T = 2\pi f_c T$.

Forming a general two-zero transfer function in factored form gives

$$\begin{aligned} H(z) &= b_0(1 - Re^{j\theta_c}z^{-1})(1 - Re^{-j\theta_c}z^{-1}) \\ &= b_0[1 - 2R\cos(\theta_c)z^{-1} + R^2z^{-2}] \end{aligned}$$

from which we identify $b_1/b_0 = -2R\cos(\theta_c)$ and $b_2/b_0 = R^2$, so that

$$y(n) = b_0\{x(n) - [2R\cos(\theta_c)]x(n-1) + R^2x(n-2)\}$$

is again the difference equation of the general two-zero filter with complex zeros. The frequency ω, is now viewed as a *notch frequency*, or *antiresonance frequency*. The closer R is to 1, the narrower the notch centered at ω_c.

The approximate relation between bandwidth and R given in Eq. (B.5) for the two-pole resonator now applies to the *notch width* in the two-zero filter.

Figure B.8 gives some two-zero frequency responses obtained by setting b_0 to 1 and varying R. The value of θ_c, is again $\pi/4$. Note that the response is exactly analogous to the two-pole resonator with notches replacing the resonant peaks. Since the plots are on a linear magnitude scale, the two-zero amplitude response appears as the reciprocal of a two-pole response. On a dB scale, the two-zero response is an upside-down two-pole response.

B.1.5   Complex Resonator

Normally when we need a resonator, we think immediately of the two-pole resonator. However, there is also a *complex one-pole resonator* having the transfer function

$$H(z) = \frac{g}{1 - pz^{-1}} \tag{B.6}$$

where $p = Re^{j\theta_c}$ is the single complex pole, and g is a scale factor. In the time domain, the complex one-pole resonator is implemented as

$$y(n) = gx(n) + py(n-1).$$

Since p is complex, the output $y(n)$ is generally complex even when the input $x(n)$ is real.

Since the impulse response is the inverse z transform of the transfer function, we can write down the impulse response of the complex one-pole resonator by recognizing Eq. (B.6) as the closed-form sum of an infinite geometric series, yielding

$$h(n) = u(n)gp^n,$$

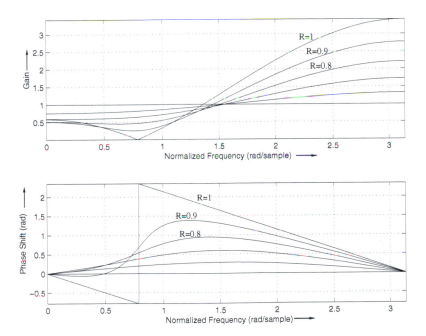

Figure B.8: Frequency response of the two-zero filter
$$y(n) = x(n) - 2R\cos(\theta_c)x(n-1) + R^2 x(n-2)$$
with θ_c fixed at $\pi/4$ and for various values of R. (a) Amplitude response.
(b) Phase response.

where, as always, $u(n)$ denotes the *unit step function*:

$$u(n) \triangleq \begin{cases} 1, & n \geq 0 \\ 0, & n < 0 \end{cases}$$

Thus, the impulse response is simply a scale factor g times the geometric sequence p^n with the pole p as its "term ratio". In general, $p^n = R^n e^{j\omega_c nT}$ is a sampled, exponentially decaying sinusoid at radian frequency $\omega_c = \theta_c/T$. By setting p somewhere on the unit circle to get

$$p \triangleq e^{j\omega_c T},$$

we obtain a *complex sinusoidal oscillator* at radian frequency ω_c rad/sec. If we like, we can extract the real and imaginary parts separately to create both a sine-wave and a cosine-wave output:

$$\begin{aligned} \mathrm{re}\left\{h(n)\right\} &= u(n)g\cos(\omega_c nT) \\ \mathrm{im}\left\{h(n)\right\} &= u(n)g\sin(\omega_c nT) \end{aligned}$$

These may be called *phase-quadrature sinusoids*, since their phases differ by 90 degrees. The phase quadrature relationship for two sinusoids means that they can be regarded as the real and imaginary parts of a complex sinusoid.

By allowing g to be complex,

$$g \triangleq A e^{j\phi}$$

we can arbitrarily set both the amplitude and phase of this phase-quadrature oscillator:

$$\begin{aligned} \mathrm{re}\left\{h(n)\right\} &= u(n)A\cos(\omega_c nT + \phi) \\ \mathrm{im}\left\{h(n)\right\} &= u(n)A\sin(\omega_c nT + \phi) \end{aligned}$$

The frequency response of the complex one-pole resonator differs from that of the two-pole *real* resonator in that the resonance occurs only for one positive or negative frequency ω_c, but not both. As a result, the resonance frequency ω_c is also the frequency where the *peak-gain* occurs; this is only true in general for the complex one-pole resonator. In particular, the peak gain of a real two-pole filter does not occur exactly at resonance, except when $\theta_c \triangleq \omega_c T = 0$, $\pi/2$, or π. See §B.6 for more on peak-gain versus resonance-gain (and how to normalize them in practice).

Two-Pole Partial Fraction Expansion

Note that every real two-pole resonator can be broken up into a sum of two complex one-pole resonators:

$$H(z) = \frac{g}{(1 - pz^{-1})(1 - \bar{p}z^{-1})} = \frac{g_1}{1 - pz^{-1}} + \frac{g_2}{1 - \bar{p}z^{-1}} \qquad (\text{B.7})$$

where g_1 and g_2 are constants (generally complex). In this "parallel one-pole" form, it can be seen that the peak gain is no longer equal to the resonance gain, since each one-pole frequency response is "tilted" near resonance by being summed with the "skirt" of the other one-pole resonator, as illustrated in Fig. B.9. This interaction between the positive- and negative-frequency poles is minimized by making the resonance sharper ($|p| \to 1$), and by separating the pole frequencies $0 \ll \angle p \ll \pi$. The greatest separation occurs when the resonance frequency is at one-fourth the sampling rate ($\angle p = \pi/2$). However, low-frequency resonances, which are by far the most common in audio work, suffer from significant overlapping of the positive- and negative-frequency poles.

To show Eq. (B.7) is always true, let's solve in general for g_1 and g_2 given g and p. Recombining the right-hand side over a common denominator and equating numerators gives

$$g = g_1 - g_1\bar{p}z^{-1} + g_2 - g_2pz^{-1}$$

which implies

$$g_1 + g_2 = g$$
$$g_1\bar{p} + g_2p = 0.$$

The solution is easily found to be

$$g_1 = g\frac{p}{2\text{im}\,\{p\}}$$

$$g_2 = -g\frac{\bar{p}}{2\text{im}\,\{p\}}$$

where we have assumed $\text{im}\,\{p\} \neq 0$, as necessary to have a resonator in the first place.

Breaking up the two-pole real resonator into a parallel sum of two complex one-pole resonators is a simple example of a *partial fraction expansion* (PFE) (discussed more fully in §6.8 on page 129).

Note that the inverse z transform of a sum of one-pole transfer functions can be easily written down by inspection. In particular, the impulse response of the PFE of the two-pole resonator (see Eq. (B.7)) is clearly

$$h(n) = g_1p^n + g_2\bar{p}^n, \qquad n = 0, 1, 2, \ldots$$

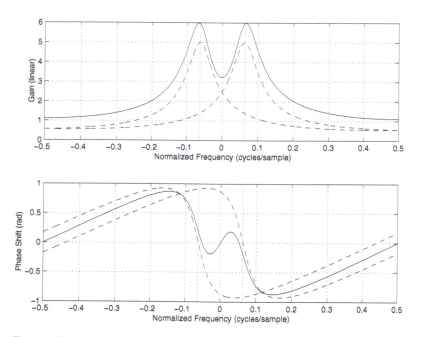

Figure B.9: Frequency response (solid lines) of the two-pole resonator
$$H(z) = 1/(1 - 2R\cos(\theta_c)z^{-1} + R^2 z^{-2}),$$
for $R = 0.8$ and $\theta_c = \pi/8$, overlaid with the frequency responses (dashed
lines) of its positive- and negative-frequency complex one-pole components. Also marked (dashed lines) are the two resonance frequencies; the
peak frequencies can be seen to lie slightly outside the resonance frequencies.

Since $h(n)$ is real, we must have $g_2 = \bar{g}_1$, as we found above without assuming it. If $|p| = 1$, then $h(n)$ is a real sinusoid created by the sum of two complex sinusoids spinning in opposite directions on the unit circle.

B.1.6   The BiQuad Section

The term "biquad" is short for "bi-quadratic", and is a common name for a two-pole, two-zero digital filter. The *transfer function* of the biquad can be defined as

$$H(z) = g\frac{1 + \beta_1 z^{-1} + \beta_2 z^{-2}}{1 + a_1 z^{-1} + a_2 z^{-2}} \tag{B.8}$$

where g can be called the *overall gain* of the biquad. Since both the numerator and denominator of this transfer function are quadratic polynomials in z^{-1} (or z), the transfer function is said to be "bi-quadratic" in z^{-1} (or z).

As derived in §B.1.3 on page 258, for real second-order polynomials having complex roots, it is often convenient to express the polynomial coefficients in terms of the radius R and angle θ of the positive-frequency pole. For example, denoting the denominator polynomial by $A(z) = 1 + a_1 z^{-1} + a_2 z^{-2}$, we have

$$A(z) = \left(1 - Re^{j\theta}z^{-1}\right)\left(1 - Re^{-j\theta}z^{-1}\right) = 1 - 2R\cos(\theta)z^{-1} + R^2 z^{-2}.$$

This representation is most often used for the denominator of the biquad, and we think of θ as the *resonance frequency* (in radians per sample— $\theta = 2\pi f_c T$, where f_c is the resonance frequency in Hz), and R determines the "Q" of the resonance (see §B.1.3 on page 261). The numerator is less often represented in this way, but when it is, we may think of the zero-angle as the *antiresonance frequency*, and the zero-radius affects the *depth* and *width* of the antiresonance (or *notch*).

As discussed on page 290, a common setting for the zeros when making a resonator is to place one at $z = 1$ (dc) and the other at $z = -1$ (half the sampling rate), *i.e.*, $\beta_1 = 0$ and $\beta_2 = -1$ in Eq. (B.8) above $\Rightarrow B(z) = 1 - z^{-2} = (1 - z^{-1})(1 + z^{-1})$. This zero placement normalizes the peak gain of the resonator if it is swept using the a_1 parameter.

Using the shift theorem for z transforms, the *difference equation* for the biquad can be written by inspection of the transfer function as

$$\begin{aligned} v(n) &= g\,x(n) \\ y(n) &= v(n) + \beta_1 v(n-1) + \beta_2 v(n-2) \\ &\quad -a_1 y(n-1) - a_2 y(n-2). \end{aligned}$$

where $x(n)$ denotes the input signal sample at time n, and $y(n)$ is the output signal. This is the form that is typically implemented in software. It is essentially the *direct-form I* implementation. (To obtain the official direct-form I structure, the overall gain g must be not be pulled out separately, resulting in feedforward coefficients $[g, g\beta_1, g\beta_2]$ instead. See Chapter 9 for more about filter implementation forms.)

B.1.7 Biquad Software Implementations

In matlab, an efficient biquad section is implemented by calling

```
outputsignal = filter(B,A,inputsignal);
```

where

$$
\begin{aligned}
\text{B} &= [g, g\beta_1, g\beta_2], \\
\text{A} &= [1, a_1, a_2].
\end{aligned}
$$

A complete C++ class implementing a biquad filter section is included in the free, open-source Synthesis Tool Kit (STK) [15]. (See the BiQuad STK class.)

Figure B.10 lists an example biquad implementation in the C programming language.

```
typedef double *pp;   // pointer to array of length NTICK
typedef word double;  // signal and coefficient data type

typedef struct _biquadVars {
    pp output;
    pp input;
    word s2;
    word s1;
    word gain;
    word a2;
    word a1;
    word b2;
    word b1;
} biquadVars;

void biquad(biquadVars *a)
{
    int i;
    dbl A;
    word s0;
    for (i=0; i<NTICK; i++) {
        A = a->gain * a->input[i];
        A -= a->a1 * a->s1;
        A -= a->a2 * a->s2;
        s0 = A;
        A += a->b1 * a->s1;
        a->output[i] = a->b2 * a->s2 + A;
        a->s2 = a->s1;
        a->s1 = s0;
    }
}
```

Figure B.10: C code implementing a biquad filter section.

B.2   Allpass Filter Sections

The *allpass filter* passes all frequencies with equal gain. This is in contrast with a lowpass filter, which passes only low frequencies, a highpass which passes high-frequencies, and a bandpass filter which passes an interval of frequencies. An allpass filter may have any phase response. The only requirement is that its amplitude response be constant. Normally, this constant is $|H(e^{j\omega T})| = 1$.

From a physical modeling point of view, a unity-gain allpass filter models a *lossless system* in the sense that it *preserves signal energy*. Specifically, if $x(n)$ denotes the input to an allpass filter $H(z)$, and if $y(n)$ denotes its output, then we have

$$\sum_{n=-\infty}^{\infty} |x(n)|^2 = \sum_{n=-\infty}^{\infty} |y(n)|^2 . \qquad (B.9)$$

This equation says that the total energy out equals the total energy in. No energy was created or destroyed by the filter. All an allpass filter can do is delay the sinusoidal components of a signal by differing amounts.

Appendix C starting on page 299 proves that Eq. (B.9) holds if and only if

$$|H(e^{j\omega T})| = 1, \quad \forall \omega.$$

That is, a filter $H(z)$ is lossless if and only if it is an allpass filter having a gain of 1 at every frequency ω.

B.2.1   The Biquad Allpass Section

The general biquad transfer function was given in Eq. (B.8) to be

$$H(z) = g \frac{1 + \beta_1 z^{-1} + \beta_2 z^{-2}}{1 + a_1 z^{-1} + a_2 z^{-2}} \triangleq \frac{B(z)}{A(z)}.$$

To specialize this to a second-order unity-gain allpass filter, we require

$$|H(e^{j\omega T})| = 1.$$

It is easy to show (see Problem 1 on page 307) that, given any monic denominator polynomial $A(z)$, the numerator $B(z)$ must be, in the real case,[3]

$$B(z) = z^{-2} A(z^{-1}) = a_2 + a_1 z^{-1} + z^{-2}.$$

Thus, to obtain an allpass biquad section, the numerator polynomial is simply the "flip" of the denominator polynomial. To obtain unity gain, we set $g = a_2$, $\beta_1 = a_1/a_2$, and $\beta_2 = 1/a_2$.

---

[3] In the case of complex coefficients a_i, $B(z) = \overline{a_2} + \overline{a_1} z^{-1} + z^{-2}$.

In terms of the poles and zeros of a filter $H(z) = B(z)/A(z)$, an allpass filter must have a zero at $z = 1/p$ for each pole at $z = p$. That is if the denominator $A(z)$ satisfies $A(p) = 0$, then the numerator polynomial $B(z)$ must satisfy $B(1/p) = 0$. (Show this in the one-pole case.) Therefore, defining $B(z) = A(1/z)$ takes care of this property for all roots of $A(z)$ (all poles). However, since we prefer that $B(z)$ be a polynomial in z^{-1}, we define $B(z) = z^{-N}A(1/z)$, where N is the order of $A(z)$ (the number of poles). $B(z)$ is then the flip of $A(z)$.

For further discussion and examples of allpass filters (including muliinput, multi-output allpass filters), see Appendix C. Analog allpass filters are defined and discussed in §E.8 on page 331.

B.2.2   Allpass Filter Design

There is a fairly large literature thread on the topic of *allpass filter design*. Generally, they fall into two main categories: *parametric* and *nonparametric* methods. Parametric methods can produce allpass filters with optimal group-delay characteristics [42, 41]. Nonparametric methods, while suboptimal, can design very large-order allpass filters, and errors can usually be made arbitrarily small by increasing the order [100, 70, 1], [78, pp. 60,172]. In music applications, it is usually the case that the "optimality" criterion is unknown because it depends on aspects of sound perception (see, for example, [35, 72]). As a result, perceptually weighted nonparametric methods can often outperform optimal parametric methods in terms of cost/performance. For a nonparametric method that can design very high-order allpass filters according to highly flexible criteria, see [1].

B.3   DC Blocker

The dc blocker is an indispensable tool in digital waveguide modeling [86] and other applications.[4] It is often needed to remove the dc component of the signal circulating in a delay-line loop. It is also often an important tool in multi-track recording, where dc components in the various tracks can add up and overflow the mix.

The *dc blocker* is a small recursive filter specified by the difference equation

$$y(n) = x(n) - x(n-1) + R\,y(n-1)$$

where R is a parameter that is typically somewhere between 0.9 and 1 (for

---

[4]For the reader with some background in analog circuit design, the dc blocker is the digital equivalent of the analog *blocking capacitor*.

a 44.1 kHz sampling rate, $R = 0.995$ is good). The transfer function is

$$H(z) = \frac{1 - z^{-1}}{1 - Rz^{-1}}. \tag{B.10}$$

Thus, there is a zero at dc $(z = 1)$ and a pole near dc at $z = R$. Far away from dc, the pole and zero approximately cancel each other. (Recall the graphical method for determining frequency response magnitude described in Chapter 8.)

B.3.1   DC Blocker Frequency Response

Figure B.11 shows the frequency response of the dc blocker for several values of R. The same plots are given over a log-frequency scale in Fig. B.12. The corresponding pole-zero diagrams are shown in Fig. B.13. As R approaches 1, the notch at dc gets narrower and narrower. While this may seem ideal, there is a drawback, as shown in Fig. B.14 for the case of $R = 0.9$: The impulse response duration increases as $R \to 1$. While the "tail" of the impulse response lengthens as R approaches 1, its initial magnitude decreases. At the limit, $R = 1$, the pole and zero cancel at all frequencies, the impulse response becomes an impulse, and the notch disappears.

Note that the amplitude response in Fig. B.11a and Fig. B.12a exceeds 1 at half the sampling rate. This maximum gain is given by $H(-1) = 2/(1 + R)$. In applications for which the gain must be bounded by 1 at all frequencies, the dc blocker may be scaled by the inverse of this maximum gain to yield

$$
\begin{aligned}
H(z) &= g\frac{1 - z^{-1}}{1 - Rz^{-1}} \\
y(n) &= g[x(n) - x(n-1)] + R\,y(n-1), \quad \text{where} \\
g &\triangleq \frac{1 + R}{2}.
\end{aligned}
$$

B.3.2   DC Blocker Software Implementations

In plain C, the difference equation for the dc blocker could be written as follows:

```
y = x - xm1 + 0.995 * ym1;
xm1 = x;
ym1 = y;
```

Here, x denotes the current input sample, and y denotes the current output sample. The variables xm1 and ym1 hold once-delayed input and output

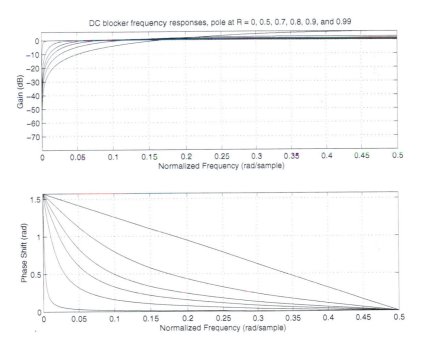

Figure B.11: Frequency response overlays for the dc blocker defined by $H(z) = (1 - z^{-1})/(1 - Rz^{-1})$ for various values of pole radius R. (a) Amplitude response. (b) Phase response.

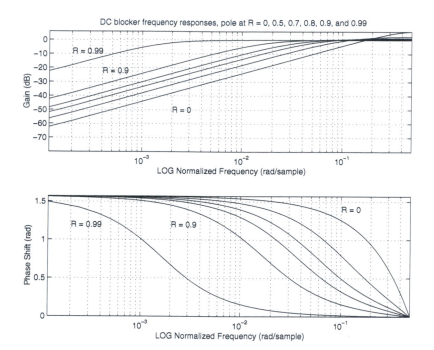

Figure B.12: Log-frequency response overlays for the dc blocker defined by $H(z) = (1 - z^{-1})/(1 - Rz^{-1})$ for various values of pole radius R. (a) Amplitude response. (b) Phase response.

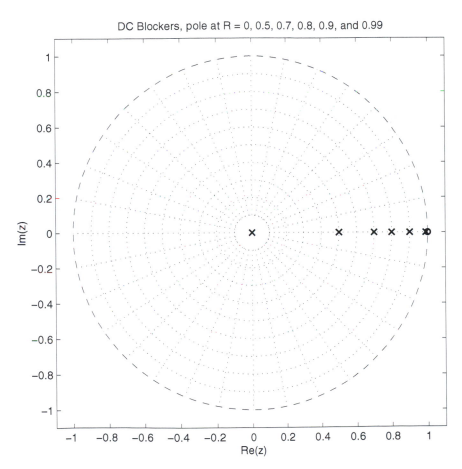

Figure B.13: Pole-zero diagram overlays for the dc blocker defined by $H(z) = (1 - z^{-1})/(1 - Rz^{-1})$ for various values of pole radius R.

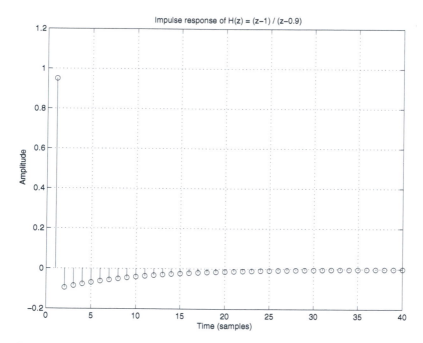

Figure B.14: Impulse response of the dc blocker defined by $H(z) = (1 - z^{-1})/(1 - 0.9z^{-1})$.

samples, respectively (and are typically initialized to zero). In this implementation, the pole is fixed at $R = 0.995$, which corresponds to an adaptation time-constant of approximately $1/(1 - R) = 200$ samples. A smaller R value allows faster tracking of "wandering dc levels", but at the cost of greater low-frequency attenuation.

A complete C++ class implementing a dc blocking filter is included in the free, open-source Synthesis Tool Kit (STK) [15]. (See the `DCBlock` STK class.)

For a discussion of issues and solutions related to fixed-point implementations, see [7].

B.4   Low and High Shelf Filters

The analog transfer function for a *low shelf* is given by [103]

$$H(s) = 1 + \frac{B_0\omega_1}{s + \omega_1} = \frac{s + \omega_1(B_0 + 1)}{s + \omega_1} \triangleq \frac{s + \omega_z}{s + \omega_1}$$

where B_0 is the dc boost amount (at $s = 0$), and the high-frequency gain $(s = \infty)$ is constrained to be 1. The *transition frequency* dividing low and high frequency regions is ω_1. See Appendix E for a development of s-plane analysis of analog (continuous-time) filters.

A *high shelf* is obtained from a low shelf by the conformal mapping $s \leftarrow 1/s$, which interchanges high and low frequencies, *i.e.*,

$$H(s) = 1 + \frac{B_\pi\omega_1}{\frac{1}{s} + \omega_1} = (1 + B_\pi)\frac{s + \frac{1}{(1+B_\pi)\omega_1}}{s + \frac{1}{\omega_1}} \triangleq \frac{\omega_z}{\omega_1} \cdot \frac{s + \frac{1}{\omega_z}}{s + \frac{1}{\omega_1}}$$

In this case, the dc gain is 1 and the high-frequency gain approaches $1 + B_\pi = \omega_z/\omega_1$.

To convert these analog-filter transfer functions to digital form, we apply the bilinear transform:

$$s = c\frac{1 - z^{-1}}{1 + z^{-1}}$$

where typically $c = 2/T$ and T denotes the sampling interval in seconds.[5]

Low and high shelf filters are typically implemented in series, and are typically used to give a little boost or cut at the extreme low or high end (of the spectrum), respectively. To provide a boost or cut near other frequencies, it is necessary to go to (at least) a second-order section, often called a "peaking equalizer," as described in §B.5 below.

---

[5] Free open-source implementations of digital shelf filters are available in `filter.lib` within the Faust distribution (see Appendix K).

Exercise

Perform the bilinear transform defined above and calculate the coefficients of a first-order *digital* low shelf filter. Find the pole and zero as a function of B_0, ω_1, and T. Set $z = 1$ and verify that you get a gain of $1 + B_0$. Set $z = -1$ and verify that you get a gain of 1 there.

B.5 Peaking Equalizers

A *peaking equalizer* filter section provides a boost or cut in the vicinity of some center frequency. It may also be called a *parametric equalizer* section. The gain far away from the boost or cut is unity, so it is convenient to combine a number of such sections in series. Additionally, a high and/or low shelf (§B.4 above) are nice to include in series with one's peaking eq sections.

The analog transfer function for a *peak filter* is given by [103, 5, 6]

$$H(s) = 1 + H_R(s)$$

where $H_R(s)$ is a two-pole resonator:

$$H_R(s) \triangleq R \cdot \frac{Bs}{s^2 + Bs + 1}$$

The transfer function can be written in the normalized form [103]

$$H(s) = \frac{s^2 + gBs + 1}{s^2 + Bs + 1},$$

where $g = 1 + R$ is approximately the desired gain at the boost (or cut), and $B = 1/Q$ is the desired bandwidth 2α at the normalized peak frequency $\omega_0 = 1$ (cf. Eq. (E.8) on page 328). When $g > 1$, a *boost* is obtained at frequency $\omega = 1$. For $g < 1$, a *cut* is obtained at that frequency. In particular, when $g = 0$, there are infinitely deep notches at $\omega = \pm 1$, and when $g = 1$, the transfer function reduces to $H(s) = 1$ (no boost or cut). The parameter B controls the *width* of the boost or cut.

It is easy to show that both zeros and both poles are on the unit circle in the left-half s plane, and when $g < 1$ (a "cut"), the zeros are closer to the $j\omega$ axis than the poles.

The bilinear transform (§I.3.1 on page 388) can be used to convert the analog peaking equalizer section to digital form. As derived in §I.3.2, the mapping constant c is best chosen as $c = \cot(\omega_d T/2)$, where ω_d is the desired peak frequency and T is the sampling interval.

Figure B.15 gives a matlab listing for a peaking equalizer section. Figure B.16 shows the resulting plot for the example "`boost(2,0.25,0.1)`."

The frequency-response display utility `myfreqz`, listed in Fig. 7.1 on page 156, can be substituted for `freqz` (better for Octave).

```
function [B,A] = boost(g,fc,bw,fs);
%BOOST - Design a digital boost filter at given gain g,
%         center frequency fc in Hz,
%         bandwidth bw in Hz (default = fs/10), and
%         sampling rate fs in Hz (default = 1).

if nargin<4, fs = 1; end
if nargin<3, bw = fs/10; end

c = cot(pi*fc/fs); % bilinear transform constant
cs = c^2;  csp1 = cs+1; Bc=bw*c; gBc=g*Bc;
nrm = 1/(csp1 + Bc); % 1/(a0 before normalization)
b0 =  (csp1 + gBc)*nrm;
b1 =  2*(1 - cs)*nrm;
b2 =  (csp1 - gBc)*nrm;
a0 =  1;
a1 =  b1;
a2 =  (csp1 - Bc)*nrm;
A = [a0 a1 a2];
B = [b0 b1 b2];

if nargout==0
  figure(1);
  myfreqz(B,A); % /l/mll/myfreqz.m
  dstr=sprintf('boost(%0.2f,%0.2f,%0.2f,%0.2f)',g,fc,bw,fs);
  subplot(2,1,1); title(['Boost Frequency Response: ',...
                   dstr],'fontsize',24);
end
```

Figure B.15: Matlab function for designing (and optionally testing) a peaking equalizer section.

A Faust implementation of the second-order peaking equalizer is available as the function `peak_eq` in `filter.lib` distributed with Faust (Appendix K).

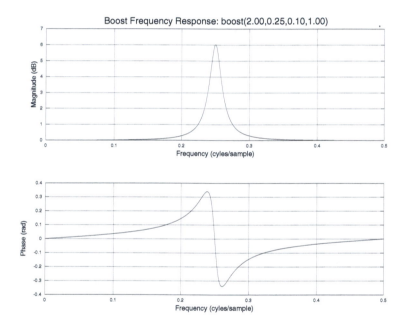

Figure B.16: Frequency response of a second-order peaking equalizer section tuned for a 6 dB peak of width $\approx f_s/10$ at center frequency $f_s/4$.

B.6 Time-Varying Two-Pole Filters

It is quite common to want to *vary* the resonance frequency of a resonator in real time. This is a special case of a *tunable filter*. In the pre-digital days of analog synthesizers, filter modules were tuned by means of *control voltages*, and were thus called *voltage-controlled filters (VCF)*. In the digital domain, control voltages are replaced by *time-varying filter coefficients*. In the time-varying case, the choice of filter structure has a profound effect on how the filter characteristics vary with respect to coefficient variations. In this section, we will take a look at the time-varying two-pole resonator.

Evaluating the transfer function of the two-pole resonator (Eq. (B.1) on page 260) at the point $e^{j\theta_c}$ on the unit circle (the filter's *resonance frequency* $\omega_c = \theta_c/T$) yields a *gain at resonance* equal to

$$
\begin{aligned}
H(e^{j\theta_c}) &= \frac{b_0}{(1 - Re^{j\theta_c}e^{-j\theta_c})(1 - Re^{-j\theta_c}e^{-j\theta_c})} \\
&= \frac{b_0}{1 - R} \cdot \frac{1}{1 - Re^{-j2\theta_c}}
\end{aligned}
\tag{B.11}
$$

For simplicity, let $b_0 = 1$ in what follows. In the special cases $\theta_c = 0$ (resonance at dc) and $\theta_c = \pi$ (resonance at $f = f_s/2$), we have

$$
H(\pm 1) = \frac{1}{(1 - R)^2}
\tag{B.12}
$$

Since R is real, we have already found the gain (amplitude response) at a dc or $f_s/2$ resonance:

$$
G(0) = G(\pi/T) \triangleq |H(\pm 1)| = \left| \frac{1}{(1 - R)^2} \right| = \frac{1}{(1 - R)^2}
$$

In the middle frequency between dc and $f_s/2$, $\theta_c = \omega_c T = \pi/2$, Eq. (B.11) with $b_0 = 1$ becomes

$$
H(j) = \frac{1}{(1 - Re^{j2\frac{\pi}{2}})(1 - R)} = \frac{1}{(1 + R)(1 - R)} = \frac{1}{1 - R^2}
$$

and, since $H(j)$ is real and positive, it coincides with the amplitude response, *i.e.*, $H(j) = G(\pi/2) = 1/(1 - R^2)$.

An important fact we can now see is that *the gain at resonance depends markedly on the resonance frequency*. In particular, the ratio of the two cases just analyzed is

$$
\left| \frac{H(1)}{H(j)} \right| = \frac{1 - R^2}{(1 - R)^2} = \frac{1 + R}{1 - R} = \frac{\text{maximum resonance gain}}{\text{minimum resonance gain}}
$$

We did not show that resonance gain is maximized at $e^{j\theta_c} = \pm 1$ and minimized at $e^{j\theta_c} = \pm j$, but this is straightforward to show, and strongly suggested by Fig. B.17 (and Fig. B.9).

Note that the ratio of the dc resonance gain to the $f_s/4$ resonance gain is *unbounded*! The sharper the resonance (the closer R is to 1), the greater the disparity in the gain.

Figure B.17 illustrates a number of resonator frequency responses for the case $R = 0.99$. (Resonators in practice may use values of R even closer to 1 than this—even the case $R = 1$ is used for making recursive digital sinusoidal oscillators [90].) For resonator tunings at dc and $f_s/2$, we predict the resonance gain to be $20 \log_{10}[1/(1 - R)^2] = -20 \log_{10}[(1 - 0.99)^2] = -40 \log_{10}(0.01) = 80$ dB, and this is what we see in the plot. When the resonance is tuned to $f_s/4$, the gain drops well below 40 dB. Clearly, we will need to compensate this gain variation when trying to use the two-pole digital resonator as a tunable filter.

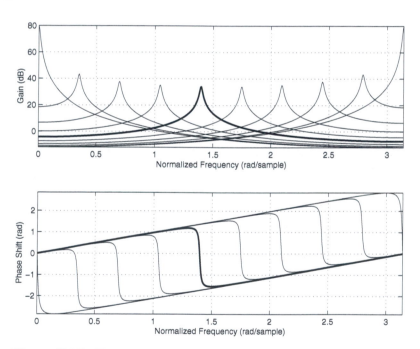

Figure B.17: Frequency response overlays for the two-pole resonator $H(z) = 1/(1 - 2R\cos(\theta_c)z^{-1} + R^2 z^{-2})$, for $R = 0.99$ and 10 values of θ_c uniformly spaced from 0 to π. The 5th case is plotted using thicker lines.

Figure B.18 shows the same type of plot for the *complex one-pole resonator* $H(z) = 1/(1 - Re^{j\theta_c}z^{-1})$, for $R = 0.99$ and 10 values of θ_c. In this case, we expect the frequency response evaluated at the center frequency to be $H(e^{j\omega_c T}) = 1/(1 - Re^{j\theta_c}e^{-j\theta_c}) = 1/(1 - R)$. Thus, the gain at resonance for the plotted example is $1/(1 - 0.99) = 100 = 40$ db for all tunings. Furthermore, for the complex resonator, the resonance gain is also exactly equal to the *peak gain*.

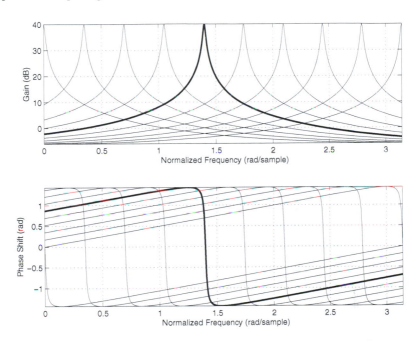

Figure B.18: Frequency response overlays for the one-pole *complex* resonator $H(z) = 1/(1 - Re^{j\theta_c}z^{-1})$, for $R = 0.99$ and 10 values of θ_c uniformly spaced from 0 to π. The 5th case is plotted using thicker lines.

B.6.1 Normalizing Two-Pole Filter Gain at Resonance

The question we now pose is how to best compensate the *tunable* two-pole resonator of §B.1.3 so that its peak gain is the same for all tunings. Looking at Fig. B.17, and remembering the graphical method for determining the amplitude response,[6] it is intuitively clear that we can help matters by adding two *zeros* to the filter, one near dc and the other near $f_s/2$. A zero exactly at dc is provided by the term $(1 - z^{-1})$ in the transfer function numerator. Similarly, a zero at half the sampling rate is provided by the term $(1 + z^{-1})$ in the numerator. The series combination of both zeros

---

[6] See §8.2 in Chapter 8.

gives the numerator $B(z) = (1 - z^{-1})(1 + z^{-1}) = 1 - z^{-2}$. The complete second-order transfer function then becomes

$$H(z) = \frac{B(z)}{A(z)} = \frac{1 - z^{-2}}{1 - 2R\cos(\theta_c)z^{-1} + R^2 z^{-2}}$$

corresponding to the difference equation

$$y(n) = x(n) - x(n-2) + [2R\cos(\theta_c)]y(n-1) - R^2 y(n-2). \qquad \text{(B.13)}$$

Checking the gain for the case $\theta_c = \pi/2$, we have

$$H(\pm 1) = 0$$

$$H(e^{j\theta_c})\big|_{\theta_c = \pi/2} = \frac{2}{1 - R^2}$$

which is better behaved, but now the response falls to zero at dc and $f_s/2$ rather than being heavily boosted, as we found in Eq. (B.12).

B.6.2   Constant Resonance Gain

It turns out it is possible to normalize *exactly* the *resonance gain* of the second-order resonator tuned by a single coefficient [89]. This is accomplished by placing the two zeros at $z = \pm\sqrt{R}$, where R is the radius of the complex-conjugate pole pair . The transfer function numerator becomes $B(z) = (1 - \sqrt{R}z^{-1})(1 + \sqrt{R}z^{-1}) = (1 - Rz^{-2})$, yielding the total transfer function

$$H(z) = \frac{B(z)}{A(z)} = \frac{1 - Rz^{-2}}{1 - 2R\cos(\theta_c)z^{-1} + R^2 z^{-2}}$$

which corresponds to the difference equation

$$y(n) = x(n) - R\,x(n-2) + [2R\cos(\theta_c)]y(n-1) - R^2 y(n-2).$$

We see there is one more multiply-add per sample (the term $-Rx(n-2)$) relative to the unnormalized two-pole resonator of Eq. (B.13). The resonance gain is now

$$\begin{aligned}
H(e^{j\theta_c}) &= \frac{1 - Re^{-j2\theta_c}}{1 - 2R\cos(\theta_c)e^{-j\theta_c} + R^2 e^{-j2\theta_c}} \\
&= \frac{1 - Re^{-j2\theta_c}}{1 - R(1 + e^{-j2\theta_c}) + R^2 e^{-j2\theta_c}} \\
&= \frac{1 - Re^{-j2\theta_c}}{(1 - R) - (1 - R)Re^{-j2\theta_c}} \\
&= \frac{1}{1 - R}
\end{aligned}$$

Thus, the gain at resonance is $1/(1-R)$ for all resonance tunings θ_c.

Figure B.19 shows a family of amplitude responses for the constant resonance-gain two-pole, for various values of θ_c and $R = 0.99$. We see an excellent improvement in the regularity of the amplitude response as a function of tuning.

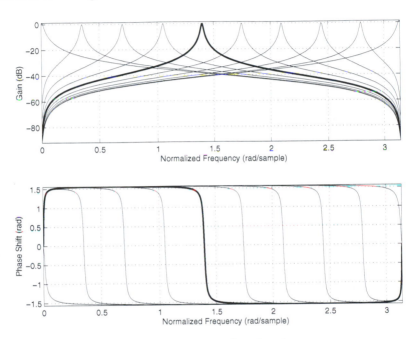

Figure B.19: Frequency response overlays for the constant resonance-gain two-pole filter $H(z) = (1-R)(1-Rz^{-2})/(1-2R\cos(\theta_c)z^{-1}+R^2z^{-2})$, for $R = 0.99$ and 10 values of θ_c uniformly spaced from 0 to π. The 5th case is plotted using thicker lines.

B.6.3   Peak Gain Versus Resonance Gain

While the constant resonance-gain filter is very well behaved, it is not ideal, because, while the *resonance gain* is perfectly normalized, the *peak gain* is not. The amplitude-response peak does not occur exactly at the resonance frequencies $\omega T = \pm\theta_c$ except for the special cases $\theta_c = 0$, $\pm\pi/2$, and π. At other resonance frequencies, the peak due to one pole is *shifted* by the presence of the other pole. When R is close to 1, the shifting can be negligible, but in more damped resonators, *e.g.*, when $R < 0.9$, there can be a significant difference between the gain at resonance and the true peak gain.

Figure B.20 shows a family of amplitude responses for the constant resonance-gain two-pole, for various values of θ_c and $R = 0.9$. We see that while the gain at resonance is exactly the same in all cases, the actual *peak* gain varies somewhat, especially near dc and $f_s/2$ when the two poles come closest together. A more pronounced variation in peak gain can be seen in Fig. B.21, for which the pole radii have been reduced to $R = 0.5$.

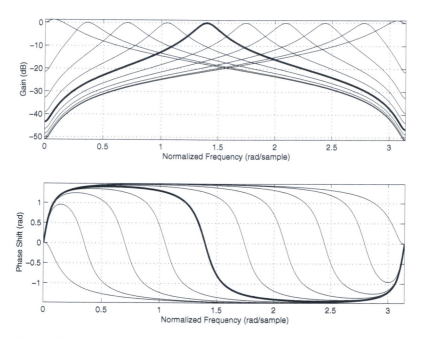

Figure B.20: Frequency response overlays for the constant resonance-gain two-pole filter $H(z) = (1-R)(1-Rz^{-2})/(1-2R\cos(\theta_c)z^{-1}+R^2z^{-2})$, for $R = 0.9$ and 10 values of θ_c uniformly spaced from 0 to π. The 5th case is plotted using thicker lines.

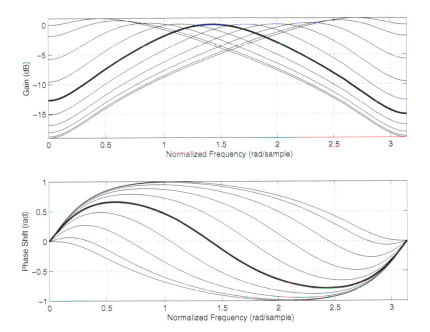

Figure B.21: Frequency response overlays for the constant resonance-gain two-pole filter $H(z) = (1-R)(1-Rz^{-2})/(1-2R\cos(\theta_c)z^{-1}+R^2z^{-2})$, for $R = 0.5$ and 10 values of θ_c uniformly spaced from 0 to π. The 5th case is plotted using thicker lines. Note the more pronounced variation in peak gain (the resonance gain does not vary).

B.6.4   Constant Peak-Gain Resonator

It is surprisingly easy to normalize exactly the *peak gain* in a second-order resonator tuned by a single coefficient [94]. The filter structure that accomplishes this is the one we already considered in §B.6.1:

$$H(z) = \frac{B(z)}{A(z)} = \frac{1 - z^{-2}}{1 - 2R\cos(\theta_c)z^{-1} + R^2 z^{-2}} \qquad (B.14)$$

That is, the two-pole resonator normalized by zeros at $z = \pm 1$ has the constant peak-gain property when it has resonant peaks in its response at all. Note, however, that the peak-gain frequency and the pole-resonance frequency (cf. §B.6.3), are generally two different things, as elaborated below. This structure has the added bonus that its difference equation requires only one more addition relative to the unnormalized two-pole resonator, and no new multiply.

Real-time audio "plugins" based on the constant-peak-gain resonator are developed in Appendix K.

The peak gain is $2/(1 - R^2)$, so multiplying the transfer function by $(1 - R^2)/2$ normalizes the peak gain to one for all tunings. It can also be shown [94] that the peak gain coincides with the *variance gain* when the resonator is driven by white noise. That is, if the variance of the driving noise is σ^2, the variance of the noise at the resonator output is $2\sigma^2/(1-R^2)$. Therefore, scaling the resonator input by $g = \sqrt{(1 - R^2)/2}$ will normalize the resonator such that the output signal power equals the input signal power when the input signal is white noise.

Frequency response overlays for the constant-peak-gain resonator are shown in Fig. B.23 ($R = 0.99$), Fig. B.20 ($R = 0.9$), and Fig. B.21 ($R = 0.5$). While the peak frequency may be far from the resonance tuning in the more heavily damped examples, the peak gain is always normalized to unity. The normalized radian frequency $\psi \in [-\pi, \pi]$ at which the peak gain occurs is related to the pole angle $\theta_c \in [-\pi, \pi]$ by [94]

$$\cos(\theta_c) = \frac{1 + R^2}{2R} \cos(\psi). \qquad (B.15)$$

When the right-hand side of the above equation exceeds 1 in magnitude, there is no (real) solution for the pole frequency θ_c. This happens, for example, when R is less than 1 and ψ is too close to 0 or π. Conversely, given any pole angle $\theta_c \in (0, \pi)$, there always exists a solution for the peak frequency $\psi = \arccos[2R\cos(\omega_c)/(1 + R^2)]$, since $|2R/(1 + R^2)| \le 1$ when $R \in [0, 1]$. However, when R is small, the peak frequency can be far from the pole resonance frequency, as shown in Fig. B.22.

Thus, R must be close to 1 to obtain a resonant peak near dc (a case commonly needed in audio work) or half the sampling rate (rarely needed

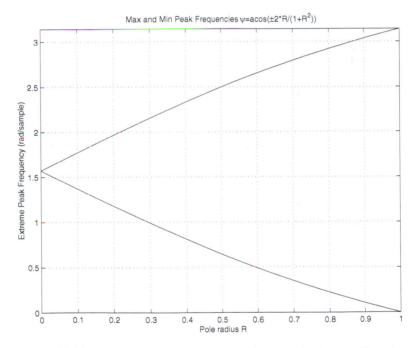

Figure B.22: Upper and lower peak-gain frequency limits as a function of pole radius R ($\arccos[\pm 2R/(1 + R^2)]$).

in practice). When R is much less than 1, the peak frequency ψ cannot leave a small interval near one-fourth the sampling rate, as can be seen at the far left in Fig. B.22.

Figure B.22 predicts that for $R = 0.5$, the lowest peak-gain frequency should be around $\psi \geq 0.515$ radian per sample. Figure B.21 agrees with this prediction.

As Figures B.23 through B.25 show, the peak gain remains constant even at very low and very high frequencies, to the extent they are reachable for a given R. The zeros at dc and $f_s/2$ preclude the possibility of peaks at exactly those frequencies, but for R near 1, we can get very close to having a peak at dc or $f_s/2$, as shown in Figures B.19 and B.20.

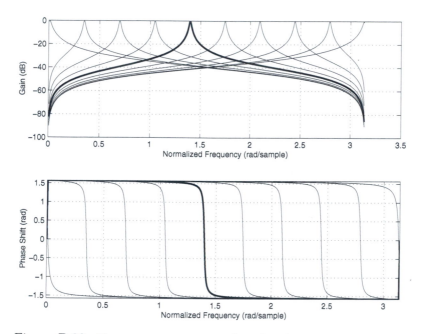

Figure B.23: Frequency response overlays for the constant peak-gain two-pole filter $H(z) = [(1-R^2)/2](1-z^{-2})/(1-2R\cos(\theta_c)z^{-1}+R^2z^{-2})$, for $R = 0.99$ and 10 values of θ_c uniformly spaced from 0 to π. The 5th case is plotted using thicker lines.

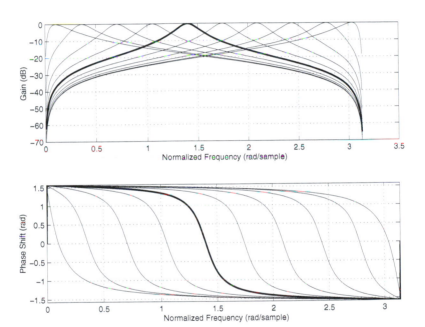

Figure B.24: Frequency response overlays for the constant peak-gain two-pole filter $H(z) = [(1 - R^2)/2](1 - z^{-2})/(1 - 2R\cos(\theta_c)z^{-1} + R^2z^{-2})$, for $R = 0.9$ and 10 values of θ_c uniformly spaced from 0 to π. The 5th case is plotted using thicker lines.

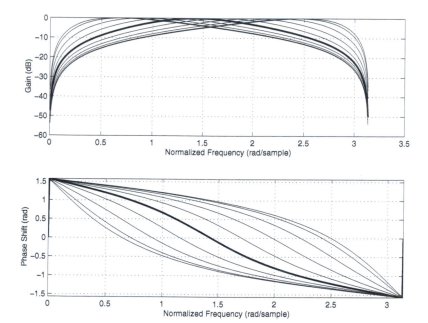

Figure B.25: Frequency response overlays for the constant peak-gain two-pole filter $H(z) = [(1 - R^2)/2](1 - z^{-2})/(1 - 2R\cos(\theta_c)z^{-1} + R^2 z^{-2})$, for $R = 0.5$ and 10 values of θ_c uniformly spaced from 0 to π. The 5th case is plotted using thicker lines.

B.6.5   Four-Pole Tunable Lowpass/Bandpass Filters

As a practical note, it is worth mentioning that in popular analog synthesizers (both real and virtual[7]), VCFs are typically *fourth order* rather than second order as we have studied here. Perhaps the best known VCF is the *Moog VCF*. The four-pole Moog VCF is configured to be a lowpass filter with an optional resonance near the cut-off frequency. When the resonance is strong, it functions more like a resonator than a lowpass filter. Various methods for digitizing the Moog VCF are described in [95]. It turns out to be nontrivial to preserve all desirable properties of the analog filter (such as frequency response, order, and control structure), when translated to digital form by standard means.

B.7   Elementary Filter Problems

1. *Resonator 3dB bandwidth*
   In Eq. (B.5), pole radius R was related to 3dB-bandwidth B (Hz) by the expression
   $$R \approx e^{-\pi BT}$$
   which was derived in §E.6. In [10], a related formula is given:
   $$BT \approx \frac{1-R}{\pi\sqrt{R}} \qquad\qquad (B.16)$$

   (a) Show that these formulas become identical as $R \to 1$ or $T \to 0$.

   (b) Derive Eq. (B.16). [Hint: Work directly with the squared amplitude response in the z-plane.]

   (c) Determine which is more accurate, and by how much.

2. *When peak gain = resonance gain*
   For a two-pole digital resonator as described in §B.1.3, determine which center frequencies f_c yield peak gain at resonance. In other words, for which resonator tunings does the peak gain occur at the resonant frequency? [Hint: there are at least four such frequencies.]

3. Prove that
   $$\left| \frac{2R}{1+R^2} \right| \le 1$$
   for all $R \in [0, 1]$.

---

[7]The term *virtual analog synthesis* refers to digital implementations of classic analog synthesizers.

4. For the constant-peak-gain resonator described in §B.6.4 on page 290, substitute Eq. (B.15) into Eq. (B.14) and evaluate $H(z)$ at $z = \exp(j\psi)$ to show that the gain at frequency $\omega = \psi$ is equal to $2/(1 - R^2)$ for all $R \in [0, 1)$ and for all θ_c.

5. Extend the previous problem to prove that the gain at frequency ψ is a *local maximum*. [Hint: Evaluate $H(z)$ at $z = \exp[j(\psi \pm \epsilon)]$ and show that the gain decreases when ϵ deviates however slightly from 0.]

6. *FIR DC blocker*
   The mean of a length N signal $x(n)$ is given by

   $$\mu_x = \frac{1}{N} \sum_{n=0}^{N-1} x(n)$$

   Therefore, we can remove the "short-term dc component" of a signal (of any length) using the FIR filter

   $$y(n) = x(n) - \mu_x(n), \quad \text{where}$$
   $$\mu_x(n) = \mu_x(n-1) + g[x(n) - x(n-N)], \quad n = 0, 1, 2, \ldots,$$

   where $g = 1/N$, and we define $x(n) = 0$ for $n < 0$.

   (a) Determine the *impulse response* of this FIR filter, $h(n)$.
   (b) What is the duration of the *transient response*? I.e., if the input signal $x[n]$ is a sinusoid starting at time 0, at what time (in samples) does the filter reach *steady state*?
   (c) Find the *transfer function* $H(z)$.
   (d) Determine the *poles and zeros* of $H(z)$.
   (e) Sketch the *amplitude response* of $H(z)$.
   (f) Sketch the *phase response* of $H(z)$.

7. *Recursive DC blocker*
   The mean of a signal $x(n)$ can also be estimated by any recursive lowpass filter with unity dc gain and gain less than 1 away from dc. A family of one-pole mean-estimators is given by

   $$\mu_x(n) = g\,x(n) + R\mu_x(n-1)$$

   where g is chosen to give unity dc gain, $0 < R < 1$, and a dc blocker based on this mean-estimator is given as before by

   $$y(n) = x(n) - \mu_x(n)$$

(a) Find the *transfer function* $H(z)$ of this recursive filter.

(b) Determine the *difference equation* expressing $y(n)$ as a recursion involving present and past values of x and y. (I.e., eliminate $\mu_x(n)$).

(c) Determine the *impulse response* $h(n)$.

(d) What is the *time-constant of decay* of the impulse response $h(n)$?

(e) Determine the *poles and zeros* of $H(z)$.

(f) Find the value of g which gives unity gain at dc.

(g) With g given by the previous problem, what is the gain at half the sampling rate $f_s/2$?

(h) Sketch the *amplitude response* of $H(z)$.

(i) Sketch the *phase response* of $H(z)$.

8. *Adaptive Recursive DC blocker*
   Consider the mean estimator given by

$$\mu_x(n) \;=\; [1 - R(n)]x(n) + R(n)\mu_x(n-1), \quad \text{where}$$
$$R(n) \;\triangleq\; 1 - \frac{1}{n+1}, \quad n = 0, 1, 2, \ldots$$

This can be interpreted as a time-varying mean estimator as in the previous problem, but where the pole at $z = R$ asymptotically approaches 1. Consider now the dc blocker formed by

$$y(n) = x(n) - \mu_x(n)$$

(a) Determine the *difference equation* expressing $y(n)$ as a recursion involving present and past values of x and y. (Eliminate $\mu_x(n)$).

(b) Is this dc blocker linear?

(c) Is it time invariant?

(d) Determine the *impulse response* $h(n)$.

(e) Suppose the input signal is $x(n) = u(n)$ (unit step signal), find $y(n)$.

(f) If the input signal is again a unit step $u(n)$, what is $\lim_{n \to \infty} y[n]$?

Appendix C

Allpass Filters

This appendix addresses the general problem of characterizing *all* digital allpass filters, including multi-input, multi-output (MIMO) allpass filters. As a result of including the MIMO case, the mathematical level is a little higher than usual for this book. The reader in need of more background is referred to [84, 37, 98].[1]

Our first task is to show that losslessness implies allpass.

Definition: A linear, time-invariant filter $H(z)$ is said to be *lossless* if it *preserves signal energy* for every input signal. That is, if the input signal is $x(n)$, and the output signal is $y(n) = (h * x)(n)$, then we have

$$\sum_{n=-\infty}^{\infty} |y(n)|^2 = \sum_{n=-\infty}^{\infty} |x(n)|^2.$$

In terms of the L^2 signal norm $\| \cdot \|_2$, this can be expressed more succinctly as

$$\| y \|_2^2 = \| x \|_2^2.$$

Notice that only stable filters can be lossless, since otherwise $\| y \|$ can be infinite while $\| x \|$ is finite. We further assume all filters are *causal*[2] for simplicity. It is straightforward to show the following:

Theorem: A stable, linear, time-invariant (LTI) filter transfer function $H(z)$ is lossless if and only if

$$\left| H(e^{j\omega}) \right| = 1, \quad \forall \omega.$$

---

[1]The Web version of this book contains automatically installed hyperlinks to more elementary tutorials, such as regarding matrices.

[2]Recall that a filter is said to be causal if its impulse response $h(n)$ is zero for $n < 0$.

That is, the frequency response must have magnitude 1 everywhere over the unit circle in the complex z plane.

Proof: We allow the signals $x(n), y(n)$ and filter impulse response $h(n)$ to be complex. By Parseval's theorem [84] for the DTFT, we have,[3] for any signal $x \leftrightarrow X$,

$$\| x \|_2 = \| X \|_2$$

i.e.,

$$\| x \|_2^2 \triangleq \sum_{n=-\infty}^{\infty} |x(n)|^2 = \frac{1}{2\pi} \int_{-\pi}^{\pi} |X(e^{j\omega})|^2 \, d\omega \triangleq \| X \|_2^2.$$

Thus, Parseval's theorem enables us to restate the definition of losslessness in the frequency domain:

$$\| X \|_2^2 = \| Y \|_2^2 = \| H \cdot X \|_2^2$$

where $Y = HX$ because the filter H is LTI. Thus, H is lossless by definition if and only if

$$\frac{1}{2\pi} \int_{-\pi}^{\pi} |X(e^{j\omega})|^2 \, d\omega = \frac{1}{2\pi} \int_{-\pi}^{\pi} |H(e^{j\omega})|^2 \, |X(e^{j\omega})|^2 \, d\omega. \qquad (\text{C.1})$$

Since this must hold for all $X(e^{j\omega})$, we must have $|H(e^{j\omega})| = 1$ for all ω, except possibly for a set of measure zero (*e.g.*, isolated points which do not contribute to the integral) [73]. If $H(z)$ is finite order and stable, $H(e^{j\omega})$ is continuous over the unit circle, and its modulus is therefore equal to 1 for all $\omega \in [-\pi, \pi]$. $\square$

We have shown that every lossless filter is allpass. Conversely, every unity-gain allpass filter is lossless.

C.1   Allpass Examples

- The simplest allpass filter is a unit-modulus gain

$$H(z) = e^{j\phi}$$

where ϕ can be any phase value. In the real case ϕ can only be 0 or π, in which case $H(z) = \pm 1$.

---

[3]Note that the time-domain norm $\| y \|_2$ is *unnormalized* (which it must be) while the frequency-domain norm $\| Y \|_2$ is *normalized* by $1/\sqrt{2\pi}$. This is the cleanest choice of L^2 norm definitions for present purposes.

- A lossless FIR filter can consist only of a single nonzero tap:

$$H(z) = e^{j\phi} z^{-K}$$

  for some fixed integer K, where ϕ is again some constant phase, constrained to be 0 or π in the real-filter case. Since we are considering only causal filters here, $K \geq 0$. As a special case of this example, a unit delay $H(z) = z^{-1}$ is a simple FIR allpass filter.

- The transfer function of every finite-order, causal, lossless IIR digital filter (recursive allpass filter) can be written as

$$H(z) = e^{j\phi} z^{-K} \frac{\tilde{A}(z)}{A(z)}$$

  where $K \geq 0$,

$$A(z) \triangleq 1 + a_1 z^{-1} + a_2 z^{-2} + \cdots + a_N z^{-N},$$

  and

$$\begin{aligned}
\tilde{A}(z) &\triangleq z^{-N} \overline{A}(z^{-1}) \\
&= \overline{a_N} + \overline{a_{N-1}} z^{-1} + \overline{a_{N-2}} z^{-2} + \cdots + \overline{a_1} z^{-(N-1)} + z^{-N}.
\end{aligned}$$

  We may think of $\tilde{A}(z)$ as the *flip* of $A(z)$. For example, if $A(z) = 1 + 1.4 z^{-1} + 0.49 z^{-2}$, we have $\tilde{A}(z) = 0.49 + 1.4 z^{-1} + z^{-2}$. Thus, $\tilde{A}(z)$ is obtained from $A(z)$ by simply reversing the order of the coefficients and conjugating them when they are complex.

- For analog filters, the general finite-order allpass transfer function is

$$H(s) = e^{j\phi} \frac{A(-s)}{A(s)}$$

  where $K \geq 0$, $A(s) = s^N + a_1 s^{N-1} + \cdots + a_{N-1} s + a_N$. The polynomial $A(-s)$ can be obtained by negating every other coefficient in $A(z)$, and multiplying by z^N. In analog, a pure delay of τ seconds corresponds to the transfer function

$$e^{-s\tau} = 1 - \tau s + \frac{\tau^2}{2} s^2 + \cdots$$

  which is infinite order. Given a pole p_i (root of $A(s)$ at $s = p_i$), the polynomial $A(-s)$ has a root at $s = -p_i$. Thus, the poles and zeros can be paired off as a cascade of terms such as

$$H_i(s) = \frac{s + p_i}{s - p_i}.$$

The frequency response of such a term is

$$H_i(j\omega) = \frac{j\omega + p_i}{j\omega - p_i} = -\frac{p_i + j\omega}{p_i + j\omega}$$

which is obviously unit magnitude.

C.2 Paraunitary Filters[4]

Another way to express the allpass condition $\left|H(e^{j\omega})\right| = 1$ is to write

$$\overline{H(e^{j\omega})}H(e^{j\omega}) = 1, \quad \forall\omega.$$

This form generalizes by analytic continuation (see §D.2 on page 311) to $\tilde{H}(z)H(z)$ over the entire the z plane, where $\tilde{H}(z)$ denotes the paraconjugate of $H(z)$:

Definition: The *paraconjugate* of a transfer function may be defined as the *analytic continuation of the complex conjugate* from the unit circle to the whole z plane:

$$\tilde{H}(z) \triangleq \overline{H}(z^{-1})$$

where $\overline{H}(z)$ denotes complex conjugation of the *coefficients only* of $H(z)$ *and not the powers of* z. For example, if $H(z) = 1 + jz^{-1}$, then $\overline{H}(z) = 1 - jz^{-1}$. We can write, for example,

$$\overline{H}(z) \triangleq \overline{H(\overline{z})}$$

in which the conjugation of z serves to cancel the outer conjugation.

Examples:

- $H(z) = 1 + z^{-1} \quad \Rightarrow \quad \tilde{H}(z) = 1 + z$

- $H(z) = 1 + 2jz^{-1} + 3z^{-2} \quad \Rightarrow \quad \tilde{H}(z) = 1 - 2jz + 3z^2$

We refrain from conjugating z in the definition of the paraconjugate because $\overline{z}$ is not analytic in the complex-variables sense. Instead, we *invert* z, which *is* analytic, and which reduces to complex conjugation on the unit circle.

The paraconjugate may be used to characterize allpass filters as follows:

Theorem: A causal, stable, filter $H(z)$ is allpass if and only if

$$\tilde{H}(z)H(z) = 1$$

---

[4]The remainder of this appendix is relatively advanced and can be omitted without loss of continuity in what follows.

Note that this is equivalent to the previous result on the unit circle since

$$\tilde{H}(e^{j\omega})H(e^{j\omega}) \triangleq \overline{H}(1/e^{j\omega})H(e^{j\omega}) = \overline{H(e^{j\omega})}H(e^{j\omega})$$

C.3   Multi-Input, Multi-Output (MIMO) Allpass Filters

To generalize lossless filters to the multi-input, multi-output (MIMO) case, we must generalize conjugation to MIMO transfer function *matrices*:

Theorem: A $p \times q$ transfer function matrix $\mathbf{H}(z)$ is *lossless* if and only if its frequency-response matrix $\mathbf{H}(e^{j\omega})$ is *unitary*, *i.e.*,

$$\mathbf{H}^*(e^{j\omega})\mathbf{H}(e^{j\omega}) = \mathbf{I}_q \qquad\qquad (\text{C.2})$$

for all ω, where $\mathbf{I}_q$ denotes the $q \times q$ identity matrix, and $\mathbf{H}^*(e^{j\omega})$ denotes the *Hermitian transpose* (complex-conjugate transpose) of $\mathbf{H}(e^{j\omega})$:

$$\mathbf{H}^*(e^{j\omega}) \triangleq \overline{\mathbf{H}^T(e^{j\omega})}$$

Let $\underline{y}_p(n)$ denote the length p output vector at time n, and let $\underline{x}_q(n)$ denote the input q-vector at time n. Then in the frequency domain we have $\underline{Y}_p(e^{j\omega}) = \mathbf{H}(e^{j\omega})\underline{X}_q(e^{j\omega})$, which implies

$$\underline{Y}_p^*\underline{Y}_p = \underline{X}_q^* \underbrace{\mathbf{H}^*(e^{j\omega})\mathbf{H}(e^{j\omega})}_{\mathbf{I}_q} \underline{X}_q = \underline{X}^*\underline{X},$$

or

$$\sum_{i=1}^{p}\left|Y_i(e^{j\omega})\right|^2 = \sum_{i=1}^{q}\left|X_i(e^{j\omega})\right|^2 .$$

Integrating both sides of this equation with respect to ω yields that the total energy in equals the total energy out, as required by the definition of losslessness.

We have thus shown that in the MIMO case, losslessness is equivalent to having a unitary frequency-response matrix. A MIMO allpass filter is therefore any filter with a unitary frequency-response matrix.

Note that $\mathbf{H}^*(e^{j\omega})\mathbf{H}(e^{j\omega})$ is a $q \times q$ matrix product of a $q \times p$ times a $p \times q$ matrix. If $q > p$, then the rank must be deficient. Therefore, $p \geq q$. (There must be at least as many outputs as there are inputs, but it's ok to have extra outputs.)

C.3.1   Paraunitary MIMO Filters

In §C.2, we generalized the allpass property $1 = \left|H(e^{j\omega})\right|^2 = H(e^{j\omega})H(e^{-j\omega})$ to the entire complex plane as

$$\tilde{H}(z)H(z) = 1,$$

where $\tilde{H}$ is defined as the paraconjugate of H. In the MIMO case, the paraconjugate is the same, but including a matrix transpose operation:

MIMO Paraconjugate

Definition: The paraconjugate of $\mathbf{H}(z)$ is defined as

$$\tilde{\mathbf{H}}(z) \triangleq \mathbf{H}^*(z^{-1})$$

where $\mathbf{H}^*(z)$ denotes transpose of $\mathbf{H}(z)$ followed by complex-conjugation of the *coefficients* within $\mathbf{H}^T(z)$ (and not the powers of z). For example, if

$$\mathbf{H}(z) = \begin{bmatrix} 1 + jz^{-1} \\ 1 + z^{-2} \end{bmatrix}$$

then

$$\tilde{\mathbf{H}}(z) = \begin{bmatrix} 1 - jz & 1 + z^2 \end{bmatrix}$$

MIMO Paraunitary Condition

With the above definition for paraconjugation of a MIMO transfer-function matrix, we may generalize the MIMO allpass condition Eq. (C.2) to the entire z plane as follows:

Theorem: Every lossless $p \times q$ transfer function matrix $\mathbf{H}(z)$ is paraunitary, *i.e.*,

$$\tilde{\mathbf{H}}(z)\mathbf{H}(z) = \mathbf{I}_q$$

By construction, every paraunitary matrix transfer function is *unitary* on the unit circle for all ω. Away from the unit circle, the paraconjugate $\tilde{\mathbf{H}}(z)$ is the unique analytic continuation of $\overline{\mathbf{H}^T(e^{j\omega})}$ (the Hermitian transpose of $\mathbf{H}(e^{j\omega})$).

Example: The normalized DFT matrix is an $N \times N$ order zero paraunitary transformation. This is because the normalized DFT matrix, $\mathbf{W} = [W_N^{nk}]/\sqrt{N}$, $n, k = 0, \ldots, N-1$, where $W_N \triangleq e^{-j2\pi/N}$, is a *unitary* matrix:

$$\frac{\mathbf{W}^*}{\sqrt{N}}\frac{\mathbf{W}}{\sqrt{N}} = \mathbf{I}_N$$

Properties of Paraunitary Systems

Paraunitary systems are essentially multi-input, multi-output (MIMO) all-pass filters. Let $\mathbf{H}(z)$ denote the $p \times q$ matrix transfer function of a paraunitary system. Some of its properties include the following [98]:

- In the square case ($p = q$), the matrix determinant, $\det[\mathbf{H}(z)]$, is an *allpass filter*.

- Therefore, if a square $\mathbf{H}(z)$ contains FIR elements, its determinant is a simple delay: $\det[\mathbf{H}(z)] = z^{-K}$ for some integer K.

Properties of Paraunitary Filter Banks

An N-channel filter bank can be viewed as an $N \times 1$ MIMO filter

$$
\mathbf{H}(z) = \begin{bmatrix} H_1(z) \\ H_2(z) \\ \vdots \\ H_N(z) \end{bmatrix}
$$

A *paraunitary filter bank* must therefore obey

$$
\tilde{\mathbf{H}}(z)\mathbf{H}(z) = 1
$$

More generally, we allow paraunitary filter banks to scale and/or delay the input signal [98]:

$$
\tilde{\mathbf{H}}(z)\mathbf{H}(z) = c_K z^{-K}
$$

where K is some nonnegative integer and $c_K \neq 0$.

We can note the following properties of paraunitary filter banks:

- A *synthesis filter bank* $\mathbf{F}(z)$ corresponding to analysis filter bank $\mathbf{H}(z)$ is defined as that filter bank which inverts the analysis filter bank, *i.e.*, satisfies

$$
\mathbf{F}(z)\mathbf{H}(z) = 1.
$$

Clearly, not every filter bank will be invertible in this way. When it is, it may be called a *perfect reconstruction filter bank*. When a filter bank transfer function $\mathbf{H}(z)$ is paraunitary, its corresponding synthesis filter bank is simply the paraconjugate filter bank $\tilde{\mathbf{H}}(z)$, or

$$
\mathbf{F}(z) = \tilde{\mathbf{H}}(z).
$$

- The channel filters $H_k(z)$ in a paraunitary filter bank are *power complementary*:

$$\left|H_1(e^{j\omega})\right|^2 + \left|H_2(e^{j\omega})\right|^2 + \cdots + \left|H_N(e^{j\omega})\right|^2 = 1$$

  This follows immediately from looking at the paraunitary property on the unit circle.

- When $\mathbf{H}(z)$ is FIR, the corresponding synthesis filter matrix $\tilde{\mathbf{H}}(z)$ is also FIR. Note that this implies an FIR filter-matrix can be inverted by another FIR filter-matrix. This is in stark contrast to the case of single-input, single-output FIR filters, which must be inverted by IIR filters, in general.

- When $\mathbf{H}(z)$ is FIR, each synthesis filter, $F_k(z) = \tilde{\mathbf{H}}_k(z)$, $k = 1, \ldots, N$, is simply the FLIP of its corresponding analysis filter $H_k(z) = \mathbf{H}_k(z)$:

$$f_k(n) = h_k(L - n)$$

  where L is the filter length. (When the filter coefficients are complex, FLIP includes a complex conjugation as well.)

  This follows from the fact that paraconjugating an FIR filter amounts to simply flipping (and conjugating) its coefficients.

  Note that only trivial FIR filters can be paraunitary in the single-input, single-output (SISO) case. In the MIMO case, on the other hand, paraunitary systems can be composed of FIR filters of any order.

- FIR analysis and synthesis filters in paraunitary filter banks have the *same amplitude response*.

  This follows from the fact that $\text{FLIP}(h) \leftrightarrow \overline{H}$, *i.e.*, flipping an FIR filter impulse response $h(n)$ conjugates the frequency response, which does not affect its amplitude response $|H(e^{j\omega})|$.

C.3.2   Paraunitary Filter Examples

The *Haar filter bank* is defined as

$$\mathbf{H}(z) = \frac{1}{\sqrt{2}} \left[\begin{array}{c} 1 + z^{-1} \\ 1 - z^{-1} \end{array} \right]$$

The paraconjugate of $\mathbf{H}(z)$ is

$$\tilde{\mathbf{H}}(z) = \left[\begin{array}{cc} 1 + z & 1 - z \end{array} \right] / \sqrt{2}$$

so that

$$\tilde{\mathbf{H}}(z)\mathbf{H}(z) = \begin{bmatrix} 1+z & 1-z \end{bmatrix} \begin{bmatrix} 1+z^{-1} \\ 1-z^{-1} \end{bmatrix} = 1$$

Thus, the Haar filter bank is paraunitary. This is true for any power-complementary filter bank, since when $\tilde{\mathbf{H}}(z)$ is $N \times 1$, power-complementary and paraunitary are the same property.

For more about paraunitary filter banks, see Chapter 6 of [98].

C.4   Allpass Problems

1. The BiQuad Allpass Section

   (a) Show that every second-order filter having transfer function

   $$H(z) = \frac{a_2 + a_1 z^{-1} + z^{-2}}{1 + a_1 z^{-1} + a_2 z^{-2}}$$

   is a unit-gain allpass filter. That is, show that $|H(e^{j\omega})| = 1$, for all a_1 and a_2. (Typically, a_1 and a_2 are chosen such that the filter is stable, but this is not necessary for the result to hold.)

   (b) Find the *zeros* of the filter as a function of the poles. In other words, given two poles, what is the rule for placing the zeros in order to obtain an allpass filter?

   (c) Find the phase response of the zeros in terms of the phase response of the poles.

.

Appendix D

Introduction to Laplace Transform Analysis

The *one-sided Laplace transform* of a signal $x(t)$ is defined by

$$X(s) \triangleq \mathcal{L}_s\{x\} \triangleq \int_0^\infty x(t)e^{-st}dt$$

where t is real and $s = \sigma + j\omega$ is a complex variable. The one-sided Laplace transform is also called the *unilateral* Laplace transform. There is also a *two-sided*, or *bilateral*, Laplace transform obtained by setting the lower integration limit to $-\infty$ instead of 0. Since we will be analyzing only *causal*[1] linear systems using the Laplace transform, we can use either. However, it is customary in engineering treatments to use the one-sided definition.

When evaluated along the $s = j\omega$ axis (*i.e.*, $\sigma = 0$), the Laplace transform reduces to the unilateral *Fourier transform*:

$$X(j\omega) = \int_0^\infty x(t)e^{-j\omega t}dt.$$

The Fourier transform is normally defined bilaterally ($0 \leftarrow -\infty$ above), but for causal signals $x(t)$, there is no difference. We see that the Laplace transform can be viewed as a generalization of the Fourier transform from the real line (a simple frequency axis) to the entire complex plane. We say that the Fourier transform is obtained by evaluating the Laplace transform along the $j\omega$ axis in the complex s plane.

---

[1] A signal $x(t)$ is said to be causal if it is zero for all $t < 0$. A system is said to be causal if its response to an input never occurs before the input is received; thus, an LTI filter is a causal system whenever its impulse response $h(t)$ is a causal signal.

An advantage of the Laplace transform is the ability to transform signals which have no Fourier transform. To see this, we can write the Laplace transform as

$$X(s) = \int_0^\infty x(t)e^{-(\sigma+j\omega)t}\,dt = \int_0^\infty \left[x(t)e^{-\sigma t}\right]e^{-j\omega t}\,dt.$$

Thus, the Laplace transform can be seen as the Fourier transform of an *exponentially windowed* input signal. For $\sigma > 0$ (the so-called "*strict right-half plane*" (RHP)), this exponential weighting forces the Fourier-transformed signal toward zero as $t \to \infty$. As long as the signal $x(t)$ does not increase faster than $\exp(Bt)$ for some B, its Laplace transform will exist for all $\sigma > B$. We make this more precise in the next section.

D.1   Existence of the Laplace Transform

A function $x(t)$ has a Laplace transform whenever it is of *exponential order*. That is, there must be a real number B such that

$$\lim_{t\to\infty} \left|x(t)e^{-Bt}\right| = 0$$

As an example, every exponential function $Ae^{\alpha t}$ has a Laplace transform for all finite values of A and α. Let's look at this case more closely.

The Laplace transform of a causal, growing exponential function

$$x(t) = \begin{cases} Ae^{\alpha t}, & t \geq 0 \\ 0, & t < 0 \end{cases},$$

is given by

$$X(s) \triangleq \int_0^\infty x(t)e^{-st}\,dt = \int_0^\infty Ae^{\alpha t}e^{-st}\,dt = A\int_0^\infty e^{(\alpha-s)t}\,dt$$

$$= \left. \frac{A}{\alpha-s}e^{(\alpha-s)t}\right|_0^\infty = \frac{A}{\alpha-s}e^{(\alpha-\sigma-j\omega)\infty} - \frac{A}{\alpha-s}$$

$$= \begin{cases} \frac{A}{s-\alpha}, & \sigma > \alpha \\ \text{(indeterminate)}, & \sigma = \alpha \\ \infty, & \sigma < \alpha \end{cases}$$

Thus, the Laplace transform of an exponential $Ae^{\alpha t}$ is $A/(s-\alpha)$, but this is defined only for $\operatorname{re}\{s\} > \alpha$.

D.2   Analytic Continuation

It turns out that the domain of definition of the Laplace transform can be extended by means of *analytic continuation* [14, p. 259]. Analytic continuation is carried out by expanding a function of $s \in \mathbf{C}$ about all points in its domain of definition, and extending the domain of definition to all points for which the series expansion converges.

In the case of our exponential example

$$X(s) = \frac{A}{\alpha - s}, \quad (\text{re}\,\{s\} > \alpha) \tag{D.1}$$

the Taylor series expansion of $X(s)$ about the point $s = s_0$ in the s plane is given by

$$
\begin{aligned}
X(s) &= X(s_0) + (s - s_0)X'(s_0) + (s - s_0)^2 \frac{X''(s_0)}{2} + (s - s_0)^3 \frac{X'''(s_0)}{3!} + \cdots \\
&\triangleq \sum_{n=0}^{\infty} (s - s_0)^n \frac{X^{(n)}(s_0)}{n!}
\end{aligned}
$$

where, writing $X(s)$ as $(\alpha - s)^{-1}$ and using the chain rule for differentiation,

$$X'(s_0) \triangleq X^{(1)}(s_0) \triangleq \frac{dX(s)}{ds}\bigg|_{s=s_0} = (-1)(\alpha - s)^{-2}(-1)\big|_{s=s_0} = \frac{1}{(\alpha - s)^2}$$

$$X''(s_0) \triangleq X^{(2)}(s_0) \triangleq \frac{d^2 X(s)}{ds^2}\bigg|_{s=s_0} = (-2)(\alpha - s)^{-3}(-1)\big|_{s=s_0} = \frac{2}{(\alpha - s)^3}$$

$$X'''(s_0) \triangleq X^{(3)}(s_0) \triangleq \frac{d^3 X(s)}{ds^3}\bigg|_{s=s_0} = (-3)(2)(\alpha - s)^{-4}(-1)\big|_{s=s_0} = \frac{3!}{(\alpha - s)^4}$$

and so on. We also used the *factorial notation* $n! \triangleq n(n-1)(n-2)\cdots 3 \cdot 2 \cdot 1$, and we defined the special cases $0! \triangleq 1$ and $X^{(0)}(s_0) \triangleq X(s_0)$, as is normally done. The series expansion of $X(s)$ can thus be written

$$
\begin{aligned}
X(s) &= \frac{1}{\alpha - s_0} + \frac{s - s_0}{(\alpha - s_0)^2} + \frac{(s - s_0)^2}{(\alpha - s_0)^3} + \cdots \\
&= \sum_{n=0}^{\infty} \frac{(s - s_0)^n}{(\alpha - s_0)^{n+1}}.
\end{aligned}
\tag{D.2}
$$

We now ask for what values of s does the series Eq. (D.2) *converge*? The value $s = \alpha$ is particularly easy to check, since

$$X(\alpha) = \sum_{n=0}^{\infty} \frac{(\alpha - s_0)^n}{(\alpha - s_0)^{n+1}} = \sum_{n=0}^{\infty} \frac{1}{\alpha - s_0} = \infty \frac{1}{\alpha - s_0}.$$

Thus, the series clearly does *not* converge for $s = \alpha$, no matter what our choice of s_0 might be. We must therefore accept the point at infinity for $H(\alpha)$. This is eminently reasonable since the closed form Laplace transform we derived, $H(s) = 1/(\alpha - s)$ *does* "blow up" at $s = \alpha$. The point $s = \alpha$ is called a *pole* of $H(s) = 1/(\alpha - s)$.

More generally, let's apply the *ratio test* for the convergence of a geometric series. Since the nth term of the series is

$$\frac{(s - s_0)^n}{(\alpha - s_0)^{n+1}}$$

the ratio test demands that the ratio of term $n+1$ over term n have absolute value less than 1. That is, we require

$$1 > \left| \frac{(s - s_0)^{n+1}}{(\alpha - s_0)^{n+2}} \middle/ \frac{(s - s_0)^n}{(\alpha - s_0)^{n+1}} \right| = \left| \frac{s - s_0}{\alpha - s_0} \right|,$$

or,

$$\boxed{|s - s_0| < |\alpha - s_0|.}$$

We see that the region of convergence is a circle about the point $s = s_0$ having radius approaching but not equal to $|\alpha - s_0|$. Thus, the circular disk of convergence is centered at $s = s_0$ and extends to, but does not touch, the *pole* at $s = \alpha$.

The *analytic continuation* of the domain of Eq. (D.1) is now defined as the *union* of the disks of convergence for all points $s_0 \neq \alpha$. It is easy to see that a sequence of such disks can be chosen so as to define all points in the s plane except at the pole $s = \alpha$.

In summary, the Laplace transform of an exponential $x(t) = Ae^{\alpha t}$ is

$$X(s) = \frac{A}{s - \alpha}$$

and the value is well defined and finite for all $s \neq \alpha$.

Analytic continuation works for any finite number of poles of finite order,[2] and for an infinite number of distinct poles of finite order. It breaks down only in pathological situations such as when the Laplace transform is singular everywhere on some closed contour in the complex plane. Such pathologies do not arise in practice, so we need not be concerned about them.

---

[2]The *order of a pole* is its multiplicity. For example, the function $H(s) = \frac{1}{(s-p)^3}$ has a pole at $s = p$ of order 3.

D.3   Relation to the z Transform

The Laplace transform is used to analyze *continuous-time* systems. Its discrete-time counterpart is the z transform:

$$X_d(z) \triangleq \sum_{n=0}^{\infty} x_d(nT)z^{-n}$$

If we define $z = e^{sT}$, the z transform becomes proportional to the Laplace transform of a sampled continuous-time signal:

$$X_d(e^{sT}) = \sum_{n=0}^{\infty} x_d(nT)e^{-snT}$$

As the sampling interval T goes to zero, we have

$$\lim_{T\to 0} X_d(e^{sT})T = \lim_{\Delta t\to 0} \sum_{n=0}^{\infty} x_d(t_n)e^{-st_n}\Delta t = \int_0^{\infty} x_d(t)e^{-st}dt \triangleq X(s)$$

where $t_n \triangleq nT$ and $\Delta t \triangleq t_{n+1} - t_n = T$.

In summary,

> the z transform (times the sampling interval T) of a discrete time signal $x_d(nT)$ approaches, as $T \to 0$, the Laplace transform of the underlying continuous-time signal $x_d(t)$.

Note that the z plane and s plane are generally related by

$$\boxed{z = e^{sT}.}$$

In particular, the discrete-time frequency axis $\omega_d \in (-\pi/T, \pi/T)$ and continuous-time frequency axis $\omega_a \in (-\infty, \infty)$ are related by

$$\boxed{e^{j\omega_d T} = e^{j\omega_a T}.}$$

For the mapping $z = e^{sT}$ from the s plane to the z plane to be invertible, it is necessary that $X(j\omega_a)$ be zero for all $|\omega_a| \geq \pi/T$. If this is true, we say $x(t)$ is *bandlimited to half the sampling rate*. As is well known, this condition is necessary to prevent *aliasing* when sampling the continuous-time signal $x(t)$ at the rate $f_s = 1/T$ to produce $x(nT)$, $n = 0, 1, 2, \ldots$ (see [84, Appendix G]).

D.4   Laplace Transform Theorems

D.4.1   Linearity

The Laplace transform is a *linear operator*. To show this, let $w(t)$ denote a linear combination of signals $x(t)$ and $y(t)$,

$$w(t) = \alpha x(t) + \beta y(t),$$

where α and β are real or complex constants. Then we have

$$
\begin{aligned}
W(s) \; &\triangleq \; \mathcal{L}_s\{w\} \triangleq \mathcal{L}_s\{\alpha x(t) + \beta y(t)\} \\
&\triangleq \; \int_0^\infty [\alpha x(t) + \beta y(t)]\, e^{-st} dt \\
&= \; \alpha \int_0^\infty x(t) e^{-st} dt + \beta \int_0^\infty y(t) e^{-st} dt \\
&\triangleq \; \alpha X(s) + \beta Y(s).
\end{aligned}
$$

Thus, linearity of the Laplace transform follows immediately from the linearity of integration.

D.4.2   Differentiation

The *differentiation theorem* for Laplace transforms states that

$$\dot{x}(t) \leftrightarrow sX(s) - x(0),$$

where $\dot{x}(t) \triangleq \frac{d}{dt} x(t)$, and $x(t)$ is any differentiable function that approaches zero as t goes to infinity. In operator notation,

$$\boxed{\mathcal{L}_s\{\dot{x}\} = sX(s) - x(0).}$$

Proof: This follows immediately from integration by parts:

$$
\begin{aligned}
\mathcal{L}_s\{\dot{x}\} \; &\triangleq \; \int_0^\infty \dot{x}(t) e^{-st} dt \\
&= \; x(t) e^{-st} \Big|_0^\infty - \int_0^\infty x(t)(-s) e^{-st} dt \\
&= \; sX(s) - x(0)
\end{aligned}
$$

since $x(\infty) = 0$ by assumption.

Corollary: *Integration Theorem*

$$\boxed{\mathcal{L}_s\left\{\int_0^t x(\tau)d\tau\right\} = \frac{X(s)}{s}}$$

Thus, successive time derivatives correspond to successively higher powers of s, and successive integrals with respect to time correspond to successively higher powers of $1/s$.

D.5   Laplace Analysis of Linear Systems

The differentiation theorem can be used to convert differential equations into *algebraic* equations, which are easier to solve. We will now show this by means of two examples.

D.5.1   Moving Mass

Figure D.1 depicts a free mass driven by an external force along an ideal frictionless surface in one dimension. Figure D.2 shows the *electrical equivalent circuit* for this scenario in which the external force is represented by a voltage source emitting $f(t)$ *volts*, and the mass is modeled by an *inductor* having the value $L = m$ *Henrys*.

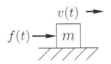

Figure D.1: Physical diagram of an external force driving a mass along a frictionless surface.

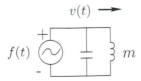

Figure D.2: Electrical equivalent circuit of the force-driven mass in Fig. D.1.

From Newton's second law of motion "$f = ma$", we have

$$f(t) = m\,a(t) \overset{\Delta}{=} m\,\dot{v}(t) \overset{\Delta}{=} m\,\ddot{x}(t).$$

Taking the unilateral Laplace transform and applying the differentiation theorem twice yields

$$
\begin{aligned}
F(s) &= m\,\mathcal{L}_s\{\ddot{x}\} \\
&= m\left[s\mathcal{L}_s\{\dot{x}\} - \dot{x}(0)\right] \\
&= m\left\{ s\left[s\,X(s) - x(0)\right] - \dot{x}(0)\right\} \\
&= m\left[s^2\,X(s) - s\,x(0) - \dot{x}(0)\right].
\end{aligned}
$$

Thus, given

- $F(s) =$ Laplace transform of the driving force $f(t)$,
- $x(0) =$ initial mass position, and
- $\dot{x}(0) \triangleq v(0) =$ initial mass velocity,

we can solve algebraically for $X(s)$, the Laplace transform of the mass position for all $t \geq 0$. This Laplace transform can then be inverted to obtain the mass position $x(t)$ for all $t \geq 0$. This is the general outline of how Laplace-transform analysis goes for *all* linear, time-invariant (LTI) systems. For nonlinear and/or time-varying systems, Laplace-transform analysis cannot, strictly speaking, be used at all.

If the applied external force $f(t)$ is zero, then, by linearity of the Laplace transform, so is $F(s)$, and we readily obtain

$$
X(s) = \frac{x(0)}{s} + \frac{\dot{x}(0)}{s^2} = \frac{x(0)}{s} + \frac{v(0)}{s^2}.
$$

Since $1/s$ is the Laplace transform of the Heaviside unit-step function

$$
u(t) \triangleq \begin{cases} 0, & t < 0 \\ 1, & t \geq 0 \end{cases},
$$

we find that the position of the mass $x(t)$ is given for all time by

$$
x(t) = x(0)\,u(t) + v(0)\,t\,u(t).
$$

Thus, for example, a nonzero initial position $x(0) = x_0$ and zero initial velocity $v(0) = 0$ results in $x(t) = x_0$ for all $t \geq 0$; that is, the mass "just sits there".[3] Similarly, any initial velocity $v(0)$ is integrated with respect to time, meaning that the mass moves forever at the initial velocity.

---

[3] Note that, mathematically, our solution specifies that the mass position is zero prior to time 0. Since we are using the unilateral Laplace transform, there is really "no such thing" as time less than zero, so this is consistent. Using the *bilateral* Laplace transform, the same solution is obtained if the mass is at position $x = 0$ for all negative time $t < 0$, and the driving force $f(t)$ imparts a *doublet* having "amplitude" $x_0 m$ at time 0, *i.e.*, $f(t) = x_0 m\dot{\delta}(t) \leftrightarrow F(s) = x_0 ms$, and all initial conditions are taken to be zero (as they must be for the bilateral Laplace transform). A *doublet* is defined as the time-derivative of the *impulse* signal (defined in Eq. (E.5) on page 324). In other words, impulsive inputs at time 0 can be used to set up arbitrary initial conditions. Specifically, the input $f(t) = x_0 m\dot{\delta}(t) + v_0 m\delta(t)$ slams the system into initial state (x_0, v_0) at time 0.

To summarize, this simple example illustrated use the Laplace transform to solve for the motion of a simple physical system (an ideal mass) in response to initial conditions (no external driving forces). The system was described by a differential equation which was converted to an algebraic equation by the Laplace transform.

D.5.2 Mass-Spring Oscillator Analysis

Consider now the mass-spring oscillator depicted physically in Fig. D.3, and in equivalent-circuit form in Fig. D.4.

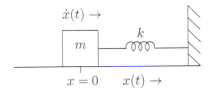

Figure D.3: An ideal mass m sliding on a frictionless surface, attached via an ideal spring k to a rigid wall. The spring is at rest when the mass is centered at $x = 0$.

Figure D.4: Equivalent circuit for the mass-spring oscillator.

By Newton's second law of motion, the force $f_m(t)$ applied to a mass equals its mass times its acceleration:

$$f_m(t) = m\ddot{x}(t).$$

By Hooke's law for ideal springs, the compression force $f_k(t)$ applied to a spring is equal to the spring constant k times the displacement $x(t)$:

$$f_k(t) = kx(t)$$

By Newton's third law of motion ("every action produces an equal and opposite reaction"), we have $f_k = -f_m$. That is, the compression force f_k applied by the mass to the spring is equal and opposite to the accelerating force f_m exerted in the negative-x direction by the spring on the mass. In other words, the forces at the mass-spring contact-point sum to zero:

$$
\begin{aligned}
f_m(t) + f_k(t) &= 0 \\
\Rightarrow m\ddot{x}(t) + kx(t) &= 0
\end{aligned}
$$

We have thus derived a second-order differential equation governing the motion of the mass and spring. (Note that $x(t)$ in Fig. D.3 is both the position of the mass and compression of the spring at time t.)

Taking the Laplace transform of both sides of this differential equation gives

$$
\begin{aligned}
0 &= \mathcal{L}_s\{m\ddot{x} + kx\} \\
&= m\mathcal{L}_s\{\ddot{x}\} + k\mathcal{L}_s\{x\} \quad \text{(by linearity)} \\
&= m\left[s\mathcal{L}_s\{\dot{x}\} - \dot{x}(0)\right] + kX(s) \quad \text{(by the differentiation theorem)} \\
&= m\left\{s\left[sX(s) - x(0)\right] - \dot{x}(0)\right\} + kX(s) \quad \text{(diff. theorem again)} \\
&= ms^2 X(s) - msx(0) - m\dot{x}(0) + kX(s).
\end{aligned}
$$

To simplify notation, denote the initial position and velocity by $x(0) = x_0$ and $\dot{x}(0) = \dot{x}_0 = v_0$, respectively. Solving for $X(s)$ gives

$$
X(s) = \frac{sx_0 + v_0}{s^2 + \frac{k}{m}} \triangleq \frac{r}{s + j\omega_0} + \frac{\bar{r}}{s - j\omega_0}, \quad \omega_0 \triangleq \sqrt{k/m}, \quad \text{and}
$$

$$
r = \frac{x_0}{2} + j\frac{v_0}{2\omega_0} \triangleq R_r e^{j\theta_r}, \quad \text{with}
$$

$$
R_r \triangleq \frac{\sqrt{v_0^2 + \omega_0^2 x_0^2}}{2\omega_0}, \qquad \theta_r \triangleq \tan^{-1}\left(\frac{v_0}{\omega_0 x_0}\right)
$$

denoting the modulus and angle of the pole residue r, respectively. From §D.1, the inverse Laplace transform of $1/(s + a)$ is $e^{-at}u(t)$, where $u(t)$ is the Heaviside unit step function at time 0. Then by linearity, the solution for the motion of the mass is

$$
\begin{aligned}
x(t) &= re^{-j\omega_0 t} + \bar{r}e^{j\omega_0 t} = 2\mathrm{re}\left\{re^{-j\omega_0 t}\right\} = 2R_r \cos(\omega_0 t - \theta_r) \\
&= \frac{\sqrt{v_0^2 + \omega_0^2 x_0^2}}{\omega_0} \cos\left[\omega_0 t - \tan^{-1}\left(\frac{v_0}{\omega_0 x_0}\right)\right].
\end{aligned}
$$

If the initial velocity is zero ($v_0 = 0$), the above formula reduces to $x(t) = x_0 \cos(\omega_0 t)$ and the mass simply oscillates sinusoidally at frequency $\omega_0 = \sqrt{k/m}$, starting from its initial position x_0. If instead the initial position is $x_0 = 0$, we obtain

$$
\begin{aligned}
x(t) &= \frac{v_0}{\omega_0} \sin(\omega_0 t) \\
\Rightarrow v(t) &= v_0 \cos(\omega_0 t).
\end{aligned}
$$

Appendix E

Analog Filters

For our purposes, an *analog filter* is any filter which operates on *continuous-time* signals. In other respects, they are just like digital filters. In particular, linear, time-invariant (LTI) analog filters can be characterized by their (continuous) impulse response $h(t)$, where t is time in seconds. Instead of a difference equation, analog filters may be described by a *differential equation*. Instead of using the z transform to compute the transfer function, we use the *Laplace transform* (introduced in Appendix D). Every aspect of the theory of digital filters has its counterpart in that of analog filters. In fact, one can think of analog filters as simply the limiting case of digital filters as the sampling-rate is allowed to go to infinity.

In the real world, analog filters are often electrical models, or "analogues", of mechanical systems working in continuous time. If the physical system is LTI (*e.g.*, consisting of elastic springs and masses which are constant over time), an LTI analog filter can be used to model it. Before the widespread use of digital computers, physical systems were simulated on so-called "analog computers." An analog computer was much like an analog synthesizer providing modular building-blocks (such as "integrators") that could be patched together to build models of dynamic systems.

E.1 Example Analog Filter

Figure E.1 shows a simple analog filter consisting of one resistor (R Ohms) and one capacitor (C Farads). The voltages across these elements are $v_R(t)$ and $v_C(t)$, respectively, where t denotes time in seconds. The filter input is the externally applied voltage $v_e(t)$, and the filter output is taken to be $v_C(t)$. By Kirchoff's loop constraints [20], we have

$$v_e(t) = v_R(t) + v_C(t), \tag{E.1}$$

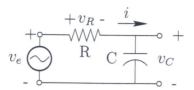

Figure E.1: Simple RC lowpass.

and the loop current is $i(t)$.

E.2 Capacitors

A *capacitor* can be made physically using two parallel conducting plates which are held close together (but not touching). Electric charge can be stored in a capacitor by applying a voltage across the plates.

The defining equation of a capacitor C is

$$q(t) = Cv(t) \qquad\qquad \text{(E.2)}$$

where $q(t)$ denotes the capacitor's *charge* in *Coulombs*, C is the *capacitance* in *Farads*, and $v(t)$ is the *voltage drop* across the capacitor in volts. Differentiating with respect to time gives

$$i(t) = C\frac{dv(t)}{dt},$$

where $i(t) \triangleq dq(t)/dt$ is now the *current* in *Amperes*. Note that, by convention, the current is taken to be positive when flowing from plus to minus across the capacitor (see the arrow in Fig. E.1 which indicates the direction of current flow—there is only one current $i(t)$ flowing clockwise around the loop formed by the voltage source, resistor, and capacitor when an external voltage v_e is applied).

Taking the Laplace transform of both sides gives

$$I(s) = CsV(s) - Cv(0),$$

by the differentiation theorem for Laplace transforms (§D.4.2 on page 314). Assuming a zero initial voltage across the capacitor at time 0, we have

$$R_C(s) \triangleq \frac{V(s)}{I(s)} = \frac{1}{Cs}.$$

We call this the *driving-point impedance* of the capacitor. The driving-point impedance facilitates *steady state analysis* (zero initial conditions) by allowing the capacitor to be analyzed like a simple resistor, with value $1/(Cs)$ Ohms.

Mechanical Equivalent of a Capacitor is a Spring

The mechanical analog of a capacitor is the *compliance of a spring*. The voltage $v(t)$ across a capacitor C corresponds to the force $f(t)$ used to displace a spring. The charge $q(t)$ stored in the capacitor corresponds to the displacement $x(t)$ of the spring. Thus, Eq. (E.2) corresponds to *Hooke's law for ideal springs*:

$$x(t) = \frac{1}{k} f(t),$$

where k is called the *spring constant* or *spring stiffness*. Note that Hooke's law is usually written as $f(t) = k\,x(t)$. The quantity $1/k$ is called the *spring compliance*.

E.3   Inductors

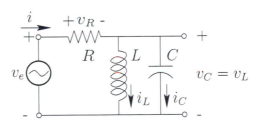

Figure E.2: An RLC filter, input $= v_e(t)$, output $= v_C(t) = v_L(t)$.

An *inductor* can be made physically using a coil of wire, and it stores magnetic flux when a current flows through it. Figure E.2 shows a circuit in which a resistor R is in series with the parallel combination of a capacitor C and inductor L.

The defining equation of an inductor L is

$$\phi(t) = Li(t) \tag{E.3}$$

where $\phi(t)$ denotes the inductor's stored magnetic flux at time t, L is the inductance in *Henrys* (H), and $i(t)$ is the *current* through the inductor coil in *Amperes* (A), where an Ampere is a Coulomb (of electric charge) per second. Differentiating with respect to time gives

$$v(t) = L\frac{di(t)}{dt}, \tag{E.4}$$

where $v(t) = d\phi(t)/dt$ is the voltage across the inductor in volts. Again, the current $i(t)$ is taken to be positive when flowing from plus to minus through the inductor.

Taking the Laplace transform of both sides gives

$$V(s) = LsI(s) - LI(0),$$

by the differentiation theorem for Laplace transforms.

Assuming a zero initial current in the inductor at time 0, we have

$$R_L(s) \triangleq \frac{V(s)}{I(s)} = Ls.$$

Thus, the *driving-point impedance* of the inductor is Ls. Like the capacitor, it can be analyzed in steady state (initial conditions neglected) as a simple resistor with value Ls Ohms.

Mechanical Equivalent of an Inductor is a Mass

The mechanical analog of an inductor is a *mass*. The voltage $v(t)$ across an inductor L corresponds to the force $f(t)$ used to accelerate a mass m. The current $i(t)$ through in the inductor corresponds to the velocity $\dot{x}(t)$ of the mass. Thus, Eq. (E.4) corresponds to *Newton's second law* for an ideal mass:

$$f(t) = ma(t),$$

where $a(t)$ denotes the *acceleration* of the mass m.

From the defining equation $\phi = Li$ for an inductor [Eq. (E.3)], we see that the stored magnetic flux in an inductor is analogous to mass times velocity, or *momentum*. In other words, magnetic flux may be regarded as electric-charge momentum.

E.4   RC Filter Analysis

Referring again to Fig. E.1 on page 320, let's perform an *impedance analysis* of the simple RC lowpass filter.

E.4.1   Driving Point Impedance

Taking the Laplace transform of both sides of Eq. (E.1) gives

$$V_e(s) = V_R(s) + V_C(s) = R\,I(s) + \frac{1}{Cs}I(s)$$

where we made use of the fact that the impedance of a capacitor is $1/(Cs)$, as derived above. The driving point impedance of the whole RC filter is thus

$$R_d(s) \triangleq \frac{V_e(s)}{I(s)} = R + \frac{1}{Cs}.$$

Alternatively, we could simply note that impedances always sum in series and write down this result directly.

E.4.2 Transfer Function

Since the input and output signals are defined as $v_e(t)$ and $v_C(t)$, respectively, the *transfer function* of this analog filter is given by, using *voltage divider rule*,

$$H(s) = \frac{V_C(s)}{V_e(s)} = \frac{\frac{1}{Cs}}{R + \frac{1}{Cs}}, = \frac{1}{RCs + 1} = \frac{1}{RC}\frac{1}{s + \frac{1}{RC}} \triangleq \frac{1}{\tau}\frac{1}{s + \frac{1}{\tau}}.$$

The parameter $\tau \triangleq RC$ is called the *RC time constant*, for reasons we will soon see.

E.4.3 Impulse Response

In the same way that the impulse response of a digital filter is given by the inverse z transform of its transfer function, the impulse response of an *analog* filter is given by the inverse *Laplace* transform of its transfer function, *viz.*,

$$h(t) = \mathcal{L}_t^{-1}\{H(s)\} = \tau e^{-t/\tau} u(t)$$

where $u(t)$ denotes the *Heaviside unit step function*

$$u(t) \triangleq \begin{cases} 1, & t \geq 0 \\ 0, & t < 0. \end{cases}$$

This result is most easily checked by taking the Laplace transform of an exponential decay with time-constant $\tau > 0$:

$$\mathcal{L}_s\{e^{-t/\tau}\} \triangleq \int_0^\infty e^{-t/\tau} e^{-st} dt = \int_0^\infty e^{-(s+1/\tau)t} dt$$

$$= \frac{-1}{s + 1/\tau} e^{-(s+1/\tau)t} \bigg|_0^\infty$$

$$= \frac{1}{s + 1/\tau} = \frac{RC}{RCs + 1}.$$

In more complicated situations, any rational $H(s)$ (ratio of polynomials in s) may be expanded into first-order terms by means of a *partial fraction expansion* (see §6.8 on page 129) and each term in the expansion inverted by inspection as above.

E.4.4   The Continuous-Time Impulse

The continuous-time impulse response was derived above as the inverse-Laplace transform of the transfer function. In this section, we look at how the *impulse* itself must be defined in the continuous-time case.

An *impulse* in continuous time may be loosely defined as any "generalized function" having *"zero width"* and *unit area* under it. A simple valid definition is

$$\delta(t) \triangleq \lim_{\Delta \to 0} \begin{cases} \frac{1}{\Delta}, & 0 \le t \le \Delta \\ 0, & \text{otherwise.} \end{cases} \tag{E.5}$$

More generally, an impulse can be defined as the limit of *any* pulse shape which maintains unit area and approaches zero width at time 0. As a result, the impulse under every definition has the so-called *sifting property* under integration,

$$\int_{-\infty}^{\infty} f(t)\delta(t)dt = f(0), \tag{E.6}$$

provided $f(t)$ is continuous at $t = 0$. This is often taken as the *defining property* of an impulse, allowing it to be defined in terms of non-vanishing function limits such as

$$\delta(t) \triangleq \lim_{\Omega \to \infty} \frac{\sin(\Omega t)}{\pi t}.$$

An impulse is not a function in the usual sense, so it is called instead a *distribution* or *generalized function* [13, 44]. (It is still commonly called a "delta function", however, despite the misnomer.)

E.4.5   Poles and Zeros

In the simple RC-filter example of §E.4.3, the transfer function is

$$H(s) = \frac{1}{s + 1/\tau} = \frac{RC}{RCs + 1}.$$

Thus, there is a single *pole* at $s = -1/\tau = -RC$, and we can say there is one *zero at infinity* as well. Since resistors and capacitors always have positive values, the time constant $\tau = RC$ is always non-negative. This means the impulse response is always an exponential *decay*—never a growth. Since the pole is at $s = -1/\tau$, we find that it is *always in the left-half s plane*. This turns out to be the case also for any *complex* analog one-pole filter. By consideration of the partial fraction expansion of any $H(s)$, it is clear that, for stability of an analog filter, *all poles must lie in the left half of the complex s plane*. This is the analog counterpart of the requirement for digital filters that all poles lie inside the unit circle.

E.5 RLC Filter Analysis

Referring now to Fig. E.2 on page 321, let's perform an *impedance analysis* of that RLC network.

E.5.1 Driving Point Impedance

By inspection, we can write

$$R_d(s) = R + Ls \left\|\frac{1}{Cs}\right. = R + \frac{L/C}{Ls + \frac{1}{Cs}} = R + \frac{Ls}{1 + LCs^2} = R + \frac{1}{C}\frac{s}{s^2 + \frac{1}{LC}}.$$

where $\|$ denotes "in parallel with," and we used the general formula, memorized by any electrical engineering student,

$$\boxed{R_1 \| R_2 = \frac{R_1 R_2}{R_1 + R_2}.}$$

That is, the impedance of the *parallel combination* of impedances R_1 and R_2 is given by the product divided by the sum of the impedances.

E.5.2 Transfer Function

The transfer function in this example can similarly be found using voltage divider rule:

$$H(s) = \frac{V_C(s)}{V_e(s)} = \frac{\left(Ls \left\| \frac{1}{Cs}\right.\right)}{R + \left(Ls \left\| \frac{1}{Cs}\right.\right)} = \frac{1}{RC}\frac{s}{s^2 + \frac{1}{RC}s + \frac{1}{LC}} \triangleq 2\eta \cdot \frac{s}{s^2 + 2\eta s + \omega_0^2}$$

E.5.3 Poles and Zeros

From the quadratic formula, the two poles are located at

$$s = -\eta \pm \sqrt{\eta^2 - \omega_0^2} \triangleq -\frac{1}{2RC} \pm \sqrt{\left(\frac{1}{2RC}\right)^2 - \frac{1}{LC}}$$

and there is a zero at $s = 0$ and another at $s = \infty$. If the damping R is sufficienly small so that $\eta^2 < \omega_0^2$, then the poles form a complex-conjugate pair:

$$s = -\eta \pm j\sqrt{\omega_0^2 - \eta^2}$$

Since $\eta = 1/(2RC) > 0$, the poles are always in the left-half plane, and hence the analog RLC filter is always stable. When the damping is zero, the poles go to the $j\omega$ axis:

$$s = \pm j\omega_0$$

E.5.4   Impulse Response

The impulse response is again the inverse Laplace transform of the transfer function. Expanding $H(s)$ into a sum of complex one-pole sections,

$$H(s) = 2\eta \cdot \frac{s}{s^2 + 2\eta s + \omega_0^2} = \frac{r_1}{s - p_1} + \frac{r_2}{s - p_2} = \frac{(r_1 + r_2)s - (r_1 p_2 + r_2 p_1)}{s^2 - (p_1 + p_2) + p_1 p_2},$$

where $p_{1,2} \overset{\Delta}{=} -\eta \pm \sqrt{\eta^2 - \omega_0^2}$. Equating numerator coefficients gives

$$\begin{aligned} r_1 + r_2 &= 2\eta = \frac{1}{RC} \\ r_1 p_2 + r_2 p_1 &= 0. \end{aligned}$$

This pair of equations in two unknowns may be solved for r_1 and r_2. The impulse response is then

$$h(t) = r_1 e^{p_1 t} u(t) + r_2 e^{p_2 t} u(t).$$

E.6   Relating Pole Radius to Bandwidth

Consider the *continuous-time complex one-pole resonator* with s-plane transfer function

$$H(s) = \frac{-\sigma_p}{s - p}.$$

where $s = \sigma + j\omega$ is the Laplace-transform variable, and $p \overset{\Delta}{=} \sigma_p + j\omega_p$ is the single complex pole. The numerator scaling has been set to $-\sigma_p$ so that the frequency response is normalized to unity gain at resonance:

$$H(j\omega_p) = \frac{-\sigma_p}{j\omega_p - \sigma_p - j\omega_p} = \frac{-\sigma_p}{-\sigma_p} = 1.$$

The amplitude response at all frequencies is given by

$$G(\omega) \triangleq |H(j\omega)| = \frac{|\sigma_p|}{|j\omega - p|} = \frac{|\sigma_p|}{\sqrt{(\omega - \omega_p)^2 + \sigma_p^2}}.$$

Without loss of generality, we may set $\omega_p = 0$, since changing ω_p merely translates the amplitude response with respect to ω. (We could alternatively define the translated frequency variable $\nu \triangleq \omega - \omega_p$ to get the same simplification.) The squared amplitude response is now

$$G^2(\omega) = \frac{\sigma_p^2}{\omega^2 + \sigma_p^2}.$$

Note that

$$G^2(0) = 1 = 0 \text{ dB},$$
$$G^2(\pm\sigma_p) = \frac{1}{2} = -3 \text{ dB}.$$

This shows that the *3-dB bandwidth* of the resonator in radians per second is $2|\sigma_p|$, or twice the absolute value of the real part of the pole. Denoting the 3-dB bandwidth in Hz by B, we have derived the relation $2\pi B = 2|\sigma_p|$, or

$$B = \frac{|\sigma_p|}{\pi} = \frac{|\text{re}\{p\}|}{\pi}.$$

Since a -3 dB attenuation is the same thing as a power scaling by $1/2$, the 3-dB bandwidth is also called the *half-power bandwidth*.

It now remains to "digitize" the continuous-time resonator and show that relation Eq. (8.7) follows. The most natural mapping of the s plane to the z plane is

$$z = e^{sT},$$

where T is the sampling period. This mapping follows directly from sampling the Laplace transform to obtain the z transform. It is also called the *impulse invariant transformation* [68, pp. 216–219], and for digital poles it is the same as the *matched z transformation* [68, pp. 224–226]. Applying the matched z transformation to the pole p in the s plane gives the *digital pole*

$$p_d = R_d e^{j\theta_d} \triangleq e^{pT} = e^{(\sigma_p + j\omega_p)T} = e^{\sigma_p T} e^{j\omega_p T}$$

from which we identify

$$R_d = e^{\sigma_p T} = e^{-\pi BT}$$

and the relation between pole radius R_d and analog 3-dB bandwidth B (in Hz) is now shown. Since the mapping $z = e^{sT}$ becomes exact as $T \to 0$, we have that B is also the 3-dB bandwidth of the digital resonator in the limit as the sampling rate approaches infinity. In practice, it is a good approximate relation whenever the digital pole is close to the unit circle ($R_d \approx 1$).

E.7   Quality Factor (Q)

The *quality factor* (Q) of a two-pole resonator is defined by [20, p. 184]

$$Q \overset{\Delta}{=} \frac{\omega_0}{2\alpha} \tag{E.7}$$

where ω_0 and α are parameters of the resonator transfer function:

$$H(s) = g\frac{2\alpha s}{s^2 + 2\alpha s + \omega_0^2} \overset{\Delta}{=} g\frac{\frac{\omega_0}{Q}s}{s^2 + \frac{\omega_0}{Q}s + \omega_0^2} \overset{\Delta}{=} g\frac{\tilde{s}}{\tilde{s}^2 + \frac{1}{Q}\tilde{s} + 1}, \quad \tilde{s} \overset{\Delta}{=} \frac{s}{\omega_0} \tag{E.8}$$

Note that Q is defined in the context of *continuous-time* resonators, so the transfer function $H(s)$ is the Laplace transform (instead of the z transform) of the *continuous* (instead of discrete-time) impulse-response $h(t)$. An introduction to Laplace-transform analysis appears in Appendix D. The parameter α is called the *damping constant* (or "damping factor") of the second-order transfer function, and ω_0 is called the *resonant frequency* [20, p. 179]. The resonant frequency ω_0 coincides with the physical oscillation frequency of the resonator impulse response when the damping constant α is zero. For light damping, ω_0 is approximately the physical frequency of impulse-response oscillation (2π times the zero-crossing rate of sinusoidal oscillation under an exponential decay). For larger damping constants, it is better to use the imaginary part of the pole location as a definition of resonance frequency (which is exact in the case of a single complex pole). (See §B.6 on page 283 for a more complete discussion of resonators, in the discrete-time case.)

By the quadratic formula, the poles of the transfer function $H(s)$ are given by

$$p = -\alpha \pm \sqrt{\alpha^2 - \omega_0^2} \overset{\Delta}{=} -\alpha \pm \alpha_d. \tag{E.9}$$

Therefore, the poles are complex only when $Q > 1/2$. Since real poles do not resonate, we have $Q > 1/2$ for any resonator. The case $Q = 1/2$ is called *critically damped*, while $Q < 1/2$ is called *overdamped*. A resonator ($Q > 1/2$) is said to be *underdamped*, and the limiting case $Q = \infty$ is simply *undamped*.

Relating to the notation of the previous section, in which we defined one of the complex poles as $p \triangleq \sigma_p + j\omega_p$, we have

$$\sigma_p = -\alpha \tag{E.10}$$

$$\omega_p = \sqrt{\omega_0 - \alpha^2}. \tag{E.11}$$

For resonators, ω_p coincides with the classically defined quantity [20, p. 624]

$$\omega_d \triangleq \omega_p = \sqrt{\omega_0^2 - \alpha^2} = \frac{\alpha_d}{j}.$$

Since the imaginary parts of the complex resonator poles are $\pm\omega_d$, the zero-crossing rate of the resonator impulse response is ω_d/π crossings per second. Moreover, ω_d is very close to the peak-magnitude frequency in the resonator amplitude response. If we eliminate the negative-frequency pole, ω_d/π becomes *exactly* the peak frequency. In other words, as a measure of resonance peak frequency, ω_d only neglects the interaction of the positive- and negative-frequency resonance peaks in the frequency response, which is usually negligible except for highly damped, low-frequency resonators. For any amount of damping ω_d/π gives the impulse-response zero-crossing rate exactly, as is immediately seen from the derivation in the next section.

E.7.1   Decay Time is Q Periods

Another well known rule of thumb is that the Q of a resonator is the number of "periods" under the exponential decay of its impulse response. More precisely, we will show that, for $Q \gg 1/2$, the impulse response decays by the factor $e^{-\pi}$ in Q cycles, which is about 96 percent decay, or -27 dB.

The impulse response corresponding to Eq. (E.8) is found by inverting the Laplace transform of the transfer function $H(s)$. Since it is only second order, the solution can be found in many tables of Laplace transforms. Alternatively, we can break it up into a sum of first-order terms which are invertible by inspection (possibly after rederiving the Laplace transform of an exponential decay, which is very simple). Thus we perform the partial fraction expansion of Eq. (E.8) to obtain

$$H(s) = \frac{g_1}{s - p_1} + \frac{g_2}{s - p_2}$$

where p_i are given by Eq. (E.9), and some algebra gives

$$g_1 = -g\frac{p_1}{p_2 - p_1} \tag{E.12}$$

$$g_2 = g\frac{p_2}{p_2 - p_1} \tag{E.13}$$

as the respective residues of the poles p_i.

The impulse response is thus

$$h(t) = g_1 e^{p_1 t} + g_2 e^{p_2 t}.$$

Assuming a resonator, $Q > 1/2$, we have $p_2 = \bar{p}_1$, where $p_1 = \sigma_p + j\omega_p = -\alpha + j\omega_d$ (using notation of the preceding section), and the impulse response reduces to

$$h(t) = g_1 e^{p_1 t} + \bar{g}_1 e^{\bar{p}_1 t} = A e^{-\alpha t} \cos(\omega_p t + \phi)$$

where A and ϕ are overall amplitude and phase constants, respectively.[1]

We have shown so far that the impulse response $h(t)$ decays as $e^{-\alpha t}$ with a sinusoidal radian frequency $\omega_p = \omega_d$ under the exponential envelope. After Q periods at frequency ω_p, time has advanced to

$$t_Q = Q \frac{2\pi}{\omega_p} \approx \frac{2\pi Q}{\omega_0} = \frac{\pi}{\alpha},$$

where we have used the definition Eq. (E.7) $Q \triangleq \omega_0/(2\alpha)$. Thus, after Q periods, the amplitude envelope has decayed to

$$e^{-\alpha t_Q} = e^{-\pi} \approx 0.043 \ldots$$

which is about 96 percent decay. The only approximation in this derivation was

$$\omega_p = \sqrt{\omega_0^2 - \alpha^2} \approx \omega_0$$

which holds whenever $\alpha \ll \omega_0$, or $Q \gg 1/2$. (See Problem 6 on page 172.)

E.7.2   Q as Energy Stored over Energy Dissipated

Yet another meaning for Q is as follows [20, p. 326]

$$Q = 2\pi \frac{\text{Stored Energy}}{\text{Energy Dissipated in One Cycle}}$$

where the resonator is freely decaying (unexcited).

Proof. The total stored energy at time t is equal to the total energy of the remaining response. After an impulse at time 0, the stored energy in a second-order resonator is

$$\mathcal{E}(0) = \int_0^\infty h^2(t)dt \propto \int_0^\infty e^{-2\alpha t}dt = \frac{1}{2\alpha}.$$

---

[1]**Exercise:** Determine A and ϕ and check your result by performing the Laplace transform and comparing to Eq. (E.8).

The energy dissipated in the first period $P = 2\pi/\omega_p$ is $\mathcal{E}(0) - \mathcal{E}(P)$, where

$$
\begin{aligned}
\mathcal{E}(P) &= \int_P^\infty h^2(t)dt \propto \int_P^\infty e^{-2\alpha t}dt \\
&= \left. -\frac{1}{2\alpha}e^{-2\alpha t}\right|_P^\infty \\
&= \frac{e^{-2\alpha P}}{2\alpha} \\
&= \frac{e^{-2\alpha(2\pi/\omega_p)}}{2\alpha}.
\end{aligned}
$$

Assuming $Q \gg 1/2$ as before, $\omega_p \approx \omega_0$ so that

$$
\mathcal{E}(P) \approx \frac{e^{-2\pi/Q}}{2\alpha}.
$$

Assuming further that $Q \gg 2\pi$, we obtain

$$
\mathcal{E}(0) - \mathcal{E}(P) \approx \frac{1}{2\alpha}\left(1 - e^{-\frac{2\pi}{Q}}\right) \approx \frac{1}{2\alpha}\frac{2\pi}{Q}.
$$

This is the energy dissipated in one cycle. Dividing this into the total stored energy at time zero, $\mathcal{E}(0) = 1/(2\alpha)$, gives

$$
\frac{\mathcal{E}(0)}{\mathcal{E}(0) - \mathcal{E}(P)} \approx \frac{Q}{2\pi}
$$

whence

$$
Q = 2\pi\frac{\mathcal{E}(0)}{\mathcal{E}(0) - \mathcal{E}(P)}
$$

as claimed. Note that this rule of thumb requires $Q \gg 2\pi$, while the one of the previous section only required $Q \gg 1/2$.

E.8   Analog Allpass Filters

It turns out that analog allpass filters are considerably simpler mathematically than digital allpass filters (discussed in §B.2 on page 272). In fact, when working with digital allpass filters, it can be fruitful to convert to the analog case using the bilinear transform (§I.3.1 on page 388), so that the filter may be manipulated in the analog s plane rather than the digital z plane. The analog case is simpler because analog allpass filters may be described as having a zero at $s = -\bar{p}$ for every pole at $s = p$, while digital allpass filters must have a zero at $z = 1/\bar{p}$ for every pole at $z = p$. In particular, the transfer function of every first-order analog allpass filter can be written as

$$H(s) = e^{j\phi}\frac{s + \overline{p}}{s - p}$$

where $\phi \in [-\pi, \pi)$ is any constant phase offset. To see why $H(s)$ must be allpass, note that its frequency response is given by

$$H(j\omega) = e^{j\phi}\frac{j\omega + \overline{p}}{j\omega - p} = -e^{j\phi}\frac{\overline{j\omega - p}}{j\omega - p},$$

which clearly has modulus 1 for all ω (since $|\overline{z}/z| = 1$, $\forall z \neq 0$). For real allpass filters, complex poles must occur in conjugate pairs, so that the "allpass rule" for poles and zeros may be simplified to state that a zero is required at *minus* the location of every pole, *i.e.*, every *real* first-order allpass filter is of the form

$$H(s) = \pm\frac{s + p}{s - p},$$

and, more generally, every real allpass transfer function can be factored as

$$H(s) = \pm\frac{(s + p_1)(s + p_2)\cdots(s + p_N)}{(s - p_1)(s - p_2)\cdots(s - p_N)}. \tag{E.14}$$

This simplified rule works because every complex pole p_i is accompanied by its conjugate $p_k = \overline{p_i}$ for some $k \in [1 : N]$.

Multiplying out the terms in Eq. (E.14), we find that the numerator polynomial $B(s)$ is simply related to the denominator polynomial $A(s)$:

$$H(s) = \pm(-1)^N\frac{A(-s)}{A(s)} = \pm(-1)^N\frac{s^N - a_{N-1}s^{N-1} + \cdots - a_1 s + a_0}{s^N + a_{N-1}s^{N-1} + \cdots + a_1 s + a_0}$$

Since the roots of $A(s)$ must be in the left-half s-plane for stability, $A(s)$ must be a *Hurwitz polynomial*, which implies that all of its coefficients are nonnegative. The polynomial

$$A(-s) = A\left(e^{j\pi}s\right)$$

can be seen as a π-rotation of $A(s)$ in the s plane; therefore, its roots must have non-positive real parts, and its coefficients form an alternating sequence.

As an example of the greater simplicity of analog allpass filters relative to the discrete-time case, the graphical method for computing phase response from poles and zeros (§8.3 on page 181) gives immediately that the phase response of every real analog allpass filter is equal to *twice* the phase response of its numerator (plus π when the frequency response is negative at dc). This is because the angle of a vector from a pole at $s = p$ to the point $s = j\omega$ along the frequency axis is π minus the angle of the vector from a zero at $s = -p$ to the point $j\omega$.

Lossless Analog Filters

As discussed in §B.2, the an allpass filter can be defined as any filter that *preserves signal energy* for every input signal $x(t)$. In the continuous-time case, this means

$$\| x \|_2^2 \triangleq \int_{-\infty}^{\infty} |x(t)|^2 \, dt = \int_{-\infty}^{\infty} |y(t)|^2 \, dt \triangleq \| y \|_2^2$$

where $y(t)$ denotes the output signal, and $\| y \|$ denotes the L^2 norm of y. Using the Rayleigh energy theorem (Parseval's theorem) for Fourier transforms [87], energy preservation can be expressed in the frequency domain by

$$\| X \|_2 = \| Y \|_2$$

where X and Y denote the Fourier transforms of x and y, respectively, and frequency-domain L^2 norms are defined by

$$\| X \|_2 \triangleq \sqrt{\frac{1}{2\pi} \int_{-\infty}^{\infty} |X(j\omega)|^2 \, d\omega}.$$

If $h(t)$ denotes the impulse response of the allpass filter, then its transfer function $H(s)$ is given by the Laplace transform of h,

$$H(s) = \int_0^{\infty} h(t) e^{-st} dt,$$

and we have the requirement

$$\| X \|_2 = \| Y \|_2 = \| H \cdot X \|_2 .$$

Since this equality must hold for every input signal x, it must be true in particular for complex sinusoidal inputs of the form $x(t) = \exp(j2\pi f_x t)$, in which case [87]

$$
\begin{aligned}
X(f) &= \delta(f - f_x) \\
Y(f) &= H(j2\pi f_x)\delta(f - f_x),
\end{aligned}
$$

where $\delta(f)$ denotes the Dirac "delta function" or continuous impulse function (§E.4.3). Thus, the allpass condition becomes

$$\| X \|_2 = \| Y \|_2 = |H(j2\pi f_x)| \cdot \| X \|_2$$

which implies

$$|H(j\omega)| = 1, \quad \forall \omega \in (-\infty, \infty). \tag{E.15}$$

Suppose H is a rational analog filter, so that

$$H(s) = \frac{B(s)}{A(s)}$$

where $B(s)$ and $A(s)$ are polynomials in s:

$$
\begin{aligned}
B(s) &= b_M s^M + b_{M-1} s^{M-1} + \cdots + b_1 s + b_0 \\
A(s) &= s^N + a_{N-1} s^{N-1} + \cdots + a_1 s + a_0
\end{aligned}
$$

(We have normalized $B(s)$ so that $A(s)$ is monic ($a_N = 1$) without loss of generality.) Equation (E.15) implies

$$|A(j\omega)| = |B(j\omega)|, \quad \forall \omega \in (-\infty, \infty).$$

If $M = N = 0$, then the allpass condition reduces to $|b_0| = |a_0| = 1$, which implies

$$b_0 = e^{j\phi} a_0 = e^{j\phi}$$

where $\phi \in [-\pi, \pi)$ is any real phase constant. In other words, b_0 can be any unit-modulus complex number. If $M = N = 1$, then the filter is allpass provided

$$|b_1 j\omega + b_0| = |j\omega + a_0|, \quad \forall \omega \in (-\infty, \infty).$$

Since this must hold for all ω, there are only two solutions:

1. $b_0 = a_0$ and $b_1 = 1$, in which case $H(s) = B(s)/A(s) = 1$ for all s.

2. $b_0 = \overline{a_0}$ and $b_1 = 1$, i.e.,

$$B(j\omega) = e^{j\phi}\overline{A(j\omega)}.$$

Case (1) is trivially allpass, while case (2) is the one discussed above in the introduction to this section.

By analytic continuation, we have

$$1 = |H(j\omega)| = |H(j\omega)|^2 = H(s)\overline{H(s)}\Big|_{s=j\omega}$$

If $h(t)$ is real, then $\overline{H(j\omega)} = H(-j\omega)$, and we can write

$$1 = H(s)H(-s)\big|_{s=j\omega}.$$

To have $H(s)H(-s) = 1$, every pole at $s = p$ in $H(s)$ must be canceled by a zero at $s = p$ in $H(-s)$, which is a zero at $s = -p$ in $H(s)$. Thus, we have derived the simplified "allpass rule" for real analog filters.

Appendix F

Matrix Filter Representations

This appendix introduces various *matrix representations* for digital filters, including the important *state space formulation*. Additionally, elementary *system identification* based on a matrix description is described.

F.1   Introduction

It is illuminating to look at *matrix representations* of digital filters.[1] Every *linear* digital filter can be expressed as a *constant matrix* $\mathbf{h}$ multiplying the input signal $\underline{x}$ (the *input vector*) to produce the output signal (vector) $\underline{y}$, *i.e.*,

$$\underline{y} = \mathbf{h}\underline{x}.$$

For simplicity (in this appendix only), we will restrict attention to *finite-length* inputs $\underline{x}^T = [x_0, \ldots, x_{N-1}]$ (to avoid infinite matrices), and the output signal will also be length N. Thus, the filter matrix $\mathbf{h}$ is a square $N \times N$ matrix, and the input/output signal vectors are $N \times 1$ column vectors.

More generally, any finite-order *linear operator* can be expressed as a matrix multiply. For example, the Discrete Fourier Transform (DFT) can be represented by the "DFT matrix" $[e^{-j2\pi kn/N}]$, where the column index n and row index k range from 0 to $N-1$ [84, p. 111].[2] Even infinite-order

---

[1] A short tutorial on *matrices* appears in [84], available online at
http://ccrma.stanford.edu/~jos/mdft/Matrices.html.

[2] http://ccrma.stanford.edu/~jos/mdft/Matrix_Formulation_DFT.html.

linear operators are often thought of as matrices having infinite extent. In summary, if a digital filter is *linear*, it can be represented by a *matrix*.

F.2   General Causal Linear Filter Matrix

To be *causal*, the filter output at time $n \in [0, N-1]$ cannot depend on the input at any times m greater than n. This implies that a causal filter matrix must be *lower triangular*. That is, it must have zeros above the main diagonal. Thus, a causal linear filter matrix $\mathbf{h}$ will have entries that satisfy $h_{mn} = 0$ for $n > m$.

For example, the general 3×3 causal, linear, digital-filter matrix operating on three-sample sequences is

$$\mathbf{h} = \begin{bmatrix} h_{00} & 0 & 0 \\ h_{10} & h_{11} & 0 \\ h_{20} & h_{21} & h_{22} \end{bmatrix}$$

and the input-output relationship is of course

$$\begin{bmatrix} y_0 \\ y_1 \\ y_2 \end{bmatrix} = \begin{bmatrix} h_{00} & 0 & 0 \\ h_{10} & h_{11} & 0 \\ h_{20} & h_{21} & h_{22} \end{bmatrix} \begin{bmatrix} x_0 \\ x_1 \\ x_2 \end{bmatrix}, \tag{F.1}$$

or, more explicitly,

$$\begin{aligned} y_0 &= h_{00}x_0 \\ y_1 &= h_{10}x_0 + h_{11}x_1 \\ y_2 &= h_{20}x_0 + h_{21}x_1 + h_{22}x_2. \end{aligned} \tag{F.2}$$

While Eq. (F.2) covers the general case of linear, causal, digital filters operating on the space of three-sample sequences, it includes *time varying* filters, in general. For example, the gain of the "current input sample" changes over time as h_{00}, h_{11}, h_{22}.

F.3   General LTI Filter Matrix

The general linear, *time-invariant* (LTI) matrix is *Toeplitz*. A *Toeplitz matrix* is *constant along all its diagonals*. For example, the general 3×3 LTI matrix is given by

$$\mathbf{h} = \begin{bmatrix} h_0 & h_{-1} & h_{-2} \\ h_1 & h_0 & h_{-1} \\ h_2 & h_1 & h_0 \end{bmatrix}$$

and restricting to causal LTI filters yields

$$
\mathbf{h} = \begin{bmatrix} h_0 & 0 & 0 \\ h_1 & h_0 & 0 \\ h_2 & h_1 & h_0 \end{bmatrix}.
$$

Note that the gain of the "current input sample" is now fixed at h_0 for all time. Also note that we can handle only length 3 FIR filters in this representation, and that the output signal is "cut off" at time $n = 3$. The cut-off time is one sample after the filter is fully "engaged" by the input signal (all filter coefficients see data). Even if the input signal is zero at time $n = 3$ and beyond, the filter should be allowed to "ring" for another two samples. We can accommodate this by appending two zeros to the input and going with a 5×5 *banded Toeplitz filter matrix*:

$$
\begin{bmatrix} y_0 \\ y_1 \\ y_2 \\ y_3 \\ y_4 \end{bmatrix} = \begin{bmatrix} h_0 & 0 & 0 & 0 & 0 \\ h_1 & h_0 & 0 & 0 & 0 \\ h_2 & h_1 & h_0 & 0 & 0 \\ 0 & h_2 & h_1 & h_0 & 0 \\ 0 & 0 & h_2 & h_1 & h_0 \end{bmatrix} \begin{bmatrix} x_0 \\ x_1 \\ x_2 \\ 0 \\ 0 \end{bmatrix} \tag{F.3}
$$

We could add more rows to obtain more output samples, but the additional outputs would all be zero.

In general, if a causal FIR filter is length N_h, then its order is $N_h - 1$, so to avoid "cutting off" the output signal prematurely, we must append at least $N_h - 1$ zeros to the input signal. Appending zeros in this way is often called *zero padding*, and it is used extensively in spectrum analysis [84]. As a specific example, an order 5 causal FIR filter (length 6) requires 5 samples of zero-padding on the input signal to avoid output truncation.

If the FIR filter is *noncausal*, then zero-padding is needed *before* the input signal in order not to "cut off" the "pre-ring" of the filter (the response before time $n = 0$).

To handle arbitrary-length input signals, keeping the filter length at 3 (an order 2 FIR filter), we may simply use a longer banded Toeplitz filter matrix:

$$
\mathbf{h} = \begin{bmatrix} h_0 & 0 & 0 & 0 & 0 & 0 & \cdots \\ h_1 & h_0 & 0 & 0 & 0 & 0 & \cdots \\ h_2 & h_1 & h_0 & 0 & 0 & 0 & \cdots \\ 0 & h_2 & h_1 & h_0 & 0 & 0 & \cdots \\ 0 & 0 & h_2 & h_1 & h_0 & 0 & \cdots \\ 0 & 0 & 0 & h_2 & h_1 & h_0 & \\ \vdots & \vdots & \vdots & & \ddots & \ddots & \ddots \end{bmatrix}
$$

A complete matrix representation of an LTI digital filter (allowing for infinitely long input/output signals) requires an infinite Toeplitx matrix, as indicated above. Instead of working with infinite matrices, however, it is more customary to speak in terms of *linear operators* [56]. Thus, we may say that every LTI filter corresponds to a *Toeplitz linear operator*.

F.4 Cyclic Convolution Matrix

An infinite Toeplitz matrix implements, in principle, *acyclic convolution* (which is what we normally mean when we just say "convolution"). In practice, the convolution of a signal x and an impulse response h, in which both x and h are more than a hundred or so samples long, is typically implemented fastest using *FFT convolution* (*i.e.*, performing fast convolution using the Fast Fourier Transform (FFT) [84][3]). However, the FFT computes *cyclic convolution* unless sufficient zero padding is used [84]. The matrix representation of cyclic (or "circular") convolution is a *circulant matrix*, e.g.,

$$\mathbf{h} = \begin{bmatrix} h_0 & 0 & 0 & 0 & h_2 & h_1 \\ h_1 & h_0 & 0 & 0 & 0 & h_2 \\ h_2 & h_1 & h_0 & 0 & 0 & 0 \\ 0 & h_2 & h_1 & h_0 & 0 & 0 \\ 0 & 0 & h_2 & h_1 & h_0 & 0 \\ 0 & 0 & 0 & h_2 & h_1 & h_0 \end{bmatrix}.$$

As in this example, each row of a circulant matrix is obtained from the previous row by a circular right-shift. Circulant matrices are thus always Toeplitz (but not vice versa). Circulant matrices have many interesting properties.[4] For example, the eigenvectors of an $N \times N$ circulant matrix are the DFT sinusoids for a length N DFT [84]. Similarly, the eigenvalues may be found by simply taking the DFT of the first row.

The DFT eigenstructure of circulant matrices is directly related to the DFT convolution theorem [84]. The above 6×6 circulant matrix $\mathbf{h}$, when multiplied times a length 6 vector $\underline{x}$, implements cyclic convolution of $\underline{x}$ with $\underline{h} = [h_0, h_1, h_3, 0, 0, 0]$. Using the DFT to perform the circular convolution can be expressed as

$$\underline{y} = \underline{x} \circledast \underline{h} = \text{IDFT}(\text{DFT}(\underline{x}) \cdot \text{DFT}(\underline{h})),$$

where '$\circledast$' denotes circular convolution. Let $\mathbf{S}$ denote the matrix of sampled DFT sinusoids for a length N DFT: $\mathbf{S}[k, n] \triangleq e^{j2\pi kn/N}$. Then $\mathbf{S}^*$ is the

---

[3]http://ccrma.stanford.edu/~jos/mdft/
[4]http://en.wikipedia.org/wiki/Circulant_matrix

DFT matrix, where '$*$' denotes Hermitian transposition (transposition and complex-conjugation). The DFT of the length-N vector $\underline{x}$ can be written as $\underline{X} = \mathbf{S}^* \underline{x}$, and the corresponding inverse DFT is $\underline{x} = (1/N)\mathbf{S}\underline{X}$. The DFT-eigenstructure of circulant matrices provides that a real $N \times N$ circulant matrix $\mathbf{h}$ having top row $\underline{h}^T$ satisfies $\mathbf{h}\mathbf{S} = \mathbf{S} \cdot \text{diag}(\underline{H})$, where $\underline{H} = \mathbf{S}^* \underline{h}$ is the length N DFT of $\underline{h}$, and $\text{diag}(\underline{H})$ denotes a diagonal matrix with the elements of $\underline{H}$ along the diagonal. Therefore, $\text{diag}(\underline{H}) = \mathbf{S}^{-1}\mathbf{h}\mathbf{S} = (1/N)\mathbf{S}^* \mathbf{h}\mathbf{S}$. By the DFT convolution theorem,

$$y = \underline{h} \circledast \underline{x} \quad \Leftrightarrow \quad \underline{Y}[k] = \underline{H}[k]\,\underline{X}[k], \; \forall k \in [0, N-1]$$
$$\Leftrightarrow \quad \underline{Y} = \text{diag}(\underline{H})\,\underline{X} = (1/N)\mathbf{S}^* \mathbf{h}\,\mathbf{S}\,\underline{X}.$$

Premultiplying by the IDFT matrix $(1/N)\mathbf{S}$ yields

$$\underline{y} = (1/N)\mathbf{S}\underline{Y} = (1/N)\mathbf{S}\mathbf{S}^* \mathbf{h}\,(1/N)\mathbf{S}\underline{X} = \mathbf{h}\underline{x}.$$

Thus, the DFT convolution theorem holds if and only if the circulant convolution matrix $\mathbf{h}$ has eigenvalues $\underline{H}$ and eigenvectors given by the columns of $\mathbf{S}$ (the DFT sinusoids).

F.5   Inverse Filters

Note that the filter matrix $\mathbf{h}$ is often *invertible* [58]. In that case, we can effectively run the filter *backwards*:

$$\underline{x} = \mathbf{h}^{-1}\underline{y}$$

However, an invertible filter matrix does *not* necessarily correspond to a *stable* inverse-filter when the lengths of the input and output vectors are allowed to grow larger. For example, the inverted filter matrix may contain truncated *growing* exponentials, as illustrated in the following `matlab` example:

```
> h = toeplitz([1,2,0,0,0],[1,0,0,0,0])
h =
   1   0   0   0   0
   2   1   0   0   0
   0   2   1   0   0
   0   0   2   1   0
   0   0   0   2   1
> inv(h)
ans =
      1      0      0      0      0
```

$$
\begin{array}{rrrrr}
-2 & 1 & 0 & 0 & 0 \\
4 & -2 & 1 & 0 & 0 \\
-8 & 4 & -2 & 1 & 0 \\
16 & -8 & 4 & -2 & 1
\end{array}
$$

The inverse of the FIR filter $h = [1, 2]$ is in fact unstable, having impulse response $h_i(n) = (-2)^n$, $n = 0, 1, 2, \ldots$, which grows to ∞ with n.

Another point to notice is that the inverse of a banded Toeplitz matrix is not banded (although the inverse of lower-triangular [causal] matrix remains lower triangular). This corresponds to the fact that the inverse of an FIR filter is an IIR filter.

F.6   State Space Realization

Above, we used a matrix multiply to represent convolution of the filter input signal with the filter's impulse response. This only works for FIR filters since an IIR filter would require an infinite impulse-response matrix. IIR filters have an extensively used matrix representation called *state space form* (or "state space realizations"). They are especially convenient for representing filters with *multiple inputs* and *multiple outputs* (MIMO filters). An order N digital filter with p inputs and q outputs can be written in state-space form as follows:

$$
\begin{aligned}
\underline{x}(n+1) &= A\underline{x}(n) + B\underline{u}(n) \\
\underline{y}(n) &= C\underline{x}(n) + D\underline{u}(n)
\end{aligned}
\tag{F.4}
$$

where $\underline{x}(n)$ is the length N *state vector* at discrete time n, $\underline{u}(n)$ is a $p \times 1$ vector of inputs, and $y(n)$ the $q \times 1$ output vector. A is the $N \times N$ *state transition matrix*, and it determines the *dynamics* of the system (its *poles*, or resonant *modes*).

State-space models are described further in Appendix G. Here, we will only give an illustrative example and make a few observations:

State Space Filter Realization Example

The digital filter having difference equation

$$
y(n) = u(n-1) + u(n-2) + 0.5\, y(n-1) - 0.1\, y(n-2) + 0.01\, y(n-3)
$$

can be realized in state-space form as follows:[5]

$$
\begin{bmatrix} x_1(n+1) \\ x_2(n+1) \\ x_3(n+1) \end{bmatrix} = \begin{bmatrix} 0 & 1 & 0 \\ 0 & 0 & 1 \\ 0.01 & -0.1 & 0.5 \end{bmatrix} \begin{bmatrix} x_1(n) \\ x_2(n) \\ x_3(n) \end{bmatrix} + \begin{bmatrix} 0 \\ 0 \\ 1 \end{bmatrix} u(n)
$$

$$
\underline{y}(n) = \begin{bmatrix} 0 & 1 & 1 \end{bmatrix} \begin{bmatrix} x_1(n) \\ x_2(n) \\ x_3(n) \end{bmatrix} \tag{F.5}
$$

Thus, $\underline{x}(n) = [x_1(n), x_2(n), x_3(n)]^T$ is the vector of state variables at time n, $B = [0,0,1]^T$ is the state-input gain vector, $C = [0,1,1]$ is the vector of state-gains for the output, and the direct-path gain is $D = 0$.

This example is repeated using matlab in §G.7.8 on page 362 (after we have covered *transfer functions*).

A general procedure for converting any difference equation to state-space form is described in §G.7 on page 352. The particular state-space model shown in Eq. (F.5) happens to be called *controller canonical form*, for reasons discussed in Appendix G. The set of all state-space realizations of this filter is given by exploring the set of all *similarity transformations* applied to any particular realization, such as the control-canonical form in Eq. (F.5). Similarity transformations are discussed in §G.8, and in books on linear algebra [58].

Note that the state-space model replaces an Nth-order difference equation by a *vector first-order difference equation*. This provides elegant simplifications in the theory and analysis of digital filters. For example, consider the case $B = C = I$, and $D = 0$, so that Eq. (F.4) reduces to

$$
\underline{y}(n+1) = A\underline{y}(n) + \underline{u}(n), \tag{F.6}
$$

where A is the $N \times N$ transition matrix, and both $\underline{u}(n)$ and $\underline{y}(n)$ are $N \times 1$ signal vectors. (This filter has N inputs and N outputs.) This vector first-order difference equation is analogous to the following scalar first-order difference equation:

$$
y(n+1) = ay(n) + u(n)
$$

The response of this filter to its initial state $y(0)$ is given by

$$
y(n) = a^n y(0), \quad n = 0, 1, 2, 3, \ldots .
$$

(This is the *zero-input response* of the filter, *i.e.*, $u(n) \equiv 0$.) Similarly, setting $\underline{u}(n) = 0$ to in Eq. (F.6) yields

$$
\underline{y}(n) = A^n \underline{y}(0), \quad n = 0, 1, 2, 3, \ldots .
$$

---

[5]While this example is easily done by hand, the matlab function `tf2ss` can be used more generally ("transfer function to state space" conversion).

Thus, an Nth-order digital filter "looks like" a first-order digital filter when cast in state-space form.

F.7   Time Domain Filter Estimation

System identification is the subject of identifying filter coefficients given measurements of the input and output signals [46, 78]. For example, one application is *amplifier modeling*, in which we measure (1) the normal output of an electric guitar (provided by the pick-ups), and (2) the output of a microphone placed in front of the amplifier we wish to model. The guitar may be played in a variety of ways to create a collection of input/output data to use in identifying a model of the amplifier's "sound." There are many commercial products which offer "virtual amplifier" presets developed partly in such a way.[6] One can similarly model electric guitars themselves by measuring the pick signal delivered to the string (as the input) and the normal pick-up-mix output signal. A separate identification is needed for each switch and tone-control position. After identifying a sampling of models, ways can be found to interpolate among the sampled settings, thereby providing "virtual" tone-control knobs that respond like the real ones [101].

In the notation of the §F.1, assume we know $\underline{x}$ and $\underline{y}$ and wish to solve for the filter impulse response $\underline{h}^T = [h_0, h_1, \ldots, h_{N_h - 1}]$. We now outline a simple yet practical method for doing this, which follows readily from the discussion of the previous section.

Recall that convolution is *commutative*. In terms of the matrix representation of §F.3 on page 336, this implies that the input signal and the filter can switch places to give

$$\underbrace{\begin{bmatrix} y_0 \\ y_1 \\ y_2 \\ y_3 \\ y_4 \\ y_5 \\ y_6 \\ \vdots \end{bmatrix}}_{\underline{y}} = \underbrace{\begin{bmatrix} x_0 & 0 & 0 & 0 & 0 \\ x_1 & x_0 & 0 & 0 & 0 \\ x_2 & x_1 & x_0 & 0 & 0 \\ x_3 & x_2 & x_1 & x_0 & 0 \\ x_4 & x_3 & x_2 & x_1 & x_0 \\ x_5 & x_4 & x_3 & x_2 & x_1 \\ x_6 & x_5 & x_4 & x_3 & x_2 \\ \vdots & \vdots & \vdots & \vdots & \vdots \end{bmatrix}}_{\mathbf{x}} \underbrace{\begin{bmatrix} h_0 \\ h_1 \\ h_2 \\ h_3 \\ h_4 \end{bmatrix}}_{\underline{h}},$$

---

[6]The methods discussed in this section are intended for LTI system identification. Many valued guitar-amplifier modes, of course, provide highly *nonlinear distortion*. Identification of nonlinear systems is a relatively advanced topic with lots of special techniques [24, 17, 97, 4, 86].

or

$$y = \mathbf{x}\underline{h}. \tag{F.7}$$

Here we have indicated the general case for a length $N_h = 5$ causal FIR filter, with input and output signals that go on forever. While $\mathbf{x}$ is not invertible because it is not square, we can solve for $\underline{h}$ under general conditions by taking the *pseudoinverse* of $\mathbf{x}$. Doing this provides a *least-squares system identification* method [46].

The *Moore-Penrose pseudoinverse* is easy to derive.[7] First multiply Eq. (F.7) on the left by the transpose of $\mathbf{x}$ in order to obtain a "square" system of equations:

$$\mathbf{x}^T \underline{y} = \mathbf{x}^T \mathbf{x}\underline{h}$$

Since $\mathbf{x}^T\mathbf{x}$ is a square $N_h \times N_h$ matrix, it is invertible under general conditions, and we obtain the following formula for $\underline{h}$:

$$\boxed{\underline{h} = \left(\mathbf{x}^T\mathbf{x}\right)^{-1}\mathbf{x}^T\underline{y}} \tag{F.8}$$

Thus, $\left(\mathbf{x}^T\mathbf{x}\right)^{-1}\mathbf{x}^T$ is the *Moore-Penrose pseudoinverse* of $\mathbf{x}$.

If the input signal x is an *impulse* $\delta(n)$ (a 1 at time zero and 0 at all other times), then $\mathbf{x}^T\mathbf{x}$ is simply the identity matrix, which is its own inverse, and we obtain $\underline{h} = \underline{y}$. We expect this by definition of the impulse response. More generally, $\mathbf{x}^T\mathbf{x}$ is invertible whenever the input signal is "sufficiently exciting" at all frequencies. An LTI filter frequency response can be identified only at frequencies that are excited by the input, and the accuracy of the estimate at any given frequency can be improved by increasing the input signal power at that frequency. [46].

F.7.1   Effect of Measurement Noise

In practice, measurements are never perfect. Let $\hat{y} = y + \underline{e}$ denote the measured output signal, where $\underline{e}$ is a vector of "measurement noise" samples. Then we have

$$\hat{\underline{y}} = \underline{y} + \underline{e} = \mathbf{x}\underline{h} + \underline{e}.$$

By the *orthogonality principle* [38], the least-squares estimate of $\underline{h}$ is obtained by orthogonally projecting $\hat{\underline{y}}$ onto the space spanned by the columns of $\mathbf{x}$. Geometrically speaking, choosing $\underline{h}$ to minimize the Euclidean distance between $\hat{\underline{y}}$ and $\mathbf{x}\underline{h}$ is the same thing as choosing it to minimize the sum of squared estimated measurement errors $||\underline{e}||^2$. The distance from

---

[7]There are many possible definitions of pseudoinverse for a matrix $\mathbf{x}$. The Moore-Penrose pseudoinverse is perhaps most natural because it gives the *least-squares solution* to the set of simultaneous linear equations $\underline{y} = \mathbf{x}\underline{h}$, as we show later in this section.

$\mathbf{x}\underline{h}$ to $\hat{y}$ is minimized when the *projection error* $\underline{e} = \hat{y} - \mathbf{x}\underline{h}$ is orthogonal to every column of $\mathbf{x}$, which is true if and only if $\mathbf{x}^T\underline{e} = 0$ [84]. Thus, we have, applying the orthogonality principle,

$$0 = \mathbf{x}^T\underline{e} = \mathbf{x}^T(\underline{y} - \mathbf{x}\underline{h}) = \mathbf{x}^T\underline{y} - \mathbf{x}^T\mathbf{x}\underline{h}.$$

Solving for $\underline{h}$ yields Eq. (F.8) as before, but this time we have derived it as the least squares estimate of $\underline{h}$ in the presence of output measurement error.

It is also straightforward to introduce a *weighting function* in the least-squares estimate for $\underline{h}$ by replacing $\mathbf{x}^T$ in the derivations above by $\mathbf{x}^T R$, where R is any positive definite matrix (often taken to be diagonal and positive). In the present time-domain formulation, it is difficult to choose a weighting function that corresponds well to *audio perception*. Therefore, in audio applications, frequency-domain formulations are generally more powerful for linear-time-invariant system identification. A practical example is the frequency-domain equation-error method described in §I.4.4 on page 393 [78].

F.7.2   Matlab System Identification Example

The Octave output for the following small matlab example is listed in Fig. F.1:

```
delete('sid.log'); diary('sid.log'); % Log session
echo('on');        % Show commands as well as responses
N = 4;             % Input signal length
%x = rand(N,1)     % Random input signal - snapshot:
x = [0.056961, 0.081938, 0.063272, 0.672761]'
h = [1 2 3]';      % FIR filter
y = filter(h,1,x) % Filter output
xb = toeplitz(x,[x(1),zeros(1,N-1)]) % Input matrix
hhat = inv(xb' * xb) * xb' * y % Least squares estimate
% hhat = pinv(xb) * y % Numerically robust pseudoinverse
hhat2 = xb\y % Numerically superior (and faster) estimate
diary('off'); % Close log file
```

One fine point is the use of the syntax "$\underline{h} = \mathbf{x} \backslash \underline{y}$", which has been a matlab language feature from the very beginning [82]. It is usually more accurate (and faster) than multiplying by the explicit pseudoinverse. It uses the QR decomposition to convert the system of linear equations into upper-triangular form (typically using Householder reflections), determine the effective rank of $\mathbf{x}$, and backsolve the reduced triangular system (starting at the bottom, which goes very fast) [29, §6.2].[8]

---

[8]Say help slash in Matlab.

```
+ echo('on');         % Show commands as well as responses
+ N = 4;              % Input signal length
+ %x = rand(N,1)      % Random input signal - snapshot:
+ x = [0.056961, 0.081938, 0.063272, 0.672761]'
x =
   0.056961
   0.081938
   0.063272
   0.672761

+ h = [1 2 3]';       % FIR filter
+ y = filter(h,1,x) % Filter output
y =
   0.056961
   0.195860
   0.398031
   1.045119

+ xb = toeplitz(x,[x(1),zeros(1,N-1)]) % Input matrix
xb =
   0.05696   0.00000   0.00000   0.00000
   0.08194   0.05696   0.00000   0.00000
   0.06327   0.08194   0.05696   0.00000
   0.67276   0.06327   0.08194   0.05696

+ hhat = inv(xb' * xb) * xb' * y % Least squares estimate
hhat =
   1.0000
   2.0000
   3.0000
   3.7060e-13

+ % hhat = pinv(xb) * y % Numerically robust pseudoinverse
+ hhat2 = xb\y % Numerically superior (and faster) estimate
hhat2 =
   1.0000
   2.0000
   3.0000
   3.6492e-16
```

Figure F.1: Time-domain system-identification matlab example.

Appendix G

State Space Filters

An important representation for discrete-time linear systems is the *state-space* formulation

$$
\begin{aligned}
\underline{y}(n) &= C\underline{x}(n) + D\underline{u}(n) \\
\underline{x}(n+1) &= A\underline{x}(n) + B\underline{u}(n)
\end{aligned}
\tag{G.1}
$$

where $\underline{x}(n)$ is the length N *state vector* at discrete time n, $\underline{u}(n)$ is a $q \times 1$ vector of inputs, and $\underline{y}(n)$ the $p \times 1$ output vector. A is the $N \times N$ *state transition matrix*,[1] and it determines the *dynamics* of the system (its *poles* or resonant *modes*).

The state-space representation is especially powerful for *multi-input, multi-output* (MIMO) linear systems, and also for *time-varying* linear systems (in which case any or all of the matrices in Eq. (G.1) may have time subscripts n) [37]. State-space models are also used extensively in the field of *control systems* [28].

An example of a Single-Input, Single-Ouput (SISO) state-space model appears in §F.6 on page 340.

---

[1] A short tutorial on *matrices* appears in [84], available online at http://ccrma.stanford.edu/~jos/mdft/Matrices.html.

G.1   Markov Parameters

The *Markov parameter sequence* for a state-space model is a kind of *matrix impulse response* that easily found by direct calculation using Eq. (G.1):

$$
\begin{aligned}
\mathbf{h}(0) &= C\underline{x}(0) + D\underline{\delta}(0) = D \\[4pt]
\underline{x}(1) &= A\underline{x}(0) + B\underline{\delta}(0) = B \\
\mathbf{h}(1) &= CB \\[4pt]
\underline{x}(2) &= A\underline{x}(1) + B\underline{\delta}(1) = AB \\
\mathbf{h}(2) &= CAB \\[4pt]
\underline{x}(3) &= A\underline{x}(2) + B\underline{\delta}(2) = A^2 B \\
\mathbf{h}(3) &= CA^2 B \\[4pt]
&\ \ \vdots \\[4pt]
\mathbf{h}(n) &= CA^{n-1}B, \quad n > 0
\end{aligned}
$$

Note that we have assumed $\underline{x}(0) = 0$ (*zero initial state* or *zero initial conditions*). The notation $\underline{\delta}(n)$ denotes a $q \times q$ matrix having $\delta(n)$ along the diagonal and zeros elsewhere.[2] Since the system input is a $q \times 1$ vector, we may regard $\underline{\delta}(n)$ as a sequence of q successive input vectors, each providing an impulse at one of the input components.

The impulse response of the state-space model can be summarized as

$$
\boxed{\ \mathbf{h}(n) = \begin{cases} D, & n = 0 \\ CA^{n-1}B, & n > 0 \end{cases}\ }
\tag{G.2}
$$

The impulse response terms $CA^n B$ for $n \geq 0$ are known as the *Markov parameters* of the state-space model.

Note that each "sample" of the impulse response $\mathbf{h}(n)$ is a $p \times q$ matrix.[3] Therefore, it is not a possible output signal, except when $q = 1$. A better name might be "impulse-matrix response". It can be viewed as a sequence of q outputs, each $p \times 1$. In §G.4 below, we'll see that $\mathbf{h}(n)$ is the inverse z transform of the matrix transfer-function of the system.

Given an arbitrary input signal $\underline{u}(n)$ (and zero intial conditions $\underline{x}(0) = 0$), the output signal is given by the *convolution* of the input signal with

---

[2] *I.e.*, $\underline{\delta}(n) = \delta(n)I_{q \times q}$, where $I_{q \times q}$ is the $q \times q$ identity matrix, and $\delta(n)$ denotes the discrete-time impulse signal (which is 1 at time $n = 0$ and zero for all $n \neq 0$).

[3] To emphasize something is a matrix, it is often typeset in a **boldface** font. In this appendix, however, capital letters are more often used to denote matrices.

the impulse response:

$$\underline{y}_u(n) = (\mathbf{h} * \underline{u})(n) = \begin{cases} D\underline{u}(0), & n = 0 \\ \sum_{m=0}^n C A^{m-1} B\underline{u}(n - m), & n > 0 \end{cases} \qquad \text{(G.3)}$$

G.2   Response from Initial Conditions

The response of a state-space model to *initial conditions*, *i.e.*, its *initial state* $\underline{x}(0)$ is given by, again using Eq. (G.1),

$$\underline{y}_x(n) = C A^{n-1}\underline{x}(0), \quad n = 0, 1, 2, \ldots . \qquad \text{(G.4)}$$

G.3   Complete Response

The *complete response* of a linear system consists of the superposition of (1) its response to the input signal $\underline{u}(n)$ and (2) its response to initial conditions $\underline{x}(0)$:

$$\underline{y}(n) = \underline{y}_u(n) + \underline{y}_x(n),$$

where $\underline{y}_u(n)$ was defined in Eq. (G.3) and $\underline{y}_x(n)$ was defined in Eq. (G.4) above.

G.4   Transfer Function of a State Space Filter

The *transfer function* can be defined as the z transform of the impulse response:

$$H(z) \triangleq \sum_{n=0}^\infty h(n)z^{-n} = D + \sum_{n=1}^\infty \left(C A^{n-1} B \right) z^{-n} = D + z^{-1} C \left[\sum_{n=0}^\infty \left(z^{-1} A \right)^n \right] B$$

Using the closed-form sum of a matrix geometric series,[4] we obtain

$$\boxed{H(z) = D + C \left(zI - A \right)^{-1} B.} \qquad \text{(G.5)}$$

Note that if there are p inputs and q outputs, $H(z)$ is a $p \times q$ *transfer-function matrix* (or "matrix transfer function").

---

[4]Let $S(R) \triangleq \sum_{n=0}^\infty R^n$, where R is a square matrix. Then $S(R) - R\,S(R) = I \Rightarrow S(R) = (I - R)^{-1}$.

Example State Space Filter Transfer Function

In this example, we consider a second-order filter ($N = 2$) with two inputs ($p = 2$) and two outputs ($q = 2$):

$$A = g \begin{bmatrix} c & -s \\ s & c \end{bmatrix} \quad \text{with } c^2 + s^2 = 1 \text{ and } 0 < g < 1$$

$$B = \begin{bmatrix} 1 & 0 \\ 0 & 1 \end{bmatrix} \quad C = \begin{bmatrix} 1 & 0 \\ 0 & 1 \end{bmatrix} \quad D = \begin{bmatrix} 0 & 0 \\ 0 & 0 \end{bmatrix}$$

so that

$$\begin{bmatrix} x_1(n+1) \\ x_2(n+1) \end{bmatrix} = g \begin{bmatrix} c & -s \\ s & c \end{bmatrix} \begin{bmatrix} x_1(n) \\ x_2(n) \end{bmatrix} + \begin{bmatrix} 1 & 0 \\ 0 & 1 \end{bmatrix} \begin{bmatrix} u_1(n) \\ u_2(n) \end{bmatrix},$$

$$\begin{bmatrix} y_1(n) \\ y_2(n) \end{bmatrix} = \begin{bmatrix} 1 & 0 \\ 0 & 1 \end{bmatrix} \begin{bmatrix} x_1(n) \\ x_2(n) \end{bmatrix}.$$

From Eq. (G.5), the transfer function of this MIMO digital filter is then

$$H(z) = C(zI - A)^{-1}B = (zI - A)^{-1} = \begin{bmatrix} z - gc & gs \\ -gs & z - gc \end{bmatrix}^{-1}$$

$$= \frac{1}{z^2 - 2gcz + g^2c^2 + g^2s^2} \begin{bmatrix} z - gc & -gs \\ gs & z - gc \end{bmatrix}$$

$$= \begin{bmatrix} \dfrac{z^{-1} - gcz^{-2}}{1 - 2gcz^{-1} + g^2z^{-2}} & -\dfrac{sz^{-2}}{1 - 2gcz^{-1} + g^2z^{-2}} \\ \dfrac{gsz^{-2}}{1 - 2gcz^{-1} + g^2z^{-2}} & \dfrac{z^{-1} - gcz^{-2}}{1 - 2gcz^{-1} + g^2z^{-2}} \end{bmatrix}.$$

Note that when $g = 1$, the state transition matrix A is simply a 2D rotation matrix, rotating through the angle θ for which $c = \cos(\theta)$ and $s = \sin(\theta)$. For $g < 1$, we have a type of *normalized second-order resonator* [51], and g controls the "damping" of the resonator, while $\theta = 2\pi f_r/f_s$ controls the resonance frequency f_r. The resonator is "normalized" in the sense that the filter's state has a constant L^2 norm ("preserves energy") when $g = 1$ and the input is zero:

$$\| \underline{x}(n+1) \| \overset{\Delta}{=} \sqrt{x_1^2(n+1) + x_2^2(n+1)} = \| A\underline{x}(n) \| \equiv \| \underline{x}(n) \| \quad \text{(G.6)}$$

since a rotation does not change the L^2 norm, as can be readily checked.

In this two-input, two-output digital filter, the input $u_1(n)$ drives state $x_1(n)$ while input $u_2(n)$ drives state $x_2(n)$. Similarly, output $y_1(n)$ is $x_1(n)$, while $y_2(n)$ is $x_2(n)$. The two-by-two transfer-function matrix $H(z)$ contains entries for each combination of input and output. Note that all component transfer functions have the same poles. This is a general property of physical linear systems driven and observed at arbitrary points: the resonant modes (poles) are always the same, but the zeros vary as the input or output location are changed. If a pole is not visible using a particular input/output pair, we say that the pole has been "canceled" by a zero associated with that input/output pair. In control-theory terms, the pole is "uncontrollable" from that input, or "unobservable" from that output, or both.

G.5 Transposition of a State Space Filter

Above, we found the transfer function of the general state-space model to be

$$H(z) = D + C\,(zI - A)^{-1}\,B.$$

By the rules for transposing a matrix, the *transpose* of this equation gives

$$H^T(z) = D^T + B^T\,(zI - A^T)^{-1}\,C^T.$$

The system (A^T, C^T, B^T, D^T) may be called the *transpose* of the system (A, B, C, D). The transpose is obtained by interchanging B and C in addition to transposing all matrices.

When there is only one input and output signal (the SISO case), $H(z)$ is a scalar, as is D. In this case we have

$$H(z) = D + B^T\,(zI - A^T)^{-1}\,C^T.$$

That is, the transfer function of the transposed system is the *same* as the untransposed system in the scalar case. It can be shown that transposing the state-space representation is equivalent to *transposing the signal flow graph* of the filter [75]. The equivalence of a flow graph to its transpose is established by *Mason's gain theorem* [49, 50]. See §9.1.3 on page 204 for more on this topic.

G.6 Poles of a State Space Filter

In this section, we show that the *poles of a state-space model* are given by the *eigenvalues* of the state-transition matrix A.

Beginning again with the transfer function of the general state-space model,

$$H(z) = D + C \left(zI - A \right)^{-1} B,$$

we may first observe that the poles of $H(z)$ are either the same as or some subset of the poles of

$$H_p(z) \triangleq (zI - A)^{-1}.$$

(They are the same when all modes are *controllable* and *observable* [37].) By Cramer's rule for matrix inversion, the denominator polynomial for $(zI - A)^{-1}$ is given by the *determinant*

$$D(z) \triangleq \det(zI - A)$$

where $\det(Q)$ denotes the *determinant* of the square matrix Q. (The determinant of Q is also often written $|Q|$.) In linear algebra, the polynomial $D(z) = |zI - A|$ is called the *characteristic polynomial* for the matrix A. The roots of the characteristic polynomial are called the *eigenvalues* of A.
    Thus, *the eigenvalues of the state transition matrix A are the poles of the corresponding linear time-invariant system.* In particular, note that the poles of the system do not depend on the matrices B, C, D, although these matrices, by placing system zeros, can cause pole-zero cancellations (unobservable or uncontrollable modes).

G.7 Difference Equations to State Space

Any explicit LTI difference equation (§5.1) can be converted to state-space form. In state-space form, many properties of the system are readily obtained. For example, using standard utilities (such as in Matlab), there are functions for computing the *modes* of the system (its poles), an equivalent *transfer-function* description, *stability* information, and whether or not modes are "observable" and/or "controllable" from any given input/output point.
    Every nth order scalar (ordinary) difference equation may be reformulated as a *first order vector* difference equation. For example, consider the second-order difference equation

$$y(n) = u(n) + 2u(n-1) + 3u(n-2) - \frac{1}{2}y(n-1) - \frac{1}{3}y(n-2). \quad \text{(G.7)}$$

We may define a vector first-order difference equation—the "state space representation"—as discussed in the following sections.

G.7.1   Converting to State-Space Form by Hand

Converting a digital filter to state-space form is easy because there are various "canonical forms" for state-space models which can be written by inspection given the strictly proper transfer-function coefficients.

The canonical forms useful for transfer-function to state-space conversion are *controller canonical form* (also called *control* or *controllable canonical form*) and *observer canonical form* (or *observable canonical form*) [28, p. 80], [37]. These names come from the field of *control theory* [28] which is concerned with designing feedback laws to control the dynamics of real-world physical systems. State-space models are used extensively in the control field to model physical systems.

The name "controller canonical form" reflects the fact that the input signal can "drive" all modes (poles) of the system. In the language of control theory, we may say that all of the system poles are *controllable* from the input $u(n)$. In observer canonical form, all modes are guaranteed to be *observable*. Controllability and observability of a state-space model are discussed further in §G.7.3 below.

The following procedure converts any causal LTI digital filter into state-space form:

1. Determine the filter transfer function $H(z) = B(z)/A(z)$.

2. If $H(z)$ is not strictly proper ($b_0 \neq 0$), "pull out" the delay-free path to obtain a feed-through gain b_0 in parallel with a strictly proper transfer function.

3. Write down the state-space representation by inspection using controller canonical form for the strictly proper transfer function. (Or use the matlab function `tf2ss`.)

We now elaborate on these steps for the general case:

1. The general causal IIR filter

$$y(n) = b_0\, u(n) \; + \; b_1\, u(n-1) + \cdots + b_{N_b}\, u(n-N_b) \quad \text{(G.8)}$$
$$- \; a_1\, y(n-1) - \cdots - a_{N_a}\, y(n-N_a) \quad \text{(G.9)}$$

has transfer function

$$H(z) \triangleq \frac{Y(z)}{U(z)} = \frac{b_0 + b_1\, z^{-1} + \cdots + b_{N_b}\, z^{-N_b}}{1 + a_1\, z^{-1} + \cdots + a_{N_a}\, z^{-N_a}}. \quad \text{(G.10)}$$

2. By convention, state-space descriptions handle any delay-free path from input to output via the direct-path coefficient D in Eq. (G.1).

This is natural because the delay-free path does not affect the state of the system.

A causal filter contains a delay-free path if its impulse response $h(n)$ is nonzero at time zero, *i.e.*, if $h(0) \neq 0$.[5] In such cases, we must "pull out" the delay-free path in order to implement it in parallel, setting $D = h(0) = b_0$ in the state-space model.

In our example, one step of long division yields

$$
\begin{aligned}
H(z) \quad &= \quad b_0 + \frac{(b_1 - b_0 a_1)\, z^{-1} + \cdots + (b_N - b_0 a_N)\, z^{-N}}{1 + a_1\, z^{-1} + \cdots + a_{N_a}\, z^{-N_a}}, \\
&\overset{\Delta}{=} \quad b_0 + \frac{\beta_1\, z^{-1} + \cdots + \beta_N\, z^{-N}}{1 + a_1\, z^{-1} + \cdots + a_{N_a}\, z^{-N_a}}, \qquad \text{(G.11)}
\end{aligned}
$$

where $N \overset{\Delta}{=} \max(N_a, N_b)$, with $a_i \overset{\Delta}{=} 0$ for $i > N_a$, and $b_i \overset{\Delta}{=} 0$ for $i > N_b$.

3. The controller canonical form is then easily written as follows:

$$
A \;=\;
\begin{bmatrix}
-a_1 & -a_2 & \cdots & -a_{N-1} & -a_N \\
1 & 0 & \cdots & 0 & 0 \\
0 & 1 & \cdots & 0 & 0 \\
\vdots & & \ddots & \vdots & \vdots \\
0 & 0 & & 1 & 0
\end{bmatrix}
\qquad
B \;=\;
\begin{bmatrix}
1 \\
0 \\
0 \\
\vdots \\
0
\end{bmatrix}
$$

$$
C \;=\; \begin{bmatrix} \beta_1 & \beta_2 & \cdots & \beta_N \end{bmatrix} \qquad D = b_0 \qquad\qquad \text{(G.12)}
$$

An alternate controller canonical form is obtained by applying the similarity transformation (see §G.8 below) which simply reverses the order of the state variables. Any permutation of the state variables would similarly yield a controllable form. The transpose of a controllable form is an observable form.

One might worry that choosing controller canonical form may result in unobservable modes. However, this will not happen if $B(z)$ and $A(z)$ have no common factors. In other words, if there are no pole-zero cancellations in the transfer function $H(z) = B(z)/A(z)$, then either controller or observer canonical form will yield a controllable and observable state-space model.

We now illustrate these steps using the example of Eq. (G.7):

1. The transfer function can be written, by inspection, as

$$
H(z) = \frac{1 + 2z^{-1} + 3z^{-2}}{1 + \frac{1}{2}z^{-1} + \frac{1}{3}z^{-2}}. \qquad\qquad \text{(G.13)}
$$

---

[5]Equivalently, a causal transfer function $H(z) = B(z)/A(z)$ contains a delay-free path whenever $H(\infty) \neq 0$, since $H(\infty) = b_0 = h(0)$.

2. We need to convert Eq. (G.13) to the form

$$H(z) = b_0 + \frac{\beta_1 z^{-1} + \beta_2 z^{-2}}{1 + \frac{1}{2}z^{-1} + \frac{1}{3}z^{-2}}. \tag{G.14}$$

Obtaining a common denominator and equating numerator coefficients with Eq. (G.13) yields

$$
\begin{aligned}
b_0 &= 1, \\
\beta_1 &= 2 - \frac{1}{2} = \frac{3}{2}, \text{ and} \\
\beta_2 &= 3 - \frac{1}{3} = \frac{8}{3}.
\end{aligned}
\tag{G.15}
$$

The same result is obtained using long division (or synthetic division).

3. Finally, the controller canonical form is given by

$$
\begin{aligned}
A &\triangleq \begin{bmatrix} -\frac{1}{2} & -\frac{1}{3} \\ 1 & 0 \end{bmatrix} \\
B &\triangleq \begin{bmatrix} 1 \\ 0 \end{bmatrix} \\
C^T &\triangleq \begin{bmatrix} 3/2 & 8/3 \end{bmatrix} \\
D &\triangleq 1.
\end{aligned}
\tag{G.16}
$$

G.7.2 Converting Signal Flow Graphs to State-Space Form by Hand

The procedure of the previous section quickly converts any *transfer function* to state-space form (specifically, controller canonical form). When the starting point is instead a signal flow graph, it is usually easier to go directly to state-space form by *labeling each delay-element output as a state variable* and writing out the state-space equations by inspection of the flow graph.

For the example of the previous section, suppose we are given Eq. (G.14) in *direct-form II* (DF-II), as shown in Fig. G.1. It is important that the filter representation be *canonical with respect to delay, i.e.,* that the number of delay elements equals the order of the filter. Then the third step (writing down controller canonical form by inspection) may replaced by the following more general procedure:

1. Assign a state variable to the output of each delay element (indicated in Fig. G.1).

2. Write down the state-space representation by inspection of the flow graph.

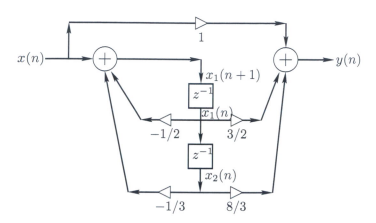

Figure G.1: Direct-form-II representation of the difference equation in Eq. (G.7), after pulling out the direct path as given in Equations (G.14–G.15).

The state-space description of the difference equation in Eq. (G.7) is given by Eq. (G.16). We see that controller canonical form follows immediately from the direct-form-II digital filter realization, which is fundamentally an all-pole filter followed by an all-zero (FIR) filter (see §9.1.2 on page 202). By starting instead from the *transposed direct-form-II* (TDF-II) structure, the *observer canonical form* is obtained [28, p. 87]. This is because the zeros effectively precede the poles in a TDF-II realization, so that they may introduce nulls in the input spectrum, but they cannot cancel output from the poles (*e.g.*, from initial conditions). Since the other two digital-filter direct forms (DF-I and TDF-I—see Chapter 9 for details) are not canonical with respect to delay, they are not used as a basis for deriving state-space models.

G.7.3   Controllability and Observability

Since the output $y(n)$ in Fig. G.1 is a linear combination of the input and states $x_i(n)$, one or more poles can be *canceled* by the zeros induced by this linear combination. When that happens, the canceled modes are said to be *unobservable*. Of course, since we started with a transfer function, any pole-zero cancellations should be dealt with at that point, so that the state space realization will always be *controllable and observable*. If a mode is uncontrollable, the input cannot affect it; if it is unobservable, it has no effect on the output. Therefore, there is usually no reason to include unobservable or uncontrollable modes in a state-space model.[6]

A physical example of uncontrollable and unobservable modes is provided by the plucked vibrating string of an *electric guitar* with one (very thin) magnetic pick-up. In a vibrating string, considering only one plane of vibration, each quasi-harmonic[7] overtone corresponds to a *mode of vibration* [86] which may be modeled by a pair of complex-conjugate poles in a digital filter which models a particular point-to-point transfer function of the string. All modes of vibration having a *node* at the plucking point are *uncontrollable* at that point, and all modes having a node at the pick-up are *unobservable* at that point. If an ideal string is plucked at its midpoint, for example, all even numbered harmonics will not be excited, because they all have vibrational nodes at the string midpoint. Similarly, if the pick-up is located one-fourth of the string length from the bridge, every fourth string harmonic will be "nulled" in the output. This is why plucked and struck strings are generally excited near one end, and why magnetic pick-ups are located near the end of the string.

A basic result in control theory is that a system in state-space form is *controllable* from a scalar input signal $u(n)$ if and only if the matrix

$$\left[B, \, AB, \, A^2 B, \, \ldots, \, A^{N-1} B\right]$$

has full rank (*i.e.*, is invertible). Here, B is $N \times 1$. For the general $N \times q$ case, this test can be applied to each of the q columns of B, thereby testing controllability from each input in turn. Similarly, a state-space system is *observable* from a given output if and only if

$$\begin{bmatrix} C \\ CA \\ CA^2 \\ \ldots \\ CA^{N-1} \end{bmatrix}$$

is nonsingular (*i.e.*, invertible), where C is $1 \times N$. In the p-output case, C can be considered the row corresponding to the output for which observability is being checked.

---

[6] An exception arises when the model may be *time varying*. A time varying C matrix, for example, will cause time-varying zeros in the system. These zeros may momentarily cancel poles, rendering them unobservable for a short time.

[7] The overtones of a vibrating string are never exactly harmonic because all strings have some finite *stiffness*. This is why we call them "overtones" instead of "harmonics." A perfectly flexible ideal string may have exactly harmonic overtones [55].

G.7.4   A Short-Cut to Controller Canonical Form

When converting a transfer function to state-space form by hand, the step of pulling out the direct path, like we did in going from Eq. (G.13) on page 354 to Eq. (G.14), can be bypassed [28, p. 87].

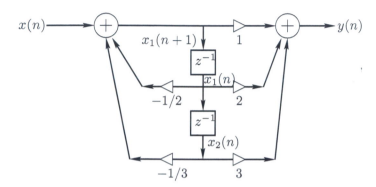

Figure G.2: Direct-form-II realization of Eq. (G.7) on page 352. Note that this form has a delay-free path from input to output.

Figure G.2 gives the standard direct-form-II structure for a second-order IIR filter. Unlike Fig. G.1 on page 356, it includes a direct path from the input to the output. The filter coefficients are all given directly by the transfer function, Eq. (G.13).

This form can be converted directly to state-space form by carefully observing all paths from the input and state variables to the output. For example, $x_1(n)$ reaches the output through gain 2 on the right, but also via gain $-1/2 \cdot 1$ on the left and above. Therefore, its contribution to the output is $(2 - 1/2)x_1(n) = (3/2)x_1(n)$, as obtained in the DF-II realization with direct-path pulled out shown in Fig. G.1 on page 356. The state variable $x_2(n)$ reaches the output with gain $3 - 1/3 \cdot 1 = 8/3$, again as we obtained before. Finally, it must also be observed that the gain of the direct path from input to output is 1.

G.7.5   Matlab Direct-Form to State-Space Conversion

Matlab and Octave support state-space models with functions such as

- `tf2ss` - transfer-function to state-space conversion

- `ss2tf` - state-space to transfer-function conversion

Note that while these utilities are documented primarily for use with continuous-time systems, they are also used for discrete-time systems.

Let's repeat the previous example using Matlab:

```
>> num = [1 2 3]; % transfer function numerator
>> den = [1 1/2 1/3]; % denominator coefficients
>> [A,B,C,D] = tf2ss(num,den)

A =
   -0.5000    -0.3333
    1.0000         0

B =
      1
      0

C =   1.5000      2.6667

D =   1

>> [N,D] = ss2tf(A,B,C,D)

N = 1.0000      2.0000      3.0000

D = 1.0000      0.5000      0.3333
```

The `tf2ss` and `ss2tf` functions are documented online at The Mathworks *help desk*[8] as well as within Matlab itself (say `help tf2ss`). In Octave, say `help tf2ss` or `help -i tf2ss`.

G.7.6   State Space Simulation in Matlab

Since matlab has first-class support for matrices and vectors, it is quite simple to implement a state-space model in Matlab using no support functions whatsoever, *e.g.*,

```
% Define the state-space system parameters:
A = [0 1; -1 0]; % State transition matrix
B = [0; 1];  C = [0 1];  D = 0; % Input, output, feed-around

% Set up the input signal, initial conditions, etc.
x0 = [0;0];                % Initial state (N=2)
Ns = 10;              % Number of sample times to simulate
u = [1, zeros(1,Ns-1)]; % Input signal (an impulse at time 0)
```

---

[8]http://www.mathworks.com/access/helpdesk/help/toolbox/signal/tf2ss.shtml

```
y = zeros(Ns,1);          % Preallocate output signal for n=0:Ns-1

% Perform the system simulation:
x = x0;                   % Set initial state
for n=1:Ns-1              % Iterate through time
  y(n) = C*x + D*u(n); % Output for time n-1
  x = A*x + B*u(n);      % State transitions to time n
end
y' % print the output y (transposed)
% ans =
%  0    1    0  -1   0   1   0  -1   0   0
```

The restriction to indexes beginning at 1 is unwieldy here, because we want
to include time $n = 0$ in the input and output. It can be readily checked
that the above examples has the transfer function

$$H(z) = \frac{z^{-1}}{1 + z^{-2}},$$

so that the following matlab checks the above output using the built-in
filter function:

```
NUM = [0 1];
DEN = [1 0 1];
y = filter(NUM,DEN,u)
% y =
%  0    1    0  -1   0   1   0  -1   0   1
```

To eliminate the unit-sample delay, i.e., to simulate $H(z) = 1/(1 + z^{-2})$ in
state-space form, it is necessary to use the D (feed-around) coefficient:

```
[A,B,C,D] = tf2ss([1 0 0], [1 0 1])
% A =
%    0    1
%   -1   -0
%
% B =
%    0
%    1
%
% C =
%   -1    0
%
% D = 1
```

```
x = x0;                     % Reset to initial state
for n=1:Ns-1
  y(n) = C*x + D*u(n);
  x = A*x + B*u(n);
end
y'
% ans =
% 1   0   -1   0   1   0   -1   0   1   0
```

Note the use of trailing zeros in the first argument of tf2ss (the transfer-function numerator-polynomial coefficients) to make it the same length as the second argument (denominator coefficients). This is *necessary* in tf2ss because the same function is used for both the continous- and discrete-time cases. Without the trailing zeros, the numerator will be extended by zeros on the *left*, *i.e.*, "right-justified" relative to the denominator.

G.7.7   Other Relevant Matlab Functions

Related Signal Processing Toolbox functions include

- tf2sos — Convert digital filter transfer function parameters to second-order sections form. (See §9.2 on page 207.)

- sos2ss — Convert second-order filter sections to state-space form.[9]

- tf2zp — Convert transfer-function filter parameters to zero-pole-gain form.

- ss2zp — Convert state-space model to zeros, poles, and a gain.

- zp2ss — Convert zero-pole-gain filter parameters to state-space form.

In Matlab, say lookfor state-space to find your state-space support utilities (there are many more than listed above). In Octave, say help -i ss2tf and keep reading for more functions (the above list is complete, as of this writing).

---

[9] As of this writing, this function does not exist in Octave or Octave Forge, but it is easily simulated using sos2tf followed by tf2ss.

G.7.8　Matlab State-Space Filter Conversion Example

Here is the example of §F.6 on page 340 repeated using matlab.[10]　The
difference equation

$$y(n) = u(n-1) + u(n-2) + 0.5\,y(n-1) - 0.1\,y(n-2) + 0.01\,y(n-3)$$

corresponds to the transfer function

$$H(z) = \frac{B(z)}{A(z)} = \frac{z^{-1} + z^{-2}}{1 - 0.5\,z^{-1} + 0.1\,z^{-2} - 0.01\,z^{-3}},$$

so that in matlab the filter is represented by the vectors

```
NUM = [0   1   1    0   ]; % NUM and DEN should be same length
DEN = [1 -0.5 0.1 -0.01];
```

The tf2ss function converts from "transfer-function" form to state-space
form:

```
[A,B,C,D] = tf2ss(NUM,DEN)
A =
     0.00000    1.00000    0.00000
     0.00000    0.00000    1.00000
     0.01000   -0.10000    0.50000

B =
   0
   0
   1

C =
   0   1   1

D = 0
```

G.8　Similarity Transformations

A *similarity transformation* is a *linear change of coordinates*. That is, the
original N-dimensional state vector $\underline{x}(n)$ is recast in terms of a new coordinate basis. For any *linear transformation* of the coordinate basis, the

---

[10]Specifically, this example was computed using Octave's tf2ss. Matlab gives a different but equivalent form in which the state variables are ordered in reverse. The effect
is a permutation given by flipud(fliplr(M)), where M denotes the matrix A, B, or C. In
other words, the two state-space models are obtained from each other using the similarity
transformation matrix T=[0 0 1; 0 1 0; 1 0 0] (a simple permutation matrix).

transformed state vector $\tilde{x}(n)$ may be computed by means of a matrix multiply. Denoting the matrix of the desired one-to-one linear transformation by E, we can express the change of coordinates as

$$x(n) \triangleq E\tilde{x}(n)$$

or $\tilde{x}(n) = E^{-1}x(n)$, if we prefer, since the inverse of a one-to-one linear transformation always exists.

Let's now apply the linear transformation E to the general N-dimensional state-space description in Eq. (G.1). Substituting $x(n) \triangleq E\tilde{x}(n)$ in Eq. (G.1) gives

$$\begin{aligned} E\tilde{x}(n+1) &= A\,E\tilde{x}(n) + B\underline{u}(n) \\ y(n) &= CE\tilde{x}(n) + D\underline{u}(n) \end{aligned} \qquad \text{(G.17)}$$

Premultiplying the first equation above by E^{-1}, we have

$$\begin{aligned} \tilde{x}(n+1) &= \left(E^{-1}AE\right)\tilde{x}(n) + \left(E^{-1}B\right)\underline{u}(n) \\ y(n) &= (CE)\,\tilde{x}(n) + D\underline{u}(n). \end{aligned} \qquad \text{(G.18)}$$

Defining

$$\begin{aligned} \tilde{A} &= E^{-1}AE \\ \tilde{B} &= E^{-1}B \\ \tilde{C} &= CE \\ \tilde{D} &= D \end{aligned} \qquad \text{(G.19)}$$

we can write

$$\begin{aligned} \tilde{x}(n+1) &= \tilde{A}\,\tilde{x}(n) + \tilde{B}\,\underline{u}(n) \\ y(n) &= \tilde{C}\,\tilde{x}(n) + \tilde{D}\,\underline{u}(n) \end{aligned} \qquad \text{(G.20)}$$

The transformed system describes the same system as in Eq. (G.1) relative to new state-variable coordinates. To verify that it's really the same system, from an input/output point of view, let's look at the transfer function using Eq. (G.5):

$$\begin{aligned} \tilde{H}(z) &= \tilde{D} + \tilde{C}(zI - \tilde{A})^{-1}\tilde{B} \\ &= D + (CE)\left(zI - E^{-1}AE\right)^{-1}\left(E^{-1}B\right) \\ &= D + C\left[E\left(zI - E^{-1}AE\right)E^{-1}\right]^{-1}B \\ &= D + C\left(zI - A\right)^{-1}B \\ &= H(z) \end{aligned}$$

Since the eigenvalues of A are the poles of the system, it follows that the eigenvalues of $\tilde{A} = E^{-1}AE$ are the same. In other words, eigenvalues are unaffected by a similarity transformation. We can easily show this directly: Let $\underline{e}$ denote an eigenvector of A. Then by definition $A\underline{e} = \lambda\underline{e}$, where λ is the eigenvalue corresponding to $\underline{e}$. Define $\underline{\tilde{e}} = E^{-1}\underline{e}$ as the transformed eigenvector. Then we have

$$\tilde{A}\underline{\tilde{e}} = \tilde{A}(E^{-1}\underline{e}) = (E^{-1}AE)(E^{-1}\underline{e}) = E^{-1}A\underline{e} = E^{-1}\lambda\underline{e} = \lambda\underline{\tilde{e}}.$$

Thus, the transformed eigenvector is an eigenvector of the transformed A matrix, and the eigenvalue is unchanged.

The transformed Markov parameters, $\tilde{C}\tilde{A}^n\tilde{B}$, are obviously the same also since they are given by the inverse z transform of the transfer function $\tilde{H}(z)$. However, it is also easy to show this by direct calculation:

$$\begin{aligned} \tilde{h}(n) &= \tilde{C}\tilde{A}^n\tilde{B} = (CE)(E^{-1}AE)(E^{-1}AE)\cdots(E^{-1}AE)(E^{-1}B) \\ &= \tilde{C}\tilde{A}^n\tilde{B} = C(EE^{-1})A(EE^{-1})\cdots A(EE^{-1})B \\ &= CA^nB \end{aligned}$$

G.9   Modal Representation

When the state transition matrix A is *diagonal*, we have the so-called *modal representation*. In the single-input, single-output (SISO) case, the general diagonal system looks like

$$\begin{bmatrix} x_1(n+1) \\ x_2(n+1) \\ \vdots \\ x_{N-1}(n+1) \\ x_N(n+1) \end{bmatrix} = \begin{bmatrix} \lambda_1 & 0 & 0 & \cdots & 0 \\ 0 & \lambda_2 & 0 & \cdots & 0 \\ \vdots & \vdots & \ddots & \vdots & \vdots \\ 0 & 0 & 0 & \lambda_{N-1} & 0 \\ 0 & 0 & 0 & 0 & \lambda_N \end{bmatrix} \begin{bmatrix} x_1(n) \\ x_2(n) \\ \vdots \\ x_{N-1}(n) \\ x_N(n) \end{bmatrix} + \begin{bmatrix} b_1 \\ b_2 \\ \vdots \\ b_{N-1} \\ b_N \end{bmatrix} u(n)$$

$$\begin{aligned} y(n) &= C\underline{x}(n) + du(n) \\ &= [c_1, c_2, \ldots, c_N]\underline{x}(n) + du(n). \end{aligned} \tag{G.21}$$

Since the state transition matrix is diagonal, the modes are *decoupled*, and we can write each mode's time-update independently:

$$\begin{aligned} x_1(n+1) &= \lambda_1 x_1(n) + b_1 u(n) \\ x_2(n+1) &= \lambda_2 x_2(n) + b_2 u(n) \\ &\vdots \\ x_N(n+1) &= \lambda_N x_N(n) + b_N u(n) \\ y(n) &= c_1 x_1(n) + c_2 x_2(n) + \cdots + c_N x_N(n) + du(n) \end{aligned}$$

Thus, the diagonalized state-space system consists of N *parallel one-pole systems*. See §9.2.2 on page 209 and §6.8.7 on page 141 regarding the conversion of direct-form filter transfer functions to parallel (complex) one-pole form.

G.9.1   Diagonalizing a State-Space Model

To obtain the *modal representation*, we may *diagonalize* any state-space representation. This is accomplished by means of a particular *similarity transformation* specified by the *eigenvectors* of the state transition matrix A. An *eigenvector* of the square matrix A is any vector $\underline{e}_i$ for which

$$A\underline{e}_i = \lambda_i \underline{e}_i,$$

where λ_i may be complex. In other words, when the matrix E of the similarity transformation is composed of the eigenvectors of A,

$$E = [\underline{e}_1 \ \cdots \ \underline{e}_N],$$

the transformed system will be *diagonalized*, as we will see below.

A system can be diagonalized whenever the eigenvectors of A are *linearly independent*. This always holds when the system poles are *distinct*. It may or may not hold when poles are *repeated*.

To see how this works, suppose we are able to find N linearly independent eigenvectors of A, denoted $\underline{e}_i$, $i = 1, \ldots, N$. Then we can form an $N \times N$ matrix E having these eigenvectors as columns. Since the eigenvectors are linearly independent, E is full rank and can be used as a one-to-one linear transformation, or *change-of-coordinates* matrix. From Eq. (G.19), we have that the transformed state transition matrix is given by

$$\tilde{A} = E^{-1}AE$$

Since each column $\underline{e}_i$ of E is an eigenvector of A, we have $A\underline{e}_i = \lambda_i \underline{e}_i$, $i = 1, \ldots, N$, which implies

$$AE = E\Lambda,$$

where

$$\Lambda \triangleq \begin{bmatrix} \lambda_1 & & 0 \\ & \ddots & \\ 0 & & \lambda_N \end{bmatrix}$$

is a diagonal matrix having the (complex) eigenvalues of A along the diagonal. It then follows that

$$\tilde{A} = E^{-1}AE = E^{-1}E\Lambda = \Lambda,$$

which shows that the new state transition matrix is diagonal and made up of the eigenvalues of A.

The transfer function is now, from Eq. (G.5), in the SISO case,

$$\begin{aligned} H(z) &= d + \tilde{C}\,(zI - \Lambda)^{-1}\,\tilde{B} \\ &= d + \frac{\tilde{c}_1 b_1 z^{-1}}{1 - \lambda_1 z^{-1}} + \frac{\tilde{c}_2 \tilde{b}_2 z^{-1}}{1 - \lambda_2 z^{-1}} + \cdots + \frac{\tilde{c}_N \tilde{b}_N z^{-1}}{1 - \lambda_N z^{-1}} \\ &= d + \sum_{i=1}^{N} \frac{\tilde{c}_i \tilde{b}_i z^{-1}}{1 - \lambda_i z^{-1}}. \end{aligned} \qquad (G.22)$$

We have incidentally shown that the eigenvalues of the state-transition matrix A are the poles of the system transfer function. When it is *diagonal*, *i.e.*, when $A = \operatorname{diag}(\lambda_1, \ldots, \lambda_N)$, the state-space model may be called a *modal representation* of the system, because the poles appear explicitly along the diagonal of A and the system's dynamic modes are decoupled.

Notice that the diagonalized state-space form is essentially equivalent to a *partial-fraction expansion* form (§6.8). In particular, the *residue* of the ith pole is given by $c_i b_i$. When complex-conjugate poles are combined to form real, second-order blocks (in which case A is block-diagonal with 2×2 blocks along the diagonal), this is corresponds to a partial-fraction expansion into real, second-order, parallel filter sections.

G.9.2   Finding the Eigenvalues of A in Practice

Small problems may be solved by hand by solving the system of equations

$$AE = E\Lambda.$$

The Matlab built-in function `eig()` may be used to find the eigenvalues of A (system poles) numerically.[11]

G.9.3   Example of State-Space Diagonalization

For the example of Eq. (G.7), we obtain the following results:

```
>> % Initial state space filter from example above:
>> A = [-1/2, -1/3; 1, 0]; % state transition matrix
>> B = [1; 0];
>> C = [2-1/2, 3-1/3];
```

---

[11] If the Matlab Control Toolbox is available, there are higher level routines for manipulating state-space representations; type "`lookfor state-space`" in Matlab to obtain a summary, or do a search on the Mathworks website. Octave tends to provide its control-related routines in the base distribution of Octave.

```
>> D = 1;
>>
>> eig(A) % find eigenvalues of state transition matrix A

ans =
  -0.2500 + 0.5204i
  -0.2500 - 0.5204i

>> roots(den) % find poles of transfer function H(z)

ans =
  -0.2500 + 0.5204i
  -0.2500 - 0.5204i

>> abs(roots(den)) % check stability while we're here

ans =
    0.5774
    0.5774
```

% The system is stable since each pole has magnitude < 1.

Our second-order example is already in *real* 2×2 form, because it is only second order. However, to illustrate the computations, let's obtain the eigenvectors and compute the *complex* modal representation:

```
>> [E,L] = eig(A)   % [Evects,Evals] = eig(A)

E =

  -0.4507 - 0.2165i   -0.4507 + 0.2165i
        0 + 0.8660i         0 - 0.8660i


L =

  -0.2500 + 0.5204i           0
        0               -0.2500 - 0.5204i

>> A * E - E * L   % should be zero (A * evect = eval * evect)

ans =
  1.0e-016 *
```

```
          0 + 0.2776i          0 - 0.2776i
          0                    0
```

% Now form the complete diagonalized state-space model (complex):

```
>> Ei = inv(E); % matrix inverse
>> Ab = Ei*A*E % new state transition matrix (diagonal)

Ab =
  -0.2500 + 0.5204i    0.0000 + 0.0000i
  -0.0000             -0.2500 - 0.5204i

>> Bb = Ei*B    % vector routing input signal to internal modes

Bb =
  -1.1094
  -1.1094

>> Cb = C*E     % vector taking mode linear combination to output

Cb =
  -0.6760 + 1.9846i   -0.6760 - 1.9846i

>> Db = D        % feed-through term unchanged

Db =
     1
```

% Verify that we still have the same transfer function:

```
>> [numb,denb] = ss2tf(Ab,Bb,Cb,Db)

numb =
   1.0000              2.0000 + 0.0000i   3.0000 + 0.0000i

denb =
   1.0000              0.5000 - 0.0000i   0.3333

>> num = [1, 2, 3]; % original numerator
>> norm(num-numb)

ans =
```

```
   1.5543e-015

>> den = [1, 1/2, 1/3]; % original denominator
>> norm(den-denb)

ans =
   1.3597e-016
```

G.9.4   Properties of the Modal Representation

The vector $\tilde{B}$ in a modal representation (Eq. (G.21)) specifies how the modes are *driven* by the input. That is, the ith mode receives the input signal $u(n)$ weighted by $\tilde{b}_i$. In a computational model of a drum, for example, $\tilde{B}$ may be changed corresponding to different striking locations on the drumhead.

The vector $\tilde{C}$ in a modal representation (Eq. (G.21)) specifies how the modes are to be *mixed* into the output. In other words, $\tilde{C}$ specifies how the output signal is to be created as a *linear combination* of the mode states:

$$y(n) = \tilde{C}\underline{\tilde{x}}(n) = \tilde{c}_1\tilde{x}_1(n) + \tilde{c}_2\tilde{x}_2(n) + \cdots + \tilde{c}_N\tilde{x}_N(n)$$

In a computational model of an electric guitar string, for example, $\tilde{C}$ changes whenever a different pick-up is switched in or out (or is moved [99]).

The modal representation is not *unique* since $\tilde{B}$ and $\tilde{C}$ may be scaled in compensating ways to produce the same transfer function. (The diagonal elements of $\tilde{A}$ may also be permuted along with $\tilde{B}$ and $\tilde{C}$.) Each element of the state vector $\underline{\tilde{x}}(n)$ holds the state of a single first-order mode of the system.

For oscillatory systems, the diagonalized state transition matrix must contain *complex* elements. In particular, if mode i is both oscillatory and *undamped* (lossless), then an excited state-variable $\tilde{x}_i(n)$ will oscillate *sinusoidally*, after the input becomes zero, at some frequency ω_i, where

$$\lambda_i = e^{j\omega_i T}$$

relates the system eigenvalue λ_i to the oscillation frequency ω_i, with T denoting the sampling interval in seconds. More generally, in the damped case, we have

$$\lambda_i = R_i e^{j\omega_i T}$$

where R_i is the pole (eigenvalue) radius. For stability, we must have

$$|R_i| < 1.$$

In practice, we often prefer to combine complex-conjugate pole-pairs to form a real, "block-diagonal" system; in this case, the transition matrix $\tilde{A}$ is block-diagonal with two-by-two real matrices along its diagonal of the form

$$\mathbf{A}_i = \begin{bmatrix} 2R_iC_i & -R_i^2 \\ 1 & 0 \end{bmatrix}$$

where $R_i = |\lambda_i|$ is the pole radius, and $2R_iC_i \triangleq 2R_i\cos(\omega_i T) = \lambda_i + \overline{\lambda}_i = 2\mathrm{re}\{\lambda_i\}$. Note that, for real systems, a real second order block requires only two multiplies (one in the lossless case) per time update, while a complex second-order system requires two *complex* multiplies. The function cdf2rdf() in the Matlab Control Toolbox can be used to convert complex diagonal form to real block-diagonal form.

G.10 Repeated Poles

The above summary of state-space diagonalization works as stated when the modes (poles) of the system are distinct. When there are two or more resonant modes corresponding to the same "natural frequency" (eigenvalue of A), then there are two further subcases: If the eigenvectors corresponding to the repeated eigenvalue (pole) are *linearly independent*, then the modes are independent and can be treated as distinct (the system can be diagonalized). Otherwise, we say the equal modes are *coupled*.

The coupled-repeated-poles situation is detected when the matrix of eigenvectors V returned by the eig matlab function [*e.g.*, by saying [V,D] = eig(A)] turns out to be *singular*. Singularity of V can be defined as when its *condition number* [cond(V)] exceeds some threshold, such as 1E7. In this case, the linearly dependent eigenvectors can be replaced by so-called *generalized eigenvectors* [58]. Use of that similarity transformation then produces a "block diagonalized" system instead of a diagonalized system, and one of the blocks along the diagonal will be a $k \times k$ matrix corresponding to the pole repeated k times.

Connecting with the discussion regarding repeated poles in §6.8.5 on page 136, the $k \times k$ Jordan block corresponding to a pole repeated k times plays exactly the same role of repeated poles encountered in a partial-fraction expansion, giving rise to terms in the impulse response proportional to $n\lambda^n$, $n^2\lambda^n$, and so on, up to $n^{k-1}\lambda^n$, where λ denotes the repeated pole itself (*i.e.*, the repeated eigenvalue of the state-transition matrix A).

G.10.1   Jordan Canonical Form

The *block diagonal* system having the eigenvalues along the diagonal and ones in some of the superdiagonal elements (which serve to couple repeated eigenvalues) is called *Jordan canonical form*. Each block size corresponds to the multiplicity of the repeated pole. As an example, a pole p_i of multiplicity $m_i = 3$ could give rise to the following 3×3 *Jordan block*:

$$
D_i = \begin{bmatrix} p_i & 1 & 0 \\ 0 & p_i & 1 \\ 0 & 0 & p_i \end{bmatrix}
$$

The ones along the superdiagonal serve to couple the states corresponding to p_i and generate polynomial amplitude envelopes multiplying the sampled exponential p_i^n.[12] Note, however, that a pole of multiplicity three can also

---

[12] In general, we can write an order k Jordan block J_i corresponding to eigenvalue p as

$$
J = pI + \Delta
$$

where I denotes the $k \times k$ identity matrix, and

$$
\Delta \triangleq \begin{bmatrix} 0 & 1 & 0 & \cdots & 0 \\ 0 & 0 & 1 & \cdots & 0 \\ \vdots & \vdots & \ddots & \ddots & \vdots \\ 0 & 0 & 0 & \ddots & 1 \\ 0 & 0 & 0 & \cdots & 0 \end{bmatrix}.
$$

Note that Δ^n, for $n = 0, 1, 2, \ldots, k-1$ has ones along the nth superdiagonal and zeros elsewhere. Also, $\Delta^n = 0$ for $n \geq k$. By the *binomial theorem*,

$$
J^n = (pI + \Delta)^n = p^n I + np^{n-1}\Delta + \frac{n(n-1)}{2}p^{n-2}\Delta^2 + \frac{n(n-1)(n-1)}{3!}p^{n-3}\Delta^3 + \cdots
$$
$$
+ \binom{n}{k} p^k \Delta^{n-k} + \cdots + np\Delta^{n-1} + \Delta^n,
$$

where $\binom{n}{k} \triangleq n!/[k!(n-k)!]$ denotes the *binomial coefficient* (also called "n choose k" in probability theory). Thus,

$$
J^n = \begin{bmatrix} p^n & np^{n-1} & \frac{n(n-1)}{2}p^{n-2} & \cdots & \cdots & 0 \\ 0 & p^n & np^{n-1} & \frac{n(n-1)}{2}p^{n-2} & \cdots & 0 \\ \vdots & & \ddots & & \ddots & \\ 0 & 0 & 0 & & & np^{n-1} \\ 0 & 0 & 0 & & & p^n \end{bmatrix},
$$

where the zeros in the upper-right corner are valid for sufficiently large n, and otherwise the indicated series is simply truncated.

yield two Jordan blocks, such as

$$D_i = \begin{bmatrix} p_i & 1 & 0 \\ 0 & p_i & 0 \\ 0 & 0 & p_i \end{bmatrix}$$

or even three Jordan blocks of order 1. The number of Jordan blocks associated with a single pole p_i is equal to the number of linearly independent eigenvectors of the transition matrix associated with eigenvalue p_i. If all eigenvectors of A are linearly independent, the system can be diagonalized after all, and any repeated roots are "uncoupled" and behave like non-repeated roots (no polynomial amplitude envelopes).

Interestingly, neither Matlab nor Octave seem to have a numerical function for computing the Jordan canonical form of a matrix. Matlab will try to do it *symbolically* when the matrix entries are given as exact rational numbers (ratios of integers) by the `jordan` function, which requires the Maple symbolic mathematics toolbox. Numerically, it is generally difficult to distinguish between poles that are repeated exactly, and poles that are merely close together. The `residuez` function sets a numerical threshold below which poles are treated as repeated.

G.11   State-Space Analysis Example: The Digital Waveguide Oscillator

As an example of state-space analysis, we will use it to determine the frequency of oscillation of the system of Fig. G.3 [90].

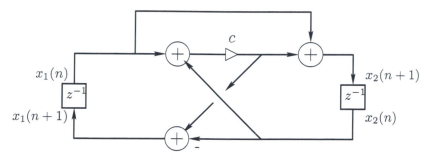

Figure G.3: The second-order digital waveguide oscillator.

Note the assignments of unit-delay outputs to state variables $x_1(n)$ and $x_2(n)$. From the diagram, we see that

$$x_1(n+1) = c[x_1(n) + x_2(n)] - x_2(n) = c\,x_1(n) + (c-1)x_2(n)$$

and

$$x_2(n+1) = x_1(n) + c[x_1(n) + x_2(n)] = (1+c)x_1(n) + c\,x_2(n)$$

In matrix form, the state time-update can be written

$$\begin{bmatrix} x_1(n+1) \\ x_2(n+1) \end{bmatrix} = \underbrace{\begin{bmatrix} c & c-1 \\ c+1 & c \end{bmatrix}}_{A} \begin{bmatrix} x_1(n) \\ x_2(n) \end{bmatrix}$$

or, in vector notation,

$$\underline{x}(n+1) = A\,\underline{x}(n).$$

We have two natural choices of output, $x_1(n)$ and $x_2(n)$:

$$y_1(n) \triangleq x_1(n) = [1,0]\underline{x}(n)$$
$$y_2(n) \triangleq x_2(n) = [0,1]\underline{x}(n)$$

A basic fact from linear algebra is that the *determinant* of a matrix is equal to the *product of its eigenvalues*. As a quick check, we find that the determinant of A is

$$\det A = c^2 - (c+1)(c-1) = c^2 - (c^2-1) = 1.$$

Since an undriven sinusoidal oscillator must not lose energy, and since every lossless state-space system has unit-modulus eigenvalues (consider the modal representation), we expect $|\det A| = 1$.

Note that $\underline{x}(n) = A^n\underline{x}(0)$. If we diagonalize this system to obtain $\tilde{A} = E^{-1}AE$, where $\tilde{A} = \text{diag}[\lambda_1, \lambda_2]$, and E is the matrix of eigenvectors of A, then we have

$$\underline{\tilde{x}}(n) = \tilde{A}^n\,\underline{\tilde{x}}(0) = \begin{bmatrix} \lambda_1^n & 0 \\ 0 & \lambda_2^n \end{bmatrix} \begin{bmatrix} \tilde{x}_1(0) \\ \tilde{x}_2(0) \end{bmatrix}$$

where $\underline{\tilde{x}}(n) \triangleq E^{-1}\underline{x}(n)$ denotes the state vector in these new "modal coordinates". Since $\tilde{A}$ is diagonal, the modes are decoupled, and we can write

$$\tilde{x}_1(n) = \lambda_1^n\,\tilde{x}_1(0)$$
$$\tilde{x}_2(n) = \lambda_2^n\,\tilde{x}_2(0).$$

If this system is to generate a real sampled sinusoid at radian frequency ω, the eigenvalues λ_1 and λ_2 must be of the form

$$\lambda_1 = e^{j\omega T}$$
$$\lambda_2 = e^{-j\omega T},$$

(in either order) where ω is real, and T denotes the sampling interval in seconds.

Thus, we can determine the frequency of oscillation ω (and verify that the system actually oscillates) by determining the eigenvalues λ_i of A. Note that, as a prerequisite, it will also be necessary to find two linearly independent eigenvectors of A (columns of E).

G.11.1   Finding the Eigenstructure of A

Starting with the defining equation for an eigenvector $\underline{e}$ and its corresponding eigenvalue λ,

$$A\underline{e}_i = \lambda_i \underline{e}_i, \quad i = 1, 2$$

we get

$$\begin{bmatrix} c & c-1 \\ c+1 & c \end{bmatrix} \begin{bmatrix} 1 \\ \eta_i \end{bmatrix} = \begin{bmatrix} \lambda_i \\ \lambda_i \eta_i \end{bmatrix}. \tag{G.23}$$

We normalized the first element of $\underline{e}_i$ to 1 since $g\underline{e}_i$ is an eigenvector whenever $\underline{e}_i$ is. (If there is a missing solution because its first element happens to be zero, we can repeat the analysis normalizing the second element to 1 instead.)

Equation (G.23) gives us two equations in two unknowns:

$$c + \eta_i(c-1) = \lambda_i \tag{G.24}$$
$$(1+c) + c\eta_i = \lambda_i \eta_i \tag{G.25}$$

Substituting the first into the second to eliminate λ_i, we get

$$1 + c + c\eta_i = [c + \eta_i(c-1)]\eta_i = c\eta_i + \eta_i^2(c-1)$$
$$\Rightarrow 1 + c = \eta_i^2(c-1)$$
$$\Rightarrow \eta_i = \pm\sqrt{\frac{c+1}{c-1}}.$$

Thus, we have found both eigenvectors

$$\underline{e}_1 = \begin{bmatrix} 1 \\ \eta \end{bmatrix}, \quad \underline{e}_2 = \begin{bmatrix} 1 \\ -\eta \end{bmatrix}, \quad \text{where}$$

$$\eta \triangleq \sqrt{\frac{c+1}{c-1}}.$$

They are linearly independent provided $\eta \neq 0 \Leftrightarrow c \neq -1$ and finite provided $c \neq 1$.

We can now use Eq. (G.24) to find the eigenvalues:

$$\lambda_i = c + \eta_i(c-1) = c \pm \sqrt{\frac{c+1}{c-1}(c-1)^2} = c \pm \sqrt{c^2 - 1}$$

Assuming $|c| < 1$, the eigenvalues are

$$\lambda_i = c \pm j\sqrt{1 - c^2} \qquad\qquad (G.26)$$

and so this is the range of c corresponding to sinusoidal oscillation. For $|c| > 1$, the eigenvalues are real, corresponding to exponential growth and decay. The values $c = \pm 1$ yield a repeated root (dc or $f_s/2$ oscillation).

Let us henceforth assume $-1 < c < 1$. In this range $\theta \triangleq \arccos(c)$ is real, and we have $c = \cos(\theta)$, $\sqrt{1 - c^2} = \sin(\theta)$. Thus, the eigenvalues can be expressed as follows:

$$\begin{aligned}
\lambda_1 &= c + j\sqrt{1 - c^2} = \cos(\theta) + j\sin(\theta) = e^{j\theta}\\
\lambda_2 &= c - j\sqrt{1 - c^2} = \cos(\theta) - j\sin(\theta) = e^{-j\theta}
\end{aligned}$$

Equating λ_i to $e^{j\omega_i T}$, we obtain $\omega_i T = \pm\theta$, or $\omega_i = \pm\theta/T = \pm f_s\theta = \pm f_s \arccos(c)$, where f_s denotes the sampling rate. Thus the relationship between the coefficient c in the digital waveguide oscillator and the frequency of sinusoidal oscillation ω is expressed succinctly as

$$\boxed{c = \cos(\omega T).}$$

We see that the coefficient range (-1,1) corresponds to frequencies in the range $(-f_s/2, f_s/2)$, and that's the complete set of available digital frequencies.

We have now shown that the system of Fig. G.3 oscillates sinusoidally at any desired digital frequency ω rad/sec by simply setting $c = \cos(\omega T)$, where T denotes the sampling interval.

G.11.2   Choice of Output Signal and Initial Conditions

Recalling that $\tilde{x} = E\underline{\tilde{x}}$, the output signal from any diagonal state-space model is a linear combination of the modal signals. The two immediate outputs $x_1(n)$ and $x_2(n)$ in Fig. G.3 are given in terms of the modal signals $\tilde{x}_1(n) = \lambda_1^n \tilde{x}_1(0)$ and $\tilde{x}_2(n) = \lambda_2^n \tilde{x}_2(0)$ as

$$\begin{aligned}
y_1(n) &= [1, 0]\underline{x}(n) = [1, 0]\begin{bmatrix} 1 & 1 \\ \eta & -\eta \end{bmatrix}\underline{\tilde{x}}(n)\\
&= [1, 1]\underline{\tilde{x}}(n) = \lambda_1^n \tilde{x}_1(0) + \lambda_2^n \tilde{x}_2(0)
\end{aligned}$$

$$\begin{aligned}
y_2(n) &= [0, 1]\underline{x}(n) = [0, 1]\begin{bmatrix} 1 & 1 \\ \eta & -\eta \end{bmatrix}\underline{\tilde{x}}(n)\\
&= [\eta, -\eta]\underline{\tilde{x}}(n) = \eta\lambda_1^n \tilde{x}_1(0) - \eta\lambda_2^n \tilde{x}_2(0).
\end{aligned}$$

The output signal from the first state variable $x_1(n)$ is

$$
\begin{aligned}
y_1(n) &= \lambda_1^n \tilde{x}_1(0) + \lambda_2^n \tilde{x}_2(0) \\
&= e^{j\omega n T} \tilde{x}_1(0) + e^{-j\omega n T} \tilde{x}_2(0).
\end{aligned}
$$

The *initial condition* $\underline{x}(0) = [1,0]^T$ corresponds to modal initial state

$$
\underline{\tilde{x}}(0) = E^{-1} \begin{bmatrix} 1 \\ 0 \end{bmatrix} = \frac{-1}{2\eta} \begin{bmatrix} -\eta & -1 \\ -\eta & 1 \end{bmatrix} \begin{bmatrix} 1 \\ 0 \end{bmatrix} = \begin{bmatrix} 1/2 \\ 1/2 \end{bmatrix}.
$$

For this initialization, the output y_1 from the first state variable x_1 is simply

$$
y_1(n) = \frac{e^{j\omega n T} + e^{-j\omega n T}}{2} = \cos(\omega n T).
$$

A similar derivation can be carried out to show that the output $y_2(n) = x_2(n)$ is proportional to $\sin(\omega n T)$, *i.e.*, it is in *phase quadrature* with respect to $y_1(n) = x_1(n)$). Phase-quadrature outputs are often useful in practice, *e.g.*, for generating complex sinusoids.

References

Further details on state-space analysis of linear systems may be found in [102, 37]. More Matlab exercises and some supporting theory may be found in [10, Chapter 5].

G.12   State Space Problems

1. Find a state space description (A, B, C, D) for the digital filter

$$
y(n) = u(n - 5)
$$

2. Transpose the signal flow graph of the DF-II filter in Fig. G.1 on page 356, find its state-space representation, and show that it is the *transpose* of the system given in Eq. (G.16) on page 355.

3. Prove that controller canonical form, as given in Eq. (G.12) on page 354 has the desired transfer function, using Eq. (G.5) on page 349 with $D = 0$. [Hint: Set up the linear system of equations $(zI - A)\underline{x} = B$ and use Cramer's rule [58] to solve for $\underline{x}$ (easy because B has only one nonzero entry); next form $Y(z) = C\underline{x}U(z)$ and determine the transfer function $H(z) = Y(z)/U(z)$.]

4. Show that a 2D rotation does not change the L^2 norm of a length 2 vector. (See Eq. (G.6) on page 350.)

Appendix H

A View of Linear Time Varying Digital Filters

As discussed in Appendix F starting on page 335, linear time-varying (LTV) digital filters may be represented as matrix operators on the linear space of discrete time signals. Using the matrix representation, this appendix provides an interpretation of LTV filters that the author has found conceptually useful. In this interpretation, the input signal is first expanded into a linear combination of orthogonal basis signals. Then the LTV filter can be seen as replacing each basis signal with a new (arbitrary) basis signal. In particular, when the input-basis is taken to be sinusoidal, as in the Discrete Fourier Transform (DFT), one may readily design a time varying filter to emit any prescribed waveform in response to each frequency component of an input signal.

H.1   Introduction

The most common type of filter dealt with in practice is a linear, causal, and time-invariant operator on the vector space consisting of arbitrary real-valued functions of time. Since we are dealing with the space of functions of time, we will use the terms *vector, function,* and *signal* interchangeably. When time is a continuous variable, the vector space is infinite-dimensional even when time is restricted to a finite interval. Digital filters are simpler in many ways theoretically because finite-time digital signals occupy a finite-dimensional vector space. Furthermore, every linear operator on the space of digital signals may be represented as a matrix.[1] If the range of time is restricted to N samples then the arbitrary linear operator is an N by N matrix. In the discussion that follows, we will be exclusively concerned with the digital domain. Every linear filter will be representable as a matrix, and every signal will be expressible as a column vector.

Linearity implies the superposition principle which is presently indispensible for a general filter response analysis. The superposition principle states that if a signal X is represented as a linear combination of signals $\{x_1, x_2, \ldots\}$, then the response Y of any linear filter H may written as the same linear combination of the signals $\{y_1, y_2, \ldots\}$ where $y_i = Hx_i$. More generally,

$$Y = HX = H \sum_{i=-\infty}^{\infty} \alpha_i x_i = \sum_{i=-\infty}^{\infty} \alpha_i H x_i = \sum_{i=-\infty}^{\infty} \alpha_i y_i.$$

A set of signals that can be used to express every signal in the space is called a set of *basis functions*. An example of a basis set is the familiar set of sinusoids at all frequencies. The most crucial use of linearity for our purposes is the representation of an arbitrary linear filter as a matrix operator.

Causality means that the filter output does not depend on future inputs. This is necessary in analog filters where time is a real entity, but for digital filters causality is highly unnecessary unless the filter must operate in real-time. Requiring a filter to be causal results in a triangular matrix representation.

A time-invariant filter is one whose response does not depend on the time of excitation. This allows *superposition in time* in addition to the superposition of component functions given by linearity. A matrix representing a linear time-invariant filter is Toeplitz (each diagonal is constant). The chief value of time-invariance is that it allows a linear filter to represented by its *impulse response* which, for digital filters, is the response elicited by the signal $(1, 0, 0, \ldots)$. A deeper consequence of superposition in time together with superposition of component signal responses is the fact that every stable linear time invariant filter emits a sinusoid at frequency f in response to an input sinusoid at frequency f after sufficient time for start-up transients to settle. For this reason sinusoids are called *eigenfunctions* of linear time-invariant systems. Another way of putting it is that a linear time-invariant filter can only modify a sinusoidal input

---

[1] Recursive filters are brought into this framework in the time-invariant case by dealing directly with their impulse response, or the so called *moving average* representation. Linear time-varying recursive filters have a matrix representation, but it is not easy to find. In general one must symbolically implement the equation $y_n = \sum_{i=-\infty}^{\infty} h_{ni} x_i + \sum_{j=1}^{\infty} \beta_{nj} y_{n-j}$ and collect coefficients of x_i.

by a constant scaling of its amplitude and a constant offset in its phase. This is the rationale behind Fourier analysis. The Laplace transform of the impulse response gives the *transfer function* and the Fourier transform of the impulse response is the *frequency response*. It is important to note that relaxing time-invariance only prevents us from using superposition in time. Consequently, while we can no longer uniquely characterize a filter in terms of its impulse response, we may still characterize it in terms of its **basis function response**.

This will be developed below for the particular basis functions used in the Discrete Fourier Transform (DFT). These basis functions are defined for the N-dimensional discrete-time signal space as

$$W_N^n(k) = e^{j2\pi \frac{kn}{N}}, \qquad k, n = 0, 1, 2, \ldots N - 1$$

where n is the time index, and k is the discrete frequency index. To be more concrete we could define $\omega_k = 2\pi f_s k/N$ as the kth raidan frequency and $t_n = nT$ as the time of the nth sample, where the sampling rate $f_s = 1/T$. Note that $W_N^n(k)$ is a sampled version of the continuous time sinusoidal basis function $e^{j\omega t}$ used in the Fourier transform. There are no eigenfunctions for general time-varying filters and so there is no fundamental reason to prefer the Fourier basis over any other basis. The basis set may be chosen according to the most natural decomposition of the input signal space without a penalty in complexity.

H.2   Derivation

For notational simplicity, we restrict exposition to the three-dimensional case. The general linear digital filter equation $Y = HX$ is written in three dimensions as

$$\begin{bmatrix} y_0 \\ y_1 \\ y_2 \end{bmatrix} = \begin{bmatrix} h_{00} & h_{01} & h_{02} \\ h_{10} & h_{11} & h_{12} \\ h_{20} & h_{21} & h_{22} \end{bmatrix} \begin{bmatrix} x_0 \\ x_1 \\ x_2 \end{bmatrix}.$$

where x_i is regarded as the input sample at time i, and y_i is the output sample at time i. The general causal time-invariant filter appears in three-space as

$$H = \begin{bmatrix} h_0 & 0 & 0 \\ h_1 & h_0 & 0 \\ h_2 & h_1 & h_0 \end{bmatrix}.$$

Consider the non-causal time-varying filter defined by

$$C_3(k) = 1/3 \begin{bmatrix} 1 & W_3^1(k) & W_3^2(k) \\ 1 & W_3^1(k) & W_3^2(k) \\ 1 & W_3^1(k) & W_3^2(k) \end{bmatrix}.$$

We may call $C_3(k)$ the *collector matrix* corresponding to the kth frequency. We have

$$C_3(0) \;=\; \frac{1}{3} \begin{bmatrix} 1 & 1 & 1 \\ 1 & 1 & 1 \\ 1 & 1 & 1 \end{bmatrix},$$

$$C_3(1) \;=\; \frac{1}{3} \begin{bmatrix} 1 & e^{j2\pi\frac{1}{3}} & e^{j2\pi\frac{2}{3}} \\ 1 & e^{j2\pi\frac{1}{3}} & e^{j2\pi\frac{2}{3}} \\ 1 & e^{j2\pi\frac{1}{3}} & e^{j2\pi\frac{2}{3}} \end{bmatrix} = \frac{1}{3} \begin{bmatrix} 1 & e^{j\frac{2\pi}{3}} & e^{-j\frac{2\pi}{3}} \\ 1 & e^{j\frac{2\pi}{3}} & e^{-j\frac{2\pi}{3}} \\ 1 & e^{j\frac{2\pi}{3}} & e^{-j\frac{2\pi}{3}} \end{bmatrix},$$

$$C_3(2) \;=\; \frac{1}{3} \begin{bmatrix} 1 & e^{j2\pi\frac{2}{3}} & e^{j2\pi\frac{4}{3}} \\ 1 & e^{j2\pi\frac{2}{3}} & e^{j2\pi\frac{4}{3}} \\ 1 & e^{j2\pi\frac{2}{3}} & e^{j2\pi\frac{4}{3}} \end{bmatrix} = \frac{1}{3} \begin{bmatrix} 1 & e^{-j\frac{2\pi}{3}} & e^{j\frac{2\pi}{3}} \\ 1 & e^{-j\frac{2\pi}{3}} & e^{j\frac{2\pi}{3}} \\ 1 & e^{-j\frac{2\pi}{3}} & e^{j\frac{2\pi}{3}} \end{bmatrix}.$$

The top row of each matrix is recognized as a basis function for the order three DFT (equispaced vectors on the unit circle). Accordingly, we have the orthogonality and spanning properties of these vectors. So let us define a basis for the signal space $\{x_0, x_1, x_2\}$ by

$$x_0 \overset{\Delta}{=} \begin{bmatrix} 1 \\ 1 \\ 1 \end{bmatrix}, \qquad x_1 \overset{\Delta}{=} \begin{bmatrix} 1 \\ e^{j\frac{2\pi}{3}} \\ e^{-j\frac{2\pi}{3}} \end{bmatrix}, \qquad x_2 \overset{\Delta}{=} \begin{bmatrix} 1 \\ e^{-j\frac{2\pi}{3}} \\ e^{j\frac{2\pi}{3}} \end{bmatrix}.$$

Then every component of $C_3(k)x_k = 1$ and every component of $C_3(k)x_j = 0$ when $k \neq j$. Now since any signal X in $\Re^3$ may be written as a linear combination of $\{x_1, x_2, x_3\}$, we find that

$$C_3(k)X = C_3(k)\sum_{i=0}^{2}\alpha_i x_i = \sum_{i=0}^{2}\alpha_i C_3(k)x_i = \alpha_k \begin{bmatrix} 1 \\ 1 \\ 1 \end{bmatrix}.$$

Consequently, we observe that $C_N(k)$ is a matrix which annihilates all input basis components but the kth. Now multiply $C_N(k)$ on the left by a diagonal matrix $D(k)$ so that the product of $D(k)C_N(k)$ times x_k gives an arbitrary column vector (d_1, d_2, d_3). Then every linear time-varying filter G

is expressible as a sum of these products as we will show below. In general, the decomposition for every filter on $\Re^N$ is simply

$$G = \sum_{k=0}^{N-1} D(k)C_N(k). \qquad (H.1)$$

The uniqueness of the decomposition is easy to verify: Suppose there are two distinct decompositions of the form Eq. (H.1). Then for some k we have different D(k)'s. However, this implies that we can get two distinct outputs in response to the kth input basis function which is absurd.

That every linear time-varying filter may be expressed in this form is also easy to show. Given an arbitrary filter matrix of order N, measure its response to each of the N basis functions (sine and cosine replace $e^{j\omega t}$) to obtain a set of N by 1 column vectors. The output vector due to the kth basis vector is precisely the diagonal of $D(k)$.

H.3 Summary

A representation of an arbitrary linear time-varying digital filter has been constructed which characterizes such a filter as having the ability to generate an arbitrary output in response to each basis function in the signal space. The representation was obtained by casting the filter in moving-average form as a matrix, and studying its response to individual orthogonal basis functions which were chosen here to be complex sinusoids. The overall conclusion is that time-varying filters may be used to convert from a set of orthogonal signals (such as tones at distinct frequencies) to a set of unconstrained waveforms in a one-to-one fashion. Linear combinations of these orthogonal signals are then transformed by the LTV filter to the same linear combination of the transformed basis signals.

Appendix I

Recursive Digital Filter Design

The subject of *digital filter design* is enormous—much larger than we can hope to address in this book. However, a surprisingly large number of applications can be addressed using small filter sections which are easily designed by hand, as exemplified in Appendix B. This appendix describes some of the "classic" methods for IIR filter design based on the *bilinear transformation of prototype analog filters*, followed by the simple but powerful *weighted equation error method* for general purpose IIR design. For further information on digital filter design, see the documentation for the Matlab Toolboxes for Signal Processing and Filter Design, and/or [64, 68, 60, 78].

I.1   Lowpass Filter Design

We have discussed in detail (Chapter 1) the simplest lowpass filter, $y(n) = x(n) + x(n-1)$ having the transfer function $H(z) = 1 + z^{-1}$ with one zero at $z = -1$ and one pole at $z = 0$. From the graphical method for visualizing the amplitude response (§8.2 on page 177), we see that this filter totally rejects signal energy at half the sampling rate, while lower frequencies experience higher gains, reaching a maximum at $\omega = 0$. We also see that the pole at $z = 0$ has no effect on the amplitude response.

A *high quality* lowpass filter should look more like the "box car" amplitude response shown in Fig. 1.1 on page 3. While it is impossible to achieve this ideal response exactly using a finite-order filter, we can come arbitrarily close. We can expect the amplitude response to improve if we add another pole or zero to the implementation.

Perhaps the best known "classical" methods for lowpass filter designs
are those derived from analog *Butterworth, Chebyshev,* and *Elliptic Function*
filters [64]. These generally yield IIR filters with the same number
of poles as zeros. When an *FIR* lowpass filter is desired, different design
methods are used, such as the *window method* [68, p. 88] (Matlab functions
`fir1` and `fir2`), *Remez exchange algorithm* [68, pp. 136–140], [64, pp. 89–
106] (Matlab functions `remez` and `cremez`), *linear programming* [93], [68,
p. 140], and *convex optimization* [67]. This section will describe only Butterworth IIR lowpass design in some detail. For the remaining classical
cases (Chebyshev, Inverse Chebyshev, and Elliptic), see, *e.g.*, [64, Chapter
7] and/or Matlab/Octave functions `butter`, `cheby1`, `cheby2`, and `ellip`.

I.2   Butterworth Lowpass Design

Almost all methods for filter design are *optimal* in some sense, and the
choice of optimality determines nature of the design. *Butterworth filters*
are optimal in the sense of having a *maximally flat amplitude response*, as
measured using a Taylor series expansion about dc [64, p. 162]. Of course,
the trivial filter $H(z) = 1$ has a perfectly flat amplitude response, but that's
an allpass, not a lowpass filter. Therefore, to constrain the optimization
to the space of lowpass filters, we need *constraints* on the design, such as
$H(1) = 1$ and $H(-1) = 0$. That is, we may require the dc gain to be 1,
and the gain at half the sampling rate to be 0.

It turns out Butterworth filters (as well as Chebyshev and Elliptic
Function filter types) are much easier to design as *analog filters* which are
then converted to digital filters. This means carrying out the design over
the s plane instead of the z plane, where the s plane is the complex plane
over which analog filter transfer functions are defined. The analog transfer
function $H_a(s)$ is very much like the digital transfer function $H(z)$, except
that it is interpreted relative to the analog frequency axis $s = j\omega_a$ (the "$j\omega$
axis") instead of the digital frequency axis $z = e^{j\omega_d T}$ (the "unit circle").
In particular, analog filter poles are stable if and only if they are all in
the *left-half* of the s plane, *i.e.*, their real parts are *negative*. An introduction to Laplace transforms is given in Appendix D, and an introduction to
converting analog transfer functions to digital transfer functions using the
bilinear transform appears in §I.3.

Butterworth Lowpass Poles and Zeros

When the maximally flat optimality criterion is applied to the general (ana-
log) squared amplitude response $G_a^2(\omega_a) \triangleq |H_a(j\omega_a)|^2$, a surprisingly sim-

ple result is obtained [64]:

$$G_a^2(\omega_a) = \frac{1}{1 + \omega_a^{2N}} \qquad (\text{I.1})$$

where N is the desired order (number of poles). This simple result is obtained when the response is taken to be maximally flat at $\omega_a = \infty$ as well as dc (*i.e.*, when both $G_a^2(\omega_a)$ and $G_a^2(1/\omega_a)$ are maximally flat at dc).[1] Also, an arbitrary scale factor for ω_a has been set such that the cut-off frequency (-3dB frequency) is $\omega_c = 1$ rad/sec.

The *analytic continuation* (§D.2) of $G_a^2(\omega_a)$ to the whole s-plane may be obtained by substituting $\omega_a = s/j$ to obtain

$$H_a(s)H_a(-s) = \frac{1}{1 + \left(\frac{s}{j}\right)^{2N}} = \frac{1}{1 + (-1)^N s^{2N}}$$

The $2N$ poles of this expression are simply the roots of unity when N is odd, and the roots of -1 when N is even. Half of these poles s_k are in the left-half s-plane (re$\{s_k\} < 0$) and thus belong to $H_a(s)$ (which must be stable). The other half belong to $H_a(-s)$. In summary, the poles of an Nth-order Butterworth lowpass prototype are located in the s-plane at $s_k = \sigma_k + j\omega_k = e^{-j\theta_k}$, where [64, p. 168]

$$\begin{aligned} \sigma_k &= -\sin(\theta_k) \\ \omega_k &= \cos(\theta_k) \end{aligned} \qquad (\text{I.2})$$

with

$$\theta_k \triangleq \frac{(2k+1)\pi}{2N}$$

for $k = 0, 1, 2, \ldots, N-1$. These poles may be quickly found graphically by placing $2N$ poles uniformly distributed around the unit circle (in the s plane, not the z plane—this is not a frequency axis) in such a way that each complex pole has a complex-conjugate counterpart.

---

[1] In other words, matching leading terms in the Taylor series expansion of G_a^2 about $\omega_a = 0$ determines the poles as a function of the zeros, leaving the zeros unconstrained. It is shown in [64] that any filter of the form

$$G_a^2(\omega_a) = \frac{B(\omega_a)}{B(\omega_a) + b_{2N}\omega_a^{2N}}$$

is maximally flat at dc, where $B(\omega_a) \triangleq b_0 + b_2\omega_a^2 + b_4\omega_a^4 + \cdots + b_{2M}\omega_a^{2M}$, with $M < N$ necessary to force a zero at $\omega_a = \infty$. Choosing maximum flatness also at $\omega_a = \infty$ pushes all the zeros out to infinity, giving the simple form in Eq. (I.1). It is noted in [64] how the more general class of Butterworth lowpass filters can be used to provide maximum flatness at dc while obtaining more general spectral shapes, such as notches at specific finite frequencies.

A Butterworth lowpass filter additionally has N zeros at $s = \infty$. Under the bilinear transform $s = c(z-1)/(z+1)$, these all map to the point $z = -1$, which determines the numerator of the digital filter as $(1 + z^{-1})^N$.

Given the poles and zeros of the analog prototype, it is straightforward to convert to digital form by means of the bilinear transformation.

Example: Second-Order Butterworth Lowpass

In the second-order case, we have, for the analog prototype,

$$H_a(s) = \frac{1}{(s+a)(s+\bar{a})}$$

where, from Eq. (I.2), $a = e^{j\pi/4}$, so that

$$H_a(s) = \frac{1}{(s + e^{j\pi/4})(s + e^{-j\pi/4})} = \frac{1}{s^2 + \sqrt{2}s + 1} \tag{I.3}$$

To convert this to digital form, we apply the bilinear transform

$$s = c\frac{1 - z^{-1}}{1 + z^{-1}}$$

(from Eq. (I.9) on page 388), where, as discussed in §I.3, we set

$$c = \cot(\omega_c T/2) \triangleq \frac{\cos(\omega_c T/2)}{\sin(\omega_c T/2)}$$

to obtain a digital cut-off frequency at ω_c radians per second. For example, choosing $\omega_c T = \pi/2$ (a cut off at one-fourth the sampling rate), we get

$$c = \frac{\cos(\pi/4)}{\sin(\pi/4)} = 1$$

and the digital filter transfer function is

$$
\begin{aligned}
H_d(z) &= H_a\left(\frac{1 - z^{-1}}{1 + z^{-1}}\right) = \frac{1}{\left(\frac{1-z^{-1}}{1+z^{-1}}\right)^2 + \sqrt{2}\left(\frac{1-z^{-1}}{1+z^{-1}}\right) + 1} & (I.4) \\[2ex]
&= \frac{(1 + z^{-1})^2}{(1 - 2z^{-1} + z^{-2}) + (\sqrt{2} - \sqrt{2}z^{-2}) + (1 + 2z^{-1} + z^{-2})} & (I.5) \\[2ex]
&= \frac{(1 + z^{-1})^2}{(2 + \sqrt{2}) + (2 - \sqrt{2})z^{-2}} & (I.6) \\[2ex]
&= \frac{1}{2 + \sqrt{2}}\frac{(1 + z^{-1})^2}{1 + \frac{2-\sqrt{2}}{2+\sqrt{2}}z^{-2}} & (I.7)
\end{aligned}
$$

Note that the numerator is $(1 + z^{-1})^2$, as predicted earlier. As a check, we can verify that the dc gain is 1:

$$H_d(1) = \frac{2^2}{2 + \sqrt{2} + 2 - \sqrt{2}} = 1$$

It is also immediately verified that $H_d(-1) = 0$, *i.e.*, that there is a (double) notch at half the sampling rate.

In the analog prototype, the cut-off frequency is $\omega_a = 1$ rad/sec, where, from Eq. (I.1), the amplitude response is $G_a(j) = 1/\sqrt{2}$. Since we mapped the cut-off frequency precisely under the bilinear transform, we expect the digital filter to have precisely this gain. The digital frequency response at one-fourth the sampling rate is

$$H_d(j) = \frac{(1 - j)^2}{2 + \sqrt{2} - (2 - \sqrt{2})} = -\frac{j}{\sqrt{2}}, \tag{I.8}$$

and $20 \log_{10}(|H_d(j)|) = -3$ dB as expected.

Note from Eq. (I.8) that the phase at cut-off is exactly -90 degrees in the digital filter. This can be verified against the pole-zero diagram in the z plane, which has two zeros at $z = -1$, each contributing $+45$ degrees, and two poles at $z = \pm j \sqrt{\frac{2 - \sqrt{2}}{2 + \sqrt{2}}}$, each contributing -90 degrees. Thus, the calculated phase-response at the cut-off frequency agrees with what we expect from the digital pole-zero diagram.

In the s plane, it is not as easy to use the pole-zero diagram to calculate the phase at $\omega_a = 1$, but using Eq. (I.3), we quickly obtain

$$H_a(j \cdot 1) = \frac{1}{j^2 + \sqrt{2}j + 1} = -\frac{j}{\sqrt{2}},$$

and exact agreement with $H_d(e^{j\pi/2})$ [Eq. (I.8)] is verified.

A related example appears in §9.2.4 on page 215.

I.3   Digitizing Analog Filters with the Bilinear Transformation

The desirable properties of many filter types (such as lowpass, highpass, and bandpass) are preserved very well by the $s \leftrightarrow z$ mapping called the *bilinear transform*.

I.3.1   Bilinear Transformation

The *bilinear transform* may be defined by

$$s \;=\; c\frac{1 - z^{-1}}{1 + z^{-1}} \tag{I.9}$$

$$z^{-1} \;=\; \frac{1 - s/c}{1 + s/c} \tag{I.10}$$

where c is an arbitrary positive constant that we may set to map one analog frequency precisely to one digital frequency. In the case of a lowpass or highpass filter, c is typically used to set the *cut-off frequency* to be identical in the analog and digital cases.

I.3.2   Frequency Warping

It is easy to check that the bilinear transform gives a one-to-one, order-preserving, *conformal map* [57] between the analog frequency axis $s = j\omega_a$ and the digital frequency axis $z = e^{j\omega_d T}$, where T is the sampling interval. Therefore, the amplitude response takes on exactly the same values over both axes, with the only defect being a *frequency warping* such that equal increments along the unit circle in the z plane correspond to larger and larger bandwidths along the $j\omega$ axis in the s plane [88]. Some kind of frequency warping is obviously unavoidable in any one-to-one map because the analog frequency axis is infinite while the digital frequency axis is finite. The relation between the analog and digital frequency axes may be derived immediately from Eq. (I.9) as

$$
\begin{aligned}
j\omega_a &= c\frac{1 - e^{-j\omega_d T}}{1 + e^{-j\omega_d T}} = c\frac{e^{j\omega_d T} - 1}{e^{j\omega_d T} + 1} \\
&= c\frac{e^{j\omega_d T/2}\left(e^{j\omega_d T/2} - e^{-j\omega_d T/2}\right)}{e^{j\omega_d T/2}\left(e^{j\omega_d T/2} + e^{-j\omega_d T/2}\right)} \\
&= jc\frac{\sin(\omega_d T/2)}{\cos(\omega_d T/2)} \\
&= jc\tan(\omega_d T/2).
\end{aligned}
$$

Given an analog cut-off frequency $\omega_a = \omega_c$, to obtain the same cut-off frequency in the digital filter, we set

$$c = \omega_c \cot(\omega_c T/2)$$

I.3.3   Analog Prototype Filter

Since the digital cut-off frequency may be set to any value, irrespective of the analog cut-off frequency, it is convenient to set the analog cut-off frequency to $\omega_c = 1$. In this case, the bilinear-transform constant c is simply set to

$$c = \cot(\omega_c T/2)$$

when carrying out mapping Eq. (I.9) to convert the analog prototype to a digital filter with cut-off at frequency ω_c.

Examples

Examples of using the bilinear transform to "digitize" analog filters may be found in §I.2 on page 386 and [64, 5, 6, 103, 86]. Bilinear transform design is also inherent in the construction of *wave digital filters* [25, 86].

I.4   Filter Design by Minimizing the L2 Equation-Error Norm

One of the simplest formulations of recursive digital filter design is based on minimizing the *equation error*. This method allows matching of both spectral phase and magnitude. Equation-error methods can be classified as variations of *Prony's method* [48]. Equation error minimization is used very often in the field of *system identification* [46, 30, 78].

The problem of fitting a digital filter to a given spectrum may be formulated as follows:

Given a continuous complex function $H(e^{j\omega})$, $-\pi < \omega \le \pi$, corresponding to a causal[2] desired frequency-response, find a stable digital filter of the form

$$\hat{H}(z) \triangleq \frac{\hat{B}(z)}{\hat{A}(z)},$$

where

$$\hat{B}(z) \triangleq \hat{b}_0 + \hat{b}_1 z^{-1} + \cdots + \hat{b}_{n_b} z^{-n_b}$$
$$\hat{A}(z) \triangleq 1 + \hat{a}_1 z^{-1} + \cdots + \hat{a}_{n_a} z^{-n_a},$$

with n_b, n_a given, such that some norm of the error

$$J(\hat{\theta}) \triangleq \left\| H(e^{j\omega}) - \hat{H}(e^{j\omega}) \right\|$$

is minimum with respect to the filter coefficients

$$\hat{\theta}^T \triangleq \left[\hat{b}_0, \hat{b}_1, \dots, \hat{b}_{n_b}, \hat{a}_1, \hat{a}_2, \dots, \hat{a}_{n_a} \right]^T,$$

which are constrained to lie in a subset $\hat{\Theta} \subset \Re^N$, where $N \triangleq n_a + n_b + 1$. When explicitly stated, the filter coefficients may be complex, in which case $\hat{\Theta} \subset \mathbf{C}^N$.

The approximate filter $\hat{H}$ is typically *constrained* to be stable, and since positive powers of z do not appear in $\hat{B}(z)$, stability implies causality. Consequently, the impulse response of the filter $\hat{h}(n)$ is zero for $n < 0$. If H were noncausal, all impulse-response components $h(n)$ for $n < 0$ would be approximated by zero.

---

[2] $H(e^{j\omega})$ is said to be *causal* if $h(n) \triangleq \int_{-\pi}^{\pi} H(e^{j\omega}) e^{j\omega n} d\omega/2\pi = 0$ for $n < 0$.

I.4.1   Equation Error Formulation

The *equation error* is defined (in the frequency domain) as

$$E_{ee}(e^{j\omega}) \triangleq \hat{A}(e^{j\omega})H(e^{j\omega}) - \hat{B}(e^{j\omega})$$

By comparison, the more natural frequency-domain error is the so-called *output error*:

$$E_{oe}(e^{j\omega}) \triangleq H(e^{j\omega}) - \frac{\hat{B}(e^{j\omega})}{\hat{A}(e^{j\omega})}$$

The names of these errors make the most sense in the time domain. Let $x(n)$ and $y(n)$ denote the filter input and output, respectively, at time n. Then the equation error is the error in the *difference equation*:

$$
\begin{aligned}
e_{ee}(n) =\ & y(n) + \hat{a}_1 y(n-1) + \cdots + \hat{a}_{n_a} y(n - n_a) \\
- & \hat{b}_0 x(n) - \hat{b}_1 x(n-1) - \cdots - \hat{b}_{n_b} x(n - n_b)
\end{aligned}
$$

while the output error is the difference between the ideal and approximate filter *outputs*:

$$
\begin{aligned}
e_{oe}(n) =\ & y(n) - \hat{y}(n) \\
\hat{y}(n) =\ & \hat{b}_0 x(n) + \hat{b}_1 x(n-1) + \cdots + \hat{b}_{n_b} x(n - n_b) \\
& -\hat{a}_1 \hat{y}(n-1) - \cdots - \hat{a}_{n_a} \hat{y}(n - n_a)
\end{aligned}
$$

Denote the L^2 norm of the equation error by

$$J_E(\hat{\theta}) \triangleq \left\| \hat{A}(e^{j\omega})H(e^{j\omega}) - \hat{B}(e^{j\omega}) \right\|_2, \tag{I.11}$$

where $\hat{\theta}^T = [\hat{b}_0, \hat{b}_1, \ldots, \hat{b}_{n_b}, \hat{a}_1, \ldots, \hat{a}_{n_a}]$ is the vector of unknown filter coefficients. Then the problem is to minimize this norm with respect to $\hat{\theta}$. What makes the equation-error so easy to minimize is that it is *linear in the parameters*. In the time-domain form, it is clear that the equation error is linear in the unknowns $\hat{a}_i, \hat{b}_i$. When the error is linear in the parameters, the sum of squared errors is a *quadratic form* which can be minimized using one iteration of Newton's method. In other words, minimizing the L^2 norm of any error which is linear in the parameters results in a set of linear equations to solve. In the case of the equation-error minimization at hand, we will obtain $n_b + n_a + 1$ linear equations in as many unknowns.

Note that (I.11) can be expressed as

$$J_E(\hat{\theta}) = \left\| \left| \hat{A}(e^{j\omega}) \right| \cdot \left| H(e^{j\omega}) - \hat{H}(e^{j\omega}) \right| \right\|_2.$$

Thus, the equation-error can be interpreted as a *weighted output error* in which the frequency weighting function on the unit circle is given by $|\hat{A}(e^{j\omega})|$. Thus, the weighting function is determined by the filter *poles*, and the error is weighted *less* near the poles. Since the poles of a good filter-design tend toward regions of high spectral energy, or toward "irregularities" in the spectrum, it is evident that the equation-error criterion assigns less importance to the most prominent or structured spectral regions. On the other hand, far away from the roots of $\hat{A}(z)$, good fits to *both phase and magnitude* can be expected. The weighting effect can be eliminated through use of the *Steiglitz-McBride algorithm* [45, 78] which iteratively solves the weighted equation-error solution, using the canceling weight function from the previous iteration. When it converges (which is typical in practice), it must converge to the output error minimizer.

I.4.2 Error Weighting and Frequency Warping

Audio filter designs typically benefit from an *error weighting function* that weights frequencies according to their audibility. An oversimplified but useful weighting function is simply $1/\omega$, in which low frequencies are deemed generally more important than high frequencies. Audio filter designs also typically improve when using a *frequency warping*, such as described in [88, 78] (and similar to that in §I.3.2). In principle, the effect of a frequency-warping can be achieved using a weighting function, but in practice, the numerical performance of a frequency warping is often much better.

I.4.3 Stability of Equation Error Designs

A problem with equation-error methods is that *stability* of the filter design is *not guaranteed*. When an unstable design is encountered, one common remedy is to reflect unstable poles inside the unit circle, leaving the magnitude response unchanged while modifying the phase of the approximation in an ad hoc manner. This requires polynomial factorization of $\hat{A}(z)$ to find the filter poles, which is typically more work than the filter design itself.

A better way to address the instability problem is to repeat the filter design employing a *bulk delay*. This amounts to replacing $H(e^{j\omega})$ by

$$H_\tau(e^{j\omega}) \triangleq e^{-\omega\tau} H(e^{j\omega}), \quad \tau > 0,$$

and minimizing $|| \hat{A}(e^{j\omega}) H_\tau(e^{j\omega}) - \hat{B}(e^{j\omega}) ||_2$. This effectively *delays* the desired impulse response, *i.e.*, $h_\tau(n) = h(n - \tau)$. As the bulk delay is increased, the likelihood of obtaining an unstable design decreases, for reasons discussed in the next paragraph.

Unstable equation-error designs are especially likely when $H(e^{j\omega})$ is *noncausal*. Since there are no constraints on where the poles of $\hat{H}$ can be, one can expect unstable designs for desired frequency-response functions having a linear phase trend with positive slope.

In the other direction, experience has shown that best results are obtained when $H(z)$ is *minimum phase*, *i.e.*, when all the zeros of $H(z)$ are inside the unit circle. For a given magnitude, $|H(e^{j\omega})|$, minimum phase gives the maximum concentration of impulse-response energy near the time origin $n = 0$. Consequently, the impulse-response tends to start large and decay immediately. For non-minimum phase H, the impulse-response $h(n)$ may be small for the first $n_b + 1$ samples, and the equation error method can yield very poor filters in these cases. To see why this is so, consider a desired impulse-response $h(n)$ which is zero for $n \leq n_b$, and arbitrary thereafter. Transforming J_E^2 into the time domain yields

$$
\begin{aligned}
J_E^2(\hat{\theta}) &= \left\| \hat{a} * h(n) - \hat{b}(n) \right\|_2^2 \\
&= \sum_{n=0}^{\infty} \left(\hat{a} * h(n) - \hat{b}(n) \right)^2 \\
&= \sum_{n=0}^{n_b} \hat{b}_n^2 + \sum_{n=n_b+1}^{\infty} \left(\hat{a} * h(n) \right)^2 ,
\end{aligned}
$$

where "$*$" denotes convolution, and the additive decomposition is due the fact that $\hat{a} * h(n) = 0$ for $n \leq n_b$. In this case the minimum occurs for $\hat{B}(z) = 0 \Rightarrow \hat{H}(z) \equiv 0$! Clearly this is not a particularly good fit. Thus, the introduction of bulk-delay to guard against unstable designs is limited by this phenomenon.

It should be emphasized that for minimum-phase $H(e^{j\omega})$, equation-error methods are very effective. It is simple to convert a desired magnitude response into a minimum-phase frequency-response by use of cepstral techniques [22, 60] (see also the appendix below), and this is highly recommended when minimizing equation error. Finally, the error weighting by $|\hat{A}(e^{j\omega_k})|$ can usually be removed by a few iterations of the Steiglitz-McBride algorithm.

I.4.4   An FFT-Based Equation-Error Method

The algorithm below minimizes the equation error in the frequency-domain. As a result, it can make use of the FFT for speed. This algorithm is implemented in Matlab's `invfreqz()` function when no iteration-count is specified. (The iteration count gives that many iterations of the Steiglitz-

McBride algorithm, thus transforming equation error to output error after a few iterations. There is also a time-domain implementation of the
Steiglitz-McBride algorithm called `stmcb()` in the Matlab Signal Processing Toolbox, which takes the desired impulse response as input.)

Given a desired spectrum $H(e^{j\omega_k})$ at equally spaced frequencies $\omega_k = 2\pi k/N, k = 0, \ldots, N-1$, with N a power of 2, it is desired to find a rational
digital filter with n_b zeros and n_a poles,

$$\hat{H}(z) \triangleq \frac{\hat{B}(z)}{\hat{A}(z)} \triangleq \frac{\sum_{k=0}^{n_b} b_k z^{-k}}{\sum_{k=0}^{n_a} a_k z^{-k}},$$

normalized by $a_0 = 1$, such that

$$J_E^2 = \sum_{k=0}^{N-1} \left| \hat{A}(e^{j\omega_k}) H(e^{j\omega_k}) - \hat{B}(e^{j\omega_k}) \right|^2$$

is minimized.

Since J_E^2 is a quadratic form, the solution is readily obtained by equating the gradient to zero. An easier derivation follows from minimizing equation error variance in the time domain and making use of the orthogonality
principle [36]. This may be viewed as a system identification problem where
the known input signal is an impulse, and the known output is the desired
impulse response. A formulation employing an *arbitrary* known input is
valuable for introducing complex weighting across the frequency grid, and
this general form is presented. A detailed derivation appears in [78, Chapter
2], and here only the final algorithm is given:

Given spectral output samples $Y(e^{j\omega_k})$ and input samples $U(e^{j\omega_k})$, we
minimize

$$J_E^2 = \sum_{k=0}^{N-1} \left| \hat{A}(e^{j\omega_k}) Y(e^{j\omega_k}) - \hat{B}(e^{j\omega_k}) U(e^{j\omega_k}) \right|^2.$$

If $|U(e^{j\omega_k})|^2$ is to be used as a weighting function in the filter-design prob-
lem, then we set $Y(e^{j\omega_k}) = H(e^{j\omega_k}) U(e^{j\omega_k})$.

Let $\underline{x}[n_1 : n_2]$ denote the column vector determined by $x(n)$, for $n = n_1, \ldots, n_2$ filled in from top to bottom, and let $T(\underline{x}[n_1 : n_2])$ denote the
size $n_2 - n_1 + 1$ symmetric Toeplitz matrix consisting of $\underline{x}[n_1 : n_2]$ in its
first column. A nonsymmetric Toeplitz matrix may be specified by its
first column and row, and we use the notation $T(\underline{x}[n_1 : n_2], \underline{y}^T[m_1 : m_2])$ to
denote the $n_2 - n_1 + 1$ by $m_2 - m_1 + 1$ Toeplitz matrix with left-most
column $\underline{x}[n_1 : n_2]$ and top row $\underline{y}^T[m_1 : m_2]$. The inverse Fourier transform
of $X(e^{j\omega_k})$ is defined as

$$x(n) = \text{FFT}^{-1} X(e^{j\omega_k}) \triangleq \frac{1}{N} \sum_{k=0}^{N-1} X(e^{j\omega_k}) e^{j\omega_k n}.$$

The scaling by $1/N$ is optional since it has no effect on the solution. We require three correlation functions involving U and Y,

$$\underline{R}_{uu}(n) \triangleq \mathrm{FFT}^{-1} \left| U(e^{j\omega_k}) \right|^2$$
$$\underline{R}_{yy}(n) \triangleq \mathrm{FFT}^{-1} \left| Y(e^{j\omega_k}) \right|^2$$
$$\underline{R}_{yu}(n) \triangleq \mathrm{FFT}^{-1} Y(e^{j\omega_k}) \overline{U(e^{j\omega_k})}$$
$$n = 0, 1, \dots, N-1,$$

where the overbar denotes complex conjugation, and four corresponding Toeplitz matrices,

$$R_{yy} \triangleq T(\underline{R}_{yy}[0:n_a-1])$$
$$R_{uu} \triangleq T(\underline{R}_{uu}[0:n_b])$$
$$R_{yu} \triangleq T(\underline{R}_{yu}[-1:n_b-1], \underline{R}_{yu}^T[-1:-n_a])$$
$$R_{uy} \triangleq R_{uy}^T,$$

where negative indices are to be interpreted mod N, e.g., $R_{yu}(-1) = R_{yu}(N-1)$.

The solution is then

$$\hat{\theta}^* = \begin{bmatrix} \hat{\underline{B}}^* \\ \hat{\underline{A}}^* \end{bmatrix} = \begin{bmatrix} R_{uu} & R_{uy} \\ R_{yu} & R_{yy} \end{bmatrix}^{-1} \begin{bmatrix} \underline{R}_{yu}[0:n_b] \\ \underline{R}_{yy}[1:n_a] \end{bmatrix}$$

where

$$\underline{B}^* \triangleq \begin{bmatrix} \hat{b}_0^* \\ \vdots \\ \hat{b}_{n_b}^* \end{bmatrix}, \qquad \hat{\underline{A}}^* \triangleq \begin{bmatrix} \hat{a}_0^* \\ \vdots \\ \hat{a}_{n_a}^* \end{bmatrix},$$

I.4.5 Prony's Method

There are several variations on equation-error minimization, and some confusion in terminology exists. We use the definition of *Prony's method* given by Markel and Gray [48]. It is equivalent to "Shank's method" [9]. In this method, one first computes the denominator $\hat{A}^*(z)$ by minimizing

$$J_{\hat{S}}^2(\hat{\theta}) = \sum_{n=n_b+1}^{\infty} \left(\hat{a} * h(n) - \hat{b}(n) \right)^2$$
$$= \sum_{n=n_b+1}^{\infty} \left(\hat{a} * h(n) \right)^2 .$$

This step is equivalent to minimization of *ratio error* (as used in *linear prediction*) for the all-pole part $\hat{A}(z)$, with the first $n_b + 1$ terms of the time-domain error sum discarded (to get past the influence of the zeros on the impulse response). When $n_b = n_a - 1$, it coincides with the covariance method of linear prediction [48, 47]. This idea for finding the poles by "skipping" the influence of the zeros on the impulse-response shows up in the stochastic case under the name of *modified Yule-Walker equations* [11].

Now, Prony's method consists of next minimizing L^2 output error with the pre-assigned poles given by $\hat{A}^*(z)$. In other words, the numerator $\hat{B}(z)$ is found by minimizing

$$\left\| H(e^{j\omega}) - \frac{\hat{B}(e^{j\omega})}{\hat{A}^*(e^{j\omega})} \right\|_2 ,$$

where $\hat{A}^*(e^{j\omega})$ is now known. This hybrid method is not as sensitive to the time distribution of $h(n)$ as is the pure equation-error method. In particular, the degenerate equation-error example above (in which $\hat{H} \equiv 0$ was obtained) does not fare so badly using Prony's method.

I.4.6   The Padé-Prony Method

Another variation of Prony's method, described by Burrus and Parks [9] consists of using *Padé* approximation to find the numerator $\hat{B}^*$ after the denominator $\hat{A}^*$ has been found as before. Thus, $\hat{B}^*$ is found by matching the first $n_b + 1$ samples of $h(n)$, viz., $\hat{b}_n^* = \hat{a}^* * h(n), n = 0 \dots, n_b$. This method is faster, but does not generally give as good results as the previous version. In particular, the degenerate example $h(n) = 0, n \leq n_b$ gives $\hat{H}^*(z) \equiv 0$ here as did pure equation error. This method has been applied also in the stochastic case [11].

On the whole, when $H(e^{j\omega})$ is causal and minimum phase (the ideal situation for just about any stable filter-design method), the variants on equation-error minimization described in this section perform very similarly. They are all quite fast, relative to algorithms which iteratively minimize output error, and the equation-error method based on the FFT above is generally fastest.

Appendix J

Matlab Utilities

This appendix provides software listings for various analysis utilities written in matlab. Except for plot-related commands, they should be compatible either Matlab or Octave.

J.1   Time Plots: `myplot.m`

```
function myplot(xdata, ydata, sym, ttl, xlab, ylab, grd, ...
                  lgnd, linewidth, fontsize)
% MYPLOT - Generic plot - compatibility wrapper for plot()

  if nargin<10, fontsize=12; end
  if nargin<9, linewidth=1; end
  if nargin<8, lgnd=''; end
  if nargin<7, grd=1; end
  if nargin<6, ylab=''; end
  if nargin<5, xlab=''; end
  if nargin<4, ttl=''; end
  if nargin<3, sym=''; end
  if nargin<2, ydata=xdata; xdata=0:length(ydata)-1; end

  plot(xdata,ydata,sym,'linewidth',linewidth);
  if length(ttl)>0, title(ttl,'fontsize',fontsize,...
                             'fontname','helvetica');
  end
  if length(ylab)>0, ylabel(ylab,'fontsize',fontsize,...
                                 'fontname','helvetica');
  end
  if length(xlab)>0, xlabel(xlab,'fontsize',fontsize,...
                                 'fontname','helvetica');
  end
  if grd, grid('on'); else grid('off'); end
  if length(lgnd)>0, legend(lgnd); end
```

Figure J.1: Compatibility matlab function for plotting a real-valued function—Matlab or Octave version.

J.2   Frequency Plots: freqplot.m

```
function freqplot(fdata, ydata, symbol, ttl, xlab, ylab)
% FREQPLOT - Plot a function of frequency.
%              See myplot for more features.

  if nargin<6, ylab=''; end
  if nargin<5, xlab='Frequency (Hz)'; end
  if nargin<4, ttl=''; end
  if nargin<3, symbol=''; end
  if nargin<2, fdata=0:length(ydata)-1; end

  plot(fdata,ydata,symbol); grid;
  if ttl, title(ttl); end
  if ylab, ylabel(ylab); end
  xlabel(xlab);
```

Figure J.2: Compatibility matlab function for plotting a real-valued function of frequency.

J.3   Saving Plots to Disk: saveplot.m

```
function saveplot(filename)
% SAVEPLOT - Save current plot to disk in a .png file.

cmd = ['print -dpng ',filename]; % .png graphics format
% For monochrome PostScript format:
%      cmd = ['print -deps ',filename];
% For color PostScript format:
%      cmd = ['print -depsc ',filename];
% Etc. - say 'help print' in either Matlab or Octave
disp(cmd); eval(cmd);
```

Figure J.3: Matlab/Octave function for saving a plot to disk.

J.4   Frequency Response Plots: `plotfr.m`

Figure J.4 lists a Matlab function for plotting frequency-response magnitude and phase. (See also Fig. 7.1 on page 156.) Since Octave does not yet support saving multiple "subplots" to disk for later printing, we do not have an Octave-compatible version here. At present, Matlab's graphics support is much more extensive and robust than that in Octave's (which is based on a shaky and Matlab-incompatible interface to `gnuplot`). Another free alternative to consider for making nice Matlab-style 2D plots is `matplotlib`.[1]

---

[1] `http://matplotlib.sourceforge.net/`

```
function [plothandle] = plotfr(X,f);
% PLOTFR - Plot frequency-response magnitude & phase.
%          Requires Mathworks Matlab.
%
% X = frequency response
% f = vector of corresponding frequency values

Xm = abs(X);          % Amplitude response
Xmdb = 20*log10(Xm);  % Prefer dB for audio work
Xp = angle(X);        % Phase response

if nargin<2, N=length(X); f=(0:N-1)/(2*(N-1)); end
subplot(2,1,1);
plot(f,Xmdb,'-k'); grid;
ylabel('Gain (dB)');
xlabel('Normalized Frequency (cycles/sample)');
axis tight;
text(-0.07,max(Xmdb),'(a)');

subplot(2,1,2);
plot(f,Xp,'-k'); grid;
ylabel('Phase Shift (radians)');
xlabel('Normalized Frequency (cycles/sample)');
axis tight;
text(-0.07,max(Xp),'(b)');

if exist('OCTAVE_VERSION')
  plothandle = 0; % gcf undefined in Octave
else
  plothandle = gcf;
end
```

Figure J.4: Matlab function for plotting frequency-response magnitude and phase.

J.5   Partial Fraction Expansion: `residuez.m`

Figure J.5 gives a listing of a matlab function for computing a "left-justified" partial fraction expansion (PFE) of an IIR digital filter $H(z) = B(z)/A(z)$ as described in §6.8 on page 129 (and below). This function, along with its "right justified" counterpart, `residued`, are included in the `octave-forge` matlab library for Octave.[2]

```
function [r, p, f, m] = residuez(B, A, tol)
if nargin<3, tol=0.001; end
NUM = B(:)'; DEN = A(:)';
% Matlab's residue does not return m (implied by p):
[r,p,f,m]=residue(conj(fliplr(NUM)),conj(fliplr(DEN)),tol);
p = 1 ./ p;
r = r .* ((-p) .^m);
if f, f = conj(fliplr(f)); end
```

Figure J.5: Matlab/Octave function for computing the partial fraction expansion of an IIR digital filter.

This code was written for Octave, but it also runs in Matlab if the 'm' outputs (pole multiplicity counts) are omitted (two places). The input arguments are compatible with the existing `residuez` function in the Matlab Signal Processing Toolbox.

J.5.1   Method

As can be seen from the code listing, this implementation of `residuez` simply calls `residue`, which was written to carry out the partial fraction expansions of s-plane (continuous-time) transfer functions $H(s)$:

$$
\begin{aligned}
H(s) &= \frac{B(s)}{A(s)} \\
&= \frac{b_0 s^M + b_1 s^{M-1} + \cdots + b_{M-1}s + b_M}{a_0 s^N + a_1 s^{N-1} + \cdots + a_{N-1}s + a_N} \\
&= F(s) + R(s)
\end{aligned}
$$

---

[2]On a Red Hat Fedora Core Linux system, `octave-forge` is presently in "Fedora Extras", so that one can simply type `yum install octave-forge` at a shell prompt (as root).

where $F(s)$ is the "quotient" and $R(s)$ is the "remainder" in the PFE:

$$
\begin{aligned}
F(s) &\triangleq f_0 s^L + f_1 s^{L-1} + \cdots + f_{L-1} s + f_L \\
R(s) &\triangleq \frac{r_1}{(s - p_1)_1^m} + \cdots + \frac{r_N}{(s - p_N)_N^m}
\end{aligned}
\tag{J.1}
$$

where $L = M - N$ is the order of the quotient polynomial in s, and m_i is the *multiplicity* of the ith pole. (When all poles are distinct, we have $m_i = 1$ for all i.) For $M < N$, we define $F(s) = 0$.

In the discrete-time case, we have the z-plane transfer function

$$
\begin{aligned}
H(z) &= \frac{B(z)}{A(z)} \\
&= \frac{b_0 + b_1 z^{-1} + \cdots + b_{M-1} z^{-(M-1)} + b_M z^{-M}}{a_0 + a_1 z^{-1} + \cdots + a_{N-1} z^{-(N-1)} + a_N z^{-N}}.
\end{aligned}
\tag{J.2}
$$

For compatibility with Matlab's residuez, we need a PFE of the form $H(z) = F(z) + R(z)$ such that

$$
\begin{aligned}
F(z) &\triangleq f_0 + f_1 z^{-1} + \cdots + f_{L-1} z^{-(L-1)} + f_L z^{-L} \\
R(z) &\triangleq \frac{r_1}{(1 - p_1 z^{-1})_1^m} + \cdots \frac{r_N}{(1 - p_N z^{-1})_N^m}
\end{aligned}
$$

where $L = M - N$.

We see that the s-plane case formally does what we desire if we treat z-plane polynomials as polynomials in z^{-1} instead of z. From Eq. (J.2), we see that this requires reversing the coefficient-order of B and A in the call to residue. In the returned result, we obtain terms such as

$$
\frac{\rho_i}{(s - \pi_i)^{m_i}} \triangleq \frac{\rho_i}{(z^{-1} - \pi_i)^{m_i}} = \frac{(-1)^{m_i} \rho_i \pi_i^{-m_i}}{(1 - \pi_i^{-1} z^{-1})^{m_i}}
$$

where the second form is simply the desired canonical form for z-plane PFE terms. Thus, the ith pole is

$$
p_i = \pi_i^{-1}
$$

and the ith residue is

$$
r_i = \frac{\rho_i}{(-\pi_i)^{m_i}}.
$$

Finally, the returned quotient polynomial must be flipped for the same reason that the input polynomials needed to be flipped (to convert from left-to-right descending powers of z^{-1} [s] in the returned result to ascending powers of z^{-1}).

J.5.2   Example with Repeated Poles

The following Matlab code performs a partial fraction expansion of a filter having three pairs of repeated roots (one real and two complex):[3]

```matlab
N = 1000;  % number of time samples to compute
A = [ 1 0 0 1 0 0 0.25];
B = [ 1 0 0 0 0 0 0];

% Compute "trusted" impulse response:
h_tdl = filter(B, A, [1 zeros(1, N-1)]);

% Compute partial fraction expansion (PFE):
[R,P,K] = residuez(B, A);

% PFE impulse response:
n = [0:N-1];
h_pfe = zeros(1,N);
for i = 1:size(R)
  % repeated roots are not detected exactly:
  if i>1 && abs(P(i)-P(i-1))<1E-7
    h_pfe = h_pfe + (R(i) * (n+1) .* P(i).^n);
    disp(sprintf('Pole %d is a repeat of pole %d',i,i-1));
    % if i>2 && abs(P(i)-P(i-2))<1E-7 ...
  else
    h_pfe = h_pfe + (R(i) * P(i).^n);
  end
end

err = abs(max(h_pfe-h_tdl)) % should be about 5E-8
```

---

[3]Thanks to Matt Wright for contributing the original version of this example.

J.6   Partial Fraction Expansion: `residued.m`

Figure J.6 gives a listing of a matlab function for computing a "right justified" partial fraction expansion (PFE) of an IIR digital filter $H(z) =
B(z)/A(z)$ as described in §6.8 on page 129 (and below).

The code in Fig. J.6 was written to work in Octave, and also in Matlab
if the 'm' argument is omitted (in two places).

```
function [r, p, f, e] = residued(b, a, toler)
if nargin<3, toler=0.001; end
NUM = b(:)';
DEN = a(:)';
nb = length(NUM);
na = length(DEN);
f = [];
if na<=nb
  f = filter(NUM,DEN,[1,zeros(nb-na)]);
  NUM = NUM - conv(DEN,f);
  NUM = NUM(nb-na+2:end);
end
[r,p,f2,e] = residuez(NUM,DEN,toler);
```

Figure J.6: Matlab/Octave function for computing the group delay
of a digital filter.

Method

The FIR part is first extracted, and the (strictly proper) remainder is passed
to `residuez` for expansion of the IIR part (into a sum of complex resonators). One must remember that, in this case, the impulse-response of
the IIR part $R(z)$ begins *after* the impulse-response of the FIR part $F(z)$
has finished, *i.e.*,

$$H(z) = F(z) + z^{-N_f} R(z)$$

where N_f is the length of the FIR part (order of $F(z)$ plus 1).

See §6.8.8 on page 142 for an example usage of `residued` (with a
comparison to `residuez`).

J.7   Parallel SOS to Transfer Function: `psos2tf`

Figure J.7 lists a matlab function for computing the direct-form transfer-function polynomials $B(z)/A(z)$ from *parallel* second-order section coefficients. This is in contrast to the existing function `sos2tf` which converts *series* second-order sections to transfer-function form.

```
function [B,A] = psos2tf(sos,g)

if nargin<2, g=1; end

[nsecs,tmp] = size(sos);
if nsecs<1, B=[]; A=[]; return; end
Bs = sos(:,1:3);
As = sos(:,4:6);
B = Bs(1,:);
A = As(1,:);
for i=2:nsecs
  B = conv(B,As(i,:)) + conv(A,Bs(i,:));
  A = conv(A,As(i,:));
end
```

Figure J.7: Matlab/Octave function for computing direct-form transfer-function coefficients B and A from a matrix of second-order section coefficients `sos` and overall gain factor `g`.

J.8 Group Delay Computation: grpdelay.m

Figure J.8 gives a listing of a matlab program for computing the group delay of an IIR digital filter $H(z) = B(z)/A(z)$ using the method described in §7.6.6 on page 169.

In Matlab with the Signal Processing Toolbox installed, (or Octave with the Octave Forge package installed), say 'help grpdelay' for usage documentation, and say 'type grpdelay' to additionally see test, demo, and plotting code. Here, we include only the code relevant to computation of the group delay itself.

```
function [gd,w] = grpdelay(b,a,nfft,whole,Fs)

  if (nargin<1 || nargin>5)
    usage("[g,w]=grpdelay(b [, a [, n [,'whole'[,Fs]]]])");
  end
  if nargin<5
    Fs=0; % return w in radians per sample
    if nargin<4, whole='';
    elseif ~isstr(whole)
      Fs = whole;
      whole = '';
    end
    if nargin<3, nfft=512; end
    if nargin<2, a=1; end
  end

  if strcmp(whole,'whole')==0, nfft = 2*nfft; end

  w = 2*pi*[0:nfft-1]/nfft;
  if Fs>0, w = Fs*w/(2*pi); end

  oa = length(a)-1;              % order of a(z)
  oc = oa + length(b)-1;        % order of c(z)
  c = conv(b,fliplr(a)); % c(z) = b(z)*a(1/z)*z^(-oa)
  cr = c.*[0:oc];               % derivative of c wrt 1/z
  num = fft(cr,nfft);
  den = fft(c,nfft);
  minmag = 10*eps;
  polebins = find(abs(den)<minmag);
  for b=polebins
    disp('*** grpdelay: group delay singular! setting to 0')
    num(b) = 0;
    den(b) = 1;
  end
  gd = real(num ./ den) - oa;

  if strcmp(whole,'whole')==0
    ns = nfft/2; % Matlab convention - should be nfft/2 + 1
    gd = gd(1:ns);
    w = w(1:ns);
  end

  w = w'; % Matlab returns column vectors
  gd = gd';
```

Figure J.8: Matlab/Octave function for computing the group delay of a digital filter.

J.9   Matlab listing: `fold.m`

The `fold()` function "time-aliases" the noncausal part of a function onto
its causal part. When applied to the inverse Fourier transform of a log-
spectrum, it converts non-minimum-phase zeros to minimum-phase zeros.
(See §J.11 for an example usage.)

```
function [rw] = fold(r)
% [rw] = fold(r)
% Fold left wing of vector in "FFT buffer format"
% onto right wing
% J.O. Smith, 1982-2002

  [m,n] = size(r);
  if m*n ~= m+n-1
    error('fold.m: input must be a vector');
  end
  flipped = 0;
  if (m > n)
    n = m;
    r = r.';
    flipped = 1;
  end
  if n < 3, rw = r; return;
  elseif mod(n,2)==1,
      nt = (n+1)/2;
      rw = [ r(1), r(2:nt) + conj(r(n:-1:nt+1)), ...
             0*ones(1,n-nt) ];
  else
      nt = n/2;
      rf = [r(2:nt),0];
      rf = rf + conj(r(n:-1:nt+1));
      rw = [ r(1) , rf , 0*ones(1,n-nt-1) ];
  end;

  if flipped
    rw = rw.';
  end
```

Figure J.9: Matlab/Octave `fold` function.

J.10   Matlab listing: `clipdb.m`

The `clipdb()` function prevents the log magnitude of a signal from being too large and negative. (See §J.11 for an example usage.)

```
function [clipped] = clipdb(s,cutoff)
% [clipped] = clipdb(s,cutoff)
% Clip magnitude of s at its maximum + cutoff in dB.
% Example: clip(s,-100) makes sure the minimum magnitude
% of s is not more than 100dB below its maximum magnitude.
% If s is zero, nothing is done.

clipped = s;
as = abs(s);
mas = max(as(:));
if mas==0, return; end
if cutoff >= 0, return; end
thresh = mas*10^(cutoff/20); % db to linear
toosmall = find(as < thresh);
clipped = s;
clipped(toosmall) = thresh;
```

J.11   Matlab listing: mps.m and test program

This section lists and describes the Matlab/Octave function mps which estimates a minimum-phase spectrum given only the spectral magnitude. A test program for mps together with a listing of its output are given in §J.11 below. See §11.7 on page 240 for related discussion.

Matlab listing: mps.m

```
function [sm] = mps(s)
% [sm] = mps(s)
% create minimum-phase spectrum sm from complex spectrum s
  sm = exp( fft( fold( ifft( log( clipdb(s,-100) )))));
```

The clipdb and fold utilities are listed and described in §J.10 and §J.9, respectively.

Note that mps.m must be given a *whole spectrum* in "FFT buffer format". That is, it must contain dc and positive-frequency values followed by negative frequency values and be a power of 2 in length.

The mps function works well as long as the desired frequency response is *smooth*. If there are any zeros on the frequency axis ("notches"), the corresponding minimum-phase impulse response will be *time aliased* because the corresponding exponentials in the cepstrum never decay. To suppress time-aliasing to some extent, the desired frequency response magnitude is clipped to 100 dB below its maximum. Time aliasing can be reduced by interpolating the desired frequency response s to a higher sampling density (thereby increasing the time available for exponential decay in the cepstral domain). However, for pure notches (zeros right on the unit circle), no amount of oversampling will eliminate the time aliasing completely. To avoid time aliasing in the cepstrum, such a desired spectrum must be *smoothed* before taking the log and inverse FFT. Zero-phase smoothing of the spectral magnitude is a typical choice for this purpose. When greater accuracy is required, all notch frequencies can be estimated so that terms of the form $1 - \exp[j(\theta_i - \omega)]$ can be effectively "divided out" of the desired spectrum and carried along as separate factors.

Matlab listing: tmps.m

Below is the test script (for ease of copy/paste extraction for online viewers). Following is the test script along with its output.

Note that this is a toy example intended only for checking the code on a simple example, and to illustrate how a spectrum gets passed in. In particular, the would-be minimum-phase impulse response computed by this example is clearly not even causal (thus indicating an insufficient spectral sampling density [FFT length]). Moreover, the starting spectrum (a sampled ideal lowpass-filter frequency response) has zeros on the unit circle, so there is *no sampling density* that is truly sufficient in the frequency domain (no sufficiently long FFT in the time domain).

```
spec = [1 1 1 0 0 0 1 1]'; % Lowpass cutting off at fs*3/8
format short;
mps(spec)
abs(mps(spec))
ifft(spec)
ifft(mps(spec))
```

Matlab diary: tmps.d

Below is the output of the test script with echo on in Matlab.

```
spec = [1 1 1 0 0 0 1 1]'; % Lowpass cutting off at fs*3/8
format short;
mps(spec)

ans =
   1.0000 - 0.0000i
   0.3696 - 0.9292i
  -0.2830 - 0.9591i
   0.0000 - 0.0000i
   0.0000 + 0.0000i
   0.0000 + 0.0000i
  -0.2830 + 0.9591i
   0.3696 + 0.9292i

abs(mps(spec))

ans =
   1.0000
   1.0000
   1.0000
   0.0000
   0.0000
   0.0000
   1.0000
   1.0000
```

```
ifft(spec)

ans =
   0.6250
   0.3018 - 0.0000i
  -0.1250
  -0.0518 - 0.0000i
   0.1250
  -0.0518 + 0.0000i
  -0.1250
   0.3018 + 0.0000i

ifft(mps(spec))

ans =
   0.1467 - 0.0000i
   0.5944 - 0.0000i
   0.4280 - 0.0000i
  -0.0159 - 0.0000i
  -0.0381 - 0.0000i
   0.1352 - 0.0000i
  -0.0366 - 0.0000i
  -0.2137 - 0.0000i
```

(The last four terms above would be zero if the result were causal.)

J.12   Signal Plots: `swanalplot.m`

Figure J.10 lists a Matlab script for plotting input and output signals for the simplest lowpass filter in §2.2 on page 30, used in Fig. 2.4 on page 31 to produce Fig. 2.5 on page 33. This is not really a "utility" since it relies on global variables. It is instead a script containing mundane plotting code that was omitted from Fig. 2.4 to make it fit on one page. I include it only because people keep asking for it! The script is compatible with Matlab only.

```matlab
%swanalplot.m - plots needed by swanal.m

doplots = 1; % set to 0 to skip plots
dopause = 0; % set to 1 to pause after each plot
if doplots
  figure(gcf);
  subplot(2,1,1);
  ttl=sprintf('Filter Input Sinusoid, f(%d)=%0.2f',k,f(k));
  myplot(t,s,'*k',ttl);
  tinterp=0:(t(2)-t(1))/10:t(end); % interpolated time axis
  si = ampin*cos(2*pi*f(k)*tinterp+phasein); % for plot
  text(-1.5,0,'(a)');
  hold on; plot(tinterp,si,'--k'); hold off;
  subplot(2,1,2);
  ttl='Filter Output Sinusoid';
  myplot(t,y,'*k',ttl);
  text(-1.5,0,'(b)');
  if dopause, disp('PAUSING - [RETURN] to continue . . .');
  pause; end
  saveplot(sprintf('../eps/swanal-%d.eps',k));
end
```

Figure J.10: Matlab script for plotting input/output signals in Fig. 2.5 on page 33.

J.13   Frequency Response Plot: swanalmainplot

Figure J.11 lists a matlab script for plotting (in Fig. 2.7 on page 35) the
overlay of the theoretical frequency response with that measured using simulated sine-wave analysis for the case of the simplest lowpass filter. It is
written to run in the specific context of the matlab script listed in Fig. 2.3
of §2.2 on page 30. This is not a general-purpose "utility" because it relies
on global variables defined in the calling script. This script is included only
for completeness.

```
% swanalmainplot.m
% Compare measured and theoretical frequency response.
% This script is invoked by swanalmainplot.m and family,
% and requires context set up by the caller.

figure(N+1); % figure number is arbitary

subplot(2,1,1);
ttl = 'Amplitude Response';
freqplot(f,gains,'*k',ttl,'Frequency (Hz)','Gain');
tar = 2*cos(pi*f/fs); % theoretical amplitude response
hold on; freqplot(f,tar,'-k'); hold off;
text(-0.08,mean(ylim),'(a)');

subplot(2,1,2);
ttl = 'Phase Response';
tpr = -pi*f/fs; % theoretical phase response
pscl = 1/(2*pi);% convert radian phase shift to cycles
freqplot(f,tpr*pscl,'-k',ttl,'Frequency (cycles)',...
'Phase shift (cycles)');
hold on; freqplot(f,phases*pscl,'*k'); hold off;
text(-0.08,mean(ylim),'(b)');
saveplot(plotfile); % set by caller
```

Figure J.11: Matlab script for plotting overlay of theoretical frequency response with that measured using simulated sine-wave analysis.

Appendix K

Digital Filtering in Faust and PD

This appendix describes use of the *Faust programming language*[1] by Yann Orlarey et al. at GRAME [61, 31] to generate real-time DSP plugins from a high-level specification. In addition to generating efficient inner loops, Faust supports Graphical User Interface (GUI) specification in the source code, and can emit code for various application and plugin environments.[2] Moreover, Faust can generate easy-to-read block diagrams directly from the source, illustrating signal flow and processing graphically. This appendix focuses on generating pd, LADSPA, and VST plugins from a simple Faust program specifying a resonator driven by white noise.

The software discussed in this appendix can be downloaded as a compressed tarball:

http://ccrma.stanford.edu/~jos/faust/faustpd.tar.gz

Additional software and more advanced examples can be found in [85].

K.1   A Simple Faust Program

Figure K.1 lists a minimal Faust program specifying the constant-peak-gain resonator discussed in §B.6.4 on page 290. This appendix does not

---

[1]The Faust home page is http://faust.grame.fr/. Faust is included in the Planet CCRMA distribution (http://ccrma.stanford.edu/planetccrma/software/). The examples in this appendix have been tested with Faust version 0.9.9.2a2.

[2]Faust "architecture files" and plugin-generators are currently available for Max/MSP, PD [65, 31], VST, LADSPA, ALSA-GTK, JACK-GTK, and SuperCollider, as of this writing.

cover the Faust language itself, so the Faust Tutorial,[3] or equivalent, should be considered prerequisite reading. We will summarize briefly, however, the Faust operators relevant to this example: signal processing blocks are connected in series via a colon (:), and feedback is indicated by a tilde (˜). The colon and tilde operators act on "block diagrams" to create a larger block diagram. There are also signal operators. For example, a unit-sample delay is indicated by appending a prime (') after a signal variable; thus, x' expands to x : MEM and indicates a signal obtained by delaying the signal x by one sample.

Function application applies to operator symbols as well as names; thus, for example, +(x) expands to _,x : +, and *(x) expands to _,x : *, where _ denotes a simple "wire". There is a special unary minus in Faust (as of release 0.9.9.4), so that -x is equivalent to 0 - x. However, -(x) still expands to _,x : -, which is a blockdiagram that subtracts signal x from the input signal on _ .

The with block provides local definitions in the context of the process definition.[4]

Other aspects of the language used in this example should be fairly readable to those having a typical programming background. [5]

```
process = firpart : + ˜ feedback
with {
  bw = 100; fr = 1000; g = 1; // parameters - see caption
  SR = fconstant(int fSamplingFreq, <math.h>); // Faust fn
  pi = 4*atan(1.0);      // circumference over diameter
  R = exp(0-pi*bw/SR); // pole radius [0 required]
  A = 2*pi*fr/SR;        // pole angle (radians)
  RR = R*R;
  firpart(x) = (x - x'') * g * ((1-RR)/2);
  // time-domain coefficients ASSUMING ONE PIPELINE DELAY:
  feedback(v) = 0 + 2*R*cos(A)*v - RR*v';
};
```

Figure K.1: Faust program specifying a constant-peak-gain resonator. Input parameters are the resonance frequency fr (Hz), resonance bandwidth bw (Hz), and the desired peak-gain g.

---

[3]http://www.grame.fr/pub/faust_tutorial.pdf

[4]A "with" block is not required, but it minimizes "global name pollution." In other words, a definition and its associated with block are more analogous to a C function definition in which local variables may be used. Faust statements can be in any order, so multiple definitions of the same symbol are not allowed. A with block can thus be used also to override global definitions in a local context.

[5]Facility with basic C++ programming is also assumed for this appendix.

Constants such as RR in Fig. K.1 are better thought of as *constant signals*. As a result, operators such as * (multiplication) conceptually act only on signals. Thus, the expression 2*x denotes the constant-signal $2, 2, 2, \ldots$ muliplied pointwise by the signal x. The Faust compiler does a good job of optimizing expressions so that operations are not repeated unnecessarily at run time. In summary, a Faust expression expands into a block diagram which processes causal signals,[6] some of which may be constant signals.

K.2   Generating Faust Block Diagrams

When learning the Faust language, it can be helpful to generate a block diagram using the -svg option. For example, the command

```
> faust -svg cpgr.dsp
```

creates a subdirectory of the current working directory named cpgr.dsp-svg which contains a "scalable vector graphics" (.svg) file for each block-diagram expression in cpgr.dsp.[7] For this example, there is a block diagram generated for the process line, and for each of the last five lines in the with clause (not counting the comment).

Figure K.2 shows the block diagram generated for the main process block from Fig. K.1:

```
process = firpart : + ~ feedback
```

The dot on each block indicates its standard orientation (analogous to a "pin 1" indicator on an integrated circuit chip). The small open square at the beginning of the feedback loop indicates a *unit sample delay* introduced by creating a signal loop. Needless to say, it is important to keep track of such added delays in a feedback loop.

Figure K.3 shows the block diagram generated for the firpart abstraction:

```
firpart(x) = (x - x'') * g * ((1-RR)/2);
```

Similarly, Fig. K.4 shows the block diagram generated for the feedback path:

```
feedback(v) = 0 + 2*R*cos(A)*v - RR*v';
```

If not for the added sample of delay in the feedback loop (indicated by the small open square in Fig. K.2), the feedback-path processing would have been instead 0 + 2*R*cos(A)*v' - RR*v''.

---

[6]A *causal signal* is any signal that is zero before time 0 (see §5.3).

[7]The faust2firefox script (distributed with Faust version 0.9.9.3 and later) can be used to generate SVG block diagrams and open them in the Firefox web browser.

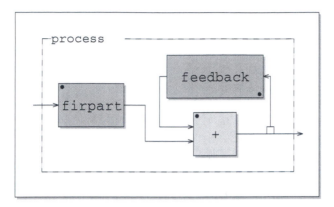

Figure K.2: Main *process* block for the constant-peak-gain resonator.

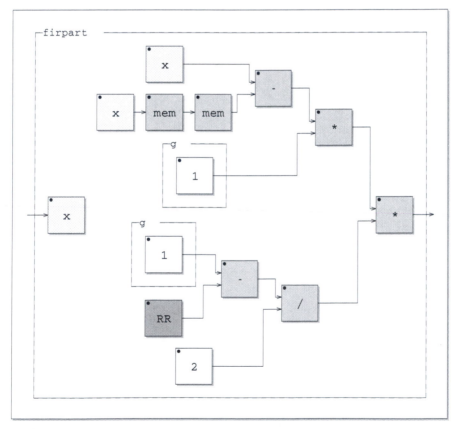

Figure K.3: FIR-part ((x - x'') * g * ((1-RR)/2)) in Faust.

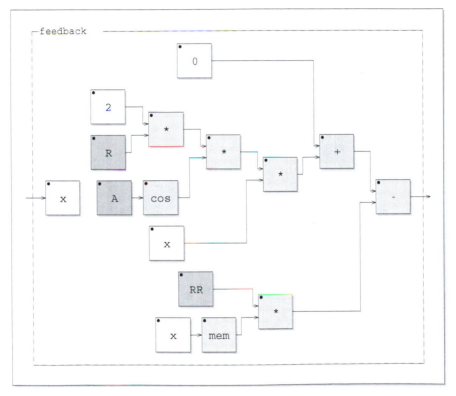

Figure K.4: Feedback block (0 + 2*R*cos(A)*x - RR*x') in Faust.

Note that the block diagrams are drawn as though all details of the expression are to be evaluated every sample. However, the Faust compiler instead computes constant expressions at init time and allocates memory locations for them. More generally, the Faust compiler separately optimizes full-rate signals at the sampling rate (calculated in the inner loop), slowly varying signals (updated at the "buffer rate" outside of the inner loop—currently every 64 samples), and constant signals (evaluated once at initialization time).

K.3   Testing a Faust Filter Section

It takes a bit of experience to write a correct Faust program on the first try. Therefore, we often have to *debug* our programs by some technique. Typically, inspecting the automatically generated block diagrams and listening to the results are tools enough for debugging Faust source code. However, sometimes it is useful to verify the output signal(s) in more detail. For this purpose, Faust has a useful "architecture file" named plot.cpp which results in generation of a main C++ program that simply prints the output signal(s) to the standard output. This printout can be used to plot the output (using, *e.g.*, gnuplot) or compare it to the output of some other program. This section gives an example of comparing the impulse response of the filter in Fig. K.1 to the output of a matlab version (Chapter 2). Specifically, we will compare the printed output from the Faust-generated program to the output of the matlab test program shown in Fig. K.5.

```
SR = 44100; % Sampling rate

fr = 1000;  % Resonant frequency
bw = 100;   % Bandwidth
g  = 1;     % Peak gain
N = 10;     % Samples to generate in test

R = exp(-pi*bw/SR); % pole radius
A = 2*pi*fr/SR;     % pole angle (radians)
firpart = g * [1 0 -1] * (1-R^2)/2;
feedback = [1 -2*R*cos(A) R^2]; % freq-domain coeffs
freqz(firpart,feedback);        % freq-response display
format long;
h = impz(firpart,feedback,N)    % print impulse response
```

Figure K.5: Constant Peak-Gain Resonator—matlab version

In our Faust program, we need a test impulse, *e.g.*,

```
process = 1-1' : firpart : + ~ feedback
with { ... <same as before> ... };
```

The signal $1 = [1, 1, 1, \ldots]$ is the unit-step signal consisting of all ones, and $1' = [0, 1, 1, \ldots]$ is the unit step delayed by one sample. Therefore, $1-1'$ is the impulse signal $\delta = [1, 0, 0, \ldots]$.

Suppose the file `cpgrir.dsp` ("Constant-Peak-Gain Resonator Impulse-Response") contains our test Faust program. Then we can generate the impulse-response printout as follows at the command line:

```
> faust -a plot.cpp -o cpgrir-print.cpp cpgrir.dsp
> g++ -Wall -g -lm -lpthread cpgrir-print.cpp -o cpgrir-print
> cpgrir-print -n 10
```

The first line generates the C++ program `cpgrir.cpp` from the Faust source file `cpgrir.dsp` using the architecture file `plot.cpp`. The second line compiles the C++ file to produce the executable program `cpgrir-print`. Finally, the third line generates and prints the first 10 samples of the output signal (anything more than the number of filter coefficients is usually enough), which is our desired impulse response:[8]

```
h = [    0.00707331   0.0139039    0.013284
         0.012405     0.0112882    0.00995947
         0.00844865   0.00678877   0.00501544
         0.00316602      ... ]
```

The matlab version produces the following impulse response:

```
h =
[ 0.00707328459864603 0.01390382707778288 0.01328399389241600
  0.01240496991806334 0.01128815312793390 0.00995943544693653
  0.00844861689634155 0.00678874919376101 0.00501542304704597
  0.00316601431505539 ... ]
```

Since matlab uses double-precision floating-point while Faust only supports single-precision `floats`, we will normally see differences after six or so decimal digits.

K.4   A Look at the Generated C++ code

Running Faust with no architecture file, *e.g.*,

---

[8]This specific output was obtained by editing `cpgrir-print.cpp` to replace %8f by %g in the print statements, in order to print more significant digits.

```
> faust cpgrir.dsp
```

causes the C++ signal-processing code to be printed on the standard output, as shown for this example in Fig. K.6. Notice how the constant subexpressions are computed only once per instance in the `instanceInit` member function. Also, even in `instanceInit`, which is only called once, repeated computation of R^2 is avoided by use of the temporary variable `fConst1`, and division by 2 is converted to multiplication by 0.5.

K.5   Generating a Pure Data (PD) Plugin

This section illustrates making a `pd` plugin using the Faust architecture file `puredata.cpp`, and Albert Gräf's `faust2pd` script (version 0.9.8.6—also included in the Planet CCRMA distribution). Familiarity with Pure Data (the `pd` program by Miller Puckette [65, 66]) is assumed in this section. Also, the original `faust2pd` paper [31] contains the most complete description of `faust2pd` at the time of this writing.

Even if one prefers writing real-time signal-processing programs in C++, C, or assembly language,[9] the ability to generate user interfaces and plugins with Faust is compellingly useful.

To illustrate automatic generation of user-interface controls, we will add two "numeric entry" fields and one "horizontal slider" to our example of Fig. K.1. These controls will allow the plugin user to vary the center-frequency, bandwidth, and peak gain of the constant-peak-gain resonator in real time. A complete listing of `cpgrui.dsp` ("Constant-Peak-Gain Resonator with User Interface") appears in Fig. K.7.

K.5.1   Generating the PD Plugin

The plugin may be compiled as follows:

```
> faust -a puredata.cpp -o cpgrui-pd.cpp cpgrui.dsp
> g++ -DPD -Wall -g -shared -Dmydsp=cpgrui \
      -o cpgrui~.pd_linux  cpgrui-pd.cpp
```

The first line uses `faust` to generate a compilable `.cpp` file, this time using the architecture file `puredata.cpp` which encapsulates the `pd` plugin

---

[9]In many cases the signal processing in Faust can occur within a "foreign function" written in C or C++ and used as a "black box" within Faust, like the `cos()` function in Fig. K.5 on page 422. However, this approach is presently limited because foreign functions can have only `float` and `int` argument types, and they can only return a `float` each sample. It is possible to set up persistent state in a foreign function by means of static variables, but this does not generalize easily to multiple instances. Therefore, more general extensions may require direct modification of the generated C++, which usually obsoletes the Faust source code.

```
class mydsp : public dsp {
private:
  float fConst0;    float fConst1;
  int   iVec0[2];   float fConst2;
  int   iVec1[3];   float fConst3;   float fRec0[3];
public:
  virtual int getNumInputs()    { return 0; }
  virtual int getNumOutputs()   { return 1; }
  static void classInit(int samplingFreq) { }
  virtual void instanceInit(int samplingFreq) {
    fSamplingFreq = samplingFreq;
    fConst0 = expf((0 - (314.159271f / fSamplingFreq)));
    fConst1 = (fConst0 * fConst0);
    for (int i=0; i<2; i++) iVec0[i] = 0;
    fConst2 = ((2 * fConst0) * cosf((2764.601562f
                             / fSamplingFreq)));
    for (int i=0; i<3; i++) iVec1[i] = 0;
    fConst3 = (0.500000f * (1 - fConst1));
    for (int i=0; i<3; i++) fRec0[i] = 0; }
  virtual void init(int samplingFreq) {
    classInit(samplingFreq);
    instanceInit(samplingFreq); }
  virtual void buildUserInterface(UI* interface) {
    interface->openVerticalBox("faust");
    interface->closeBox(); }
  virtual void compute (int count, float** input,
                                   float** output) {
    float* output0 = output[0];
    for (int i=0; i<count; i++) {
      iVec0[0] = 1;
      int iTemp0 = iVec0[1];
      iVec1[0] = (1 - iTemp0);
      fRec0[0] = (((fConst3 * (1 - (iTemp0 + iVec1[2])))
                              + (fConst2 * fRec0[1]))
                              - (fConst1 * fRec0[2]));
      output0[i] = fRec0[0];
      // post processing
      fRec0[2] = fRec0[1]; fRec0[1] = fRec0[0];
      iVec1[2] = iVec1[1]; iVec1[1] = iVec1[0];
      iVec0[1] = iVec0[0];
    }
  }
};
```

Figure K.6: C++ code emitted by the shell command
faust cpgrir.dsp (and reformatted slightly).

```
declare name "Constant-Peak-Gain Resonator";
declare author "Julius Smith";
declare version "1.0";
declare license "GPL";

/* Controls */
fr = nentry("frequency (Hz)", 1000, 20, 20000, 1);
bw = nentry("bandwidth (Hz)", 100, 20, 20000, 10);
g  = hslider("peak gain", 1, 0, 10, 0.01);

/* Constants (Faust provides these in math.lib) */
SR = fconstant(int fSamplingFreq, <math.h>);
PI = 3.1415926535897932385;

/* The resonator */
process = firpart : + ~ feedback
with {
  R = exp(0-PI*bw/SR); // pole radius [0 required]
  A = 2*PI*fr/SR;      // pole angle (radians)
  RR = R*R;
  firpart(x) = (x - x'') * (g) * ((1-RR)/2);
  // time-domain coeffs ASSUMING ONE PIPELINE DELAY:
  feedback(v) = 0 + 2*R*cos(A)*v - RR*v';
};
```

Figure K.7: Listing of cpgrui.dsp—a Faust program specifying a constant-peak-gain resonator with three user controls. Also shown are typical header declarations.

API. The second line (which wraps) compiles `cpgrui-pd.cpp` to produce the dynamically loadable (binary) object file `cpgrui~.pd_linux`, which is our signal-processing plugin for `pd`. Such `pd` plugins are also called *externals* (externally compiled loadable modules). The filename extension ".`pd_linux`" indicates that the plugin was compiled on a Linux system.

Figure K.8 shows an example test patch,[10] named `cpgrui~-help.pd`,[11] written (manually) for the generated plugin. By convention, the left inlet and outlet of a Faust-generated plugin correspond to control info and general-purpose messages. Any remaining inlets and outlets are signals.

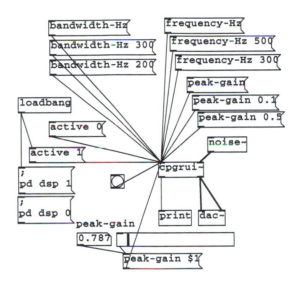

Figure K.8: Pure Data test patch `cpgrui~-help.pd` exercising features of the external `pd` plugin `cpgrui~` generated by Faust using the `puredata.cpp` architecture file.

A simple "bang" message to the control-inlet of the plugin (sent by clicking on the "button" drawn as a circle-within-square in Fig. K.8), results in a list being sent to the control (left) outlet describing all plugin controls and their current state. The `print` object in Fig. K.8 prints the received list

---

[10] All manually generated .dsp files and `pd` patches in this appendix are available at
`http://ccrma.stanford.edu/realsimple/faust/faustpd.tar.gz`.

[11] In `pd`, a dynamically loadable module (`pd` plugin) is called an *abstraction*. (This is distinct from the *one-off subpatch* which is encapsulated code within the parent patch, and which resides in the same file as the parent patch [66].) It is customary to document each abstraction with its own "help patch". The convention is to name the help patch "name-help.pd", where "name" is the name of the abstraction. Right-clicking on an object in `pd` and selecting "Help" loads the help patch in a new `pd` window.

in the main **pd** console window. For our example, we obtain the following bang-response in the **pd** console:

```
print: nentry /faust/bandwidth-Hz 100 100 20 20000 10
print: nentry /faust/frequency-Hz 1000 1000 20 20000 1
print: hslider /faust/peak-gain 1 1 0 10 0.01
```

These are the three controls we expected corresponding to the frequency, bandwidth, and gain of the resonator. However, note that the message-names generated for the controls have changed. In particular, spaces have been replaced by hyphens, and parentheses have been removed, to observe pd naming rules for messages [31].

Controls may be queried or set to new values in the plugin by sending the following **pd** *messages*:

- `frequency-Hz [newval]`
- `bandwidth-Hz [newval]`
- `peak-gain [newval]`

The longer form of the control name printed in the **pd** console, *e.g.*, `/faust/peak-gain`, is the complete "fully qualified path" that can be used to address controls within a hierarchy of nested controls and abstractions. For example, if we were to add the instance argument "foo" to the plugin (by changing the contents of the plugin box to "cpgrui~ foo" in Fig. K.8), then the path to the **peak-gain** control, for example, would become `/foo/faust/peak-gain` (see [31] and the Faust documentation for more details and examples).

In the test-patch of Fig. K.8, the various controls are exercised using **pd** *message boxes*. For example, the message "**peak-gain**" with no argument causes the plugin to print the current value of the peak-gain parameter on its control outlet. Messages with arguments, such as "**peak-gain 0.01**", set the parameter to the argument value without generating an output message. The slider and number-box output raw numbers, so they must be routed through a message-box in order to prepend the controller name ("peak-gain" in this case).

The plugin input signal (second inlet) comes from a **noise~** object in Fig. K.8, and the output signal (second outlet) is routed to both channels of the D/A converter (for center panning).

In addition to the requested controls, all plugins generated using the **puredata.cpp** architecture file respond to the boolean "**active**" message, which, when given a "false" argument such as 0, tells the plugin to bypass itself. This too is illustrated in Fig. K.8. Note that setting active to "true" at load time using a **loadbang**[12] message is not necessary; the plugin defaults to the active state when loaded and initialized—no **active** message

---

[12] The **loadbang** object sends a "bang" message when the patch finishes loading.

is needed. The `loadbang` in this patch also turns on `pd` audio computation for convenience.

K.5.2   Generating a PD Plugin-Wrapper Abstraction

The test patch of Fig. K.8 was constructed in `pd` by manually attaching user-interface elements to the left (control) inlet of the plugin. As is well described in [31], one can alternatively use the `faust2pd` script to generate a `pd` abstraction containing the plugin and its `pd` controllers. When this abstraction is loaded into `pd`, its controllers are brought out to the top level using the "graph on parent" mechanism in `pd`, as shown in Fig. K.10 on page 431.

The `faust2pd` script works from the XML file generated by Faust using the `-xml` option:

```
> faust -xml -a puredata.cpp -o cpgrui-pd.cpp cpgrui.dsp
> faust2pd cpgrui.dsp.xml
```

Adding the `-xml` option results in generation of the file `cpgrui.dsp.xml` which is then used by `faust2pd` to generate `cpgrui.pd`. Type `faust2pd` `-h` (and read [31]) to learn more of the features and options of the `faust2pd` script.

The generated abstraction can be opened in `pd` as follows:

```
> pd cpgrui.pd
```

Figure K.9 shows the result. As indicated by the `inlet~` and `outlet~` objects, the abstraction is designed to be used in place of the plugin. For this reason, we will refer to it henceforth as a *plugin wrapper*.

Notice in Fig. K.9 that a plugin wrapper forwards its control messages (left-inlet messages) to the encapsulated plugin, as we would expect (via `faust-control` and various `route` abstractions). However, it also forwards a copy of each control message to its control outlet. This convention facilitates making *cascade chains* of plugin-wrappers, as illustrated in `faust2pd` examples such as `synth.pd`.[13]

K.5.3   A PD Test Patch for the Plugin Wrapper

Figure K.10 shows `pd` patch developed (manually) to test the plugin wrapper generated by `faust2pd`. Compare this with Fig. K.8 on page 427. Notice how the three controls are brought out to the plugin-wrapper object automatically using the "graph on parent" convention for `pd` abstractions

---

[13]On a Linux system with Planet CCRMA installed, the command "`locate synth.pd`" should find it, *e.g.*, at `/usr/share/doc/faust-pd-0.9.8.6/examples/synth/synth.pd` .

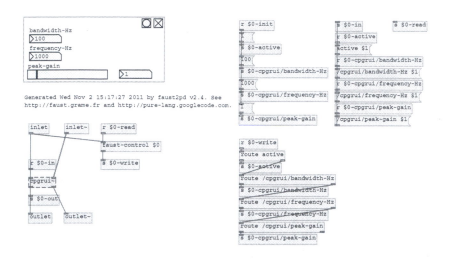

Figure K.9: Pure Data abstraction generated by **faust2pd** from the XML file emitted by Faust for the constant-peak-gain resonator (**cpgrui.dsp**).

with controllers. The bang button on the plugin resets all controls to their default values, and the toggle switch in the upper-right corner functions as a "bypass" switch (by sending the **active** message with appropriate argument). The previous mechanism of setting controls via message boxes to the control inlet still works, as illustrated. However, as shown in Fig. K.9 (or by opening the plugin-wrapper in **pd**), the control outlet simply receives a copy of everything sent to the control inlet. In particular, "bang" no longer prints a list of all controls and their settings, and controls cannot be queried. However, bang and print can be added manually in the Pd abstraction for test purposes.

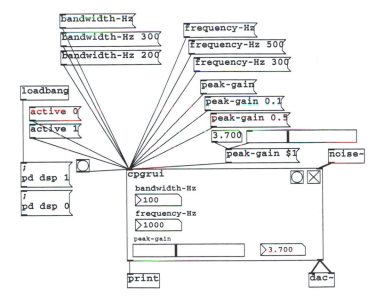

Figure K.10: Pure Data test patch (`cpgrui-help.pd`) for exercising the plugin-wrapper (`cpgrui.pd`) generated by `faust2pd` to control the **faust**-generated pd plugin (`cpgrui~.pd_linux`).

K.6 Generating a LADSPA Plugin via Faust

LADSPA stands for "Linux Audio Developer Simple Plugin API", and it is the most common audio plugin API for Linux applications. It can be considered the Linux counterpart of the widely used VST plugin standard for Windows applications. In the Planet CCRMA distribution, most of the LADSPA plugins are found in the directory /usr/lib/ladspa/. At the time of this writing, there are 161 audio plugins (.so files) in or under that directory.

To generate a LADSPA plugin from Faust source, it is merely necessary to use the ladspa.cpp architecture file, as in the following example:

```
> faust -a ladspa.cpp cpgrui.dsp -o cpgruilp.cpp
> g++ -fPIC -shared -O3 \
      -Dmydsp='Constant_Peak_Gain_Resonator' \
      cpgruilp.cpp -o cpgruilp.so
> cp cpgruilp.so /usr/local/lib/ladspa/
```

(Recall that cpgrui.dsp was listed in Fig. K.7 on page 426.) We see that the C++ compilation step calls for "position-independent code" (option -fPIC) and a "shared object" format (option -shared) in order that the file be dynamically loadable by a running program. (Recall that pd similarly required its externals to be compiled -shared.) The Faust distribution provides the make file /usr/lib/faust/Makefile.ladspacompile (among others) which documents such details.

Many Linux programs support LADSPA programs, such as the sound editor Audacity, the multitrack audio recorder/mixer Ardour, and the sequencer Rosegarden. However, for our example, we'll use a simple application-independent LADSPA effects rack called JACK Rack (select "Applications / Planet CCRMA / Jack / JACK Rack").

Figure K.11 shows the appearance of the jack-rack main window after adding[14] the plugin named Constant_Peak_Gain_Resonator. Note that the two numeric entry fields have been converted to horizontal sliders. (Vertical sliders are also converted to horizontal.) Also, the controller names have been simplified. A bug is that the default values for the controls are not set correctly when the plugin loads. (They were set manually to obtain Fig. K.11 as shown.)

To test the LADSPA plugin, any program's audio output can be routed through jack-rack to the sound-out driver (typically "ALSA PCM" these

---

[14]After running jack-rack, the LADSPA plugin was added by clicking on the menu items "Add / Uncategorised / C / Constant_Peak_Gain_Resonator". If jack-rack does not find this or other plugins, make sure your LADSPA_PATH environment variable is set. A typical setting would be /usr/local/lib/ladspa/:/usr/lib/ladspa/.

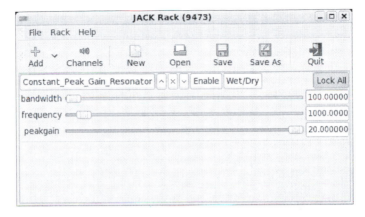

Figure K.11: JACK Rack screenshot after adding the LADSPA plugin `Constant_Peak_Gain_Resonator`. Additional LADSPA plugins can be loaded in the space below (and connected in series).

days). For example, `pd`'s audio output can be routed through `jack-rack` to `alsa_pcm` as shown in Fig. K.12.[15]

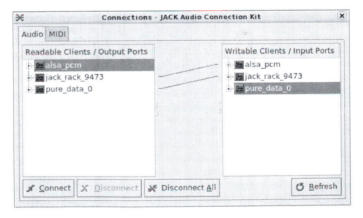

Figure K.12: JACK audio connections routing `pd` through `jack-rack` to the ALSA sound-out driver `alsa_pcm`.

---

[15]Sound routings such as this may be accomplished using the "Connect" window in `qjackctl`. In that window, there is an Audio tab and a MIDI tab, and the Audio tab is selected by default. Just click twice to select the desired source and destination and then click "Connect". Such connections can be made automatic by clicking "Patchbay" in the `qjackctl` control panel, specifying your connections, saving, then clicking "Activate". Connections can also be established at the command line using `aconnect` from the `alsa-utils` package (included with Planet CCRMA).

K.7   Generating a VST Plugin via Faust

This section describes generation of a Windows VST plugin starting from Faust code, again using the constant-peak-gain resonator example.

The *VST* (Virtual Studio Technology) plugin standard was developed by Steinberg Media Technologies (makers of Cubase). It enjoys wide usage on Windows and Macintosh platforms. The Faust distribution contains the make-file `/usr/lib/faust/Makefile.vstcompile` for compiling and installing VST plugins using Xcode on a Mac OS-X machine. For our example, however, we'll create a Windows-format VST plugin (`.dll` file) using Microsoft Visual C++. The example was tested on a *Muse Receptor*.[16]

Because the Receptor does not support mono plugins, the `process` line in the Faust source in Fig. K.7 on page 426 was modified as follows to make it stereo-compatible:

```
process = + : firpart : + ~ feedback <: (_,_)
```

This version was named `cpgrui_vst.dsp`. To generate a VST plugin, we simply use a VST architecture file:

```
faust -a vst2p4.cpp cpgrui_vst.dsp -o cpgrui_vst.cpp
```

Next, the file `cpgrui_vst.cpp` was copied over to a Windows-XP machine with Microsoft Visual Studio Express installed (including Visual C++ 2008). The programming sample "`again`" from the Steinberg VST-2.4 SDK was copied to an adjacent directory `cpgr` and trivially modified to create a compilable C++ project. (Specifically, replace `again.cpp` by `cpgrui_vst.cpp`, rename `again.vcproj` to `cpgr.vcproj`, and change all occurrences of "again" to "cpgrui_vst" in `cpgr.vcproj`, and change "Gain" to "CPGR" to rename the plugin. Finally, double-click on `cpgr.vcproj` to launch Visual C++ on the `cpgr` project.) Selecting the menu item "Build / Build cpgr" creates `cpgr/win/Debug/cpgr.dll` (the VST plugin itself). To test the plugin, it was copied into the "Unsupported Plugins" folder on the Receptor, and installed by clicking the "1 installs" button on the Receptor's Setup page. After that, the plugin could be instantiated on a Receptor "Mix" channel, as shown in Fig. K.13, and Fig. K.14 shows the automatically generated edit window of the plugin.

---

[16]The Receptor is a hardware VST plugin host designed for studio work and live musical performance. While it only supports Windows VST plugins, it is based on a Red Hat Linux operating system using `wine` for Windows compatibility. The VST plugin described in this section was tested on system version 1.6.20070717 running on Receptor hardware version 1.0. This system expects VST-2.3 plugins, and so VST-2.4 plugins cause a warning message to be printed in the Receptor's system log. However, v2.4 plugins seem to work fine in the 2.3 framework. There was a competitor to the Receptor called Plugzilla that supported both VST and LADSPA plugins, but Plugzilla no longer appears to be available.

Figure K.13: Screenshot of the Receptor Remote Control program, showing the "Mix" view. The constant-peak-gain resonator (named `cpgr`) is instantiated as a plugin processing the "Piano" source signal.

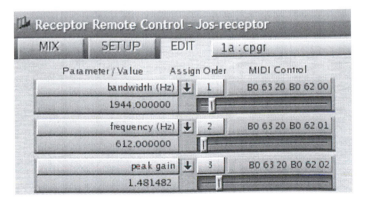

Figure K.14: Screenshot of the upper-left corner of the parameter-editing window of the Receptor's remote-control program showing the constant-peak-gain resonator parameters.

K.7.1   Bypassing Windows

Beginning with Faust version 0.9.9.4j-par, a new makefile called Makefile.w32vstcompile is distributed in the examples directory. This makefile can be adapted to work on Fedora F8 Linux as follows.

1. Download and install the following RPMs from SourceForge:

   ```
   mingw-binutils-2.18.50-6.fc8.i386.rpm
   mingw-gcc-core-4.2.1-6.fc8.i386.rpm
   mingw-gcc-g++-4.2.1-6.fc8.i386.rpm
   mingw-runtime-3.14-3.fc8.i386.rpm
   mingw-w32api-3.11-3.fc8.i386.rpm
   ```

   (Unfortunately, mingw is not in the standard yum repos yet.)

2. In Makefile.w32vstcompile, edit the VST line to say where your vstsdk2.4 directory is located, and change all occurrences of i586-mingw32msvc to i386-mingw32.

3. The plugin name defaults to "FaustFx". You can change this by declaring the **name** in your Faust source. For the example of the previous section, we could say

   ```
   declare name "CPGR";
   ```

   in place of the longer name used in Fig. K.7 on page 426. (The longer name results in a plugin called "ConstantPeakGainResonator".)

4. After the make, simply copy the dll file to the Receptor and tell the Receptor to install it on the Setup page of the Receptor Remote Control program as before (which requires Windows or a Mac). While one can press the Setup button on the Receptor front panel and rotate the Top Display Knob to "Install/Upgrade" (the next-to-last entry), there you will find "0 files" even when there is a file to install. The manual documents that it is not allowed to install plugins from the Receptor front panel, because some installs require a user interface (such as to receive an authorization code). This is an unfortunate and unnecessary restriction in our case that prevents working entirely directly with the Receptor from a Linux environment.

The Receptor's "Unsupported Plugins" directory can be mounted as follows:

```
> mkdir /mnt/receptor
> mount -t cifs <ReceptorIPA>:hard\ drive/Program\ Files/VST\ Plugins/-
            Unsupported\ Plugins /mnt/receptor
```

where '-' at the end of a line means line-continuation. (Remember to say `umount /mnt/receptor` when you are done.) The Receptor's IP Address (typically assigned by DHCP) can also be viewed by pressing the Setup button and rotating the Top Display Knob to that field.

K.8   Generating a MIDI Synthesizer for PD

The `faust2pd` script (introduced in §K.5 above) also has a mode for generating *MIDI synthesizer plugins* for `pd`. This mode is triggered by use of the `-n` option ("number of voices"). For this mode, the Faust program should be written to synthesize one voice using the following three parameters (which are driven from MIDI data in the `pd` plugin):

- `freq` - frequency of the played note (Hz)
- `gain` - amplitude of the played note (0 to 1)
- `gate` - 1 while "key is down", 0 after "key up"

The parameters `freq` and `gain` are set according to MIDI note-number and velocity, respectively, while the `gate` parameter is set to 1 on a MIDI "note-on" and back to zero upon "note-off". The `faust2pd` script handles instantiation of up to 8 instances of the synth patch, and provides the abstraction `midi-in.pd` for receiving and decoding MIDI data in `pd`.

Let's make a simple 8-voiced MIDI synthesizer based on the example Faust program `cpgrs.dsp` ("Constant-Peak-Gain Resonator Synth") listed in Fig. K.15. In addition to converting the frequency and gain parameters to the standard names, we have added a classic ADSR envelope generator (defined in Faust's `music.lib` file) which uses the new `gate` parameter, and which adds the four new envelope parameters `attack`, `decay`, `sustain`, and `release`.

Compiling the example is the same as for a `pd` plugin, except that the `-n` option is used (8 voices is the maximum):

```
> faust -xml -a puredata.cpp -o cpgrs-pd.cpp cpgrs.dsp
> g++ -DPD -Wall -g -shared -Dmydsp=cpgrs \
      -o cpgrs~.pd_linux cpgrs-pd.cpp
> faust2pd -n 8 -s -o cpgrs.pd cpgrs.dsp.xml
```

```
declare name "Constant-Peak-Gain Resonator Synth";
declare author "Julius Smith";
declare version "1.0";
declare license "GPL";

/* Standard synth controls supported by faust2pd */
freq = nentry("freq", 440, 20, 20000, 1); // Hz
gain = nentry("gain", 0.1, 0, 1, 0.01); // frac
gate = button("gate"); // 0/1

/* User Controls */
bw = hslider("bandwidth (Hz)", 100, 20, 20000, 10);

import("music.lib"); // define noise, adsr, PI, SR, et al.

/* ADSR envelope parameters */
attack  = hslider("attack", 0.01,0, 1, 0.001); // sec
decay   = hslider("decay",  0.3, 0, 1, 0.001); // sec
sustain = hslider("sustain",0.5, 0, 1, 0.01);  // frac
release = hslider("release",0.2, 0, 1, 0.001); // sec

/* Synth */
process = noise * env * gain : filter
with {
  env = gate :
        vgroup("1-adsr",
                adsr(attack, decay, sustain, release));
  filter = vgroup("2-filter", (firpart : + ~ feedback));
  R = exp(0-PI*bw/SR); // pole radius [0 required]
  A = 2*PI*freq/SR;       // pole angle (radians)
  RR = R*R;
  firpart(x) = (x - x'') * ((1-RR)/2);
  // time-domain coeffs ASSUMING ONE PIPELINE DELAY:
  feedback(v) = 0 + 2*R*cos(A)*v - RR*v';
};
```

Figure K.15: Listing of cpgrs.dsp—a Faust program specifying a simple synth patch consisting of white noise through a constant-peak-gain resonator.

K.9   MIDI Synthesizer Test Patch

The example synth is loaded into pd like any plugin-wrapper. A manually written test patch (cpgrs-help.pd) is shown in Fig. K.16. Note that the standard MIDI-synth control parameters (freq, gain, gate) are handled behind the scenes and do not appear among the plugin GUI controls.

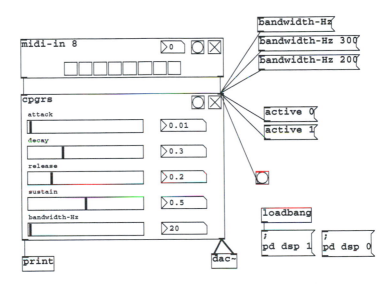

Figure K.16: Test patch for the pd synth plugin cpgrs.pd generated by faust2pd based on cpgrs.dsp in Fig. K.15.

To drive our MIDI synth, we need a source of MIDI data. Perhaps the simplest resource for this purpose is the Virtual Keyboard (vkeybd), which is standard in Red Hat Fedora 6, and in the planetccrma-menus at "Applications / Planet CCRMA / MIDI / Vkeybd"). Figure K.17 shows a screen shot of the Virtual Keyboard with its key-range and velocity controllers displayed (menu item "View / Key/Velocity"). The velocity controller sets the gain parameter, mapping MIDI velocity (0-127) to the unit interval (0-1). The key-range controller transposes the keyboard by octaves. Pressing a key determines, together with the key-range, the freq parameter in our synth. Pressing a key also sets the gate parameter to 1, and releasing it sets gate to 0. The ADSR envelope is triggered when gate transitions to 1, and it begins its "release" phase when gate transitions to 0, as is standard for ADSR envelopes triggered by a keyboard. Note that the bottom two rows of ASCII keyboard keys are mapped to virtual-keyboard keys, enabling the playing of chords in real time on the regular computer keyboard.

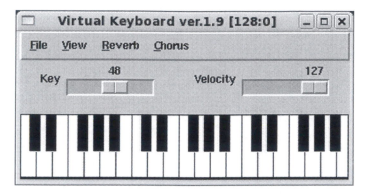

Figure K.17: The Virtual Keyboard (MIDI source).

Figure K.18 illustrates the MIDI tab of `qjackctl`'s Connect window after connecting the Virtual Keyboard MIDI output to `pd`'s MIDI input.[17]

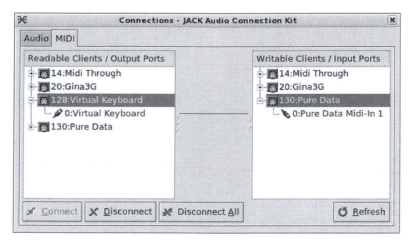

Figure K.18: JACK MIDI connections routing MIDI from the Virtual Keyboard (`vkeybd`) to `pd`'s first MIDI input port.

To play back a MIDI file (extension `.mid`), a nice way is to open it in Rosegarden ("Applications / Planet CCRMA / Sequencers / Rosegarden") and connect Rosegarden's MIDI output to `pd`'s MIDI input as above. (You can still play along on the Virtual Keyboard.)

---

[17]Pd must have at least one MIDI-input port defined at startup for this to work. For example, a typical `~/.pdrc` file might contain the following startup options for pd: `-jack -r 48000 -alsamidi -midiindev 1 -midioutdev 1 -audiooutdev 1 -outchannels 2 -path /usr/lib/pd/...`

Appendix L

Links to Online Resources

This short appendix lists some especially interesting resources available on the Web.

- For additional background on elementary mathematics and spectrum analysis, see Book I in the Music Signal Processing book series [84], available on the Web at

    http://ccrma.stanford.edu/~jos/mdft/.

- For advanced applications of digital filters to musical sound synthesis and effects, see Book III in the Music Signal Processing book series [86], available on the Web at

    http://ccrma.stanford.edu/~jos/pasp/.

- Website devoted to music applications of digital signal processing:

    http://www.dspmusic.org.

- There are some nice elementary tutorials pertaining to audio digital filtering at Harmony Central:

    http://www.harmony-central.com/

- Another tutorial on digital filters, covering some topics not covered here:

    http://www.dsptutor.freeuk.com/dfilt1.htm.

Bibliography

[1] J. Abel and J. O. Smith, "Robust design of very high-order allpass dispersion filters," *Proceedings of the Conference on Digital Audio Effects (DAFx-06), Montreal, Canada*, Sept. 2006, `http://www.dafx.de/`.

[2] M. Abramowitz and I. A. Stegun, eds., *Handbook of Mathematical Functions*, New York: Dover, 1965.

[3] S. Bilbao, *Wave and Scattering Methods for the Numerical Integration of Partial Differential Equations*, PhD thesis, Stanford University, June 2001, `http://ccrma.stanford.edu/~bilbao/`.

[4] S. Boyd, L. O. Chua, and C. A. Desoer, "Analytical foundations of Volterra series," *IMA Journal of Mathematical Control and Information*, vol. 1, pp. 243–282, 1984, `http://lanoswww.epfl.ch/studinfo/-courses/cours_nonlinear_de/extras/Volterra_3.pdf`.

[5] R. Bristow-Johnson, "The equivalence of various methods of computing biquad coefficients for audio parametric equalizers," *Audio Engineering Society Convention*, 1994, `http://www.harmony-central.com/Effects/-Articles/EQ_Coefficients/EQ-Coefficients.pdf`.

[6] R. Bristow-Johnson, "Audio EQ cookbook," 1998, `http://www.harmony-central.com/Computer/Programming/-Audio-EQ-Cookbook.txt`.

[7] R. Bristow-Johnson, "DSP trick: Fixed-point dc blocking filter with noise-shaping," *The Unofficial Comp.DSP Home Page*, June 22, 2000, `http://www.dspguru.com/comp.dsp/tricks/alg/dc_block.htm`.

[8] J. R. Buck, M. Daniel, and A. C. Singer, *Computer Explorations in Signals and Systems using Matlab*, Englewood Cliffs, NJ: Prentice-Hall, 1997, ISBN 0-13-732868-0.

[9] C. S. Burrus and T. W. Parks, "Time domain design of recursive digital filters," *IEEE Transactions on Audio and Electroacoustics*, vol. 18, pp. 137–141, June 1970.

[10] C. S. Burrus, J. H. McClellan, A. V. Oppenheim, T. W. Parks, R. W. Schafer, and H. W. Schuessler, *Computer-Based Exercises for Signal Processing Using Matlab*, Englewood Cliffs, NJ: Prentice-Hall, 1994.

[11] J. A. Cadzow, "High performance spectral estimation—a new ARMA method," *IEEE Transactions on Acoustics, Speech, Signal Processing*, vol. ASSP-28, pp. 524–529, Oct. 1980.

[12] G. C. Carter, ed., *Coherence and Time Delay Estimation*, New York: IEEE Press, 1993.

[13] D. C. Champeney, *A Handbook of Fourier Theorems*, Cambridge University Press, 1987.

[14] R. V. Churchill, *Complex Variables and Applications*, New York: McGraw-Hill, 1960.

[15] P. Cook and G. Scavone, *Synthesis ToolKit in C++, Version 4*, `http://ccrma.stanford.edu/software/stk/`, 2010, see also `http://ccrma.stanford.edu/~jos/stkintro/`.

[16] P. R. Cook, *Identification of Control Parameters in an Articulatory Vocal Tract Model, with Applications to the Synthesis of Singing*, PhD thesis, Elec. Engineering Dept., Stanford University (CCRMA), Dec. 1990, `http://www.cs.princeton.edu/~prc/`.

[17] P. R. Cook, "Non-linear periodic prediction for on-line identification of oscillator characteristics in woodwind instruments," in *Proceedings of the 1991 International Computer Music Conference, Montreal*, pp. 157–160, Computer Music Association, 1991.

[18] G. Dahlquist and Å. Björck, *Numerical Methods*, Englewood Cliffs, NJ: Prentice-Hall, 1974.

[19] J. R. Deller Jr., J. G. Proakis, and J. H. Hansen, *Discrete-Time Processing of Speech Signals*, New York: Macmillan, 1993.

[20] C. A. Desoer and E. S. Kuh, *Basic Circuit Theory*, New York: McGraw-Hill, 1969.

[21] M. Dolson, "The phase vocoder: A tutorial," *Computer Music Journal*, vol. 10, no. 4, pp. 14–27, 1986.

[22] DSP Committee, ed., *Programs for Digital Signal Processing*, New York: IEEE Press, 1979.

[23] G. Fant, *Acoustic Theory of Speech Production*, The Hague: Mouton, 1960.

[24] A. Farina, "Simultaneous measurement of impulse response and distortion with a swept-sine technique," *108th Audio Engineering Society Convention*, Feb. 19–22, 2000, Preprint 5093.

[25] A. Fettweis, "Wave digital filters: Theory and practice," *Proceedings of the IEEE*, vol. 74, pp. 270–327, Feb. 1986.

[26] J. L. Flanagan and R. M. Golden, "Phase vocoder," *Bell System Technical Journal*, vol. 45, pp. 1493–1509, Nov. 1966, Reprinted in [74, pp. 388–404].

[27] J. L. Flanagan and L. R. Rabiner, eds., *Speech Synthesis*, Stroudsburg, Penn.: Dowden, Hutchinson, and Ross, Inc., 1973.

[28] G. F. Franklin, J. D. Powell, and M. L. Workman, *Digital Control of Dynamic Systems, Third Edition*, Englewood Cliffs, NJ: Prentice-Hall, 1998.

[29] G. H. Golub and C. F. Van Loan, *Matrix Computations, 2nd Edition*, Baltimore: The Johns Hopkins University Press, 1989.

[30] G. C. Goodwin and R. L. Payne, *Dynamic System Identification*, New York: Academic Press, 1977.

[31] A. Gräf, "Interfacing Pure Data with FAUST," in *Proceedings of the 5th International Linux Audio Conference (LAC2007), TU Berlin*, *http://www.kgw.tu-berlin.de/~lac2007/proceedings.shtml*, 2007, http: //www.kgw.tu-berlin.de/~lac2007/papers/lac07_graef.pdf.

[32] A. H. Gray and J. D. Markel, "A normalized digital filter structure," *IEEE Transactions on Acoustics, Speech, Signal Processing*, vol. ASSP-23, pp. 268–277, June 1975.

[33] D. Halliday, R. Resnick, and J. Walker, *Extended, Fundamentals of Physics, 6th Edition*, New York: John Wiley and Sons, Inc., 2000.

[34] W. J. Hess, *Algorithms and Devices for Pitch Determination of Speech-Signals*, Berlin: Springer-Verlag, 1983.

[35] H. Järveläinen, V. Välimäki, and M. Karjalainen, "Audibility of inharmonicity in string instrument sounds, and implications to digital sound synthesis," in *Proceedings of the 1999 International Computer Music Conference, Beijing*, pp. 359–362, Oct. 22-27, 1999, http://www.acoustics.hut.fi/~hjarvela/publications/.

[36] T. Kailath, *Lectures on Linear Least-Squares Estimation*, New York: Springer Verlag, 1976.

[37] T. Kailath, *Linear Systems*, Englewood Cliffs, NJ: Prentice-Hall, 1980.

[38] T. Kailath, A. H. Sayed, and B. Hassibi, *Linear Estimation*, Englewood Cliffs, NJ: Prentice-Hall, Apr. 2000.

[39] J. B. Keller, "Bowing of violin strings," *Comm. Pure Applied Math.*, vol. 6, pp. 483–495, 1953.

[40] D. Klatt, "Software for a cascade/parallel formant synthesizer," *Journal of the Acoustical Society of America*, vol. 67, pp. 13–33, 1980.

[41] M. Lang, "Allpass filter design and applications," *IEEE Transactions on Signal Processing*, vol. 46, no. 9, pp. 2505–2514, 1998.

[42] M. Lang and T. I. Laakso, "Simple and robust method for the design of allpass filters using least-squares phase error criterion," *IEEE Transactions on Circuits and Systems—I: Fundamental Theory and Applications*, vol. 41, no. 1, pp. 40–48, 1994.

[43] W. R. LePage, *Complex Variables and the Laplace Transform for Engineers*, New York: Dover, 1961.

[44] M. J. Lighthill, *Introduction to Fourier Analysis*, Cambridge University Press, Jan. 1958.

[45] L. Ljung and T. L.Soderstrom, "The Steiglitz-McBride algorithm revisited—convergence analysis and accuracy aspects," *IEEE Transactions on Automatic Control*, vol. 26, pp. 712–717, June 1981, See also the function stmcb() in the Matlab Signal Processing Toolbox.

[46] L. Ljung and T. L. Soderstrom, *Theory and Practice of Recursive Identification*, Cambridge, MA: MIT Press, 1983.

[47] J. Makhoul, "Linear prediction: A tutorial review," *Proceedings of the IEEE*, vol. 63, pp. 561–580, Apr. 1975.

[48] J. D. Markel and A. H. Gray, *Linear Prediction of Speech*, New York: Springer Verlag, 1976.

[49] S. J. Mason, "Feedback theory—some properties of signal flow graphs," *Proceedings of the IRE*, vol. 41, pp. 1144–1156, Sept. 1953.

[50] S. J. Mason, "Feedback theory—further properties of signal flow graphs," *Proceedings of the IRE*, vol. 44, pp. 920–926, July 1956.

[51] M. Mathews and J. O. Smith, "Methods for synthesizing very high Q parametrically well behaved two pole filters," in *Proceedings of the Stockholm Musical Acoustics Conference (SMAC-03)*, *http://www.speech.kth.se/smac03/*, (Stockholm), Royal Swedish Academy of Music, Aug. 2003, available online, with sound examples, at http://ccrma.stanford.edu/~jos/smac03maxjos/.

[52] J. H. McClellan, R. W. Schafer, and M. A. Yoder, *DSP First: A Multimedia Approach*, Englewood Cliffs, NJ: Prentice-Hall, 1998, Tk5102.M388.

[53] F. R. Moore, "An introduction to the mathematics of digital signal processing, parts I–II," *Computer Music Journal*, vol. 2, no. 1,2, pp. 38–47,38–60, 1978, available at CCRMA (see http://ccrma.stanford.edu/overview/publications.html).

[54] J. A. Moorer, "The use of the phase vocoder in computer music applications," *Journal of the Audio Engineering Society*, vol. 26, pp. 42–45, Jan./Feb. 1978.

[55] P. M. Morse, *Vibration and Sound*, http://asa.aip.org/publications.html: American Institute of Physics, for the Acoustical Society of America, 1948, 1st edition 1936, last author's edition 1948, ASA edition 1981.

[56] A. W. Nayor and G. R. Sell, *Linear Operator Theory in Engineering and Science*, New York: Springer Verlag, 1982.

[57] Z. Nehari, *Conformal Mapping*, New York: Dover, 1952.

[58] B. Noble, *Applied Linear Algebra*, Englewood Cliffs, NJ: Prentice-Hall, 1969.

[59] A. V. Oppenheim, *Discrete-Time Signal Processing*, Englewood Cliffs, NJ: Prentice-Hall, 1989.

[60] A. V. Oppenheim and R. W. Schafer, *Digital Signal Processing*, Englewood Cliffs, NJ: Prentice-Hall, 1975.

[61] Y. Orlarey, A. Gräf, and S. Kersten, "DSP programming with FAUST, Q and SuperCollider," in *Proceedings of the 4th International Linux Audio Conference (LAC2006), ZKM Karlsruhe*, `http://lac.zkm.de/2006/proceedings.shtml`, pp. 39–40, 2006, `http://lac.zkm.de/2006/proceedings.shtml#orlarey_et_al`.

[62] J. M. Ortega, *Numerical Analysis*, New York: Academic Press, 1972.

[63] A. Papoulis, *Signal Analysis*, New York: McGraw-Hill, 1977.

[64] T. W. Parks and C. S. Burrus, *Digital Filter Design*, New York: John Wiley and Sons, Inc., June 1987, contains FORTRAN software listings.

[65] M. Puckette, *Pure Data (PD)*, `http://www.puredata.org`, July 2004.

[66] M. Puckette, *Theory and Techniques of Electronic Music*, http://www.worldscibooks.com/compsci/6277.html: World Scientific Press, May 2007, `http://www-crca.ucsd.edu/~msp/techniques.htm`.

[67] W. Putnam and J. O. Smith, "Design of fractional delay filters using convex optimization," in *Proceedings of the IEEE Workshop on Applications of Signal Processing to Audio and Acoustics, New Paltz, NY*, (New York), IEEE Press, Oct. 1997, `http://ccrma.stanford.edu/~jos/resample/optfir.pdf`.

[68] L. R. Rabiner and B. Gold, *Theory and Application of Digital Signal Processing*, Prentice-Hall, 1975.

[69] L. R. Rabiner and R. W. Schafer, *Digital Processing of Speech Signals*, Prentice-Hall, 1978.

[70] G. R. Reddy and M. N. S. Swamy, "Digital all-pass filter design through discrete hilbert transform," in *Proceedings of the International Conference on Acoustics, Speech, and Signal Processing, Albuquerque*, 1998.

[71] C. Roads, ed., *The Music Machine*, Cambridge, MA: MIT Press, 1989.

[72] D. Rocchesso and F. Scalcon, "Accurate dispersion simulation for piano strings," in *Proc. Nordic Acoustical Meeting (NAM'96)*, (Helsinki, Finland), June 12-14 1996, 9 pages.

[73] W. Rudin, *Principles of Mathematical Analysis*, New York: McGraw-Hill, 1964.

[74] R. W. Schafer and J. D. Markel, eds., *Speech Analysis*, New York: IEEE Press, 1979.

[75] H. Schmid, "Circuit transposition using signal-flow graphs," in *Proceedings of the International Symposium Circuits and Systems (ISCAS-2002), Phoenix, AZ*, vol. 2, (New York), pp. 25–28, IEEE Press, May 2002.

[76] M. R. Schroeder, "Vocoders: Analysis and synthesis of speech (a review of 30 years of applied speech research)," *Proceedings of the IEEE*, vol. 54, pp. 720–734, May 1966, Reprinted in [74, pp. 352–366].

[77] L. L. Sharf, *Statistical Signal Processing, Detection, Estimation, and Time Series Analysis*, Reading MA: Addison-Wesley, 1991.

[78] J. O. Smith, *Techniques for Digital Filter Design and System Identification with Application to the Violin*, PhD thesis, Elec. Engineering Dept., Stanford University (CCRMA), June 1983, CCRMA Technical Report STAN-M-14, http://ccrma.stanford.edu/STANM/stanms/stanm14/.

[79] J. O. Smith, "Introduction to digital filter theory," in *Digital Audio Signal Processing: An Anthology* (J. Strawn, ed.), Los Altos, California: William Kaufmann, Inc., 1985, (out of print). Book reprint available from ICMA at http://www.computermusic.org/. Original version available as Stanford CCRMA Tech. Report STAN-M-20, April 1985. A shortened version appears in [71].

[80] J. O. Smith, "Music applications of digital waveguides," Tech. Rep. STAN-M-39, CCRMA, Music Department, Stanford University, 1987, CCRMA Technical Report STAN-M-39, http://ccrma.stanford.edu/STANM/stanm39/.

[81] J. O. Smith, "Principles of digital waveguide models of musical instruments," in *Applications of Digital Signal Processing to Audio and Acoustics* (M. Kahrs and K. Brandenburg, eds.), pp. 417–466, Boston/Dordrecht/London: Kluwer Academic Publishers, 1998.

[82] J. O. Smith, *Introduction to Matlab and Octave*, http://ccrma.stanford.edu/~jos/matlab/, 2003.

[83] J. O. Smith, *Introduction to Digital Filters with Audio Applications*, http://ccrma.stanford.edu/~jos/filters/, Sept. 2007, online book.

[84] J. O. Smith, *Mathematics of the Discrete Fourier Transform (DFT), with Audio Applications, Second Edition*, http://ccrma.stanford.edu/~jos/mdft/, Apr. 2007, online book.

[85] J. O. Smith, "Virtual electric guitars and effects using FAUST and Octave," in *Proceedings of the 6th International Linux Audio Conference (LAC2008), http://lac.linuxaudio.org/*, 2008, paper: http://ccrma.stanford.edu/realsimple/faust_strings/faust_strings.pdf, presentation overheads: http://ccrma.stanford.edu/~jos/pdf/LAC2008-jos.pdf, supporting website: http://ccrma.stanford.edu/realsimple/faust_strings/.

[86] J. O. Smith, *Physical Audio Signal Processing*,
     `https://ccrma.stanford.edu/~jos/pasp/`, Dec. 2010, online book.

[87] J. O. Smith, *Spectral Audio Signal Processing*,
     `http://ccrma.stanford.edu/~jos/sasp/`, Dec. 2011, online book.

[88] J. O. Smith and J. S. Abel, "Bark and ERB bilinear transforms," *IEEE
     Transactions on Speech and Audio Processing*, pp. 697–708, Nov. 1999.

[89] J. O. Smith and J. B. Angell, "A constant-gain digital resonator tuned
     by a single coefficient," *Computer Music Journal*, vol. 6, no. 4, pp.
     36–40, 1982.

[90] J. O. Smith and P. R. Cook, "The second-order digital waveguide
     oscillator," in *Proceedings of the 1992 International Computer Music
     Conference, San Jose*, pp. 150–153, Computer Music Association, 1992,
     `http://ccrma.stanford.edu/~jos/wgo/`.

[91] J. O. Smith and P. Gossett, "A flexible sampling-rate conversion
     method," in *Proc. 1984 Int. Conf. Acoustics, Speech, and Signal
     Processing (ICASSP-84), San Diego*, vol. 2, (New York), pp.
     19.4.1–19.4.2, IEEE Press, Mar. 1984, expanded tutorial and associated
     free software available at the Digital Audio Resampling Home Page:
     `http://ccrma.stanford.edu/~jos/resample/`.

[92] A. S. Spanias, "Speech coding: A tutorial review," *Proceedings of the
     IEEE*, vol. 82, Oct. 1994.

[93] K. Steiglitz, *A Digital Signal Processing Primer with Applications to
     Audio and Computer Music*, Reading MA: Addison-Wesley, 1996.

[94] K. Steiglitz, "A note on constant-gain digital resonators," *Computer
     Music Journal*, vol. 18, no. 4, pp. 8–10, 1994.

[95] T. Stilson and J. O. Smith, "Analyzing the Moog VCF with
     considerations for digital implementation," in *Proceedings of the 1996
     International Computer Music Conference, Hong Kong*, Computer Music
     Association, 1996, `http://ccrma.stanford.edu/~stilti/`.

[96] J. C. Strikwerda, *Finite Difference Schemes and Partial Differential
     Equations*, Pacific Grove, CA: Wadsworth and Brooks, 1989.

[97] T. Tolonen, V. Välimäki, and M. Karjalainen, "Modeling of tension
     modulation nonlinearity in plucked strings," *IEEE Transactions on Speech
     and Audio Processing*, vol. SAP-8, pp. 300–310, May 2000.

[98] P. P. Vaidyanathan, *Multirate Systems and Filter Banks*, Prentice-Hall,
     1993.

[99] S. A. Van Duyne and J. O. Smith, "Implementation of a variable pick-up
     point on a waveguide string model with FM/AM applications," in
     *Proceedings of the 1992 International Computer Music Conference, San
     Jose*, pp. 154–157, Computer Music Association, 1992.

[100] B. Yegnanarayana, "Design of recursive group-delay filters by
      autoregressive modeling," *IEEE Transactions on Acoustics, Speech, Signal
      Processing*, vol. 30, pp. 632–637, Aug. 1982.

[101] D. Yeh and J. O. Smith III, "Discretization of the '59 Fender Bassman tone stack," *Proceedings of the Conference on Digital Audio Effects (DAFx-06), Montreal, Canada*, Sept. 2006, http://www.dafx.de/.

[102] L. A. Zadeh and C. A. Desoer, *Linear System Theory: The State Space Approach*, New York: McGraw-Hill, 1963, reprinted by Krieger, 1979.

[103] U. Zölzer, *Digital Audio Signal Processing*, New York: John Wiley and Sons, Inc., 1999.

Index

3-dB bandwidth, **189**, **327**

abstraction (pd), **427**
additive synthesis, **168**
affine function, **227**
allpass condition, **299**
allpass filter, **272**
    biquad case, **272**
    examples, **300**
    general case, **299**
allpass filter design, **273**
Amperes, **320**, **321**
amplifier modeling, **342**
amplitude, **244**
amplitude envelope, **168**
amplitude response, **3**, **8**, **151**
analog filters, **319**, **384**
    allpass, **331**
    capacitor impedance, **320**
    example, **319**
    example RC analysis, **322**
    example RLC analysis, **325**
    inductor impedance, **321**
    poles and zeros, **324**
    RL impulse response, **323**
    RLC impulse response, **326**
    second-order poles and zeros, **325**
    second-order transfer function, **325**
    transfer function, **323**
analog prototype, **389**
analytic continuation, 123, **311**, **385**
anticausal, **194**
anticausal exponentials, **190**
antiresonance frequency, **264**, **269**
antiresonator, **263**
antisymmetric impulse responses, **227**
antisymmetric linear-phase filters, **227**

banded Toeplitz filter matrix, **337**
bandwidth of a pole, **189**
bandwidth of a pole , **326**
bilateral Laplace transform, **309**
bilateral z transform, **122**
bilinear transformation, **388**
    frequency warping, **388**
    prototype analog filters, **383**
binomial coefficient, **371**
biquad filter section, **132**, **269**
blocking capacitor, **273**
boost, **280**
Butterworth filters, **384**
Butterworth lowpass example, **215**
Butterworth lowpass filter design example, **386**

canonical with respect to delay, **112**
capacitor, **320**
capacitor driving point impedance, **322**
capacitors as springs, **321**
carrier frequency, **163**
carrier term, **252**
carrier wave, **168**
causal, **87**, **100**, **299**
causal filters, **100**
causal signal, **122**, **419**
center frequency of a resonator, **260**
cepstrum
    complex, **193**
    minimum phase, **195**
    poles and zeros, **193**
    real, **193**
characteristic polynomial, **352**
circulant matrix, **338**
clipping, **85**
clipping dB magnitude, **411**

coefficients, difference equation, **98**
comb filter, **47**
commutativity of series filters, **129**
companding, **92**
complete response, **118**, **349**
complex amplitude, **15**
complex analysis, **85**
complex and trig identities, **246**
complex cepstrum, **193**
complex exponential, 15, **133**
complex filter, **86**, **98**
complex numbers summary, **246**
complex one-pole sections, **209**
complex resonator, **264**, **326**
complex signal, **84**
complex sinusoid, **15**
complex sinusoidal oscillator, **266**
condition number, **370**
conformal map, **388**
constant peak-gain resonator, **290**
constant resonance-gain resonator, **286**
continuous-time complex one-pole res-
     onator, **326**
controllability and observability, **356**
controllable modes, **353**
controller canonical form, 341, **353**
convex optimization, **384**
convolution, **143**, **348**
convolution filter representation, **102**,
     106
convolution is commutative, **129**
convolution operator "∗", **111**
convolution theorem for z transforms,
     124
Coulombs, **320**
cps, **243**
critically damped, **328**
current, **320**
cut filter, **280**
cut-off frequency, **3**
cycles per second, **243**
cyclic convolution, **338**

damping constant, **328**
dB clipping, **411**
dc blocker, **273**

dc blocker frequency response, **274**
dc blocking filter, **273**
decay response, **118**
decay time, **116**
decay time-constant, **189**
deconvolution, **145**
degeneracy, **136**
delay equalization, **165**
delta function, **324**
design of recursive digital filters, **383**
determinant, **352**
DFT matrix, **339**
diagonalizing a state-space model, **365**
difference equation, **97**
differentiation theorem for Laplace trans-
     forms, **314**
digital filter theory, **83**
direct form filter implementation, **270**
direct form filter implementations, **200**
discrete Fourier transform (DFT), **154**
discrete time Fourier transform (DTFT),
     150
discrete-time sinusoid, **244**
doublet, **316**
driving point impedance
     RLC network, **325**
driving-point impedance, **320**, **322**
DTFT, **150**
Durbin recursion, **185**
dynamic convolution, **94**
dynamic range compression, **92**

eigenvalues, **351**, **352**
eigenvector, **365**
electrical equivalent circuit, **315**
equation error, **391**
     definition, **391**
     minimization, **390**
equiripple, **165**
error weighting function, **392**
Euler's identity, **14**
even impulse-response filter, **220**
example elementary audio filters, **253**
exercises
     elementary filters, **295**
     elementary matlab, **45**

elementary theory, **22**
filter structures, **217**
frequency response, **171**, **196**
linearity and time-invariance, **95**
state space filters, **376**
time-domain representation, **120**
transfer function, **146**
existence of the *z* transform, **123**
explicit finite difference scheme, **98**
exponential function summary, **246**
exponential order, **310**
exponentially swept sine analysis, **7**
exponentially windowed, **310**
externals (pd), **427**

factorial notation, **311**
Farads, **320**
Fast Fourier Transform (FFT), **155**
Faust programming language, **417**
feedback coefficients, **98**
feedback signal, **87**
feedforward coefficients, **98**
FFT convolution, **113**, **338**
filter
 allpass biquad, **272**
 allpass examples, **300**
 allpass sections, **272**
 amplitude response, **151**
 antiresonator, **263**
 antisymmetric impulse response, **227**
 biquad, **269**
 causal, **100**
 checking stability, **185**
 coefficients, **98**
 complete response, **118**
 complex, **98**
 complex one-pole resonator, **264**
 constant gain at resonance, **285**
 converting to minimum phase, **240**
 converting to parallel form, **129**
 dc blocker, **273**
 definition, **85**
 difference equation, **97**
 direct-form I, **99**, **100**
 direct-form II, **99**, **202**

estimation from input/output data, **342**
even impulse response, **220**
examples, **86**
feedback, **98**
finite impulse response (FIR), **109**
first and second-order sections, **253**
forming real second-order sections from two complex one-poles, **131**
forward and backward, **228**
frequency response, **149**
frequency response in matlab, **154**
general form of finite-order, causal, linear, time-invariant case, **100**
graphical amplitude-response calculation from poles and zeros, **177**
graphical phase response, **181**
imaginary frequency response, **225**
implementation structures, **99**, **199**
 complex resonators, **209**
 parallel second-order sections, **209**
 real second-order sections, **209**
 repeated pole, **210**
 second-order sections, **207**
 series second-order sections, **207**
 transposed direct-form II, **206**
implementations
 direct-form I, **200**
 direct-form II, **202**
 transposed direct forms, **204**
internal overflow, **203**
inverse, **339**
linear, **88**
linear phase, **219**, **225**
linear time-varying, **377**
linear, time invariant, **83**
lossless, **299**
LTI, **90**
LTI matrix representation, **336**
matrix representation, **335**
minimum phase, **231**
multi-input, multi-output (MIMO) allpass filters, **303**
nonlinear example, **92**

notch, **263**
null, **263**
odd impulse response, **225**
one complex pole, **264**
one pole, **256**
one zero, **254**
order, **100**, **176**
paraconjugate, **302**
parallel combination, **127**
paraunitary, MIMO case, **304**
paraunitary, SISO case, **302**
partial fraction expansion, **129**
peaking eq, **280**
phase, **152**
phase preserving, **219**
phase response, **152**
polar form of freq. response, **152**
poles, **63**
poles and zeros, **175**
Q (quality factor), **328**
real, **98**
real, digital, **85**
recursive, **98**
reflection coefficients, **185**
resonance bandwidth of a pole, **326**
resonator, **258**
resonator bandwidth in terms of
    pole radius, **261**
resonator center frequency, **260**
series combination, **127**
shelf, **279**
shift-invariance, **90**
signal flow graph (system diagram),
    99
simplest lowpass, **1**
stability, **101**, **184**
state space realization, **340**
symmetric impulse response, **225**
theory problems, **22**
time-domain representations, **97**
time-invariance, **90**
transfer function, **121**
transposition, **204**
tunable resonator, **285**
two pole, **258**
two zero, **263**

zero phase, **220**
zeros, **63**
filter design
    analog prototype, **389**
    analog to digital conversion via bi-
        linear transform, **388**
    Butterworth, **165**, **384**
    Chebyshev, **165**
    elliptic, **157**, **165**
    equation error method, **390**
    equation error minimization in the
        frequency domain, **393**
    frequency warping, **388**
    lowpass filter, **383**
    maximally flat amplitude response,
        384
    Padè-Prony method, **396**
    Prony's method, **395**
filter-structure problems, **217**
Finite Impulse Response (FIR) digital
    filter, **109**
finite support, **111**
Finite-Impulse-Response (FIR) digital
    filter, **98**
finite-order causal LTI digital filters, **100**
FIR filter, **109**
FIR filter design, **227**
FIR part, **133**
flanger, **172**
flip theorem for z transforms, **228**
flow graph, **99**
flow graph reversal, **204**
folding a signal about index zero, **410**
formant, **211**
formant filtering, **210**
forward-backward filtering, **228**
frequencies, **243**
frequency domain, **245**
frequency response, **149**
    computation in matlab, **154**
    example in matlab, **157**
    imaginary, **225**
frequency response problems, **171**
frequency warping, **388**, **392**
frequency-domain equation-error mini-
    mization, **393**

frequency-response
    measurement, **5**
    plotting in matlab, **401**

gain at resonance, **283**
generalized eigenvectors, **370**
generalized function, **324**
geometric sequence, **133**
graphical computation of amplitude response from transfer-function poles and zeros, **177**
graphical phase response calculation, **181**
group delay, **163**
    computation, **169**
    example, **165**
    matlab function 1, **408**
    matlab function 2, **406**
group delay equals modulation delay, **163**
guard bits, **204**
GUI generation, **417**

Haar filter bank, **306**
half-angle tangent identities, **249**
half-open interval, **34**
half-power bandwidth, 189, **327**
harmonic distortion, **83**
Heaviside unit step function, **323**
Henrys, **321**
Hermitian, 220, **225**
Hertz (Hz), **243**
high shelf, **279**
Hilbert transform relations, **195**
Hooke's law for ideal springs, **321**
Hurwitz polynomial, **332**

impedance analysis, 322, **325**
implicit finite difference schemes, **98**
impulse, **100**
impulse invariant transformation, **327**
impulse response, 100, 111, **232**
    example, **102**
    state-space model, **348**
impulse signal, 56, 101, **111**
impulse, continuous time, **324**
inductor, 315, **321**
inductors as masses, **322**

infinite-impulse-response (IIR), **98**
initial conditions, **349**
initial state, **349**
initial-condition response, **118**
instantaneous frequency, **244**
instantaneous phase, **244**
intermodulation distortion, **83**
interreciprocal, **204**
inverse filter, **339**
irreducible, **141**

Jordan block, **371**
Jordan canonical form, **371**
Jordan form of a matrix, **371**

L1 norm, **120**
ladder filter, **211**
LADSPA plugins, **432**
Laplace transform
    analysis
        linear systems, **315**
        mass-spring oscillator, **317**
        moving mass, **315**
    definition, **309**
    differentiation theorem, **314**
    existence, **310**
    linearity, **314**
    relation to z transform, **313**
    response to initial conditions, **315**
    theorems, **314**
least-squares, **343**
level-dependent gain, **93**
Levinson recursion, **185**
limiter, **92**
linear algebra, **85**
linear filter, **88**
linear operator, **86**
linear phase in audio applications, **235**
linear prediction, 185
linear systems theory, **83**
linear transformation, **86**
linear, time-invariant filters, **83**
linear-phase filter, 219, **225**
    design, **227**
    examples, **226**
linearity and time invariance, **83**

problems, **95**
log-swept sine-wave analysis, **7**
logarithmic derivative, **169**
long division, **133**
lossless analog filters, **333**
lossless filter, **272**, **299**
    examples, **300**
lossless transfer function matrix, **303**
losslessness implies allpass, 299
low shelf, **279**
LTI filter matrix, **336**
LTI filters, **90**, **95**
LTI implications, **102**

magnitude frequency response, **3**, **151**
marginally stable, **185**, **186**
Markov parameters, **348**
Mason's gain formula, **204**
Mason's gain theorem, **351**
matched z transformation, **327**
math summary, **243**
matlab, **25**
matlab elementary problems, **45**
Matlab software, *see* software
matrices, **335**, **347**
matrix, **86**
matrix fraction descriptions, **86**
matrix representations, **335**
maximum-phase filters, **233**
maximum-phase sequence, **233**
median smoother, **87**
memoryless nonlinearity, **87**
message box (pd), **428**
MIMO digital filter, **86**
minimum-delay sequence, **234**
minimum-delay signals, **234**
minimum-phase
    filter, **231**
    polynomial, **232**
    sequence, **232**
minimum-phase = fastest decay, **234**
minimum-phase allpass decomposition, **234**
minimum-phase computation from spectral magnitude data, **240**

minimum-phase conversion of a spectrum, **412**
minimum-phase filter design, **240**
minimum-phase filters and signals, **240**
minimum-phase sequence, **240**
mixed-phase filter, **233**
modal representation, **364**, **365**
mode of vibration, **357**
Moog VCF, **295**
Moore-Penrose pseudoinverse, **343**
moving average, **91**
multi-input, multi-out (MIMO) digital filter, **86**
multiplicity of a pole, **137**
Muse Receptor, **434**

negative-frequency component, **18**
Newton's second law, **322**
nonlinear distortion, **342**
nonlinear filter, **92**
    analysis, **94**
nonparametric signal processing, **240**
nonrecursive digital filter, **98**
normalized second-order resonator, **350**
notch, **269**
notch filter, **11**
notch frequency, **264**
null, **11**
numerical issues, **199**

observable modes, **356**
observer canonical form, **353**, **356**
Octave software, *see* software
odd impulse response, **225**
one-off subpatch (pd), **427**
one-pole filter, **256**
one-pole resonator, complex, **264**
one-sided Laplace transform, **309**
one-zero filter, **254**
operator, **86**
operator theory, **85**
optimality in the Chebyshev sense, **165**
order of a
    filter, **100**, **176**
    pole, **312**
    polynomial, **176**

rational function, **176**
orthogonality principle, **343**
output error minimization, **391**
overdamped, **328**

Padé-Prony method for filter design, **396**
para-Hermitian conjugate, **170**
paraconjugate transfer function, **302**
parallel and series filter sections, **216**
parallel combination, **128**, **325**
parallel complex resonator, **209**
parallel second-order filter sections, **65**
parallel sos in matlab, **407**
parametric equalizer, **280**
paraunitary filter bank, **305**
paraunitary MIMO filters, **304**
partial fraction expansion, **65**, **129**, **209**,
    267
    alternate methods, **136**
    complex poles, **66**
    FIR part, **133**
    in matlab, **403**
    inversion, **132**
    repeated pole, **136**, **137**
    second order sections, **131**
    software, **142**
    summary, **141**
passband, **3**, **157**, **221**
pd
    abstraction, **427**
    externals, **427**
    plugins, **424**
    subpatch, **427**
peak filter, **280**
peak gain, **285**, **287**
peak gain versus resonance gain, **287**
peaking eq filters, **280**
perfect reconstruction filter bank, **305**
periodic signal, **243**
phase, **244**
phase delay, **160**
phase dispersion, **163**, **229**
phase offset, **244**
phase quadrature, **376**
phase response, **8**, **152**
phase unwrapping, **161**

phasor, **16**, **252**
phasor analysis, **16**, **251**, **252**
phasor representation, **16**
piecewise constant-phase filters, **221**
plot
    frequency data, **399**
    saving to disk, **400**
plugin wrapper (pd), **429**
plugins, **417**
    LADSPA, **432**
    pd, **424**
    VST, **434**
polar form of freq. response, **152**
pole, **312**
    bandwidth, **189**
    frequency, **260**
    order, **312**
    time-constant, **189**
pole-zero analysis, **63**
    problems, **196**
poles, **63**, **127**, **129**, **175**
poles and zeros, **175**
poles of a state-space model, **351**
poles outside unit circle, **190**
polynomial
    division in matlab, **145**
    long division, **145**
    multiplication, **143**
    multiplication in matlab, **143**
    order, **176**
polynomial amplitude envelopes, **138**
positive-frequency sinusoid, **18**
predelay, **134**
problems, *see* exercises
projection error, **344**
Prony's method, **395**
pseudoinverse, **343**

Q (quality factor), **328**
    relation to decay time, **329**

radians per second, **243**
ratio test, **312**
rational function, **176**
RC time constant, **323**
real filter, **10**, **85**, **98**, 131

real signal, **84**
real, even-impulse-response filter, **220**
real-frequency-response filter, **220**
Receptor, **434**
recursive filter, **87**, **98**
reflecting zeros inside unit circle, **195**
reflection coefficients, **185**
region of convergence, **190**
repeated pole, **370**
    impulse response, **138**
residue, **129**
resonance, **260**
resonant frequency, **328**
resonator, **258**
resonator bandwidth, **326**
response to initial conditions, **118**
right-half plane, **310**
ring time, **116**
ripple, **157**
rms level, **93**
roll-off, **157**
running weighted sum, **91**

samples, **243**
sampling interval, **243**
scalars, **85**
scaling property of linear systems, **88**
Schur recursion, **185**
Schur-Cohn stability test, **185**
seconds, **243**
series and parallel filter sections, **216**
series and parallel transfer functions, **127**
series connection, **128**
series second-order sections, **207**
set notation, **84**
shelf filters, **279**
shift operator, **90**
shift theorem for z transforms, **124**
shift-invariant filter, **90**
sideband images, **83**
sifting property, **324**
signal
    complex, discrete-time, **84**
    definition, **84**
    flow graph, **99**
    operator, **88**

    plotting in matlab, **398**, **416**
    real, discrete-time, **84**
    representation, **243**
signal flow graph, **48**
signal space, **84**
similarity transformation, **362**, **365**
simple lowpass filter
    analysis in matlab, **25**, **30**, **39**, **42**
    matlab implementation, **26**
simulation diagram, **4**, **99**
sinc function, **224**
sine-wave analysis, **7**, **8**, **18**
single-input, single-output (SISO) digital filters, **86**
singular matrix, **370**
sinusoid, **244**
SISO digital filter, **86**
sliding linear combination, **91**
software, **397**
    Faust programming, **417**
    Matlab
        frequency-response plot, **401**, **416**
        signal plots, **398**
    Matlab or Octave
        clipping dB magnitude, **411**
        folding a signal about index zero, **410**
        frequency plots, **399**
        frequency-response computation, **154**
        group delay computation, **408**
        minimum phase conversion, **412**
        parallel second-order sections, **407**
        partial fraction expansion, **403**, **406**
        saving plots, **400**
    Octave
        signal plots, **398**
spectrum, **244**
speech modeling, 185
speech synthesis, **210**
split-radix FFT, **42**
spring
    compliance, **321**
    constant, **321**
    stiffness, **321**

stability of a digital filter, **101**, **140**, **184**, **185**
state space filter, **347**
  analysis, **347**
  analysis example
    the digital waveguide oscillator, **372**
  complete response, **349**
  computation, **359**
  diagonalization, **365**
  example, **340**
  from difference equations, **352**
  impulse response, **348**
  matlab, **362**
  modal representation, **364**
  poles, **351**
  problems, **376**
  realization, **340**, **347**
  response from initial conditions, **349**
  similarity transformation, **362**
  transfer function, **349**
  transfer function example, **350**
  transposition, **351**
state space realization, 136
steady state
  analysis, **320**
  response, **114**
  signal, **116**
Steinberg Media Technologies, 434
step-down procedure, **185**
stopband, **3**, **157**
strict right-half plane, **310**
strictly proper transfer function, **132**
subpatch (pd), **427**
sum of sinusoids, **250**
superposition property, **88**
superposition property of linear systems, **88**, **106**
swanalmainplot, 416
swanalplot, 415
symmetric impulse response, **219**
symmetric linear-phase FIR filter, **225**
synthesis filter bank, **305**
system diagram, **48**, **99**
system function, **121**
system identification, **342**, **343**

tapped delay line, **109**
Taylor series expansion, 14
Tellegen's theorem, **204**
time constant, **189**
time constant of a pole, **189**
time domain, **245**
time reversal inverts the locations of all zeros, **233**
time-delay spectrometry, **7**
time-invariant filter, **90**
time-varying
  filter coefficients, **283**
  filter example, **94**
  two-pole digital filters, **283**
Toeplitz linear operator, **338**
Toeplitz matrix, **336**
transfer characteristics, **121**
transfer function, **112**, **121**
  factored, **127**
  matrix, **349**
  of a state space filter, **349**
  problems, **146**
  to second-order-section matlab function tf2sos, **207**
transient, **116**
transient response, **114**
transition band, **157**
transition frequency, **279**
transpose of a filter, **204**, **351**
transposed direct form I (TDF-I), **204**
transposed direct form II (TDF-II), **204**
transposing the signal flow graph, **351**
transversal filter, **109**
tremolo, **94**
trig identities, **246**
trigonometric identity summary, **248**
tunable two-pole digital filters, **283**
two's complement wrap-around, **201**
two-pole filter, **258**
two-pole partial fraction expansion, **267**
two-pole time-varying filter, **283**
two-sided Laplace transform, **309**
two-zero filter, **263**

undamped, **328**
underdamped, **328**

unilateral Laplace transform, **309**
unilateral z transform, **122**
unit step function, **102**, **266**
unstable poles, **190**
unwrapping phase, **161**

variable resonator, **285**
variable two-pole digital filters, **283**
VCF, 283
vector coordinate, **84**
vector space, **84**
vectorized algorithms, **27**
virtual analog synthesis, **295**
vocoder, **168**
voltage divider rule, **323**
voltage-controlled filters, **283**
Volterra kernels, **94**
vowel simulation, **210**
VST plugins, **434**

wave digital filters, **389**
weighting function, **392**
window method for FIR filter design,
        384

z transform, **122**
    existence, **123**
    theorems
        convolution, **124**
        shift, **124**
zero at infinity, **324**
zero initial state, **348**
zero padding, 42, **337**, 338
zero-input response, **341**
zero-phase filter, **220**
    examples, **222**, **224**
zero-state response, **118**
zeros of a filter, **63**